Unlocking Private Investment in Sustainable Infrastructure in Asia

Investment in infrastructure is essential for promoting economic growth, and while countries in Asia have enjoyed higher rates of gross domestic product growth in recent years, the region remains severely deficient in the scale and quality of sustainable infrastructure. Moreover, population growth and climate change continue to put increasing pressure on the need for strategic and farsighted development, calling for policy makers to reevaluate infrastructure governance to ensure sustainable economic growth. Currently, in developing Asia, most investment in infrastructure comes from the public sector. However, with growing fiscal deficits and other budgetary constraints, it is essential to develop alternative sources of investment for infrastructure projects. This presents opportunities to tap into the private sector, which can play an instrumental role in minimizing the funding gap through the development of stronger, more transparent public–private partnerships (PPPs) and incentivizing sustainable infrastructure investment.

This book provides a scholarly discussion on the importance of PPPs and approaches to unlock private participation in infrastructure investment based on lessons from across Asia. Among the proposed schemes are government tax incentives, development-based land value capture strategy under PPP land pooling, Viability Gap Funds, Project Development Facilities, and other guarantees. The book aims to assess the impacts and future of sustainable infrastructure investments and examines the role of governments in mobilizing financial resources and new models for unlocking private investment in sustainable infrastructure.

This book consists of fifteen original chapters on the experiences of the Central Asia Regional Economic Cooperation (CAREC) and a few other cases for promoting private investment in sustainable infrastructure. The fact that not much has been published previously on this theme makes this book a welcome and timely addition to the much needed knowledge on this subject.

Bhajan Grewal is Professor at Victoria University, Australia.

Nella Hendriyetty is Senior Economist at the Asian Development Bank Institute (ADBI).

Iskandar Abdullaev is Deputy Director Two, CAREC Institute.

Chul Ju Kim is Chairman of the Credit Coordination Committee, Republic of Korea, and Former Deputy Dean, ADBI.

Naoyuki Yoshino is Professor Emeritus, Keio University Japan and Former Dean and CEO, ADBI.

Eisa Khan Ayoob Ayoobi is Chief of the Capacity Building Division, CAREC Institute.

Routledge Studies in Development Economics

169 The Political Economy of Universal Healthcare in Africa
Evidence from Ghana
Philip C. Aka, Hassan Wahab, and Yvette M. Alex-Assensoh

170 State Building and Social Policies in Developing Countries
The Political Economy of Development
Rashed Al Mahmud Titumir

171 Taxation in the Digital Economy
New Models in Asia and the Pacific
Edited by Nella Hendriyetty, Chris Evans, Chul Ju Kim and Farhad Taghizadeh-Hesary

172 Human Capital and Gender Inequality in Middle-Income Countries
Schooling, Learning and Socioemotional Skills in the Labour Market
Elizabeth M. King and Dileni Gunewardena

173 Digital Financial Inclusion and Regulation
Ogochukwu Monye

174 Household Demand for Consumer Goods in Developing Countries
A Comparative Perspective with Developed Countries
Eliyathamby A. Selvanathan, Saroja Selvanathan and Maneka Jayasinghe

175 Unlocking Private Investment in Sustainable Infrastructure in Asia
Edited by Bhajan Grewal, Nella Hendriyetty, Iskandar Abdullaev, Chul Ju Kim, Naoyuki Yoshino and Eisa Khan Ayoob Ayoobi

176 The Political Economy of Bilateral Aid
Implications for Global Development
Peter Blunt with Cecilia Escobar and Vlassis Missos

For more information about this series, please visit: www.routledge.com/Routledge-Studies-in-Development-Economics/book-series/SE0266

Unlocking Private Investment in Sustainable Infrastructure in Asia

Edited by Bhajan Grewal, Nella Hendriyetty, Iskandar Abdullaev, Chul Ju Kim, Naoyuki Yoshino and Eisa Khan Ayoob Ayoobi

Co-publication of the Asian Development Bank Institute and Routledge

Routledge
Taylor & Francis Group
LONDON AND NEW YORK

ADBInstitute

First published 2023
by Routledge
4 Park Square, Milton Park, Abingdon, Oxon OX14 4RN

and by Routledge
605 Third Avenue, New York, NY 10158

Routledge is an imprint of the Taylor & Francis Group, an informa business

British Library Cataloguing-in-Publication Data
A catalogue record for this book is available from the British Library

Library of Congress Cataloging-in-Publication Data
Names: Grewal, Bhajan S. (Bhajan Singh), editor. | Hendriyetty, Nella, editor. | Abdullaev, Iskandar, editor. | Kim, Chul Ju, editor. | Yoshino, Naoyuki, 1950– editor. | Ayoob Ayoobi, Eisa Khan, editor.
Title: Unlocking private investment in sustainable infrastructure in Asia / edited by Bhajan Grewal, Nella Hendriyetty, Iskandar Abdullaev, Chul Ju Kim, Naoyuki Yoshino and Eisa Khan Ayoob Ayoobi.
Description: London; New York, NY: Routledge: Asian Development Bank Institute, 2023. | Series: Routledge studies in development economics | Includes bibliographical references and index. |
Identifiers: LCCN 2022024770 | ISBN 9781032133461 (hardback) | ISBN 9781032133454 (paperback) | ISBN 9781003228790 (ebook)
Subjects: LCSH: Infrastructure (Economics)–Asia. | Sustainable development–Asia. | Urban policy–Asia. | Private investments in public equity–Asia.
Classification: LCC HC415.C3 U55 2023 | DDC 338.95–dc23/eng/20220613
LC record available at https://lccn.loc.gov/2022024770

ISBN: 9781032133461 (hbk)
ISBN: 9781032133454 (pbk)
ISBN: 9781003228790 (ebk)

DOI: 10.4324/9781003228790

Typeset in Galliard
by Newgen Publishing UK

Contents

Figures

Tables

Contributors

Iskandar Abdullaev, Deputy Director Two, CAREC Institute, People's Republic of China (PRC)

Umid Abidhadjaev, Deputy Director, Center for Economic Research and Reforms, Tashkent, Uzbekistan

Yanuar Falak Abiyunus, Staff of International Taxation Policy, Fiscal Policy Agency, Ministry of Finance of Indonesia

Shakhboz Akhmedov, Senior Research Fellow, Knowledge and Research Networking, CAREC Institute, People's Republic of China

Nicolas J.A. Buchoud, Global Solutions Fellow, Founding Principal of Renaissance Urbaine.

Amar Causevic, Policy Fellow, Stockholm Environment Institute, Stockholm, Sweden

Eugene Chao, Faculty Research Associate, The Wharton Business School Finance Department

Youngho Chang, Associate Professor, School of Business, Singapore University of Social Sciences, Singapore

Dharish David, Associate Faculty, Singapore Institute of Management – Global Education (SIM-GE)

Feruzbek Davletov, Research Associate, Center for Economic Research and Reforms, Tashkent, Uzbekistan

Nauli A. Desdiani, Junior Research Associate, Institute for Economic and Social Research, Faculty of Economics and Business, University of Indonesia

Yohanna M.L. Gultom, Faculty of Economics and Business, University of Indonesia

Nella Hendriyetty, Senior Economist, Asian Development Bank Institute (ADBI)

Derek Hondo, Capacity Building and Training Coordinator, ADBI

Fredrich Kahrl received his PhD from the Energy and Resources Group at the University of California, Berkeley

Febrio Kacaribu, Head of Fiscal Policy Agency, Ministry of Finance of Indonesia

Necmettin Kaymaz, United States Country Director, Presidency of the Republic of Turkey Investment Office

Chul Ju Kim, Chairman of the Credit Coordination Committee, Republic of Korea, and Former Deputy Dean, ADBI

Keun Jung Lee, Assistant Professor, KIMEP University, Republic of Kazakhstan

Wawan Juswanto, Chief Change Management Officer, Ministry of Finance of Indonesia

Minquan Liu, Professor, School of Economics and Center for Human and Economic Development Studies, Peking University

Muhammad Ayub Mehar, Professor, Iqra University Karachi, Pakistan

Misuzu Nakamura, Capacity Building and Training Assistant, ADBI

Rakesh Padhan, Research Scholar, Department of Liberal Arts, Indian Institute of Technology Hyderabad, India

K. P. Prabheesh, Associate Professor, Department of Liberal Arts, Indian Institute of Technology Hyderabad, Telangana State, India

David Roland-Holst, Adjunct Professor in the Department of Agricultural and Resource Economics and the Department of Economics at the University of California, Berkeley

Syahda Sabrina, Research Assistant, Institute for Economic and Social Research, Faculty of Economics and Business University of Indonesia

Farhad Taghizadeh-Hesary, Associate Professor, Tokai University, Japan

Gaurav Verma, CEPT University, Ahmedabad, India

Naoyuki Yoshino, Professor Emeritus, Keio University, Tokyo, Japan, and Director of Financial Research Center, Japan

Foreword

Minister of Uzbekistan

Infrastructure plays a pivotal role in promoting economic growth. However, rapid population over the past years, coupled with the adverse impacts of climate change, has put significant strain on existing infrastructure, particularly in emerging and developing economies. The Sustainable Development Goals (SDGs), which are set out to address these global challenges and build up a better and more sustainable future, also emphasize the importance of sustainable infrastructure in combating climate change and strengthening resilience in countries, Asian region included.

The Central Asia (CA) region is a diverse region with a mixture of upper middle and low income countries. It has major strategic importance due to their geographic location and natural resource endowments. In 2001, the Central Asia Regional Economic Cooperation (CAREC) Program was established with the overarching vision of "Good Neighbors, Good Partners, and Good Prospects". In recent years, the opening up of the CA region and improving relationships among neighboring countries have led to the implementation of major infrastructure projects in the hydropower, rail and port connectivity sectors. Furthermore, Central Asian countries also rank among the most climate change vulnerable in the European and Central Asia (ECA) region[1]; thus, developing sustainable infrastructure, especially in low-carbon and climate-resilient projects, is necessary to remain a more sustained growth within the region.

It is estimated by the Asian Development Bank (ADB) that the Central Asia Regional Economic Cooperation (CAREC) region will need $79.7 billion during the 2016–2030 period in infrastructure to maintain its growth momentum, equivalent to about 7.8% of GDP for CAREC member countries.[2] Other estimates of infrastructure financing needs are broadly in the same range. Thus, large regional infrastructure investment projects in the CAREC region require recourse to additional financing sources beside the state budget, such as, private financiers, public-private partnerships (PPPs), long-term institutional investors, and appropriate risk allocations.

This book, *Unlocking Private Investment in Sustainable Infrastructure in Asia*, is introduced as a valuable reference for sustainable infrastructure development in developing Asian countries. It seeks to assess the impacts of infrastructure investments in the region. While still emphasizing the central role of public financing schemes in infrastructure improvement, it also highlights the importance of private sector participation into the process. From that basis, the book provides suggestions on how to unlock private investments in sustainable infrastructure in Asia to achieve the SDGs.

Notes

1 www.worldbank.org/en/region/eca/brief/central-asia
2 ADB. 2017. Meeting Asia's Infrastructure Needs. Manila

Foreword

ADBI/CAREC Institute

The 2030 Agenda for Sustainable Development sets out 17 goals that span the economic, social and environmental pillars of development. Among those sustainable goals, the development of sustainable and resilient infrastructure is deemed to be a central task since infrastructure is a critical component that connects all of the Sustainable Development Goals together. An efficient and well-functioning infrastructure system can undoubtedly yield significant economic, financial and social returns, generate positive externalities and strengthen climate-resilient capacity.

In recent years, to achieve sustained and inclusive growth, developing Asia is investing heavily into sustainable infrastructure, especially in low-carbon and climate-resilient projects. According to the Asian Development Bank (ADB), "developing Asia will need to invest \$26 trillion from 2016 to 2030, or ca. \$1.7 trillion per year if the region is to maintain its growth momentum, eradicate poverty, and respond to climate change."[1] This figure for the Central Asia Regional Economic Cooperation (CAREC) region only reaches \$79.7 billion. The infrastructure investment gap—the difference between investment needs and current investment levels—for CAREC developing countries exceeds 5% of their projected GDP for the 5-year period from 2016 to 2020.

Nonetheless, investing in infrastructure is perceived as being financially burdensome, complex and risky. This can make it particularly difficult to raise the financing needed to enact high quality infrastructure projects. Meanwhile, an overdependence on state budgets for such investment needs may bear a great burden on those countries' fiscal front in the long run. It is, therefore, worthwhile to re-evaluate some aspects of traditional infrastructure investment and financing and assess the efficiency of private participation as additional sources for infrastructure funding.

This book advocates a shift in perspective towards infrastructure financing. In particular, based on a scholarly discussion of the current state of infrastructure and investment needs in the Asian region, it suggests that a more strategic and efficient mobilization of resources is needed, focusing not only on public funding, but also on leveraging additional funding and participation from private sector. Furthermore, it provides a set of recommendations on how policy-makers and government agencies could unlock the private financing sources into infrastructure investments to achieve sustainable goals in the region.

Note

1 ADB. 2017. Meeting Asia's Infrastructure Needs. Manila

Acknowledgments

The editors would like to thank all contributors and those who helped with the publication of this book. In particular, we acknowledge support from Ms. Phi Thi Minh Nguyet, Mr. Derek Hondo, Ms. Dildar Zakir, Mr. Adam Majoe, Ms. Misuzu Nakamura, and the teams of Asian Development Bank Institute and CAREC Institute staff for their kind help and assistance during the publication process.

Introduction

While Asia has enjoyed healthy rates of gross domestic product (GDP) growth in recent years, it remains severely deficient with respect to the scale and quality of infrastructure. In a recent assessment, the Asian Development Bank estimated that the Asian region needed to spend $26 trillion on infrastructure between 2016 and 2030 (ADB 2017).

The focus of this book is on unlocking various sources of investments in sustainable infrastructure in Asia, including those by the private sector and public-private partnerships (PPPs). A key premise of this book is that infrastructure plays an indispensable role in promoting economic development, creating new employment, and enriching livelihoods. Given their budgetary pressures, however, governments in most Asian countries find it difficult to meet infrastructure funding requirements. It has become essential, therefore, to develop alternative sources of investment in sustainable infrastructure that requires additional climate-adjusted finances. The scholarly contributions in this book discuss important issues, including the roles of national, provincial, and local governments in mobilizing investments in sustainable infrastructure; the scope of private sector investment in infrastructure; specific PPP models for investment in infrastructure; and the development of new models for unlocking private sector investments in sustainable infrastructure.

There is no doubt that private sector investment in infrastructure is becoming increasingly common in many countries, simply because public investment is insufficient. Nevertheless, there is no one-size-fits-all way of attracting private investment into infrastructure financing, and a variety of models and approaches have been tried in different countries, with innovative approaches emerging over time. This book also underlines its central message that a multitude of issues must be addressed to attract private investments into infrastructure. These issues reside mainly in the governance of host countries, where supportive and investor-friendly regulatory frameworks must be strengthened. This book consists of 15 original chapters on the experiences of the Central Asia Regional Economic Cooperation (CAREC) and a few other cases for promoting private investment in sustainable infrastructure. The fact that not much has been published previously on this theme makes this book a welcome and timely addition to the much-needed knowledge on this subject.

DOI: 10.4324/9781003228790-1

The CAREC Program was established in 2001 with the mission of achieving shared and sustainable development under the guiding principle of "Good Neighbors, Good Partners, and Good Prospects." After Pakistan and Turkmenistan joined in 2010, CAREC now includes 11 countries: Afghanistan (population 39 million), Azerbaijan (10 million), the People's Republic of China (PRC) (1.4 billion), Georgia (4 million), Kazakhstan (19 million), the Kyrgyz Republic (6 million), Mongolia (3 million), Pakistan (221 million), Tajikistan (9 million), Turkmenistan (6 million), and Uzbekistan (33 million).

As suggested by its title, the book's main focus is on the contributions of private sector investment in sustainable infrastructure—a relatively newer topic, especially for the CAREC region countries, many of which remained deficient in infrastructure during the Soviet era, which ended in 1991. Each of the 15 chapters deals with an important set of issues or a different location-based experience. Valuable policy lessons can be learned from each case study.

Private investors are generally reluctant to invest in infrastructure due to low rates of return and high risks. Infrastructure can create big spillover effects into the region. Water supply can increase production of farmers and clean water can improve health of the population. New residential and commercial areas can also be developed with fresh water supply. Development of new residential areas will increase population, pushing up income tax revenues, including spillover tax revenues that arise from increases in agricultural production and the incomes of the farmers. Rising property values will also increase revenues from property taxes. If part of these increased tax revenues were returned to water supply companies, the rate of return on water investments would also rise. Traditionally, water operators have relied only on user charges for water supply. The rate of return from new investments in water supply would increase due to the spillover tax revenues, in addition to user charges. Acquisition of land has been another difficulty in water supply in Central Asia, as farmers often do not want to sell their land. In these circumstances, formation of land trusts can make it possible for the farmers to retain their ownership of land, but lease it to the water companies. This would also reduce the negotiation period for land acquisition.

Manila's highway, Uzbekistan's railway, and Japan's high-speed railways all have generated large spillover effects by enlarging the tax base of their respective regions, which in turn has increased tax revenues. These revenues occur even when no new taxes have been imposed or no rates have been increased; the higher revenues materialize simply because of the expansion of the tax base due to the higher production and sales of farm outputs. In the past, such additional revenues were collected and retained by the governments; no part was returned to the investors in infrastructure or to the operators. This book proposes, however, that a part of these spillover tax revenues be returned to private infrastructure investors and infrastructure operators to increase their rates of return.

Sustainable infrastructure is a multidimensional economic input that affects all segments of the economy, including agriculture, industry, commerce, trade, transport, communications, etc. Viewed in this light, sustainable infrastructure serves as an all-pervasive *enabler and connector* of human endeavors in the pursuit of production, consumption, and trade. None of the lofty policy goals, such as poverty reduction or inclusive economic development, can be achieved without supportive infrastructure. Development of sustainable infrastructure for supporting inclusive economic growth involves careful planning, management, and governance.

Investment in sustainable infrastructure is not always expected to yield immediate returns, however; it takes a long time for the full benefits of infrastructure investment to materialize. The infrastructure that people use today was created over many decades and will continue to support economic activity for many more years. Thinking about sustainable infrastructure in this way highlights two of its distinguishing features:

1. Sustainable infrastructure consists of shared goods that benefit large populations simultaneously; and
2. Economic and social benefits of sustainable infrastructure continue to flow for long periods of time.

It is useful, at this point, to note that all consumption, production, savings, and investment consist of goods and services, some of which are provided by the public sector and the rest by the private (market) sector. However, the nature of public and private goods (and services) differs in an important respect. Because private goods (and services) are bought and sold (exchanged) in the market, consumers must pay to enjoy their benefits. Public goods, on the other hand, are paid for by taxes and charges levied by the providing governments and semi-government organizations. This distinction of market prices versus taxes is important because the underlying *principle of exclusion* applies only to market goods. Those who do not pay are excluded from consumption of market goods. On the other hand, public goods (like infrastructure), are consumed collectively and exclusion from their utilization is not always easy, and involves a cost (e.g., toll roads or specific fees and charges for certain services).

If the public sector of a country is unable to finance new infrastructure, however, the alternatives are either to go without it or to find innovative ways of attracting private sector investment. But, as noted above, private investment in infrastructure is possible only if the investors can earn a reasonable return. In these cases, governments need to create (and maintain) conditions in which private investors are incentivized to invest in sustainable infrastructure. In this context, it is desirable to explore how private sector investment in infrastructure may be encouraged and regulated. This book does precisely that, and offers recommendations to a wide range of target audiences—policy makers/influencers and decision makers, etc.

In summary, private investment in sustainable infrastructure is relatively new and its success depends on the quality of governance, by way of its effectiveness in attracting private investment in infrastructure for which pricing rules are not always practical. The 15 chapters of this book cover different aspects, themes, and issues related to private sector investment in sustainable infrastructure and provide important lessons for future policies.

Chapter 1 highlights the importance of managerial oversight in the planning of urban infrastructure for making cities more livable by striking the right balance between mass transit systems and highways for cars. Three important considerations are distinguished during this balancing between conflicting urban design policies. First, there must be a clear vision about the kind of city people want because a city built around a transit system would function differently from a city built around highways for cars. Second, the decision-making criteria for investment must balance the opportunity costs of capital, shareholder value, and the vision of governance. Third, it is always useful to review selected transformational studies and investment experiences of comparable settings to learn the right lessons for mobilizing capital for successful urban investments. Managerial vision can ensure maximum value to be derived in many CAREC cities by balancing financial returns on investment with environmental, social, and governance outcomes that determine the livability of cities. Lack of managerial vision, on the other hand, would result in sub-optimal outcomes. The key message of this chapter is that livable cities must consistently implement policies that encourage transit use and discourage the use of cars.

Chapter 2 deals with the challenges facing Central Asia's energy infrastructure. The cross-border energy transmission system of Central Asia was built during the Soviet era and it is not capable of meeting the efficiency requirements of a modern energy transmission system. Meanwhile, transitioning to low carbon renewable energy infrastructure has become a priority in the CAREC region. This requires member countries to upgrade their energy infrastructure for electricity generation, storage, and transmission. Meanwhile, global demand and supply systems for energy are undergoing rapid change because energy markets are responding to member countries' transition to lower-carbon energy-use options. In this context of rapid change, the CAREC region's competitiveness in sustainable energy trade also requires that investors in the sector must be able to respond quickly and effectively to emerging trends. Thus, reconciling the CAREC region's energy transition pathways with global decarbonization trends has become a major challenge for this region. Noting that renewable energy resources (solar and wind) are much more equally distributed around the region, the chapter sets out an ambitious agenda for public-private partnerships to promote low carbon electric power development and integration for more sustainable and inclusive regional growth.

Chapter 3 deals with modernization of urban infrastructure in Central Asia, where the Smart Cities movement has rapidly grown into a major campaign, with the support of the World Bank, the United Nations Development Program, and the United Nations Economic Commission for Europe. Leading examples of urban infrastructure renewal in the CAREC region are the Tashkent 2025 Plan, Uzbekistan's Safe City project, the World Bank's Digital CASA (Central Asia South Asia) Project and the Republic of Korea's Delta City Project in Uzbekistan. Thus, the Smart Cities movement is attracting not only new investment into the CAREC region's urban infrastructure, but also technical knowledge and management skills that accompany the modernization campaigns. The environmental dimension of these cities is also important, given the priorities of Smart Cities for providing clean drinking water and environment-friendly waste management. The PRC's Belt and Road Initiative has helped rapid development of telecommunications and geo-positioning systems in Central Asia. Regional interconnectivity of power grids has also created similar changes in the energy sector. In this context of inter-dependency of cities and interconnectedness of infrastructure systems, this chapter also highlights the role of smart cities in achieving global development and environmental goals. Private investment in these cities would also need to be consistent with regional commitments to social and environmental sustainability. In turn, this could also encourage the World Bank and other international institutions to ensure that their own approaches to urbanization are supportive of Central Asia's urban transformation and sustainable urban growth in CAREC.

Chapter 4 deals with issues related to an integrated Asia-Pacific natural gas market in the CAREC region. Specifically, it explores how the infrastructure of natural gas pipelines in this region may promote sustainable development of this region's natural gas trade. The CAREC region has abundant supplies of both crude oil and natural gas. At the end of 2018, CAREC countries had 15.4% of the global proven reserves of natural gas and 3.7% of the proven reserves of crude oil. Despite the relative abundance of natural gas, however, intra-regional trade of natural gas remains quite low among the CAREC countries. How the modernization of infrastructure and natural gas trade are intertwined in the CAREC region is the focus of this chapter.

Chapter 5 analyzes the current state of irrigation in Central Asia. According to the CAREC Institute (2020), water availability in the Central Asia region is expected to drop sharply from 2,500 cubic meters per capita to 1,400 cubic meters per capita; that is, a 44% reduction. Built during the 1970s and 1980s, water infrastructure in this region is old, outdated, and dilapidated. The situation has become particularly serious since the collapse of the Soviet Union, as public financing of water infrastructure has fallen by 33% to 50%. The World Bank has estimated that Central Asia needs to invest at least $20–25 billion to upgrade its water infrastructure (World Bank 2018). While the governments do not have the required funds to invest for this improvement, private sector investors are reluctant to invest in water infrastructure due to the lack of ownership rights and the low returns on investment. As a result, the CAREC region needs an operationally efficient and holistic water governance system to address the rapidly approaching era of water scarcity.

Chapter 6 examines the nexus between investment in high quality infrastructure and its impact on economic growth by reducing costs of transportation, facilitating quicker and cheaper mobilization of goods, raising productivity, and improving business environments. This chapter reveals that, contrary to the common assumption of causality, the impact of infrastructure investment on economic growth is not uniform across Central Asia, and it varies according to each country's level and stage of development. While countries in the CAREC region are rich in natural resources, they are quite diverse in their stages of development. As a result, the findings of this analysis are country-specific. First, it is found that a robust relationship exists between higher infrastructure investment and higher economic growth in Kazakhstan. Second, infrastructure investment is found to have no growth-enhancing effect in the Kyrgyz Republic. Third, Uzbekistan is found to have a bi-directional relationship, where infrastructural investment promotes economic development but is also positively impacted by higher economic development. Finally, the modelling of this chapter finds that, in Tajikistan, infrastructure investment leads to a reduction in economic growth in the short run. In this context, it is also instructive to note that, according to ADB (2019), energy infrastructure of this region needs new investment of $33 billion by 2030 to meet domestic and international demand.

Chapter 7 traces the evolution of three stages of local public financing of infrastructure investment in the PRC and discusses the impact of infrastructure investment on economic development. In the PRC, large-scale investments in physical infrastructure have been financed mostly by provincial and municipal governments. Three successive models of local public financing in infrastructure investment are discussed in this chapter. The first model was premised on the PRC's former agricultural collectives and was abolished in the late 1970s. The second model, that is, the so-called "land financing" model, is ongoing and has been based on the leasing of public land, while the third model—a form of property tax—is currently being experimented with. "Land financing" in the PRC refers to a practice whereby a local government leases the land it owns or controls to an economic agent in need of the land for a fee, which the local government then uses to help finance its various activities, including the provision of various public infrastructures. Although the third model is not yet being widely used in the PRC, it is expected to be applied all over the country progressively. This chapter also pinpoints the risks that local government financing vehicles may impose by relying heavily on the rising prices of land for raising public revenues.

Chapter 8 aims to identify effective modes of financing logistics infrastructure and testing the effects of its magnitude and quality on economic development. Analysis of a database consisting of 219 countries for 2007–2016 reveals that the external debt to the public sector was a significant determinant of the magnitude and quality of the logistic infrastructure. No significant impact of the private sector external debt was detected on infrastructure development, however. The most significant determinant of logistic infrastructure development was the long-term public sector external debt, which is also an indicator of public participation in infrastructure projects. The indices of logistic infrastructure are quite low in CAREC countries (except the PRC), further confirming that investment in logistic infrastructure remains deficient in this region. Per capita income in the CAREC region indicates high reliance on foreign direct investment (FDI) and relatively low contribution of domestic agriculture, industry, and services.

Chapter 9 introduces the new concept of spillover taxes to finance investment in infrastructure. Recognizing that clean water shortages are a serious challenge in many parts of the world, including Central Asia, the United Nations designated, in 2016, "access to clean water" as one of the Sustainable Development Goals of the *2030 Agenda for Sustainable Development.* In Central Asia, water infrastructure remains inadequate, as most of it has not been upgraded since the end of the Soviet Era. While governments manage water systems in Central Asian countries, they do not have sufficient funds to modernize water infrastructure. As a result, this chapter argues that private sector investment is needed to upgrade and develop water infrastructure of this region. The importance of high-quality infrastructure is emphasized and it is proposed that the additional value created by infrastructure could finance the additional infrastructure and fill the existing gaps in infrastructure investment in this region.

The proposal for spillover taxes is a novel idea in public finance literature and needs further discussion. Not noted in this book, however, is the fact that the concept of spillover tax is similar to the "betterment levy" that was introduced in Punjab, India under the Betterment Charges and Acreage Rates Act, 1952, after the completion of the Bhakra Dam. The aim of this levy was to recover a portion of the cost from the farmers who had directly benefitted from the newly opened irrigation canals flowing from the Bhakra Dam. However, the spillover tax revenues proposed in this chapter are not additional taxes; they are additional revenues resulting from higher production and sales in the surrounding region, which can be attributed to the improved infrastructure. The Land Trust would promote more efficient use of land and water supply; farmers would keep the ownership of land but lease it to a privatized water company. Negotiations of land use would be simplified, lowering the costs of clean water supply. This chapter also proposes certain policy responses for governments to maintain quality infrastructure in the water sector. The recommendations range from utilizing parts of spillover tax revenues created by infrastructure investments and compensating for risk and financing further expenditures, to supporting small and medium-sized enterprises, secondary markets, adoption of smart city initiatives, and environmental protection in infrastructure development.

The role of government in attracting private investment in infrastructure is examined in Chapter 10. In order to overcome financial constraints, governments seek FDI. This motivation makes FDI an important target for economic diversification strategies of the developing countries. This chapter models inflows to determine which factors are important for attracting FDI. According to this modelling, the determinants of FDI inflows in five Central Asian countries (Kazakhstan, the Kyrgyz Republic, Tajikistan, Turkmenistan, and Uzbekistan) are GDP growth rate, inflation rate, FDI stock, exports, imports, fiscal freedom, economic freedom, population, the labor force, and the share of internet users in total population. For Kazakhstan, FDI stock, exports, inflation, and fiscal freedom are found to be important for FDI inflows. For Tajikistan, fiscal freedom matters the most for FDI inflows, while the rate of inflation is the crucial determinant for Turkmenistan.

Chapter 11 is focused on PPPs in energy projects in the developing countries of ASEAN and the CAREC region. The ASEAN region consists of the following 10 countries: Brunei Darussalam, Cambodia, Indonesia, Lao People's Democratic Republic, Malaysia, Myanmar, the Philippines, Singapore, Thailand, and Viet Nam. The CAREC region includes the following 11 countries: Afghanistan, Azerbaijan, the PRC, Georgia, Kazakhstan, the Kyrgyz Republic, Mongolia, Pakistan, Tajikistan, Turkmenistan, and Uzbekistan. Although currently relying heavily on carbon-intensive energy sources, these countries have made voluntary commitments to reduce their greenhouse gas emissions and are hastening their shift towards renewable energy. With limited public funds to finance new infrastructure projects, they have introduced innovative policies, and are incentivizing PPPs to attract private investment in green energy projects. While investments and PPPs in hydropower projects has been the trend so far in both these regions, it has been shifting quickly in recent years to solar and wind-based projects, especially in ASEAN. This chapter also considers future opportunities and challenges facing infrastructure investment in these regions.

Chapter 12 deals with the evidence-based financing of infrastructure and examines the specific case of a new railway line in Uzbekistan—the Toshguzar-Boysun-Kumkurgon line. It is reported that the new railway line has generated not only positive direct economic benefits for the region, but also new infrastructural development that served as an important driver of improved financial performance of local enterprises and institutions. The policy implications drawn from this analysis are that (i) the infrastructure development can also be important for the financial performance of existing business enterprises and institutions; and (ii) it might be rational to employ the rule of Tax Increment Financing (TIF) for financing other cases of infrastructure investment, because taxable capacity of the main beneficiary of this infrastructure development, namely the *Toshguzar-Boysun-Kumkurgon* region, was enhanced by the new investment. On this basis, the chapter supports the TIF rule, because the main beneficiary is indeed the region where this project is introduced. Because the TIF rule conforms to the theoretical principle of benefit taxation, it is both efficient and equitable according to the principles of public finance.

Chapter 13 deals with government initiatives to promote public-private partnerships for increasing investment in water infrastructure in Indonesia. Although access to clean water is acknowledged as a necessity in most countries, its provision is not among the top priorities for every local government in Indonesia. It is also true that private sector investors are not often attracted to water infrastructure. This may be partly because investing in water infrastructure is not regarded as competitive due to the expected rates of return on investment in water often being low, despite its high economic and social impact. In this context, this study of Indonesia's water infrastructure investment provides helpful insights into the ways in which a developing country might attract private sector investment in clean water infrastructure. Based on in-depth interviews with government officials and private sector counterparts, it is found that private sector investment in the water sector of Indonesia has been helped by the provision of government supports such as the Viability Gap Fund, the Project Development Facility, land acquisition, and government guarantees to hedge against financial risks. Together, these initiatives have helped to make water sector projects more attractive to private sector investors. Thus, targeted government support has played an important role in attracting private sector investment into water infrastructure in Indonesia.

Chapter 14 provides a narrative for Delhi's land-pooling policy and development-based value capture strategies as a source of finance for infrastructure in Transit-Oriented Development (TOD) areas. In India, the central, state, and local governments have always been involved in investing in relevant infrastructure. This chapter reports on the use of land-pooling as a development-based value capture tool (the purest form of land monetization) for the Territory of Delhi. Urban development authorities and urban local bodies (ULBs) in Delhi are highly dependent on taxes and fees for revenue generation. It is noted that the process of value capture is underutilized in Delhi due to the land being a central subject under India's constitution. Thus, Delhi's ULBs do not own the land and are therefore prevented from generating revenues from land ownership. This situation creates challenges for the urban government and local bodies in financing infrastructure investment. A methodology that is suggested by way of a sustainable model for developing infrastructure follows along with the value capture strategies under PPPs in Delhi's land-pooling zones. It is expected that this methodology would emerge as a way to allow local authorities and ULBs to capture land value through the provision of infrastructure around the TOD zones. In turn, this would allow the development of sustainable urban infrastructure to occur. The recommendations in the paper could make land pooling a novel approach for funding urban infrastructure, despite the fact that subnational governments in Delhi cannot own land on which infrastructure investment takes place.

Chapter 15 deals with tax incentives offered by the Indonesian government to attract private investment in infrastructure. With more than 17,000 islands, balanced regional economic development has been a challenge for Indonesia, because economic activity is heavily concentrated in Java, which accounts for more than 56% of national population and 55% of national GDP. The development of infrastructure is a critical factor for achieving regionally equitable economic growth. In recent years, infrastructure investment in Indonesia has increased sharply in response to government incentives, including tax concessions to attract private sector investment in infrastructure. This chapter evaluates the effectiveness of tax incentives and their impact on administrative policies. It considers how the private sector of Indonesia might be incentivized to invest in infrastructure. The importance of this issue arises from the fact that, while Indonesia needs to invest more than 6% of its GDP in infrastructure, budgetary allocation is only about one-half of this amount. Indonesia's government has also offered tax incentives to attract private sector investors. In addition to VAT exemption, direct tax incentives are also offered in the form of a tax holiday and a tax allowance for reducing the corporate income tax effective rate. The uptake of these tax allowances remains low, however. For example, only 167 taxpayers had utilized the legally available tax allowances between 2007 and 2020. Indeed, the perverse situation is that the amount of tax revenue foregone on account of legal tax concessions declined from Rp1.06 trillion in 2016 to Rp791 billion in 2019! This shows that tax allowances are either not well designed or not properly implemented. A third, but unlikely, possibility could be that, because tax effectiveness in Indonesia is so low to start with, most tax liability is evaded already, rendering new tax allowances virtually ineffective.

Part I

Assessing the Impacts of Investments and the Future of Sustainable Infrastructure

1 Infrastructure Investment and Managerial Oversight

A Pathway to Regional Growth

Eugene Chao and Necmettin Kaymaz

1.1 Introduction

Infrastructure is a national asset for economic productivity. Government spending on infrastructure investment, along with a significant amount of capital infill and endorsement from the multilateral banks, has become a common scheme to transform a nation's long-term competitiveness and facilitate regional integration (Bivens 2017; EIB 2018h, Leduc and Wilson 2012, 2014; Warner 2014), with examples that include the Belt and Road Initiative in the 2010–2020s; the Juncker Plan of the European Investment Bank, and the Central Asia transport strategy of the Asian Development Bank and the Central Asia Regional Economic Cooperation (CAREC) (ADB 2019a; European Commission 2018; The Economist 2018; CAREC 2020). Reviewing these transformative periods, infrastructure investment undoubtedly boosted national GDPs but left disastrous outstanding liabilities on each government's balance sheet (Hamada 2016a,b; IMF 2019; 中国发展研究基金会 2016a,b). In the realm of delivering public goods, what are the roles the government leaders, capital enablers, and state-owned enterprises (SOEs) should take? What scale and magnitude of investment are enough to achieve the intended environmental, social and governance (ESG) outcome and investment return? Which investment will create the most value? Is there an interrelation or a contradiction of investing in different infrastructure assets in terms of investment return and regional integration? What are the corresponding measures to avoid the likelihood of investment offset? How could policy formation and managerial strategy complement each other to maximize synergistic value among the investments to further empower a region's long-term competitiveness? The article distills these decisive questions, revealing the investment landscape of common city assets and the important distinction between value-creating vs. value-destroying projects.

Many countries, while investing in infrastructure, often face these challenges:

I. Prior to fund allocation, the prerequisite is to define what kind of city people want. Cities built around transit and rail, for example, are different from those built around cars and highways. How can countries create a greener and more livable city and region while increasing their return on investment

DOI: 10.4324/9781003228790-3

(ROI) and ESG outcomes? As many Central Asian cities are trying to upgrade their infrastructure, it is imperative for government leaders and capital enablers to define this.

II. Federal and state decision-makers are carrying different infrastructure investment mindsets and horizons (e.g., seasonality, five-year duration, 10-year duration, perpetuity fund, etc.). Public servants dedicate themselves to new infrastructure projects that make positive impacts on the life of citizens; however, they may overemphasize the scale of the investment at the expense of ROI. Private investors exercise their fiduciary obligation to generate return, but this may evolve into a mundane methodology: an overemphasis on driving a specific fund's return (e.g., highway fund III.) without systematic examination of its interrelation with correlating funds (e.g., rail fund III.). An inevitable phenomenon occurs: a large amount of capital is invested in infrastructure, but the city and region still faces significant externalities and economic growth leakage. Even worse, aggregate growth (economic, social, and environmental) and livability remain elusive. Without systematically examining the complex interrelation between funds within the portfolio, it requires more capital to "correct" the situation in the following rounds of investment.

III. Investment activity is the execution of policy. Mutually conflicting policies and investment decisions offset the total aggregated return. This frequently happens in emerging countries that are trying to learn from developed countries' experience. However, they are simultaneously encountering policy and investment dilemmas: is the policy formed today going to incentivize higher rail or transit usage to increase the fund's return or is it going to encourage more cars on the (toll) road without considering externality and negative spillover. A confusion of goals and means and lack of managerial oversight lead to either overspending or poorly defined goals or unintended outcomes. This happens when the investor (e.g., government, bank, etc.) is unable to differentiate between investing in value creation vs. value-destroying infrastructure projects.

Aside from addressing these investment concepts, the purpose of infrastructure is to improve people's lives. The definition of a livable city or region includes the following characteristics: economically viable and efficient, socially sound and equitable, and environmentally friendly and sustainable (Vuchic 1999, 2003; Gehl 2010). Under the CAREC 2020 strategy, 7,800 km of roads and 1,800 km of rail tracks were built by 2017. The 2030 agenda will be focusing on increasing sustainability and network quality (ADB 2019b, CAREC 2017a, b, 2020). But which investment will create the most value to the region? A debate of the necessity to invest in car-related infrastructure vs. rail-related infrastructure deserves comprehensive examinations at the policy, investment, and management levels. What are the critical roles the different transportation modes should take in increasing city functionality and regional integration? What are the decision trade-offs while investing in these assets? Table 1.1 compares the

Table 1.1 Technical, Operational, and System Characteristics of Urban Transportation Modes

Generic Class		*Private*		*Street Transit*		*Semirapid Transit*		*Rapid Transit*	
Characteristics	*Unit*	*Auto on Street*	*Auto on Freeway*	*RB*	*SCR*	*BRT*	*LRT*	*RRT*	*RGR*
Vehicle/Capacity, C_v	sps/veh	4–6, total	1.2–2.0 usable	40–120	100–180	40–120	110–250	140–280	140–210
Vehicles/Transit Unit	veh/TU	1	1	1	1–3	1	1–4	1–10	1–10
Transit Unit Capacity	sps/TU	4–6, total	1.2–2.0 usable	40–120	100–300	40–120	100–600	140–2000	140–1800
Max. Technical Speed, V	km/h	40–80	89–90	40–80	60–70	70–90	60–100	80–100	80–130
Max. Frequency, f_{max}	TU/h	600–800	1500–2000	60–120	60–120	60–90	40–90	20–40	10–30
Line Capacity, C	sps/h	720–1050	1800–2600	2400–8000	4000–15,000	4000–8000	6000–20,000	10,000–40,000	8000–35,000
Normal Operating Speed, V_o	km/h	20–50	60–90	15–25	12–20	20–40	20–45	25–60	40–70
Operating Speed at Capacity, V^c_o	km/h	10–30	20–60	6–15	5–13	15–30	15–40	24–55	38–65
Productive Capacity, P_c	10^3 sp-km/h	10–25	50–120	20–90	30–150	75–200	120–600	400–1800	500–2000
Lane Width (one-Way)	m	3.00–3.65	3.65–3.75	3.00–3.65	3.00–3.50	3.65–3.75	3.40–3.75	3.70–4.30	4.00–4.75
Vehicle Control	-	Man./vis.	Man./vis.	Man./vis.	Man./vis.	Man./vis.	Man./vis.-sig.	Man.-auto./sig.	Man./vis.-sig.
Reliability	-	Low-med	Med-high	Low-med	Low-med	High	High	Very high	Very high
Safety	-	Low	Low-med	Med	Med	High	High	Very high	Very high
Station Spacing	m	-	-	200-500	250-500	350-800	350-800	500-2000	1200-4500

Source: Authors.

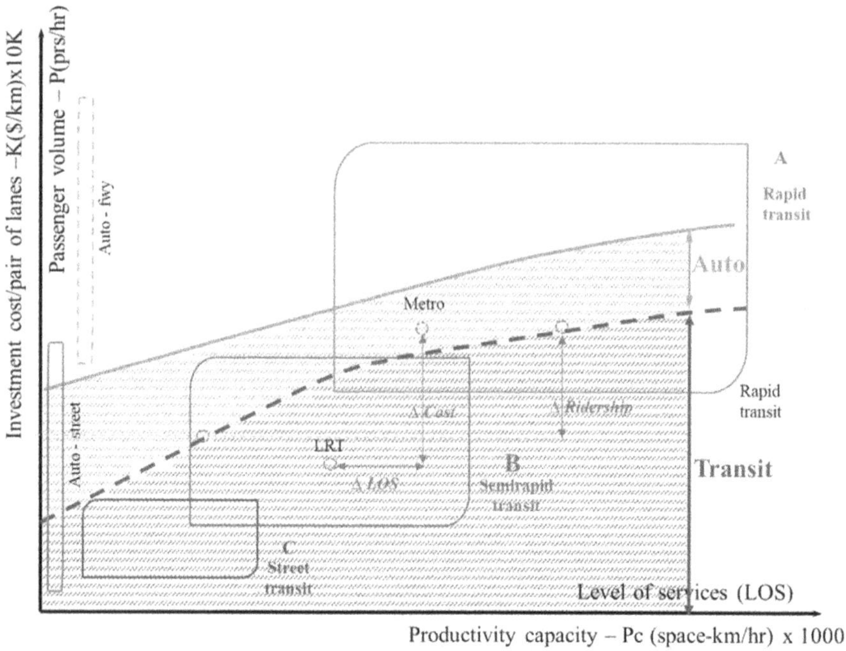

Figure 1.1 Relationships between Productive Capacity, Investment Cost, and Passenger Attraction of Different Right of Way Modes.

Source: Authors.

common modes of public transport in cities and metropolitan areas. Figure 1.1 shows the investment trade-offs between different modes (Vuchic 1981). For example, with a big budget to invest in the transit system, metro offers higher capacity with higher investment cost than light rail, which provides a greater level of services. Meanwhile, within the constant demand for public transport, the growing amount of transit investment has a positive correlation with usage, and, as the modal split from car to transit increases, fewer drivers and fewer cars on the road alleviate congestion and externalities.

1.2 Essential Challenges in City Infrastructure: Collision of Cities and Cars in a Vicious Circle

One of the essential challenges in infrastructure investment is the collision of cities and cars and the "vicious circle" it creates. Many cities do not have a full understanding of the forces (shown in Figure 1.2) that increase traffic congestion, decrease transit usage, and worsen conditions for pedestrians and for the environment. Cities make short-term improvements to their transportation systems by building more roads and parking facilities; in the long term, the problems

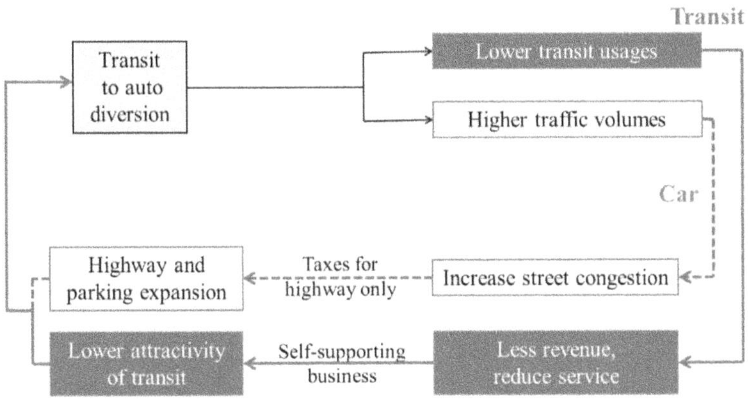

Figure 1.2 The Vicious Circle in Urban Transportation.
Source: Authors.

with their systems are more serious than these improvements can address. In the US state of Texas, Governor Rick Perry spent $2.8 billion to widen Interstate 10 from the initial eight lanes to 26 lanes (12 main, eight feeder, six high occupancy) (Aaron 2008; Schmitt 2015). Aside from the massive landmass taken, the total travel time on average increased 30% year-over-year after the completion (Cornell 2016). Simply expanding lanes worsened the situation. Incrementally, an increasing number of cities have adopted measures that lead to reduced traffic congestion and shift many trips from private cars to transit, non-motorized vehicles, and pedestrians.

1.2.1 Interrelation Between Highway and Transit Travel

A systems approach to the relationship between highways and transit explains the fundamental problem in urban transportation and corresponding policies. Figure 1.3 shows the travel time of cars on streets/highways for a given distance as the traffic volume (cars per hour) increases. The speed is constant when the traffic volume is low. As the number of cars increases, traffic speed decreases, causing travel time and costs to increase until it leads to congestion, stopped vehicles and theoretically infinite travel time. The total disutility of travel (or so-called negative spillover) increases in the same way as travel time. Transit systems have a different relationship between the number of passengers and their travel time or disutility. As also shown in Figure 1.3, when passenger volume q (trip/hr) is low (e.g., service is one bus every 30 mins), cost per person is high. As the passenger volume increases, bus frequency increases, with rail systems eventually built to increase speed and reliability and reduce cost per passenger.

Figure 1.4 shows the distribution of Q passengers traveling in a joint corridor by car (from the left) and by transit (from the right). As passengers mostly select

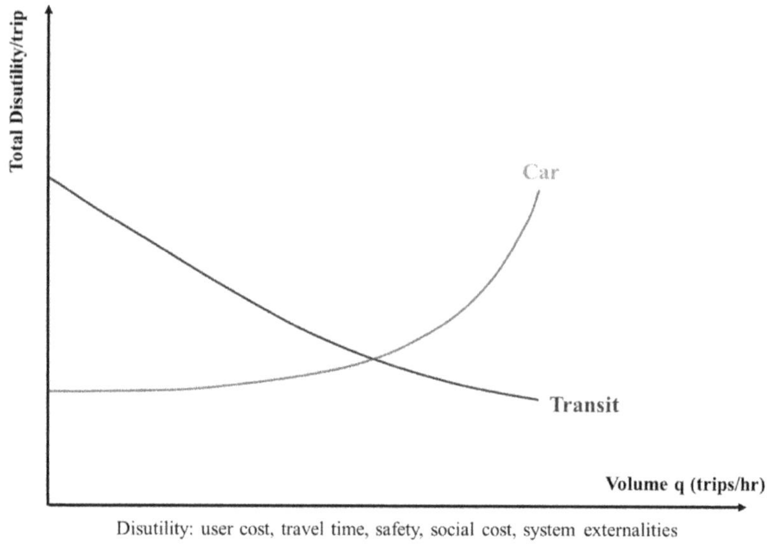

Figure 1.3 Average User Travel Disutility Curves as Functions of Number of Trips/hr. for Car and Transit.

Source: Authors.

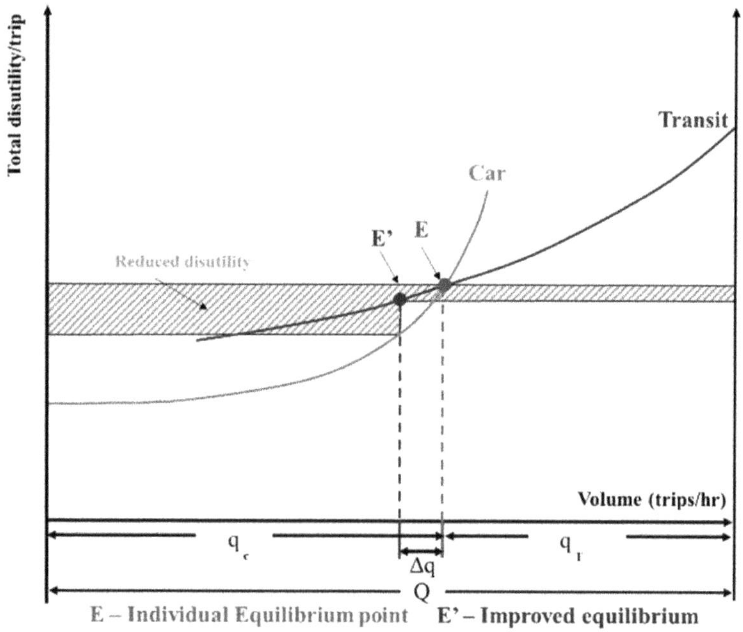

Figure 1.4 Travel Distribution between Cars and Transit.

Source: Authors.

the lower disutility mode, their distribution between car and transit will be at the equilibrium point E: q_c passengers use cars, while q_T passengers use transit. This situation can be seen in a real-world example where there is a higher capacity public transit mode and a parallel highway with congested traffic. If one could shift, for example, Δq persons per hour from their cars to the transit line, its service would be improved by greater train frequency, and congestion on the highway would be decreased. Thus, travelers on both transit and on the highway would benefit, so that shifting travelers from cars to transit optimizes the system—with minimum total disutility on both modes. However, as the diagram shows, at the situation after the shift of Δq persons, shown as point E', the disutility of individual travelers would be lower on the highway than on the transit, so that if individual travelers would decide by themselves, the Δq of them would return to the highway, or to the original equilibrium point E. Thus, the optimal condition based on individual travelers' decisions is not optimal for the entire system.

Cities with balanced transportation for livable environments understand the relationship between car and transit travel, and they apply two sets of policies to shift a substantial portion of car trips to transit trips, i.e., from individual travelers' choices toward the system optimal condition. To achieve this, cities have consistently applied two sets of transportation policies:

Policy I: Incentives to Use Transit

Policy II: Disincentives to Use Cars

Figure 1.5 shows how these two measures shift the equilibrium point from individual equilibrium (IE) toward system optimum (SO): transit incentives move the T curve down to T', whereas auto disincentives move the C curve up to C'. The result is a shift from car to transit so that the distribution between cars and transit, known as MODAL SPLIT, goes from the initial individual equilibrium toward the system optimum through the decisions of travelers, and remains stable there. The diagram shows that the total disutility of travel on both modes, which was initially at the individual equilibrium level, has been reduced to system optimum, again equal on both modes, cars and transit.

The concepts of individual equilibrium and system optimum are fundamental to determining transportation policies and corresponding investment decisions. It should be pointed out again that this examination of costs, disutilities, and intermodal trip distributions between cars and transit is conceptual. Similar to the supply-demand diagrams in economics, they are difficult to plot and interpret numerically, but they are useful for presenting the respective concepts clearly. Transportation systems operations based on individual equilibrium are much less efficient and cause more serious negative impacts than their operations at system optimum travel distribution. Cities which attempt to solve their traffic problems by building more streets, highways, and parking facilities are going into transportation conditions based on individual equilibrium. To be livable and green, cities must consistently implement the two sets of policies: incentives to

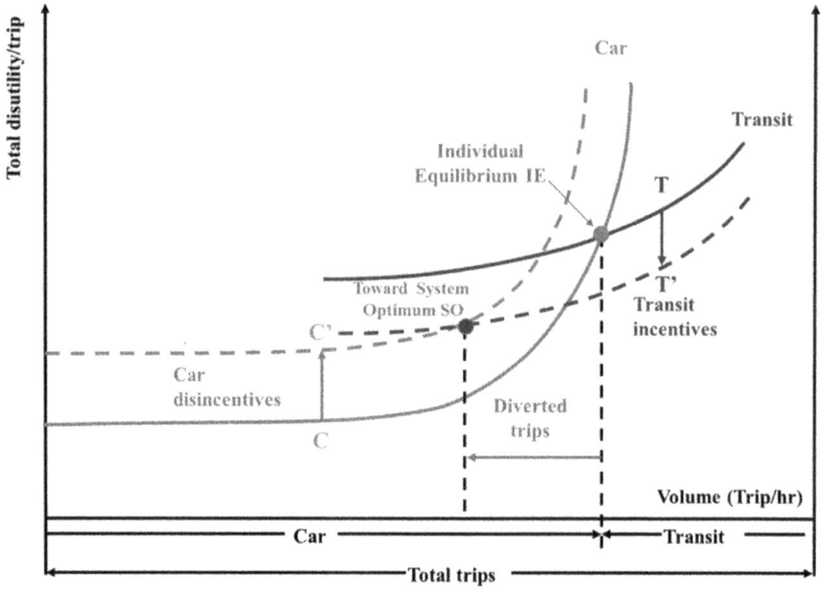

Figure 1.5 Transportation Policies for Shifting the Individual Equilibrium Point toward System Optimum.

Source: Authors.

use transit and develop a walking/human-oriented urban environment, and car-use disincentives.

1.2.2 Conflicting Policy Decisions on Investment Activity: Highway vs. Transit

Investment is generated by policy decisions. In certain cases, highway lobbyists and special interest groups have claimed that highways should be funded in equal amounts as public transit. If a city decides on a new metro line, its highway lanes would also need to expand. If a city decides to upgrade to a light rail line, a corresponding investment should be made in more roads and parking garages, etc. (IBTTA 2019; US DOT FHWA 2019). Cities that do so soon realized that their overall traffic situation does not improve, even sometimes becoming worse. These cities must again ask the fundamental question: what kind of city do people want?

Figure 1.6 explains why simultaneously investing in transit and highway infrastructure undermines cities. The purpose of infrastructure investment, besides generating returns, is to increase efficiency and decrease the cost of traveling and

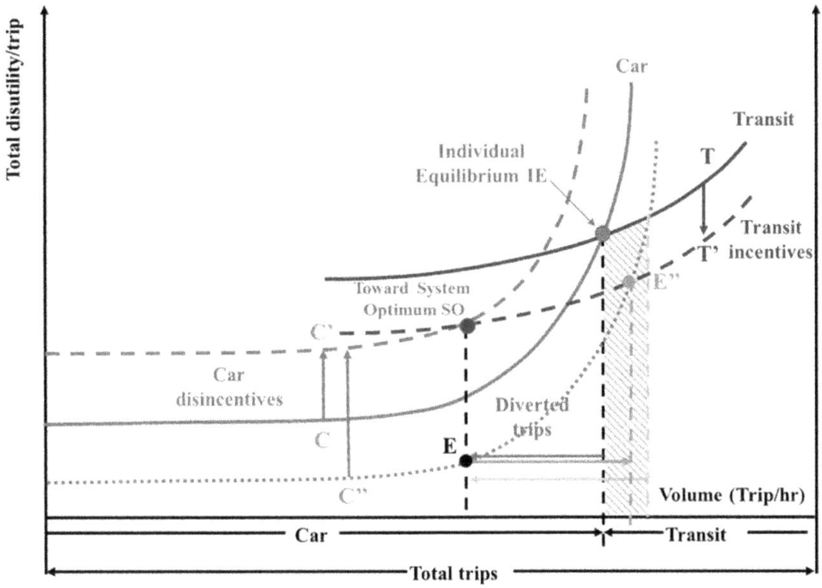

Figure 1.6 Investment Offset: Investing the Equal Amount of Capital in Public Transit and Car-Based Infrastructure.

Source: Authors.

total disutility. Investing in car-based infrastructure results in a line movement from the initial C to C'', and, in the case of transit, from T to T'. In fact, investing in car-based infrastructure results in a volume increase from E to E''; that is, more people are driving and fewer people are using transit even though the transit is efficient. The correct investment outcome is to divert a greater number of car trips to transit from E'' to system optimum; that is, to increase the total travel volume by transit. This is not meant to advocate for divestment in car-based infrastructure, but rather to advise caution regarding the dynamic movement between individual equilibrium and system optimum. If the increase in car travel causes economic leakage and lower productivity due to congestion and externalities, policy and investment decisions need to alleviate the offset.

Figure 1.6 illustrates that, if a city were to follow the advice of the highway lobbyists, and invest equally in highway and public transit, it would be unable to deliver a better outcome. Figure 1.7 explains that the more desirable outcome can be achieved when the capital put into the transit system is greater than that put into the highway infrastructure. By doing so, the total disutility on both systems has been improved and the travel volume by transit was increased from E' to E'' associated with car reduction.

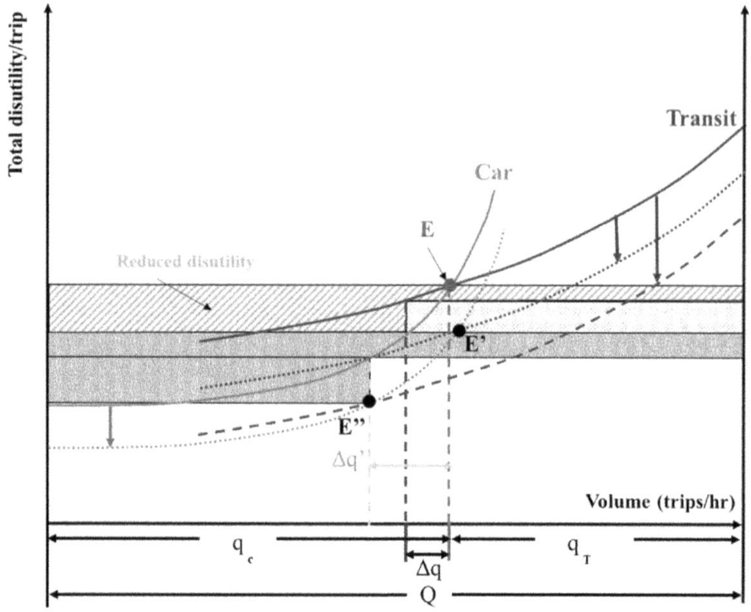

Figure 1.7 Positive Return on Investment: Capital Put into Transit is Greater than the Car-Related Infrastructure.

Source: Authors.

1.2.3 Policy Implementation: A Systematic Interplay of Control Mechanisms

Transit and walking incentives consist of a variety of physical, operational, and financial, short-term or long-term measures. Car use disincentives comprise designing complete streets, introducing pedestrian streets, zones or squares, limiting parking supply, meter parking, road pricing, gasoline taxes, etc. The above-defined policy does not mean that there should be no construction or improvements to streets and highways; rather, it means that traffic congestion should be reduced or prevented by discouraging use of cars.

An overview of the car and transit incentive and disincentives policies, investment decisions, and their mutual relationships are given in Table 1.2. Combinations of car and transit incentives and car and transit disincentives result in increased and decreased mobility, respectively, but they do not change modal split. For example, building a parallel freeway and metro line represents an investment in competing facilities without improving livability and mutually jeopardizes each return. Car incentives combined with transit disincentives, which is still influencing many cities' investment decisions, makes a city more car-dependent and less people-friendly. Car disincentives combined with transit incentives lead to greener cities and is proven to strengthen national long-term competitiveness and provides a high rate of return.

Table 1.2 Policies and Investments Toward Car and Transit Modes and Their Impacts on Intermodal Balance

Policy Type	*Investment*	*Mobility*	*Modes and Policies*
Incentives	High	Increased	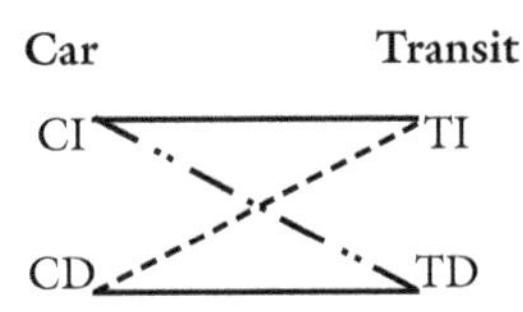
Disincentives	Low or Negative	Decreased	

Legend for policies

- - - - - - - - - -	Leads to balanced intermodal system	CI: Car Incentive
————————	May not influence intermodal relations	TI: Transit Incentive
— -- — -- —	Increases imbalance favoring car	CD: Car Disincentive
		TD: Transit Disincentive

Source: Authors.

1.3 Managerial Strategy and Performance Appraisal for Growth Management

Government, multilateral banks, SOEs, and private investors are needed to invest in infrastructure assets. The faster investors can increase revenue and deploy more capital at attractive rates, the more value they create. To determine which investment opportunity will create the most value, the investor needs to distinguish between investing in value creation vs. destruction projects. Investors must also gauge investment decisions based on scale vs. quality. Finally, as competition increases, access to higher quality investments becomes restricted. Unavoidably, investing in value destruction projects occasionally occurs. To prevent this, the investor must take countermeasures. A four-step value creation procedure delineates the corresponding measures.

1.3.1 Differentiation Between Value Creation Vs. Destruction Projects in Infrastructure Investment

In investments, the opportunity cost of capital (OCC) involves the comparison of expected returns from a project to an alternative target with similar risk attributes after the same capital and resource have been invested. OCC is what has been given up by investing in a specific project instead of the alternative. The investment decision is a trade-off, and the OCC represents a non-negotiable dichotomy of value creation vs. destruction. Recalling the concept of return on investment: infrastructure projects with an expected Return on New Invested Capital (RONIC) above the OCC are value creating; those with an expected return below the OCC are value destroying, as shown in Figure 1.8. As this example shows, then:

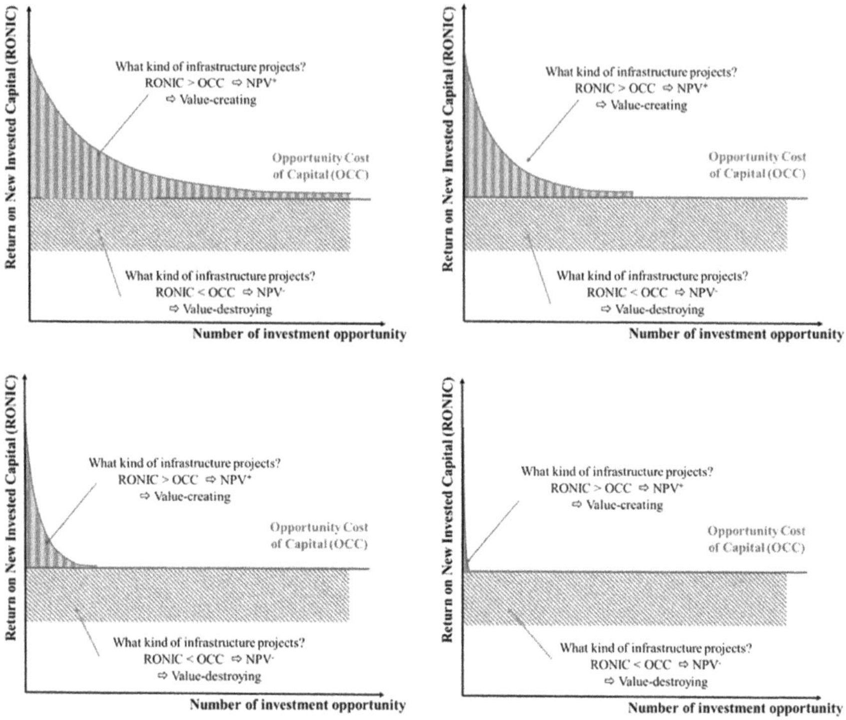

Figure 1.8 Infrastructure Investment in Value Creation vs. Destruction Projects over Economic Competitiveness.

Source: Kaiser and Young (2013).

- If RONIC is less than the OCC, growth destroys value;
- If RONIC is greater than the OCC, growth creates value;
- If RONIC equals the OCC, growth has a neutral impact on value since all investments are net present value (NPV)=0;
- If growth = 0, there is no return on new investment. The investment impact on value is none.

No matter whether the investor is a government, bank, SOE, or private investor, the expectation is to generate more RONIC than OCC. To a government, RONIC refers to the aggregate return (economic, social, and environmental) on investment and the growth of the economy and jobs. To a bank, RONIC refers to the accumulated return over the lending period. To SOEs, RONIC could mean the opportunity of business expansion and enhancement of reciprocating relationship. To an investor, RONIC could simply mean the monetary return. A project is value creating if it can generate a positive NPV over the course of the asset's lifecycle. If a government were able to consistently invest in positive-NPV projects, it would create a possibility, not a guarantee, of returns exceeding OCC. Some governments routinely earn RONIC higher than OCC while creating value with their investments. Other governments that have been unable to discern the importance of choosing positive-NPV projects have inevitably seen their RONIC fall to the level of OCC or below it.

If the government fails to act on this investment principle, it will have no access to positive-NPV projects because all growth will be coming from value-destroying projects. Any additional investment is going to destroy value (Kaiser and Young 2013). When this happens, the correct action is to divest until understanding the fundamentals. Infrastructure is the backbone of the economy and one of the common elements to rank country competitiveness. Those lacking understanding of the importance of investing in positive-NPV projects have no choice but to invest in negative-NPV projects. Sooner or later, one will face a series of diminishing returns (the blue color part of Figure 1.8) and incrementally lose global competitiveness.

1.3.2 Differentiation Between Return on Scale Vs. Return on Quality in Infrastructure Investment

Within the realm of infrastructure decisions, a common question is: how much capital is needed to invest to sustain economic growth? (Warner 2014; IMF 2015; Coutts 2016; The White House 2016; The Economist 2018). The question needs to be reframed as: how much can we grow without destroying value? While the initial question focuses on scale, the reframed question draws attention to quality and method. When growth is disconnected from value creation, growth itself leads to value destruction (Kaiser and Young 2013). Within the public sector, a common standard is to evaluate government officials by quantifying the growth achieved under their tenure. For example, within the 4-year electoral period, government officials have invested X_1 capital to open X_2 metro lines, replaced X_3 diesel buses, privatized X_4 government assets to generate X_5 upfront capital for the city, etc. (CAREC 2019a, b; Goodman and Loveman 1991; OECD 2009; TR News 2018; World Bank Group 2018). Quantifying delivered growth is a good way for officials to win another 4- or 5-year seat or move toward an upper-level position, but this is a deceptive measure because they are neither measuring the quality of growth nor ensuring they are investing in positive-NPV projects. Many officials will fight to deliver growth, even when they feel it is not the right thing to do. If the only chance for success depends on spending money without considering whether the investment will create or destroy value, and one's authority depends on speed, then this is a foregone conclusion. It is easy to find examples of governments that have set growth targets and then aggressively pursued them until they destroyed the city (in this chapter, it refers to the collision of cars and cities and the vicious circles), or at least until painful restructuring is started. This is a hazard of growth and the whole system needs to be fixed, not necessarily any particular decision-maker. Some government officials mix goals and means, presuming that, as long as money keeps flowing into infrastructure, the nation's economy, society, environment, and livability standards will keep getting better. It is common to see that they misinterpreted the causality simply by assuming that if the nation achieves high gross domestic product and increases government spending, it will pave the way to success. In fact, not all growth is good for the government, particularly when it comes to using government capital to invest in infrastructure. It depends on how much capital has been allocated to achieve the growth (Kaiser and Young 2013). Growth at what cost? Growth, but how long can it be sustained? What is the quality of growth? When a government fails to invest in positive-NPV projects and simultaneously increases the overall liability, it destroys value and is unable to deliver intended outcomes.

1.3.3 Value Destruction vs. Countermeasure: A Better Governance

Governmental obsession with growth comes in part from this confusion of casuality and of goals and means. Some governments tend to either overspend their money or spend money without clearly defined goals and expected outcomes. On the other hand, successful governments with clearly defined goals, experience above average growth in gaining the aggregate return on infrastructure investment. Additionally, these governments never reward value-destroying investment decisions and activities. When decision-makers destroy value by pursuing unprofitable growth, there are opportunities for the incumbent to add value simply by cutting investment and not safeguarding it. What should the government do when investing in a value-destroying project or executing a mutually conflicting decision? If it unfortunately happens, the correct countermeasure is a precise sequence, as shown in Figure 1.9:

- First, stop all cash from flowing into the investment unless a definitive path on how it would generate short-term profit and long-term value. Returns ambiguously delivering on a combination of these two must end.
- Second, the managerial strategy needs to separate from the short-term profit spike vs. long-term value creation to ensure every ongoing endeavor is going to drive the expected future free cash flow. A common dissection is to start with the working capital—a measurement of an organization's financial strength (e.g., national account, state budget). If there is room for improvement, the execution is going to unleash capital and free up resources, but must not compromise administrative operations and organizational management.
- Third, put capital back to work. Moving forward, managerial oversight can focus on value creation rather than alternative perspectives. Only value creation activities that generate higher expected future free cash flow than the OCC should be carried out. Only when this new mindset has proliferated should new investments and growth be reinitiated.
- Fourth, develop an investment discipline. A necessary endeavor focuses on managing and monitoring performance with a feed-in governance procedure and control mechanism to continuously drive government fund

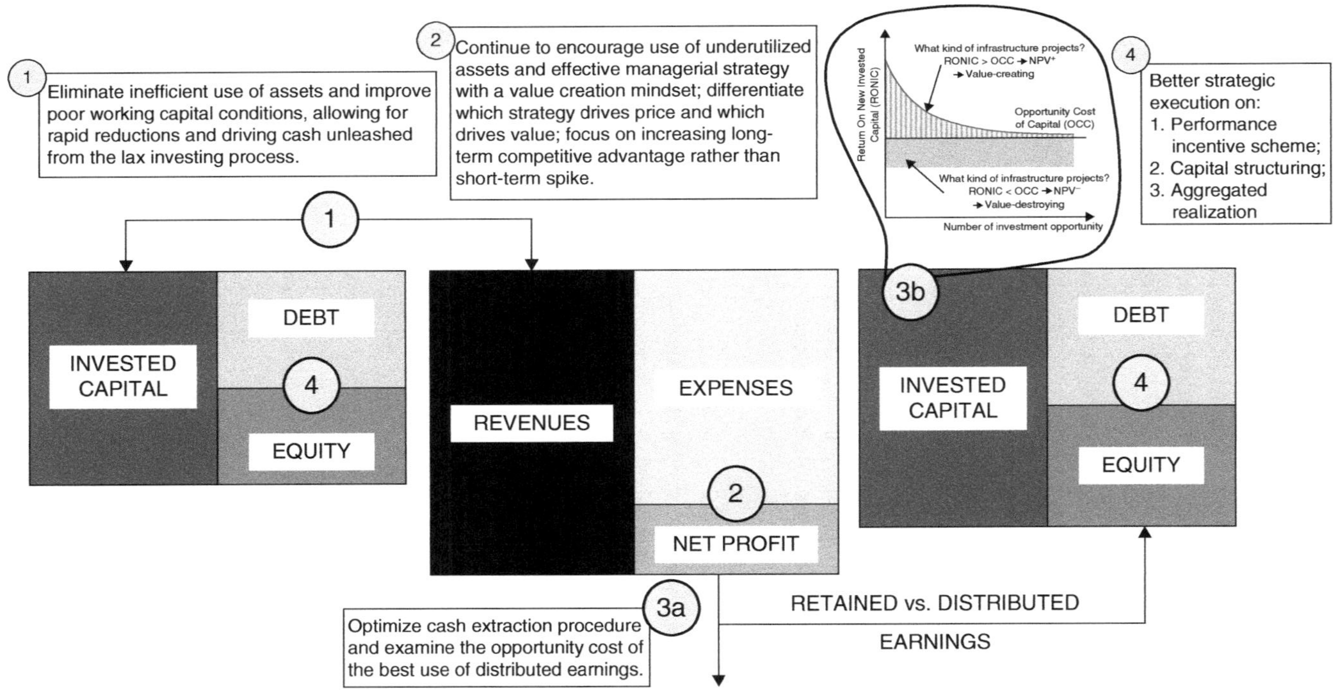

Figure 1.9 Infrastructure Value Destruction vs. Countermeasure: The 4-Step Value Creation Procedure Chart.
Source: Authors; Kaiser and Westarp (2010).

returns and anticipated growth. To uplift, one must reduce the unnecessary administrative burden and avoid the hazard of agency cost. The unnecessary administrative burden refers to competing interests in investing in infrastructure raised by institutional autonomy and independent governance. In this case, gaps in interagency collaboration and bureaucratic procedure erode efficiency gains. The hazard of agency costs refers to a high cost of exchanging information, information delays, biased decision-making due to imbalanced information, and a misallocation of capital arising from interagency or multilateral competition. At the managerial level, thoughtful leadership and supervisory mechanisms are indispensable for establishing efficient administration and effective interagency collaboration (Kaiser and Westarp 2010).

1.4 Common Mistakes in Policy Making and Capital Deployment

With the analysis of value-creation investment frameworks, interpretation of the diminishing returns of investing in negative-NPVprojects, and investigation of the countermeasures against value-destruction projects, four types of cities are identified below:

a. Confusing cities do not identify clear goals and policies and investment mechanisms; these are more willing to make small adjustments and tolerate congestion when inevitable;
b. Aggressive cities do not identify clear goals, policies, and investment mechanisms, but nevertheless aggressively dump capital into heavily subsidized kickstarter (i.e., unbankable) projects, with the unrealistic expectation that as long as they kept spending, development would occur and the city's capacity to handle that development would be maintained;
c. Progressive cities have defined clear goals and progressive policies to implement the changes needed to move toward greener cities; and
d. Transitioning cities learn from large cities in developed countries, avoiding their mistakes and adopting their successful measures. However, this "copy-and-paste" method has led to a variety of recurring issues; thus, certain countermeasures need to be adopted and finely tuned to the individual city.

The evolution of cities' growth from pedestrian-oriented to transit-guided and then to car-dependent occurred in different periods and local conditions, but many basic patterns and changes were similar. Today, many Central Asian countries in the transitioning stages (e.g., Uzbekistan) have the advantage of learning from cities that have already transitioned (ADB 2015; 2019a; Buyuk Kelajak 2019; WBG 2015, 2019a,b, 2020), adopting their solutions while avoiding their mistakes.

1.4.1 Managerial Oversight and Misused Subsidy in Infrastructure Investment

This first group of case studies demonstrates the important elements of return on "managerial oversight" and the consequence of mutually conflicting policies on investment decisions. In addition, the narrative, contrary to value creation, reveals how government entities misuse SOEs and subsidies to invest in unbankable infrastructure projects, causing the infamous scheme of debt transfer.

1.4.1.1 Mutually Conflicting Policies and Investment Offset

One common failure happens in the initial phase of investment decision by not adopting a systems approach or drafting corresponding transportation incentives and disincentive policies. It is frequently misunderstood and underestimated how policies can achieve a better modal split by slightly adjusting the equilibrium point and reducing the aggregated disutility between cars and transit. Some governments fail to incorporate externality costs into their decision process. Unfortunately, a series of distorted policies and eschewed investments generate offsetting consequences to cities' livability, as shown in Figure 1.10.

1.4.1.2 Debt Transfer Scheme

Unlike fully privatized corporations with solely revenue-driven mindsets, corporate entities with partial governmental ownership benefit from closer supervision and, more importantly, help the government facilitate and execute public policy (Buyuk

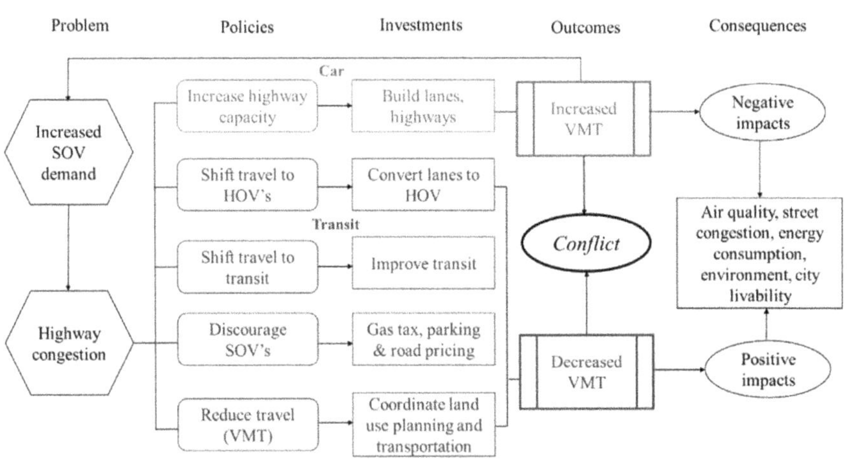

Figure 1.10 Offsetting Consequences of Conflicting Policies and Investments: Car vs. Transit.

Source: Authors.

Kelajak 2019; CDF 2018b; EBRD 2018a,b; Ernst & Young 2019; OECD 2019). SOEs function as an enforcement arm of the government to carry out initiatives, and an incumbent party to safeguard projects (Global Capital 2019; Doré 2019; IFC 2019). The fiduciary duty of SOEs is to produce a higher ESG return along with the investment. The reality, however, is sometimes more quid pro quo; many SOEs safeguard projects because the enterprise plans to win more political endorsements and expand itself. They ensure projects are built and developments are completed; government officials, meanwhile, can deliver their promised scale of investment and climb the career ladder thanks to this reciprocating system. But not every development is bankable and delivers value creation (Penyalver and Turró 2019; Turró and Penyalver 2019a, b; Tadjibaeva, D. 2019; Talatovna et al. 2019). Too often, the SOEs find themselves safeguarding an unbankable project, or even multiple unbankable projects at the same time. Besides destroying value as described in Section 3.1, these unbankable projects and businesses often require a significant amount of government subsidy. Through the heavy subsidies, the cost of operating low-productivity businesses is transferred to the government's balance sheet, rather than the corporate account. This is known as a debt transfer scheme. Figure 1.11 shows how debt transfer schemes work. The cost of operating the low-productivity businesses falls to the government. The more the government requests for unbankable projects, the more likely the SOEs are to conduct debt transfer schemes. This eventually leads to a dramatic increase in government debt, such that the state or federal administration encounters a serious exposure to bankruptcy. To reverse this trend, the precise countermeasure is the four-step value creation procedure chart shown in Figure 1.11.

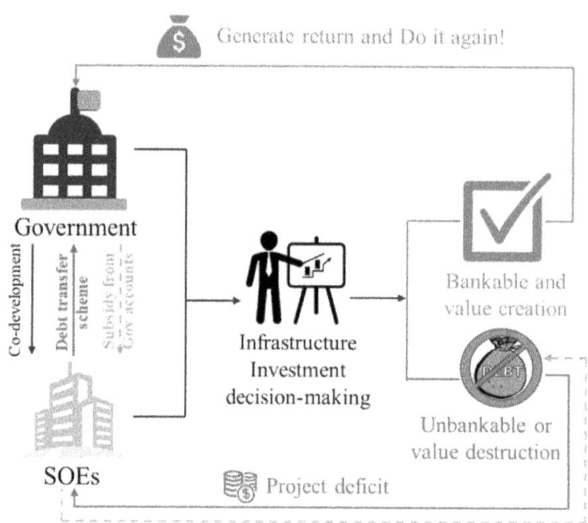

Figure 1.11 Debt Transfer Scheme in Unbankable or Value Destruction Projects. Source: Authors.

1.4.2 Administrative Burden and Hazard of Agency Cost in Infrastructure Investment

The second case study group contrasts two different cities' way of making public transportation investment decisions. The New York case reflects decentralized decision-making; by contrast, the Moscow case shows a process where policy, investment, and execution decisions are consolidated. Moscow is a good example of how a city can use infrastructure to transform its long-term competitiveness and increase its livability. Both cities still have room to scale and improve.

1.4.2.1 US Passenger Rail Case Study: New York Regional Rail System

In contrast to Russian cities, cities in the US encounter more administrative and managerial barriers across different layers of government when mobilizing infrastructure investment. For example, in New York, a global economic hub, there are six major agencies, including Amtrak, New Jersey Transit (NJT), Long Island Rail Road (LIRR), Metro-North Railroad, New York Mass Transit Agency (MTA), and bi-state Port Authority of New York and New Jersey, as shown in Figure 1.12. These agencies have their own agendas and priorities (New Jersey Commuter Organization 2016; New Jersey Business Journal 2017; North New Jersey Daily News 2017; Rethink Studio 2017a,b,c). This uncooperative inter-agency management has resulted in serious inconveniences to passengers traveling across different modes throughout the region. The lack of coordination embedded with a significant agency cost undermines regional rail investment in three different ways: overlapping spending on a same project, skewed investing priorities, and susceptibility to the efforts of lobbyists.

The city's current transit systems and network are unable to accommodate the rising demand of ridership. More people chose to move into the city for different reasons: fashion, art, music, or to make a fortune, etc. To commute in and out of Manhattan, common choices are either by rail or bus. Penn Station is a dead-end terminal in the center of midtown Manhattan that serves millions of daily commuters. The network efficiency, operating flexibility, and continuity of lines and transfers at Penn Station are low. Train movements at Penn Station are inefficient due to the design and inflexible track alignments, resulting in low fleet utilization. Penn Station is also disconnected from Grand Central Station, which links to the northeastern part of the US. Commuting in and out of Manhattan via the rail network becomes difficult. Commuters relying on low capacity Right-of-Way (ROW) C buses face even more delays. In fact, buses, on both peak and off-peak commuter times, are "parked" at the Lincoln Tunnel toll plaza. Commuters spend about an extra 60–120 minutes to enter and exit Manhattan on a daily basis (CBS NY 2015; NY Business Journal 2015; NBC NY 2017). The Port Authority is bringing commuters through the already heavily congested Lincoln Tunnel to the midtown Manhattan bus terminal, instead of using a high-capacity ROW A rail system through the Trans-Hudson Gateway tunnel to Penn Station.

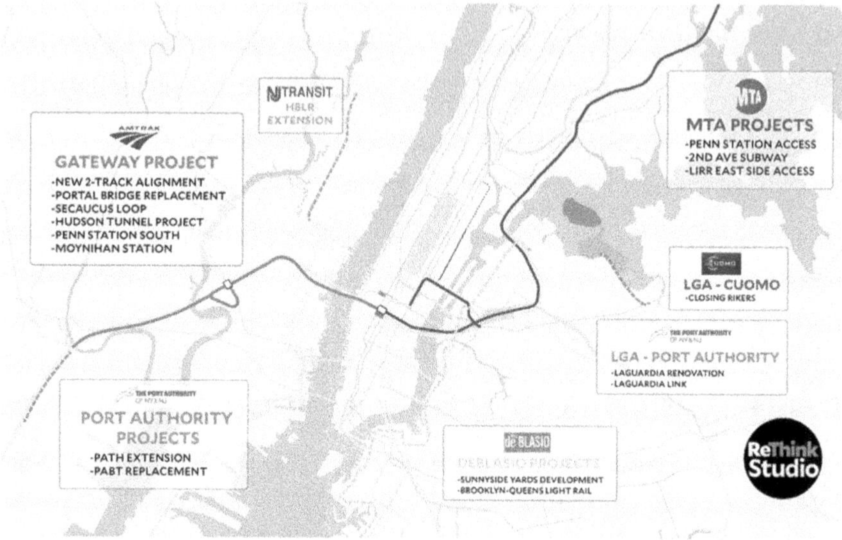

Figure 1.12 The Incumbent Transit Agencies in the New York Region.
Source: ReThinkNYC Regional Unified Network Overview.

The delays associated with these various modes of transit result in lost productivity as commuters spend unproductive time on travel.

The traveling dilemma in New York is an outcome of mutually conflicting policies that do not prioritize high-capacity modes, as well as minimum or even nonexistent interagency collaboration on regional infrastructure development and capital allocation. As an example, over the past two decades, the Gateway Tunnel project has been one of the most important rail projects in the Northeast corridor. At the state level, New York and New Jersey had to develop and invest in this bi-state project together with the federal grant. However, the states could not agree on how much each side would invest. More devastatingly, the federal government regarded the project as a state-level development. The federal and state government could not agree on the proper funding mechanism and investment process. Idling this project has been harmful to economic growth, especially as more people continue to move into the city. Contradictory policies offset anticipated outcomes and dedicated investment. Complementary policies are required instead; for instance, when investing in a rail system, a disincentive policy to discourage auto usage, or an orienting policy to direct buses on the highway to it, is necessary to achieve the expected outcome of more rail mode share and corresponding optimal use of the investment. At present, New York fails to deliver the interagency synergy and policy coordination needed to substantially improve its transit and regional rail system.

1.4.2.2 Russian Federation Intermodal Balanced Transportation System: Moscow Public Transportation

Russian cities faced a dramatic increase in private car usage during the transitional period, causing significant economic growth leakage, even stagnation, due to congestion and environmental externality. Besides Russian cities, many other cities around the globe have had a "honeymoon" phase when they made many changes to accommodate cars (wider streets, parking lots, and garages, etc.). Many cities are still building more roads and parking facilities as short-term solutions to their transportation woes, instead of defining what type of city they want and what measures they should use to achieve their goals. Even worse, some cities are using incorrect policy tools to resolve their unidentified goals. US cities like Chicago, Los Angeles, Houston, Dallas, Cleveland, etc. built wider streets and freeways for several decades, and only then invested in better transit and designed areas to re-attract pedestrians. Moscow had a shorter "honeymoon" with private cars and then began to protect and attract pedestrians, acknowledging them as indispensable elements of a livable city. These measures have been adopted at both physical and policy levels. The redesign of streets, squares, and plazas to improve intersections, together with the use of traffic engineering methods to improve traffic flow, capacity and safety with the formation of pedestrian areas, have contributed to a reduction of *probki* and improvements to overall mobility.

The city was able to successfully implement two sets of coordinated transportation policies: incentives (↑) to use public transit, walk, or use other alternative modes, and disincentives (↓) to use private cars with a dedication to creating an intermodal balanced transportation system. The city's efforts so far have included the procurement of thousands of city-wide Elektrobuses, the purchase of 100 modern articulated low-floor Skorostnyi Tramvaj (Light Rail Transit) to add to the existing Mosgortrans fleet, the examination of the electric power and service compatibility between the Elektrobus and trolleybus, the installation of dedicated lanes for prioritizing bus and LRT services, and massive investment in the Metro system: the existing Moscow central circle (MCC) and the incoming Moscow central diameter (MCD) (Moscow Transport 2017). These efforts were made with the coordination of the Treasury and the Department of Transportation and the Mayor's office (Kozlov 2017; The Russian Government 2018).

Some would say that these efforts are managerial strategies for city development with a certain involvement of transportation policy, separated from any bank's role. In fact, the banks are playing three supreme roles in investing in city's infrastructure: establishing and endorsing a favorable market for infrastructure assets, safeguarding value creation decisions and investments, and helping different government agencies build consensus policies to generate a nation's long-term competitiveness and a greater return profile. The banks need to prioritize and enforce policies in a cohesive manner; meanwhile, it must avoid enacting mutually conflicting policies and investment decisions that would offset the total return on investment.

1.5 Conclusion

Infrastructure investment can strengthen a nation's long-term competitiveness with an aggregate return on investment across the economy, society, environment, and livability. Central Asian cities and regions are facing a series of transformations. Some cities are heavily investing in infrastructure; others are trying to maintain and repair outdated assets; and still others are in the process of repositioning themselves. Infrastructure is an asset class with a significant sunk cost and an ongoing operation and maintenance commitment, which needs consistent funding to maintain a state of good repair. In the process of infrastructure investment, a common question is whether the government spending on infrastructure investment can generate long-term anticipated outcomes and strengthen national competitiveness. What scale and magnitude of government spending are enough to achieve an intended outcome? Investment is a means to accelerate growth, but growth itself is not the goal. The goal is to identify what kind of city or country people want, for example, a city built around highway or built around transit? Once the goal has been identified, the following steps are to first define which roles different participants should play and second to formulate a series of orchestrating policies, legislations (Table 1.2), and managerial strategies (Table 1.3) that focus on investing in value-creating projects with a positive-NPV, while alleviating the investment offset and externality.

When the government invests in infrastructure, the incumbent again needs to understand the importance of value-creating projects, identify the goal of the investment, assess the anticipated outcome, plan the investment procedure, allocate capital and resources, form supporting policies to encourage greater usage of the infrastructure, balance the modes of travel, mitigate the externalities, determine how to operate and maintain the infrastructure, generate a stream of revenue for the government, and, most importantly, keep investing in value-creating projects going forward. This whole process must be streamlined and efficient. Government and thought leaders are in a strong position to create a desirable investment market through a mixture of legislative policies and incentive schemes. Elected officials need to prioritize the vital few from the trivial many and enforce the few meticulously; meanwhile, they must avoid structuring mutually conflicting policies that offset the aggregate return on investment. The constructive countermeasure and control mechanism (Figure 9) must be activated when unfortunately investing in value-destroying projects. No matter whether the value created is aggregate or purely economic, the return is driven by the quality, not the scale. If one were to focus on the latter, overspending and growth leakage would take place. The role of the incumbent along with the investee's administration is to establish, foster, and expand the market with a relentless effort to strengthen a nation's long-term economy by safeguarding infrastructure investment decisions and planning city and regional development activities.

Investment activity is the execution of policy. Managerial strategy and oversight of city development and regional integration are complementary tools to

Table 1.3 Selected Managerial Strategies for Increasing an Infrastructure Asset's Competitive Advantage

Intrinsic Value	*External Growth*
Innovative products and services: Non-duplicable or patented products, or technologies to maximize network effect	**Innovative business method:** Product or service integration to capture new catchment markets and maximize synergy
Quality: Users willing to pay a higher premium for better produces and services to save travel time or increase comfort, etc	**Unique circumstance:** Unparalleled or favorable access to scarce resource, knowledge, or development right, etc
Brand: Users willing to pay a higher premium without an actual difference on product, service or tangible benefits	**Economies of scale:** Balancing return of scale vs. earnings quality, growth, and sustainable competitive advantage
User retention: Users willing to stay loyal with definitive advantages on quality, travel time saving, etc	**Operating efficiency:** Standardized lean process and control procedure
Elasticity of demand: Attention to react price fluctuation and corresponding effects without compromising return	**Barrier elimination:** Reduction of agency cost, administrative burden, and permitting process, etc

Source: Valuation – Measuring and managing the value of companies – Chapter 6 by David Wessels et.al, and author insights.

shift from individual equilibrium to system optimum. Two strategic governances can control externalities and establish an efficient travel system: one is to control the usage volume; another is to direct onto users the intrinsic cost of using the infrastructure. The implication for infrastructure investment, here, is not that cities should divest in one of the infrastructure systems, but rather they should be cautious of the dynamic movement between the individual equilibrium and system optimum. If the negativities cause economic leakage, policy and investment decisions need to act.

Acknowledgments

The corresponding author would like to thank the Senior Director at The Wharton School Alternative Investments Initiative Dr. Kevin Kaiser for the initiation and construction of the first infrastructure investment course to the MBAs in the fall of 2018 along with Eugene. Dr. Kaiser's expert insight and his theory on value creation served as an integral part of the applicable study. The corresponding author would like to thank the Moscow Deputy Mayor and Head of the Department for Transport and Road Infrastructure Development Mr. Maxim Liksutov for the exclusive invitation to visit Moscow for two and a half days in September 2018. The technical visit enabled a comprehensive understanding of the recent transformation and ongoing development in Moscow. Last, we are grateful to have numerous public transit agencies and private investors who generously shared information with us throughout several years, even decades. Although data disclosure reveals the historical fund performance and organization earnings, it could indirectly leak materialistic information and trigger unintended negativities, even dilute the outstanding cooperative relationship. To protect the accumulated relationship, we decided to cite the sources anonymously and normalize the data and still maintain the critical infrastructure investment concepts. Therefore, the figures in this chapter have been smoothened without distort any objective assessment.

References

Aaron, B. 2008. Texas Governor Rick Perry Celebrates 18 Lanes of Freedom. https://nyc.streetsblog.org/2008/10/30/texas-governor-rick-perry-celebrates-18-lanes-of-freedom (accessed 9 March 2020).

Asian Development Bank (ADB). 2014. Money Matters: Local Government Finance in the People's Republic of China. www.adb.org/sites/default/files/publication/151515/money-matters-local-government-finance-peoples-republic-china.pdf (accessed 4 August 2019).

———. 2015. Uzbekistan Factsheet. https://reliefweb.int/sites/reliefweb.int/files/resources/uzb-2015.pdf (accessed 7 March 2020).

———. 2019a. Country Partnership Strategy – Uzbekistan, 2019–2023: Supporting Economic Transformation. www.adb.org/sites/default/files/institutional-document/510251/cps-uzb-2019-2023.pdf (accessed 7 March 2020).

———. 2019b. Sector Assessment (Summary): Rail Transport. www.adb.org/sites/default/files/linked-documents/48025-003-ssa.pdf (accessed 7 March 2020).

Bivens, J. 2017. The Potential Macroeconomic Benefits from Increasing Infrastructure Investment. Economic Policy Institute. www.epi.org/publication/the-potential-macroeconomic-benefits-from-increasing-infrastructure-investment (accessed 10 January 2019).

Buyuk Kelajak (BK). 2019. Development Strategy Framework of the Republic of Uzbekistan by 2035. http://uzbekistan2035.uz/wp-content/uploads/2019/05/Концепция-Развития-Узбекистана-ENG.pdf (accessed 7 March 2020).

Central Asia Regional Economic Cooperation (CAREC). 2017a. Unlocking the Potential of Railways – A Railway Strategy for CAREC, 2017-2030. www.adb.org/sites/default/files/institutional-document/227176/carec-railway-strategy-2017-2030.pdf (accessed 25 February 2020).

———. 2017b. Connecting the Region for Shared and Sustainable Development. www.carecprogram.org/uploads/2017-CAREC-2030.pdf (accessed 25 February 2020).

———. 2019a. Transport Sector Progress Report and Work Plan 2019–2021. www.carecprogram.org/uploads/Transport-Sector-Progress-Report-Work-Plan-2019%E2%80%932021.pdf (accessed 25 February 2020).

———. 2019b. Corridor Performance Measurement Monitoring Annual Report 2018. www.carecprogram.org/uploads/CAREC-Corridor-Performance-Measurement-Monitoring-Annual-Report-2018.pdf (accessed 25 February 2020).

———. 2020. Transport Strategy 2030. www.carecprogram.org/uploads/CAREC-Transport-Strategy-2030-1.pdf (accessed 25 February 2020).

CBS New York. 2015. CBS2 Demanding Answers: Why Is Lincoln Tunnel Helix Construction Taking So Long? http://newyork.cbslocal.com/2015/07/14/lincoln-tunnel-helix-fix (accessed 14 January 2019).

Doré, D. 2019. Uzbekistan's Privatisation Programme. https://ijglobal.com/articles/141846/uzbekistans-privatisation-programme (accessed 2 March 2020).

Economist. 2018. Is China Investing Too Much in Infrastructure? http://country.eiu.com/article.aspx?articleid=866788670&Country=China&topic=Economy (accessed 23 September 2019).

European Bank for Reconstruction and Development (EBRD). 2018a. Uzbekistan Diagnostic: Assessing Progress and Challenges in Unlocking the Private Sector's Potential and Developing a Sustainable Market Economy. www.ebrd.com/documents/comms-and-bis/country-diagnostic-paper-uzbekistan.pdf (accessed 9 March 2020).

———. 2018b. Uzbekistan Country Strategy 2018-2023. www.ebrd.com/documents/strategy-and-policy-coordination/strategy-for-uzbekistan.pdf (accessed 9 March 2020).

European Commission. 2018. Pilot Project Study on Innovative Ways of Sustainable Financing Public Transport. https://op.europa.eu/en/publication-detail/-/publication/f3815f44-5fc8-11e8-ab9c-01aa75ed71a1/language-en (accessed 9 March 2020).

Ernst & Young. 2019. Doing Business in Uzbekistan. www.ey.com/Publication/vwLUAssets/ey-doing-business-in-uzbekistan-2019-e/$File/ey-doing-business-in-uzbekistan-2019-e.pdf (accessed 11 March 2020).

Gehl, J. 2010. *Cities for People*. Washington, DC: Island Press.

Global Capital. 2019. Uzbekistan is Reforming and Opening up to the World. www.globalcapital.com/Media/documents/emerging-markets/import/Uzbekistan_lowres.pdf (accessed 9 March 2020).

Goodman, J.B. and Loveman, G.W. 1991. HBS: Does Privatization Serve the Public Interest? https://hbr.org/1991/11/does-privatization-serve-the-public-interest (accessed 9 March 2020).

Government of the Russian Federation. 2018. Official Order. http://static.government.ru/media/files/MUNhgWFddP3UfF9RJASDW9VxP8zwcB4Y.pdf?fbclid=IwAR32ogu37-UPpT2LIgoCR-zWA-6R4SxAsydR5g29p7Y_krcaRxfamvZt2MA (accessed 28 January 2019).

Harada, I. 2018. China Curbs Infrastructure Spending as Local Debt Climbs. https://asia.nikkei.com/Economy/China-curbs-infrastructure-spending-as-local-debt-climbs (accessed 20 December 2020).

International Monetary Fund (IMF). 2015. Making Public Investment More Efficient. www.imf.org/external/np/pp/eng/2015/061115.pdf (accessed 23 November 2020).

International Finance Corporation (IFC). 2019. Creating Markets in Uzbekistan. www.ifc.org/wps/wcm/connect/bac596d6-322f-4e78-9368-bd3bf32c18ae/UZB+CPSD+Launch+Presentation_English.pdf?MOD=AJPERES&CVID=mA4w5R5 (accessed 11 March 2020).

Kaiser, K.M.J. and C. Westarp. 2010. Value Creation in the Private Equity and Venture Capital Industry. www.insead.edu/sites/default/files/assets/dept/centres/gpei/docs/insead-value-creation-in-private-equity-and-venture-capital-industry-working-paper-2010.pdf (accessed 1 February 2018).

Kaiser, K.M.J. and D.S. Young. 2013. *The Blue Line Imperative – What Managing for Value Really Means*. Hoboken, NJ: Wiley & Sons.

Kozlov, V. 2017. Kremlin to Launch Massive Infrastructure Projects in 2018. *Intellinews*. www.intellinews.com/kremlin-to-launch-massive-infrastructure-projects-in-2018-129318/ (accessed 26 January 2019).

Leduc, S. and D. Wilson. 2012. Roads to Prosperity or Bridges to Nowhere? Theory and Evidence on the Impact of Public Infrastructure Investment. FRBSF Working Paper 2012-04. San Francisco: Federal Reserve Bank.

Leduc, S. and D. Wilson. 2014. Infrastructure Spending as Fiscal Stimulus: Assessing the Evidence. *Review of Economics and Institutions* 5(1): 1–24.

New Jersey Commuter Organization. 2016. It's Time for NYC to Create a Regional Transit Network That Works. http://njcommuters.org/its-time-for-nyc-to-create-a-regional-transit-network-that-works (accessed 23 September 2018

New Jersey Business Journal. 2017. ReThinking the Gateway Program. www.njbiz.com/article/20171113/NJBIZ01/171119984/rethinking-the-gateway-program (accessed 23 September 2018

North New Jersey Daily News. 2017. NJ Transit Won't Take You to Queens. But Jim Venturi Will. www.northjersey.com/story/news/columnists/christopher-maag/2017/08/18/nj-transit-wont-take-you-queens-but-jim-venturi-will/538530001 (accessed 23 September 2018).

New York Business Journal. 2015. And the Award for Worst Bottleneck in N.Y.C. Traffic Goes to.... www.bizjournals.com/newyork/news/2015/11/23/and-the-award-for-worst-bottleneck-in-n-y-c.html (accessed 23 September 2018).

NBC New York. 2017. South Tube of Lincoln Tunnel Reopens, But Hour-Long Delays Remain. www.nbcnewyork.com/news/local/Delays-Crash-Inbound-South-Tube-Lincoln-Tunnel-418976494.html (accessed by 24 September 2018).

OECD. 2009. Good Practices: Privatisation in the 21st Century: Recent Experiences of OECD Countries. www.oecd.org/corporate/ca/corporategovernanceofstate-owned enterprises/48476423.pdf (accessed 4 August 2019).

———. 2019. Sustainable Infrastructure for Low-Carbon Development in Central Asia and the Caucasus: Hotspot Analysis and Needs Assessment, Green Finance and Investment. Paris: OECD Publishing. https://doi.org/10.1787/d1aa6ae9-en.

Penyalver, D. and M. Turró, 2019. A Classification for the Redistributive Effects on Investments in Transport Infrastructure. *International Journal of Transport Economics* 45(4): 695–732.

Rethink Studio. 2017a. *The Regional Unified Network. Volume 1.* New York: First Step.

———. 2017b. *The Regional Unified Network Service Map.* New York: First Step.

———. 2017c. ReThinkNYC Regional Unified Network Overview. https://vimeo.com/214381280 (9 May 2017).

Schmitt, A. 2015. The 23-Lane Katy Freeway: A Monument to Texas Transportation Futility. https://usa.streetsblog.org/2015/05/28/the-23-lane-katy-freeway-a-monument-to-texas-transportation-futility (accessed 9 March 2020).

Tadjibaeva, D. 2019. Small and Medium-Sized Enterprise Finance in Uzbekistan: Challenges and Opportunities. ADBI Working Paper 997. Tokyo: Asian Development Bank Institute.

Talatovna, G., et al. 2019. Experience of Investment Activity in the Railway System of the Republic of Uzbekistan. *International Journal of Recent Technology and Engineering* 8(4): 12651–12654.

TR News. 2018. 40 Years of Transportation Deregulation. No.315, May-June Issue. http://onlinepubs.trb.org/onlinepubs/trnews/trnews315.pdf (accessed 9 March 2020).

Turró, M. and D. Penyalver. 2019a. Hunting White Elephants on the Road. A Practical Procedure to Detect Harmful Projects of Transport Infrastructure. *Research in Transportation Economics* 75: 3–20.

———. 2019b. Measuring the Value for Money of Transport Infrastructure Procurement – An Intergenerational Approach. *Transportation Research Part A: Policy and Practice* 119: 238–254.

U.S. Department of Transportation (DOT) FHWA. 2019. Cooperative Automation: Safely Improving Highway Capacity. https://youtu.be/9Re__KRr4NU (accessed 1 February 2019).

Vuchic, V.R. 1981. *Urban Public Transportation Systems and Technology*. Englewood Cliffs, NJ: Prentice-Hall.

Vuchic, V.R. 1999. *Transportation for Livable Cities*. New Brunswick, NJ: CUPR, Rutgers University.

Vuchic, V.R. 2003. Livable Cities – Will Transportation Professionals Answer the Challenge? *Transportation Research News* Nov.-Dec.: 22–26.

Warner, A.M. 2014. Public Investment as an Engine of Growth. IMF Working Paper WP/14/148.

World Bank Group (WBG). 2015. Uzbekistan Partnership: Country Program Snapshot. www.worldbank.org/content/dam/Worldbank/document/Uzbekistan-Snapshot.pdf (accessed 27 February 2020).

———. 2018. Performance and Learning Review of the Country Partnership Framework for Uzbekistan for the Period of FY16-FY20. Report No. 126078-UZ. http://documents.worldbank.org/curated/en/139671530243060422/pdf/UZ-Performance-and-Learning-Review-SEC-06052018.pdf (accessed 27 February 2020).

———. 2019a. Uzbekistan Country Snapshot http://pubdocs.worldbank.org/en/389531571374572251/Uzbekistan-Snapshot-Oct2019.pdf (accessed 27 February 2020).

———. 2019b. Uzbekistan Country Economic Update – Toward a New Economy. http://documents.worldbank.org/curated/en/866501562572675697/Uzbekistan-Toward-a-New-Economy-Country-Economic-Update (accessed 13 January 2020).

———. 2020. The World Bank in Uzbekistan. www.worldbank.org/en/country/uzbekistan (accessed 13 January 2020).

国务院办公厅. 2015. 国务院办公厅转发财政部发展改革委人民银行关于在公共服务领域推广政府和社会资本合作模式指导意见的通知. www.gov.cn/zhengce/content/2015-05/22/content_9797.htm (accessed 3 August 2019).

国务院国有资产监督管理委员会. 2017. 央企名录. www.sasac.gov.cn/n2588035/n2641579/n2641645/index.html (accessed 4 August 2019).

财政部. 2019a. 政府和社会资本合作项目财政管理暂行办法. www.mof.gov.cn/gp/xxgkml/jrs/201610/t20161021_2512417.html (accessed 3 August 2019).

———. 2019b. 财政部关于推进政府和社会资本合作规范发展的实施意见. www.gov.cn/gongbao/content/2019/content_5411612.htm (accessed 3 August 2019).

———. 2019c. 全国PPP综合信息平台项目管理库. www.cpppc.org:8086/pppcentral/map/toPPPMap.do (accessed 3 August 2019).

中国发展研究基金会. 2016a. 地方预算绩效改革的关键点. www.pbgchina.cn/ggczgl/972.jhtml (accessed 3 August 2019).

———. 2016b. 地方财政紧张如何解决? www.pbgchina.cn/ggczgl/970.jhtml (accessed 3 August 2019).

2 Transition Pathways for Central Asian Energy Infrastructure

David Roland-Holst and Fredrich Kahrl

2.1 Introduction

Energy is one of the most important strategic resources of the Central Asian region. While energy services secure livelihoods in all Central Asia Regional Economic Cooperation (CAREC) member countries, primary energy resources offer potent development stimulus to the region's exporters and, by extension, across an ever-expanding web of regional infrastructure to their neighbors.

However, markets for Central Asian energy exports are on the verge of significant change, driven by evolving energy and climate policies. Europe, the traditional market for primary fuel exports (via the Russian Federation) has committed to achieving net zero greenhouse gas emissions by 2050. The People's Republic of China (PRC), which accounted for most export growth from CAREC over the 2010s has committed to peaking its CO_2 emissions by 2030. India, a potential new source of export growth, has embarked on aggressive policies for renewable energy and electric transport development.

Taken together, these trends imply a flattening and decline of regional demand for Central Asian oil and natural gas over the next two decades and present an important strategic challenge for Central Asian countries: How can they reorient their energy sector investment strategies to exploit emerging opportunities in regional and global energy markets, avoiding the macroeconomic risks of a global transition away from carbon fuels?

This chapter examines potential transition pathways for energy infrastructure in Central Asia that can reconcile global decarbonization trends with the region's goals for sustained and inclusive growth. It begins with a review of current estimates of regional energy resource potential, production, export infrastructure, and export market prospects, combining the most up-to-date publicly available information with our own projections.

The chapter then examines potential transition strategies using scenarios that include different assumptions about energy resource mix (oil, natural gas, wind, solar, nuclear), energy carriers (natural gas, hydrogen, electricity), distribution infrastructure (pipelines, electric power transmission systems), and export demand. We will consider both status quo policies and more innovative strategies.

DOI: 10.4324/9781003228790-4

The aim of the chapter is to improve visibility for public and private stakeholders, informing government decision makers and industry leaders alike. We argue for a more determined assessment of infrastructure investments, costs, and estimated economic benefits for the region to achieve a renewable energy transition that is both necessary and desirable. Institutional and other feasibility issues, such as market fragmentation, joint venture and foreign investment standards, and logistics will also be discussed. Bringing together this evidence, we recommend a variety of complementary policies and metrics that promote sustainability and inclusion within and across the CAREC community.

2.2 Background

2.2.1 Central Asian Energy Trade

Energy trade has played a critical role in economic development in Central Asia. The region's main energy exporters—Azerbaijan, Kazakhstan, Mongolia, Turkmenistan, and Uzbekistan—accounted for 6% of global oil trade and 14% of global natural gas trade in 2017 (IEA 2018). In energy terms, oil and gas accounted for more than 85% of the region's energy trade in 2017 (Table 2.1).

The region's major energy exporters are effectively landlocked, requiring pipeline (oil and gas) and rail (coal) infrastructure to reach export markets. Key pipeline infrastructure includes the Central Asia-PRC pipeline, which delivers natural gas from Turkmenistan, Uzbekistan, and Kazakhstan to the PRC; the Central Asia-Center pipeline, which delivers gas from Turkmenistan, Uzbekistan, and Kazakhstan to the Russian Federation; and pipelines delivering oil from Azerbaijan to ports on the Black and Mediterranean Seas. The Turkmenistan-Afghanistan-Pakistan-India pipeline, scheduled to be operational in 2020, is an export pathway to India.

Table 2.1 Net Energy Exports for the Five Largest CAREC Exporters by Energy Source, 2017

Country	*Coal*	*Oil*	*Natural Gas*	*Electricity*	*Total*
Azerbaijan	0	1,406	237	4	**1,643**
Kazakhstan	511	3,058	404	16	**3,973**
Mongolia	808	–11	0	–6	**797**
Uzbekistan	–13	6	713	2	**706**
Turkmenistan	0	180	1,850	12	**2,030**
Total	**1,306**	**4,639**	**3,204**	**28**	**9,149**

Source: International Energy Agency.

Note

Energy exports are in petajoules (PJ); one million tons oil equivalent (Mtoe) is approximately equal to 42 PJ.

The development of the Central Asia-PRC and Turkmenistan-Afghanistan-Pakistan-India pipelines reflect a pivot in global energy supply toward Asian demand over the last two decades. From 2000 to 2017, the Asia and the Pacific region accounted for 75% of the growth in global energy demand.

2.3 Emerging Challenges

Over the coming decade, as the global community moves to mitigate the risks of climate change, Central Asia's largest sources of oil and gas demand (the PRC, Europe, and India) will begin a sustained transition away from fossil fuels.

These legacy export markets have already signaled, to differing extents, a commitment to cleaner energy sources. The PRC has committed to a peak in national CO_2 emissions by 2030, combined with a goal of obtaining 20% of its primary energy from renewable sources by 2030, and policies to support transportation electrification. The European Union (exempting Poland) has committed to a carbon neutrality goal by 2050 (EC, undated), which would limit the region to minimal or even zero fossil fuel combustion. India plans to install 450 GW of renewable energy by 2030 and is laying the groundwork for transportation electrification.

Although the timing of the low-carbon transition in these regions is uncertain, the possibility of a world in which global trade in fossil fuels will be significantly diminished by mid-century is realistic. In the nearer term, and even without considering national climate policies, structural changes in oil and gas markets, including the emerging trade in liquefied natural gas, will create new challenges for CAREC energy exports (IEA 2018).

Shifts in the structure of global energy demand and energy trade will have profound implications for CAREC countries and pose a fundamental threat to their legacy growth and development strategies. Because of the long lead times needed to develop and adapt energy infrastructure, these risks need to be managed proactively, with initiatives decades in advance of emergent needs and structural changes.

2.3.1 New Opportunities

If proactively managed, shifting patterns of global energy consumption and trade can enable more inclusive economic development and stronger cooperation for the CAREC region. To realize the potential of these resources at the national level will require large-scale commitments to transmission infrastructure. Such investments, fueled by energy sector reform and public-private partnerships (PPPs), will lower sub-regional energy costs, improving both development prospects and export competitiveness.

In a future world economy dominated by renewables, the two most promising energy carriers for cross-border energy trade are likely to be electricity and hydrogen. Trade in electricity requires infrastructure for transmission and, to a lesser extent, energy storage. Trade in hydrogen requires compression or liquefication facilities, storage, and pipelines or other conveyance infrastructure.

Taking advantage of these opportunities will require laying the foundation for a transition to low- or no-carbon energy sources over the next decade, to enable the region to emerge as a leader in sustainable energy supply by mid-century. Worldwide, the most scalable sustainable primary energy resources are currently wind, solar, and hydropower. At the same time, the most promising future energy carriers are electric power and hydrogen.

2.3.1.1 Renewable Electric Power Generation

CAREC countries are rich in wind and solar resources (Obozov and Loscutof 1998; Elliot 2001; CAREC 2019). As an illustration, Table 2.2 shows mean wind speeds in the 10% windiest areas in CAREC countries relative to select neighboring countries. As renewable energy costs have fallen, several CAREC countries have set long-term goals to significantly expand renewable electricity over the coming decades, including Azerbaijan (35%–40% of electricity generation by 2030), Kazakhstan (50% by 2050), and Uzbekistan (25% by 2030).

For CAREC countries, shifting to a renewables-oriented energy infrastructure will require significant upgrades for electric power generation, storage, and transmission. Much of the existing cross-border transmission system in northern Central Asia was built during the Soviet era to enable seasonal hydropower exchange between mountainous countries in the east (Tajikistan, the Kyrgyz Republic) and fossil fuel-rich countries in the steppes (Kazakhstan, Uzbekistan). This legacy framework is not well matched to endowments of more recent

Table 2.2 Mean Wind Speed for 10% of Windiest Areas, CAREC Countries and Select Neighboring Countries

CAREC Countries	*Mean wind speed (ms/)*	*Neighboring Countries*	*Mean wind speed (ms/)*	
Afghanistan	9.5	Bulgaria	6.7	
Azerbaijan	7.8	Germany	8.5	
PRC	8.9	Greece	8.5	High
Georgia	8.2	Hungary	6.7	
Kazakhstan	8.5	India	6.6	Medium
Kyrgyz Republic	9.1	Italy	7.1	
Mongolia	8.8	Poland	7.8	Low
Pakistan	7.8	Romania	6.8	
Tajikistan	9.5	Russian Federation	8.5	
Turkmenistan	8.5	Turkey	7.3	
Uzbekistan	8.7	Ukraine	7.5	

Source: Global Wind Atlas: https://globalwindatlas.info, accessed 8 September 2020.

Note

CAREC = Central Asia Regional Economic Cooperation, PRC = People's Republic of China.

renewables (wind and solar), nor does it effectively serve intra-regional growth or the newly dominant Asian energy export markets.

More generally, the present scope and carrying capacity for CAREC's regional electricity grid is woefully inadequate in comparison to the region's potential for renewables and clean energy service exports. Apart from a limited intertie in Mongolia, the region currently does not have a single electric power transmission link to the PRC, and has only limited indirect connections with Europe, and none whatsoever with India. Electric power systems in Turkmenistan and Afghanistan are not synchronized with the rest of CAREC (Shamsiev 2018). For these reasons, a move to more sustainable energy systems in the region offers a new platform of opportunity to strengthen interconnections across the CAREC region and all its large overseas energy markets, including Kazakhstan-PRC, Mongolia-PRC, and Afghanistan-Pakistan, while reaching to Europe through Iran-Turkey and India through Pakistan.

Achieving harmonized operation across a more fully interconnected regional electricity system requires parallel improvements in hard and soft infrastructure, and concerted, large-scale commitments to investment in generation and transmission, combined with adoption of common standards for technical design, implementation, and mediation through open multilateral energy markets. Recent history offers some precedence and optimism that this can be realized. Cooperation that had sustained cross-border electricity operations under the Soviet Union broke down after 2000, but in recent years there have been renewed efforts to reestablish institutions for cross-border coordination of electricity infrastructure and operations.

2.3.1.2 The Hydrogen Option

As a non-carbon fuel, hydrogen has many attractive characteristics for adoption by conventional transport and other fuel use technologies. Hydrogen also has characteristics that make it a more flexible energy carrier, with multiple potential transport modes and longer-lasting and cheaper storage than electricity. Producing hydrogen from renewables would involve conversion losses in electrolysis, which means that, for it to be cost-competitive with electricity as an energy carrier, its delivery costs must be lower, and its storage and other flexibility benefits must be higher. Because of these complexities, the future of hydrogen conversion and delivery infrastructure remains uncertain (Staffell et al. 2019). Despite this, many leading national development partners (e.g., Japan) and private sector interests (Shell) are making determined commitments to hydrogen. This could play an essential supporting role in the middle of renewable energy transition, capturing most of the potential of natural gas with much lower greenhouse gas emission risks.

2.4 Transition Implications

This section explores the implications of a transition to renewables for energy-driven development policy in the CAREC region. It focuses on sustainable energy exports, rather than economy-wide transitions, recognizing that this transition may be slower in Central Asia than, for instance, in the PRC or Europe. The analysis is intended to explore order of magnitude estimates of physical infrastructure requirements and investment costs. It is not intended to be a forecast.

In 2017, net exports from CAREC's five major energy exporters totaled 9.2 PJ (including intraregional exports). By 2030, the International Energy Agency projects that approximately 2.5% per year growth in gas exports will increase this total to 10.3 PJ (IEA 2018). If the region were to maintain this level of delivered net exports in a world of trade in renewable energy, what would be the implications for physical infrastructure and investment needs by 2050?

The analysis considers two bookend scenarios, organized around energy carriers: (1) all energy exports are electricity, and (2) all energy exports are hydrogen. In a world of fuels produced from renewables, hydrogen can be considered a generic energy carrier that has higher conversion and transport losses than electricity. In each scenario, wind and solar energy each provide 50% of primary energy needs.

Figure 2.1 illustrates this transition, for scenario 1 (electricity). Beginning in 2030, the region's fossil fuel exports decline linearly and are completely replaced with renewable electricity exports by 2050.

Primary energy needs will vary between scenarios due to conversion and transport losses. For electricity, the analysis assumes transmission line losses of 5% (ADB 2005). For hydrogen, generic assumptions are 80% conversion efficiency for electrolysis and 10% losses in the transport process, for total losses of 30%.

Because the focus is on delivered energy exports, the analysis does not consider additional losses that may occur in the final delivery (distribution), conversion, or consumption of either energy carrier.

With these assumptions, the region would need approximately 1 to 1.5 TW of total installed wind and solar generation capacity (500–700 GW of wind, 700–900 GW of solar) by 2050 to provide 10.3 PJ per year of net energy exports. If this transition begins in 2030 (20 years), this implies an annual need of 50 to 75 GW per year. For reference, total global installed wind and solar generation capacity was 902 GW in 2017 (EIA 2019).

Current installed wind and solar costs in the region are in the order of $50/MWh (Tazhmakina 2018; Bellini 2019). This implies overnight investment costs

Table 2.3 Scenario Assumptions

Assumption	*Scenario 1 Electricity*	*Scenario 2 Hydrogen*
Share of electricity in net energy exports	100%	0%
Share of hydrogen in net energy exports	0%	100%
Wind share of primary energy	50%	50%
Solar share of primary energy	50%	50%

Source: Authors.

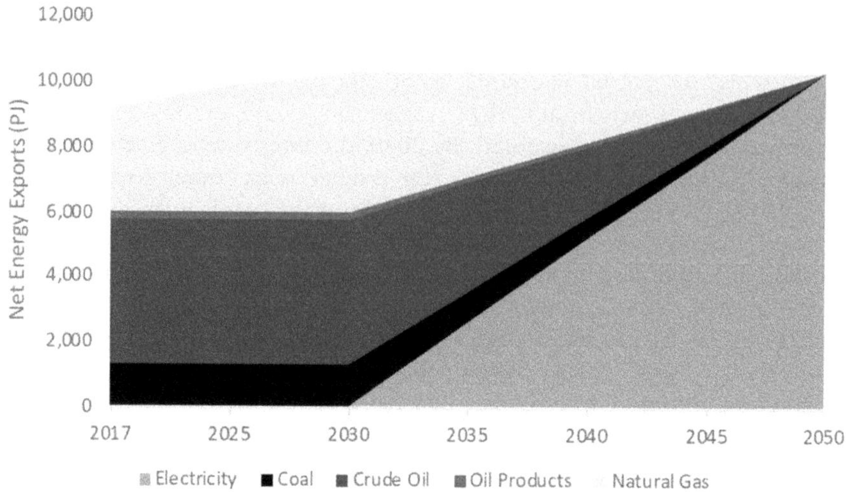

Figure 2.1 Illustration of Transition in Energy Export Mix for Scenario 1.
Note: PJ = petajoules.
Source: Author estimates from IEA data.

Table 2.4 Capacity Factor and Loss Assumptions

Assumption	*Value*
Wind net capacity factor	0.35
Solar net capacity factor	0.20
Electricity transmission losses	5%
Hydrogen conversion and transport losses	30%

Note
Capacity factors are high-level estimates based on the US National Renewable Energy Laboratory's RE Data Explorer, https://maps.nrel.gov/rede-central-asia, accessed 12 June 2020.

of approximately $500/kW to $1,000/kW (assuming an average 30% capacity factor and a capital recovery factor of 0.12), total investment costs of $500 billion to $1.5 trillion by 2050, and average annual investment costs in the order of tens of billions of dollars.

The transmission system expansion (in circuit kilometers and total capacity) needed to support TW-scale renewable energy development in the Central Asian region is uncertain, as are unit transmission costs. Transmission is generally not sized to deliver the rated capacity of wind and solar units and their peak output will generally not be coincident.

Transmission costs to support renewable generation expansion often vary significantly; in the US, for instance, costs have ranged from around $1,500/

Table 2.5 Transmission Cost Assumptions

Assumption	*Value*
Total renewable installed capacity	1,000 GW
Transmission need (distance) per GW renewable capacity	50 km/GW
Transmission need (capacity) per GW renewable capacity	20 MW/GW
Total transmission need (distance)	50,000 km
Total transmission (capacity)	20 GW
Transmission cost	$1,000/MW-km

Source: Authors.

MW-km to $10,000/MW-mile (Andrade and Balck 2016). Using an approximate transmission distance of 50 km per GW of renewable generation capacity and assuming incremental transmission capacity needs of 20 GW, based on half of the corresponding values from Texas' competitive renewable energy zone projects (Billo 2017), and a cost of $1,000/MW-km, transmission costs would be in the order of $1 trillion dollars.

Hydrogen has the potential to use existing oil and gas infrastructure and electrolyzers can be interconnected at high voltages close to renewable generation facilities. However, hydrogen would require incremental transport infrastructure investments whose costs are unclear. At a minimum, the cost of hydrogen electrolysis and transport infrastructure would need to be significantly lower than corresponding electricity infrastructure to make trade in hydrogen cost competitive.

A more likely outcome would be a hybrid approach, with some direct electricity exports and some exports using energy carriers with more flexible transport. In any case, renewable energy and transport infrastructure costs are still likely to be in the order of hundreds of billions to trillions of dollars by 2050. In part, large investment requirements are driven by the capital-intensive nature of wind and solar and the infrastructure required to store and transport them (storage and transmission are substitutes). High investment requirements do not imply that renewable energy is not cost-effective, but they do imply that finance will be critical.

In a renewables-dominant world, the dynamics and drivers of cross-border energy trade change in important and interesting ways. The fundamental driver of trade (arbitrage) remains the same, but instead of fossil fuel extraction costs and fuel quality, trade in renewable energy is driven by resource quality (capacity factors) and land availability.

For instance, consider two regions. One has excellent solar resources and an average photovoltaic capacity factor of 0.25. The other has poorer resources and an average photovoltaic capacity factor of 0.10. Assuming they have the same installed photovoltaic costs (e.g., $100/kW-yr), the trade margin between the two will be driven by differences in capacity factor. In this case, the margin ($68/MWh, or $19/GJ) is significantly higher than typical natural gas delivery costs.

Nevertheless, the viability of long-distance cross-border energy trade in a world of renewables systems will depend on transport efficiency.

The development of large quantities of wind and solar generation in the Central Asian region is likely predicated on a well-functioning regional grid that has a limited number of centralized regional system operators, real-time energy markets with short interval (5-minute) dispatch, market-based congestion management (locational marginal pricing), stochastic management of generation reserves, sophisticated wind, solar, and load forecasting, and state-of-the-art hydropower planning tools.

With regions external to CAREC countries, electricity exports at this scale would imply, at a minimum, direct current ties, short interval scheduling, and extensive scheduling and operational coordination. Energy storage can reduce the need for coordination, but it does so at a higher cost. The transition to an electricity system like the one envisioned here is a generational project, requiring multiple decades.

Although the sources of primary energy and energy carriers that will have the lowest cost 30 years into the future is unclear, there are a large number of "least-regrets" generation and transmission projects throughout the region that can serve as the building blocks of a future sustainable energy system for the region. Least regrets refers to an approach to planning under uncertainty where projects that would occur under almost any potential scenario should be pursued first (CAISO 2016). The scale of the infrastructure required to make the CAREC region competitive in sustainable energy trade suggests that these core, transformational investments should begin to expand soon.

2.5 Transition Pathways

As we have seen in the narrative above, conventional energy resources in Central Asia are abundant but very unevenly distributed across national economies. For those with favorable initial conditions, a variety of strategies are available to leverage these resources for economic growth. These options still depend, however, on conditions in other countries, including large net energy imports that are far away, as well as smaller import dependent neighboring economies. In this section, we discuss strategies for CAREC economies to diversify their energy systems in ways that can support more sustained and inclusive regional growth.

Historically, the opportunity presented by the traditional, large oil and gas importing economies of Europe and East Asia dominated CAREC regional and national energy development strategies. As we have emphasized, however, the fundamentals of global energy demand and supply are changing. In particular, Organisation for Economic Co-operation and Development (OECD) markets are beginning an extended but determined transition to lower carbon energy use, rendering them increasingly less reliable as destinations for carbon fuel exports. Because CAREC oil and gas exporters are also well endowed with renewables, they can follow the transition of their legacy destination markets, but only if they make a corresponding shift from carbon fuels to renewables and from primary energy to electric power exports. This will require substantial commitments to both hard and soft infrastructure. In the first category, this means investments in both renewable generation capacity and long-distance transmission infrastructure on a scale that is comparable to the PRC, Denmark, and other advanced renewables economies. The magnitude of such investments is large but can be met with a combination of diverted revenue from today's carbon fuel exports and public-private partnerships that recruit substantial foreign direct investment (FDI). Excellent candidates for such FDI would of course be the legacy destination markets, and, with respect to their capital markets, the requirements for these investment projects would be modest. They may also be eligible for home country investment credit because they contribute to the dual objectives of decarbonization and energy security.

On the soft infrastructure side, we have already described the challenges presented by segmented regional (and even national) electric power grids and markets. These barriers are endemic to the CAREC region, as well as the Russian Federation and the PRC domestically, but overcoming them is likely to be in the interest of all parties. Particularly when it accesses more diverse energy sources, improved continuity, and reduced costs of necessary decarbonization, grid integration can be defended as an essential source of longer-term energy security, foundational to sustainable growth and poverty reduction.

On the institutional side, open and inclusive multilateral energy systems will require a great deal of negotiation and standard setting. Particularly in cases where power market access barriers exist to protect vested interests, farsighted policy will be essential. If system integration is achieved, the dedicated public and private investment commitments needed to build out this model will likely follow. Among CAREC legacy energy exporters, this may include diversion of current conventional energy revenues, but can be significantly compensated by higher long-term renewable export revenue and lower long-term domestic energy costs.

To facilitate policy dialogue on this transition agenda, this chapter proposes a more specific hypothetical energy pathway scenario, including assumptions about energy resource mix (oil, natural gas, wind, solar, nuclear), energy carriers (natural gas, hydrogen, electricity), distribution infrastructure (pipelines, electric power transmission systems), and export demand. This represents a future very different from today, but the resources and technologies to realize it would probably be accessible to regional governments with sufficient determination. In particular, we consider a three-phase approach to regional energy transition:

1. High-carbon (2020) primary carbon fuel exports, financing growth and transition to,
2. Mid-carbon (by 2030) (natural gas and gas-fired electricity exports) financing new capacity for,
3. Low-carbon (2040–50) solar and wind capacity for carbon-free electricity and hydrogen exports).

This scenario (among others we consider) is noteworthy because endowments of renewable capacity (especially wind and solar) are much more equally distributed across CAREC than carbon fuel energy resources. Thus, the phase 2-3 transition would open opportunities for more inclusive and profitable regional energy infrastructure investment, raising the prospect of PPPs on a regional and global basis. Meanwhile, grid investments needed for more extensive supply development could also dramatically improve energy access across the region, lowering average CAREC energy access costs and offering a potent catalyst for domestic growth and diversification. In this way, energy can play the same role that manufacturing did in the dynamic East Asian economies, with export opportunities driving infrastructure investments that ultimately facilitate domestic connectivity, efficiency, and long-term, more inclusive growth.

2.6 Policy Support for Inclusive Regional Development: Renewable Energy Diffusion and the SDGs

The background presented above supports a new vision of Central Asian regional energy development, including its well-established linkages to most of the world's largest energy consumers. Carbon fuels present several sustainability challenges, including negative environmental public health impacts. A long and controversial history of carbon fuel energy subsidies was based on a simple and universal premise: lowering the cost of energy services supports economic growth. This logic does not need to be rejected to promote decarbonization, but new energy policies need to avoid the two features that make carbon fuel subsidies unsustainable: environmental damage and misallocation of public funds. The most important opportunities here would be policies that reduce the cost of low- and no-carbon energy substitutes but promoting innovation and private investment. Although these objectives are simply stated, they apply to a complex landscape that mixes technology R&D with public-private-partnerships. Success in this area is becoming much more common (e.g., transport, communication, etc.); indeed, it is a hallmark of OECD, ADB, and other multilateral effectiveness. More recent initiatives like the Belt and Road Initiative have the same potential to coordination multilateral public and private interest, more effective harmonization of these efforts could expand their economic potential dramatically.

Spelling out all the policy options that would facilitate the dual objective of lowering renewable energy costs through investment and innovation is beyond the scope of a single chapter. Instead, this section promulgates a set of objective standards for measuring progress toward the intended goal, in the hope that this can guide public and private decision makers to meet their economies' needs for access to abundant, affordable, clean energy. The logic of this goal applies with equal force to producing and consuming countries, regardless of where they are on their decarbonization pathway. Consuming countries with heavy reliance on carbon fuels need to invest in lower-cost clean energy solutions, and sourcing will be an important part of this strategy if options are limited at home. Likewise, carbon-intensive energy producers, like the leading CAREC exporters, need to invest in a future comparative advantage in wind and solar power if they want to sustain external income as conventional energy demand and/or reserves decline.

Within the CAREC region, traditional fuel exporters converting to renewable generation can be joined by their neighbors, most of whom have substantial renewables potential, investing individually in capacity and collectively in transmission to expand and integrate regional electricity resources. This process will lower costs for all CAREC producers and consumers, benefiting the lower-income regional economies most. In addition to promoting internal growth from new energy income and cost savings, CAREC regional integration and convergence will accelerate.

To facilitate this process, both for energy exporters and importers, CAREC members and their non-CAREC trading partners, we recommend assessing progress with a set of metrics designed for development progress. In 2015, the members of the UN General Assembly unanimously adopted the Sustainable Development Goals (SDGs), a set of 17 aspirational objectives (and over 150 objectively verifiable targets) for governments, international agencies, civil society, and other institutions for the next decade and a half (2016–2030). These goals (Figure 2.2) were formally incorporated into global policy dialogue to advance sustainable and inclusive economic progress.

Tying these metrics to CAREC renewable energy development can strengthen policy dialogue and improve public and private awareness of the benefits and achievements of this transition, using universally recognized metrics for sustainable growth and prosperity. Here we present only two examples of how the CAREC regional energy transition can advance the SDGs, using related metrics we will call Energy Development Indicators (EDIs).

Figure 2.2 The Sustainable Development Goals.

Source: https://sdgs.un.org/goals, accessed 8 September 2020.

2.6.1 SDG 1: No Poverty—Livelihoods and Energy

Objective: Eliminate Energy Poverty in across CAREC by 2030

Indicators

EDI 1.1 Energy Poverty—Headcount percent of energy-poor people, i.e., without electricity, and/or biomass dependent for heating.
EDI 1.2 Energy-poor population living below the national poverty line.
EDI 1.3 Poverty gap ratio (incidence x depth of energy poverty).
EDI 1.4 Share of energy poorest quintile in national consumption.

2.6.2 No Hunger—Agricultural Production and Food Security

Objective: By 2030, raise the nutritional status of all energy-poor people above the SDG minimum for dietary sufficiency.

Indicators:

EDI 2.1: Proportion of energy-poor population below minimum level of dietary energy consumption
EDI 2.2: Prevalence of underweight in energy-poor children (under 5 years of age)

2.6.2.1 Example: Renewable Energy Development Permits CAREC Natural Gas Reserves for Regional Agricultural Development

CAREC renewable energy development would release gas reserves to serve other purposes, such as agrochemical development to unlock the region's vast agricultural potential. Lower-cost local access to synthetic fertilizer[1] and other agrochemicals is an essential buttress to support CAREC's shift toward higher value agricultural products such as intensive livestock, specialty vegetables, fruits, ornamental plants, etc., has significant promise for increasing agricultural value added in Central Asia. Diversification of traditional cereal and commodity crops (e.g., cotton) toward livestock and horticulture offers unprecedented potential for agricultural productivity growth, rural poverty reduction, and more sustainable land use. By leveraging external demand and investment for agricultural modernization and supply chain development, rural majorities across Central Asia can participate indirectly in more dynamic economic growth trends now firmly established across East and Southeast Asia. To accomplish this, public and private sector resources must be coordinated to invest in higher productivity, combining low-cost land and agrochemicals with FDI-induced technology transfer.[2] The impetus from PPP like this, combined with national commitments to transport and communication infrastructure, will facilitate more inclusive market access,

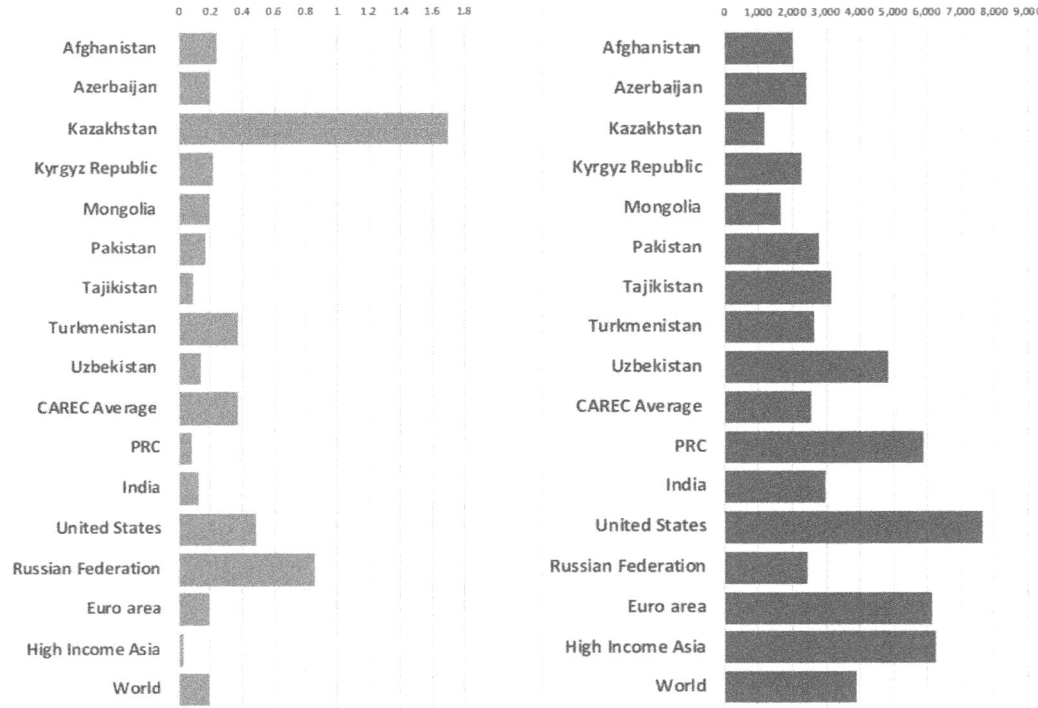

Figure 2.3 CAREC Land Is Relatively Abundant, but Productivity Is Low.

Note: CAREC = Central Asia Regional Economic Cooperation, PRC = People's Republic of China.

Source: World Bank.

technology diffusion, and agrifood supply chain integration across the CAREC region and with large expanding emerging market neighbors.[3]

Renewable energy development across CAREC would not only free natural gas for agricultural development but contribute directly to both large-scale and distributed electrification in one of the more underserved regions of the world. This would advance a number of other SDGs.

In addition to these two more detailed examples, all 17 of the SDGs are amenable to energy-oriented measures of progress. Three more general examples are discussed below:

2.7 Conclusions and Policy Recommendations

Energy is one of the most important strategic resources of the Central Asian region. While energy services secure livelihoods in all CAREC member countries, primary energy resources offer potent development stimulus to the region's exporters and, by extension, across an ever-expanding web of regional infrastructure, to their neighbors.

However, markets for Central Asian energy exports are on the verge of significant change, driven by evolving energy and climate policies. In addition to the fundamental economic challenge of relying on exports of nonrenewable resources, the region's primary sources of energy demand are beginning a determined transition away from fossil fuel-based energy. Despite these endemic risks, CARECs legacy energy exporters and most of the other countries in the region have the potential for a bright energy future. This would entail a fundamental shift from unevenly distributed carbon fuels to more widely available renewables, primarily wind and solar energy. Building out such capacity would require massive investments, but these can largely be financed with conventional export earnings and public-private investment partnerships, especially including FDI from larger-trading partners that have historically relied on CAREC for conventional energy and can transit to clean electric power from the same sources as part of their own low carbon transition.

The recommended transition would comprise three stages:

1. High-carbon (2020) primary carbon fuel exports, financing growth and transition to:
2. Mid-carbon (by 2030) (natural gas and gas-fired electricity and hydrogen exports), financing new capacity for:
3. Low-carbon (2040–50) solar and wind capacity for carbon- free electricity exports).

This strategy is noteworthy because endowments of renewable capacity (esp. wind and solar) are much more equally distributed across the CAREC than carbon fuel energy resources. Thus, phases 2 and 3 of transition would open opportunities for more inclusive and profitable regional energy infrastructure investment. Meanwhile, grid investments needed for more extensive supply development could also dramatically improve energy access across the region. In this way, energy can play the same role that manufacturing did in the dynamic East Asian economies, with export opportunities driving infrastructure investments that ultimately facilitate domestic connectivity, efficiency, and long-term, more inclusive growth.

The final recommendation of this chapter is that policy makers commit to, along with the many hard and soft infrastructure measures needed to realize the transition, a set of verifiable indicators that measure development progress. These will facilitate better-informed and more coherent policy dialogue, supporting a bold but evidence-based initiative that can deliver more sustainable and inclusive prosperity to the region.

Notes

1 Natural gas is the primary feedstock for ammonia production (99% of global ammonia tonnage). In addition to being the second-largest chemical product produced in the world, ammonia is the primary feedstock for synthetic fertilizer (72% of tonnage). Other hydrocarbon fuels can be used, but natural gas is preferred (Roland-Holst 2020).

2 See, e.g., Graff et al. (2006) for more on the pro-poor nature of such technology transfers.

3 The case for such a Central Asian agrifood development strategy is made more fully in Roland-Holst (2017).

References

Andrade, J., R. Balck. 2016. Estimation of Transmission Costs for New Generation. http://sites.utexas.edu/energyinstitute/files/2016/11/UTAustin_FCe_TransmissionCosts_2016.pdf (accessed 26 February 2020).

Asian Development Bank (ADB) 2005. Electricity Sectors in CAREC Countries: A Diagnostic Review of Regulatory Approaches and Challenges. www.adb.org/sites/default/files/publication/29932/electricity-sectors-carec-countries.pdf (accessed 26 February 2020).

Bellini, E. 2019. Italy's Eni Wins Kazakhstan's 50 MW Solar Auction with USItaly's Eni Wins Kazakhstan's 50 MW Solar Auction with US$0.032/kWh.032/kWh bid. www.pv-magazine.com/2019/12/02/italys-eni-wins-kazakhstans-50-mw-solar-auction-with-0-032-kwh-bid/ (accessed 26 February 2020).

Billo, J. 2017. The Texas Competitive Renewable Energy Zone Process. https://cleanenergysolutions.org/sites/default/files/documents/jeff-billo_webinar-ercot-crez-process.pdf (accessed 26 February 2020).

California Independent System Operator (CAISO). 2016. 2015-2016 Conceptual Statewide Transmission Plan Update. www.caiso.com/Documents/Draft2015-2016ConceptualStatewideTransmissionPlanUpdate-2016-2017TransmissionPlanningCycle.pdf (accessed 26 February 2020).

Climate Action Tracker (CAT). 2019. Country Summary: China. https://climateactiontracker.org/countries/china/ (accessed 26 February 2020).

Elliot, D., M. Schwartz, G. Scott, S. Haymes, D. Heimiller, R. George 2001) Wind Energy Resource Atlas of Mongolia. NREL/TP-500-28972. NREL, Golden.

European Commission (EC) (undated) 2050 long-term strategy. https://ec.europa.eu/clima/policies/strategies/2050_en (accessed 26 February 2020.

Graff, G., D. Roland-Holst, and D. Zilberman. 2006. Agricultural Biotechnology and Poverty Reduction in Low-Income Countries. *World Development* 34(8): 1430–1445.

International Energy Agency (IEA) 2018) World Energy Outlook. IEA/OECD, Paris.

NITI Aayog 2018) Zero Emissions Vehicles (ZEVs): Towards a Policy Framework. https://niti.gov.in/writereaddata/files/document_publication/EV_report.pdf (accessed 26 February 2020.

Obozov, A.J., W.V. Loscutof. (1998) Opportunities for Renewable Energy Sources in Central Asia Countries. NRELTP-210-25047. NREL, Golden.

Roland-Holst, D. 2017. Trade Horizons for Horticulture in Central and West Asia. Report produced for the Asian Development Bank, Manila.

Roland-Holst, D. 2020. Agricultural Energy Demand and Use. Oxford Research Encyclopedia of Environmental Science. Oxford University Press. United Kingdom. https://oxfordre.com/environmentalscience/view/10.1093/acrefore/9780199389414.001.0001/acrefore-9780199389414-e-593 (accessed 26 February 2020).

Shamsiev, Kh. A. 2018) The Interconnected Power Grid of Central Asia. www.carecprogram.org/uploads/05-The-Interconnected-Power-Grid-of-Central-Asia-Regional-Trade-Outlooks.pdf (accessed 26 February 2020.

Staffell I. et al. 2019) The role of hydrogen and fuel cells in the global energy system. *Energy and Environmental Science* 12: 463–491. https://doi.org/10.1039/C8EE01157E

Tazhmakina, B. 2018) Renewable Energy Auctions in Kazakhstan. www.unece.org/fileadmin/DAM/energy/se/pp/eneff/9th__Forum_Kiev_Nov.18/13_Novembe_2018/RE_DEVCO/02_Baltugan_Tazhmakina.pdf (accessed 26 February 2020.

United States Department of Energy (DOE). 2019. FY 2018 Progress Report for the DOE Hydrogen and Fuel Cells Program. DOE/GO-102019-5156., Washington, DC: DOE.

United States Energy Information Agency (EIA) 2019) International Data. www.eia.gov/international/data/world (accessed 26 February 2020.

3 Silk Road Smart Cities

Sustainable Growth and Recovery Drivers for Central Asia?

Nicolas J.A. Buchoud

3.1 Is There a Central Asia Smart Cities Rationale?

According to pre-COVID-19 estimates, the global market potential of smart cities was more than $2 trillion by 2025.[1] In the past years, and even as far back as the mid-1990s for Kazakhstan, Central Asian countries have started to engage in this direction.

While the development and growth of Nur-Sultan, formerly Astana, has been acknowledged since the mid-1990s, the national government has been continuously encouraged and showcased the process of information technology (IT)-based urban modernization, as recently illustrated by the promotion of Aqkol as the first integrated smart city in the country (Yergaliyeva 2019).

With economic liberalization and political reforms under way as part of the 2017–2021 plan, Uzbekistan also seeks to boost urban modernization investments, as reflected by the many projects and initiatives under way or envisioned for Tashkent and its region. From traffic management to water and sanitation to integrated, large-scale, high-end developments mobilizing private investors from the region and beyond, smart cities have become a metaphor for ambitious long-term growth plans. At different stages, urban transformation pathways depend on a unique blend of influences. In Turkmenistan, flagship large-scale government-supported "mega-projects" such as in Ashgabat seem to follow the same direction, while in Kyrgyztan and Tajikistan digital transformation is also high on the agenda, as illustrated by the adoption of the Concept of Digital Economy by the Tajik government in December 2019 (Olters 2020).

With an expected $500 billion of investments to meet the regional infrastructure needs in the next decade according to pre Covid-19 crisis estimates, Central Asia maintains a significant growth potential, with smart cities being the epicenter of expected economic transformations (ADB 2017). However, achieving sustainable growth will require more than modernizing city bus fleets, installing smart metering or multiplying traffic control smart cameras.

While there are very similar design features among urban development projects in the region's capital cities, it will take more than that to achieve a successful "silk road" model of smart cities, for three main reasons. First, the transition from rural to more urbanized countries will require comprehensive

DOI: 10.4324/9781003228790-5

land management policies, including second- and third-tier cities, as well as villages and rural settlements in overall territorial development plans. Second, while the growth potential of agglomeration economics has been well assessed in the past 10–15 years, there are growing environmental and social limits to this model, which the region must take into account as it embraces the Sustainable Development Goals (SDGs) and raises the profile of its global climate and biodiversity agendas (World Bank 2009).[2] Third, there is a specific, multi-vector, Central Asian geopolitical smart cities rationale, which does call for multilateral trade rules to support inclusive innovation and help support private investments along with state-led cooperation. The regional development is indeed shaped by multiple long-term strategies and partnerships with the Russian Federation, the People's Republic of China, the European Union, and the United States, as well as Japan, the United Arab Emirates, Saudi Arabia, or Turkey, along with many multilateral institutions and agencies.[3] These frameworks are driving competing investments in infrastructure, in particular energy, transportation, water (and sanitation) or IT, not to mention the building sector. Those investments are triggering accelerated transformations in capital cities, gradually reaching out to second- and third-tier cities, and displaying a patchwork of standards, norms, engineering systems and spheres of influence.

There are many challenges for Silk Road smart cities to become sustainability catalysts, in particular the competition between infrastructure investments and digital industry standards along several strategic partnerships, and throughout varying degrees of citizen participation in decision-making processes. We argue that, even if smart cities have recently become a game-changer in Central Asia, corresponding public and private investments should be reviewed for consistency and sustainable infrastructure rationale to secure long-term inclusive growth in the Covid-19 context (ADBI 2020; Buchoud, forthcoming).

3.2 Smart Cities as a Common Expression of Urban Modernization Across Central Asia

A systematic revision of cities and even rural municipality masterplans is currently taking place throughout provinces and districts of Uzbekistan as part of the 2017–2021 development plan. This goes along with a series of national sectoral plans to develop and modernize key national infrastructures such as railways and power grids. In this context, in the beginning of 2019, the Cabinet of Ministers of the Republic of Uzbekistan adopted a framework for the implementation of Smart City technologies, which entails the introduction of IT into various areas of city life. Pilot projects such as "Safe City" or "Smart Transport" are underway in Tashkent. The national smart city framework also includes the construction of "Tashkent City" and "Delta City" large-scale developments, as well as the development of a new administrative center for Tashkent region in the city of Nurafshan, meant to be the "first smart city in Uzbekistan."[4] While the streets of Tashkent are filled with posters of future buildings and plazas, this only echoes the rise of Nur Sultan, which has been a magnet for design, engineering

and architecture companies from across the globe. In the mid-2010s, a bilateral agreement between Kazakhstan and France allowed for the creation of a virtual city simulator of Nur Sultan, featured as a flagship initiative by French multinational companies involved in the process. More recently, investors from the Middle East have been engaged in building higher and more sophisticated buildings, such as the Abu Dhabi Plaza.

In Central Asia, cooperation about urban development is quite diverse, which makes the region a rather unique case from a global perspective.

In Uzbekistan, the Delta City project is to be implemented jointly with a Republic of Korea company for an estimated $1.4 billion. At an investment forum in Tashkent in November 2018, a memorandum was signed between the State Committee on Investments and a Singapore company for another "smart city" in the Tashkent region, targeting an ambitious $2.5 billion of investments. Meanwhile, PRC investors are scouting the country's regional centers and displaying futuristic neighborhoods such as the Smart Ecocity project in Namangan, with similar projects being showcased in Nukus in Karakalpakstan, 1,300 km away. Active discussions are also taking place in the Kyrgyz Republic, although in the past couple of years, the concept of smart cities has stirred many government debates. In Turkmenistan, physical and digital models of Ashgabat City, a smart new "city in the city," were presented to the President in the spring of 2019.

Alongside government-led new urban directions, international institutions such as the United Nations Development Programme and the United Nations Economic Commission for Europe are advocating for more structural changes along a sustainability priority, targeting large-scale investments in energy, waste, telecommunication or transportation infrastructure. The next decade will be critical in assessing how smart city initiatives can help accelerate systemic change for environment preservation, including public health, and global warming mitigation starting with the curbing of greenhouse gas emissions. From that perspective, mega-projects are only the most visible part of a deeper, ongoing urban transformation, as illustrated in Uzbekistan. Uzbek cities and regional planning tools, i.e., the "GenPlans," are being updated and developed to meet the national development priorities set up in 2017 and which echo the SDGs. However, while national and sectoral policies frequently refer to the SDGs and global environment goals, the localization of those agendas has still to be included in the technical cooperation and support agreements that largely depend on Belarus, Georgia, Azerbaijan, the Russian Federation or Kazakhstan, as far as city development and urban planning are concerned.

3.3 Quality Infrastructure as a Common Standard to Invest in Central Asian Cities

At the 2019 Tokyo Urban 20 summit, Tashkent was among the cities invited,[5] providing a good illustration of cities from Central Asia gaining institutional recognition on the global stage and beyond the traditional Community of Independent

States (CIS) countries. As a consequence of national reforms—although with significant differences in scope and intensity—the largest urban centers in the region are facing visible transformations, though in-depth changes also depend on how they will be articulated with country-wide urban reforms involving second and third tier cities, especially through infrastructure investments.

Infrastructure investments in Central Asia depend on regional factors, topped by global factors. Uzbekistan, which hosts nearly 50% of the total Central Asian population, is again a good illustration of the multiple influences linked with digitalization in the region. At the 27th Organization for Security and Co-operation in Europe Economic and Environmental Forum held in September 2019, the presentation of digital ecosystem priorities for Uzbekistan showcased smart cities as a component of digital platforms and smart solutions within a regional digital connectivity infrastructure, as part of the World Bank 'Digital Casa' project and looking for a smart city integration strategy towards 2030. Meanwhile, as a delegation of the Embassy of Uzbekistan in the United States participated in a Global Smart Cities and Communities summit (UZDaily 2019), Uzbekistan's Ministry of Development of Information Technologies and Communications and the PRC's CITIC Group and Henan Costar Group signed an agreement on the implementation of Uzbekistan's Safe City project, highlighting the PRC's role in shaping Uzbekistan's digital infrastructure (Hashimova 2019). The creation of a ministry dedicated to innovation and the implementation of smart city technologies reflect the national government's intent to meet global digital standards, though the delivery of this digital ambition depends on contracts with private providers of services and IT infrastructure from the PRC, Europe, the Russian Federation, Japan, the US, etc.

We argue that the huge diversity of technological standards embedded in the country's many key partnerships calls for a common sustainability rationale for future infrastructure investments, which the G20 "quality infrastructure" agenda could provide, as it has been approved by all major technological partner countries of Uzbekistan. As the COVID-19 pandemic is adding pressure to national budgets, and as physical infrastructure investment needs are redoubled by social infrastructure priorities, finance could provide the leverage for a regional alignment of future projects, including smart cities along quality and sustainable investment principles.

In preparation for the contribution to the ADBI-CAREC initiative on sustainable infrastructure in Central Asia, we have conducted a short assessment to find out how the global conversation on cities and urban priorities was shaped before the COVID-19 pandemic outbreak. From 2017 to the very beginning of 2020 and the 10th World Urban Forum, an estimated half million urban development professionals, journalists, researchers, people in local governments, civil society groups, etc., gathered to discuss the future of cities at more than 50 major conferences and summits. It is thus no surprise that the acceleration of the global urban conversation has reached out to Central Asia as well. Digital networks accelerate the possibility of teaming up and meeting with others, but, in an era of abundant connecting opportunities, urbanization and infrastructure systems need more than networking to deliver on societal and environmental sustainability. The institutional uncertainties about smart cities or the vivid debates about the implementation of the Tashkent 2025 Plan show that, while there is a growing appetite for smart technologies and design at institutional level, citizens' use of digital technologies might reflect different priorities, in particular more inclusion in key decision-making processes managing territorial transformations (Kudryavtseva 2018; Radio Free Europe 2020). Supporting capacity building and the development of social capital should be part of the development of common standards.

3.4 Conclusion: Rapidly Urbanizing Central Asia as a Common Space for Sustainability?

Smart cities have become a universal language for marketing and services, but long-term urban transformations and corresponding infrastructure investments are also linked with industry changes, in particular, Industry 4.0, which is based upon automation and massive data exchange in manufacturing technologies, mobility, construction or energy industries. In Central Asia, the rapid development of new telecommunication, geo-positioning, and monitoring systems provided by the PRC under the Belt and Road Initiative is gradually creating a new digital space. Similar changes also are occurring in the energy sector, with regional exchanges regarding powergrid interconnectivity. Rethinking urban innovation and smart cities with a focus on industry and not just on services should allow for a better understanding of the interdependency of cities and infrastructure systems in delivering locally on the global development and environmental goals in the region. In return, it could help structure and prioritize private investments in real estate, building, and construction along a region-wide social and environmental sustainability focus. This could only help build a way out of the Covid-19 crisis and support sustainable long-term growth. Finally, we can only encourage international institutions to also modernize their own approach of urbanization in support of Central Asia's strong systemic transformation potentials.[6]

Notes

1 www.smartcitiesworld.net/news/news/smart-cities-market-to-be-worth-over-2-trillion-by-2025-2785 (accessed 27 June 2021)

2 For recent release reviewing the approaches of agglomeration economics: *Shaping the new frontiers of sustainable (urban) infrastructure. Reviewing the long term value of infrastructure investments and enabling system change,* N. Buchoud, et al., Sept 2020, *T20 Taskforce on infrastructure investment and financing* https://t20saudiarabia.org.sa/en/briefs/Pages/Policy-Brief.aspx?pb=TF3_PB10 See also (forthcoming, Ov. 2020) The role of global cities in shaping a new sustainable economy, N.Buchoud, ISPI. In *The Future of Sustainability* ISP and *A Sustainable Urbanization And Infrastructure Response to the Covid19,* N.Buchoud, dir.n Oct. 2020

T20 Special taskforce on *Covid19 'Multidisciplinary Approaches To Complex Problems'* https://t20saudiarabia.org.sa/en/briefs/Pages/Policy-Brief.aspx?pb=TF11_PB15

3 Among the key partnerships and agreements in the region are the Eurasian Union led by the Russian Federation, the European Union-Central Asia Partnership, the New Silk Roads under the PRC's Belt and Road Initiative, and several initiatives led by the United Nations, as illustrated by the multipartner trustfund for the Aral sea recovery. In addition, numerous cooperation agreements are under way with multilateral development banks such as the Asian Development Bank or the World Bank, alongside multiple bilateral cooperation agreements implemented by partners such as the Japan International Cooperation Agency (JICA) or the German cooperation agency GiZ or the Saudi Fund for Economic Development. The Uzbekistan 2017–2021 development strategy is an illustration of ongoing, country-led economic and societal reforms in Central Asia.

4 The "Delta City" project was formerly known until July 2018 as the Hi-Tech City Innovation Center, illustrating rapid underging changes, at least before the COVID-19 pandemic.

5 The U20 is the civil society engagement group of cities of the G20.

6 As an example, the latest environmental performance review, performed every 10 years by the United Nations Economic Commission for Europe (UNECE), with recent updates in several Central Asian Countries, still relies on such rigid and formal categories as "land management" or "human settlements" instead of "territorial development." They therefore tend to underestimate the need and potential for more systemic transformation triggered by urbanization and digitalization.

References

Asian Development Bank (ADB). 2017. *Meeting Asia's Infrastructure Needs.* www.adb.org/publications/asia-infrastructure-needs (accessed 27 June 2021).

Asian Development Bank Institute (ADBI). 2020. *Building the Future of Quality Infrastructure.* Tokyo: ADBI Institute. www.adb.org/sites/default/files/publication/577031/adbi-building-future-quality-infrastructure.pdf (accessed 27 June 2021).

Buchoud, N. 2020.*Shaping the New Frontiers of Sustainable Infrastructure. Reviewing the Long-Term Value of Infrastructure Investments and Enabling System Change.* To be released.

Hashimova, U. 2019. China Dominates Digital Infrastructure in Uzbekistan. *The Diplomat,* June 28. https://thediplomat.com/2019/06/china-dominates-digital-infrastructure-in-uzbekistan/ (accessed 27 June 2021).

Kudryavtseva, T. 2018. Government of Kyrgyzstan Withdraws from Smart City Agreement. March. https://24.kg/english/78507__Government_of_Kyrgyzstan_withdraws_from_Smart_City_agreement/ (accessed 27 June 2021).

Olters, J.P. 2020. *Digital Transformation in Tajikistan as Central COVID-19 Response Policy.* www.worldbank.org/en/news/speech/2020/10/14/digital-transformation-in-tajikistan-as-central-covid-19-response-policy (accessed 27 June 2021).

Radio Free Europe. 2020. Tashkent Scraps Redistricting Plan After Rare Street Protests, August. www.rferl.org/a/tashkent-scraps-redistricting-plan-after-rare-street-protests/30779689.html accessed 27 June 2021).

SEnECA. 2019. Central Asia in 2030: SEnECA Forecasts for the Region and the Role of the European Union, Policy paper no. 13. www.seneca-eu.net/wp-content/uploads/2019/07/SEnECA_Policy_Paper_13_2019.pdf (accessed 27 June 2021).

UZ Daily. 2019. Ambassador of Uzbekistan at the Summit on the Development of Global "Smart Cities" Presented a Presentation of Ongoing Projects in the Country. August 21. https://uzdaily.uz/en/post/51392 (accessed 27 June 2021).

World Bank. 2009. World Development Report 2009: Reshaping Economic Geography. https://openknowledge.worldbank.org/handle/10986/5991 (accessed 27 June 2021).

Yergaliyeva, A. 2019. Aqkol Becomes First Smart City in Kazakhstan. *The Astana Times*, 23 January. https://astanatimes.com/2019/01/aqkol-becomes-first-smart-city-in-kazakhstan/ (accessed 27 June 2021).

4 Infrastructure Needs and Cooperation in CAREC Countries

Perspectives from a Pan-Asian Natural Gas Trade Model

Youngho Chang and Farhad Taghizadeh-Hesary*

4.1 Introduction

By making more competition possible, integration of the Asia-Pacific natural gas market has the potential to improve the equilibrium price and quantity of natural gas traded across the region, in turn enhancing overall welfare (Chang and Li 2014). The hypothetical pan-Asian natural gas trade model includes most of Asia and some countries outside the region such as the US, the Russian Federation, Tobago, a few African countries including Algeria, and a number of Middle Eastern states including Qatar and the United Arab Emirates.[1]

The Central Asia Regional Economic Cooperation (CAREC) countries have abundant natural gas, and Table 4.1 shows statistics such as proven reserves, production, consumption, exports, and imports. Though the People's Republic of China (PRC) imports natural gas in the form of liquefied natural gas (LNG), the predominant mode of trade in CAREC countries is via pipeline.

The amount of proven reserves of natural gas in CAREC countries is 35,000 bcm, about 1% of which was produced at the end of 2019. The share of the proven reserves of natural gas for the CAREC countries was 17.5% of the total energy portfolio, while the share of crude oil was only 3.6% at the end of 2019 (BP 2020).

Despite the relative abundance of natural gas in the CAREC countries, intra-region trade is not active, with the PRC and Pakistan importing LNG from outside the region. Other than in the case of these two countries, all the natural gas traded in the region is transported via natural gas pipelines.

According to the BP Statistical Review of World Energy (BP 2020), Azerbaijan exports natural gas mainly to Turkey (9.2 bcm) and a few European countries (2.0 bcm in total); Kazakhstan mainly to the Russian Federation and the PRC, and a small amount to other Commonwealth of Independent States (CIS) countries (20.6 bcm, 6.5 bcm, and 0.4 bcm, respectively); Turkmenistan mainly to the PRC (31.6 bcm); and Uzbekistan mainly to Kazakhstan, the Russian Federation, and the PRC (1.8 bcm, 6.2 bcm, and 4.9 bcm, respectively) and a small amount to other CIS countries (0.4 bcm in total). To facilitate and promote trade of

DOI: 10.4324/9781003228790-6

Table 4.1 Statistics of Natural Gas in CAREC Countries in 2019 (in billion cubic meters)

Country	*Reserves*	*Production*	*Consumption*	*Export*	*Import*	*Remark*
Azerbaijan	2,800	24.3	11.8	11.5	-	
Kazakhstan	2,700	23.4	17.9	27.5	6.9	
Turkmenistan	19,500	63.2	31.5	31.6	-	
Uzbekistan	1,200	56.3	43.4	13.2	-	
PRC	8,400	177.6	307.3	-	47.7	43.0*
Pakistan	400	33.9	45.7	-	-	
Total	**35,000**	**378.7**	**457.6**	**84.0**	**50.6**	

Source: BP Statistical Review of World Energy 2020.

Notes
CAREC = Central Asia Regional Economic Cooperation, PRC = People's Republic of China.
Import by pipeline; * import from Kazakhstan, Turkmenistan, and Uzbekistan.

natural gas in the CAREC region requires more national interconnections beyond existing ones such as Central Asia-Central Gas Pipelines (CAC).

While there have been discussions about connecting CAREC countries via more pipeline networks, none have been built in the region since CAC-5 was completed in 1988. The idea of constructing the Caspian Coastal Pipeline was mooted but has been mothballed (Global Energy Monitor Wiki 2020a). This study draws some lessons from the pan-Asian Natural Gas Trade Model (Chang and Li 2014) to explore how the CAREC region can promote intra-region trade of natural gas.

4.2 Pan-Asian Natural Gas Trade Model: Structure and Implications

The BP Statistical Review of World Energy shows that there are four key players in global natural gas trade: the Russian Federation, Norway, Qatar, and Australia (BP 2020). Natural gas from the Russian Federation and Norway is exported mainly to European countries by pipeline, while natural gas from Qatar and Australia is exported mainly to East Asian countries as LNG. Unlike the Russian Federation, which exports natural gas to European countries and other CIS countries, Norway exports natural gas only to European countries. Apart from Norway, the Netherlands exports a significant amount of natural gas to European countries (38.2 bcm).

The Russian Federation exports natural gas to most European countries. The main importing countries of Russian Federation natural gas are Germany, Italy, the Netherlands, France, and the UK. Turkey imports natural gas via pipeline from the Russian Federation. Like the Russian Federation, Norway exports natural gas via pipeline to most European countries, with the main ones being Germany, the UK, the Netherlands, and France (Belgium, Italy, and Spain import less than 10 bcm). Germany is the main importer of Dutch natural gas and

Belgium and France import a smaller amount (6.6 bcm and 4.4 bcm, respectively). Qatar exports natural gas via pipeline to the United Arab Emirates, while Australia exports natural gas only as LNG.

Qatar has very diversified LNG export destinations, including Asia and the Pacific, Europe, and Kuwait. Japan, the PRC, and the Republic of Korea are the main importing countries of Qatari LNG, while Australia exports LNG to many Asia and the Pacific economies such as Japan, the PRC, Republic of Korea and Taipei,China. For Europe and Asia and the Pacific regions that have a smaller amount of proven reserves of natural gas compared to the Middle East and the CIS, the quantity of imports is far larger than the quantity of exports, with the Asia and the Pacific region importing 334.1 bcm and exporting 177.3 bcm as LNG, and the Middle East importing 6.6 bcm and exporting 128.8 bcm as LNG.

There have been studies on how natural gas is traded at a global or regional level using the Canadian Natural Gas Allocation Model, EIA Short-Term Integrated Forecasting model from the Energy Information Administration of the US Department of Energy, Gas Market System for Trade Analysis in a Liberalizing Europe, North American Gas Trade Model, and Strategic Model of European Gas Supply, among others (Beltramo 1985, 1986; Rowse 1986; Costello 1999; Boots et al. 2003; Holz et al. 2005).

Because of a lack of studies on natural gas trade in the Asia and the Pacific region, a model was constructed that appeared to remove inefficiency and establish the price of natural gas independent from oil prices (Chang and Li 2014). Although a few exporters exist in East Asia, the majority are net importers of natural gas. The study presented two key findings: the efficient trade routes of natural gas in the region under an integrated and competitive market, and possible impacts of additional infrastructure, including pipelines and LNG terminals.

The pan-Asian natural gas trade model is a non-linear programming model (Chang and Li 2014). It is a parametric static equilibrium model, meaning it is a snapshot of natural gas trade in a specific year. The objective function of the model is to maximize the social welfare of exporting natural gas, accommodating the cost of transport. Technical and policy constraints include pipeline capacity limits and the lack of LNG terminals, the total amount of delivery from the exporting country not being more than its total production, and the total amount of reception for the importing country needing to be more than its total consumption.[2] The total amount of consumption of the importing country was computed using historical price and quantity data and the price elasticity of demand. The cost function was computed by taking two historical data points of prices and quantities for each supply country.

The pan-Asian natural gas trade model adopted two scenarios with respect to the status of the interconnections of infrastructure for trading natural gas via pipeline or as LNG in the region. First, a competitive equilibrium was derived by assuming that there is an integrated market with current trade patterns such as trade links, prices, and quantities. Second, an extended competitive equilibrium was derived assuming that there is an integrated market with new infrastructure that has been completed and connected. Compared to the current trade flows, those under an integrated and competitive natural gas market showed that inefficient trade links were removed. An integrated and competitive market with new infrastructure for natural gas in the region showed the changes of the trade routes such as new and deleted ones.

4.3 Energy Landscape and Infrastructure in CAREC Countries

The BP Statistical Review of World Energy presents that countries in the CAREC region have relatively more abundant amount of natural gas compared to crude oil. However, there is not much intra-trade of natural gas in the region mainly due to a lack infrastructure. Table 4.2 shows a snapshot of intra-regional natural gas trade. All the intra-region trade of natural gas is done via pipelines, not LNG. Considering the landlocked nature of the region, trade via pipeline appears to the best mode. There could be some potential for intra-trade of natural gas in the region.

As shown in Table 4.2, Turkey is the main export destination for Azerbaijan,[3] with no intra-regional trade. The Russian Federation is the main destination for exports, with the PRC a distant second for Kazakhstan. Turkmenistan, the largest producer of natural gas in the CAREC region, exports to the PRC only, while Uzbekistan is the most diversified among four countries, with the Russian Federation being the largest exporter, followed by the PRC and Kazakhstan. In sum, the natural gas market in the region is small and very concentrated and dependent on the PRC.

The CAC gas pipeline, which spans 3,666 km, links the Turkmenistan/Uzbekistan border and Jingbian in the PRC and can constitute a new Silk Road supported by the Belt-Road Initiative (FT 2016). The three parallel pipelines

Table 4.2 Intraregional Natural Gas Trade in CAREC Countries (in billion cubic meters)

To\From	*Azerbaijan*	*Kazakhstan*	*Russian Federation*	*Turkmenistan*	*Uzbekistan*	*Total*
Belarus			19.0			19.0
Kazakhstan			5.1		1.8	6.9
Russian Federation		20.6			6.2	26.8
Other CIS		0.4	4.8		0.4	5.6
Other Middle East	0.3					0.3
PRC		6.5	0.3	31.6	4.9	43.3
Total	0.3	27.5	29.2	31.6	13.2	101.9
Turkey	9.2					

Source: BP Statistical Review of World Energy 2020.

Note

CAREC = Central Asia Regional Economic Cooperation, CIS = Commonwealth of Independent States, PRC = People's Republic of China.

run from Saman-Depe on the Turkmenistan/Uzbekistan border east to Olot, Shymkent, and Alataw Pass to Horgos, Xinjiang Province, PRC (Global Energy Monitor Wiki 2020a).

Uzbekistan, Tajikistan, and the Kyrgyz Republic signed agreements to build a fourth CAC gas pipeline in September 2013. It is expected to increase Turkmenistan's gas exports to the PRC from 55 bcm per year to 85 bcm. In January 2020, it was reported that construction was suspended. The pipeline was expected to be completed by 2022.

The CAC gas pipeline is a Gazprom-controlled system that runs from Turkmenistan via Uzbekistan and Kazakhstan to the Russian Federation. The pipeline runs from Dauletabad gas field and Okarem, Turkmenistan through Shatlyk gas field, Khiva, Kungrad, Cheleken, and Beyneu to Alexandrov Gay, the Russian Federation. The eastern branch includes the CAC 1, 2, 4, and 5 pipelines, which start from the southeastern gas fields of Turkmenistan. The western branch consists of the CAC 3 pipeline and a project to build a new parallel Caspian pipeline. The western branch runs from the Caspian Sea coast of Turkmenistan to the north. The branches meet in western Kazakhstan. From there, the pipelines run north where they are connected to the Russian natural gas pipeline system (Global Energy Monitor Wiki 2020b).

In 2007, the Russian Federation, Turkmenistan, and Kazakhstan agreed to construct the Caspian Coastal Pipeline that is parallel to the existing CAC 3 pipeline. The Caspian Coastal Pipeline was supposed to start in 2009 but the project has been halted.

4.4 Prospects for Intra-Region Natural Gas Trade in the CAREC Region

Chow and Hendrix (2010) presented some lessons regarding pipeline development in Central Asia that still shed some light on infrastructure needs and cooperation in the CAREC region. First, international politics can sometimes help the development of pipelines, but appear not to determine the outcome, and, more often, block sensible commerce. When expected gains from a decision following international politics outweigh economic gains, the decision becomes distorted. Venezuela exported crude oil to its neighboring countries at prices far lower than the global price. This decision allowed Venezuela to gain votes from those countries in the international political arena, but forced it to sacrifice the expected economic gains it otherwise would have gotten. Such a decision and ensuing action eventually led Venezuela to financial collapse. Second, having bankable volumes is the key to building pipelines. Third, one committed and capable player rather than multiple players appears to be better for successful pipeline projects. The completion of Nord Stream could support why having one committed and capable player is the key to success. A counterexample can be seen from the delay in constructing the South Stream or Nabucco Pipeline. The PRC can be considered the pivotal player in promoting and completing the interconnectivity in the CAREC region (Pirani 2012; 2019). Fourth, diversifying supply and routes is good, but the price of having such a system should be paid by those who get the most benefits. Fifth, as more players came from differing backgrounds, the construction of pipelines has complicated regional connectivity issues (Kubicek 2013). In sum, it is imperative to show that CAREC countries should pursue "cooperative competition," in which they will increase the size of the regional natural gas market first and compete openly to get a fair share of it afterwards. Geoeconomics, not geopolitics, should be the key principle to connect CAREC countries via pipelines (Chen and Fazilov 2018; Fazilov and Chen 2013).

The pan-Asian gas trade model can be applied to the CAREC countries. CAREC's abundant natural gas hints that integrating energy markets through building new infrastructure will bring benefits to the region. Both exporting and importing countries can benefit from intra-region natural gas trade under the coordinated cooperation and competition among the CAREC governments.

The road to the assured connectivity and cooperative competition in the region can be stated as follows. First, the region needs to carry out a simulation study of linking national and regional natural gas markets by applying the pan-Asian gas trade model (Chang and Li 2014) or other feasibility studies and strategic analysis (c.f., Bowden 2019; Hu 2014; Guo et al. 2019; Han 2016; Mantel 2015; Mathiesen 2010). Second, with the simulation results, the region needs to identify the best possible routes. Third, the region can present various options of integrating national and regional natural gas markets via pipeline for intergovernmental implementation discussions. With robust and solid economic analyses and sound and viable technologies, what remains to complete the interconnectivity is the political will of leaders in the region.

4.5 Conclusions and Policy Recommendations

Compared to crude oil, natural gas is relatively abundant in the CAREC region, but infrastructure for transporting it in the region is still ineffective. An integrated gas trade model for pan-Asian countries can verify whether and how cooperation can bring the benefit to countries in the CAREC region (Chang and Li 2014).

Integrating natural gas markets through new natural gas infrastructure will bring benefits to the region. Apart from this, both exporting and importing countries can benefit from intra-region natural gas trade under the coordinated cooperation among the governments in the CAREC region and assured connectivity. The region is advised to carry out a simulation study to explore the best ways to implement "cooperative competition" by applying robust economic principles and mature technologies, and putting collective economics gains before regional or international politics.

Notes

* School of Business, Singapore University of Social Sciences, 463 Clementi Road, Singapore 599494. Tel: +65-6248-0159; email: yhchang@suss.edu.sg

1 The hypothetical pan-Asian natural trade model includes non-Asian nations to replicate the actual natural gas infrastructure and trade patterns in the Asia and the Pacific region as closely as possible.
2 For the full description of the model, please refer to Chang and Li (2014): "Towards an integrated Asia-Pacific natural gas market."
3 This is possibly due to a close relationship between Azerbaijan and Turkey. Turkey aided Azerbaijan during the recent border dispute and war between Azerbaijan and Armenia in 2020.

References

Beltramo, M.A. 1985. Interfuel Substitution and Natural Gas Trade in North America. PhD. Dissertation. Stanford University

Beltramo, M.A., A. Manne, and J. Weyant 1986. A North American Gas Trade Model (GTM). *Energy Journal* 7(3): 15–32.

Boots, M.G., F.A.M. Rijkers, and B.F. Hobbs. 2003. GASTALE: An Oligopolistic Model of Production and Trade in the European Gas Market. Energy Research Center of the Netherlands (ECN), ECN-R-03-001.

Bowden, J. 2019. *SE Europe Gas Markets: Toward Integration*. OIES Paper 150. Oxford: The Oxford Institute for Energy Studies.

BP. 2020. *BP Statistical Review of World Energy* 2020. London, UK.

Chang, Y. and Y. Li. 2014. Towards an Integrated Asia-Pacific Natural Gas Market. In *Energy Market Integration in East Asia: Deepening Understanding and Moving Forward*, edited by Yanrui Wu, Fukunari Kimura, and Xunpeng Shi, pp. 163–187. London: Routledge.

Chen, X. and F. Fazilov 2018. Re-centering Central Asia: China's New Great Game in the Old Eurasian Heartland. *Palgrave Communications* 4(71): 4–12.

Chow, E.C. and L.E. Hendrix. 2010. Central Asia's Pipelines: Field of Dreams and Reality. NBR Special Report #23. Seattle: The National Bureau of Asian Research.

Costello, D. 1999. *Short-Term Integrated Forecasting (STIFS) Model*. Washington, DC: Energy Information Administration, US Department of Energy.

Fazilov, F. and X. Chen. 2013. China and Central Asia: A Significant New Energy Nexus. *The European Financial Review*, April-May: 38–43.

FT. 2016. Map: Connecting Central Asia. *Financial Times*, 10 May 2016. www.ft.com/content/ee5cf40a-15e5-11e6-9d98-00386a18e39d (accessed 15 November 2020).

Global Energy Monitor Wiki. 2020a. Central Asia-China Gas Pipeline. https://gem.wiki/Central_Asia-China_Gas_Pipieline (accessed 15 November 2020).

Global Energy Monitor Wiki. 2020b. Central Asia-Center Gas Pipeline. https://gem.wiki/Central_Asia-Center_Gas_Pipieline (accessed 15 November 2020).

Guo, F.-F., C.-F. Huang, and X.-L. Wu. 2019. Strategic Analysis on the Construction of a New Energy Corridor China-Pakistan-Iran-Turkey. *Energy Reports* 5: 828–841.

Han, W. 2016. *Towards a Cooperative Framework for a China-Central Asia Energy Transit Community*. ECSKC Occasional Paper Series. Brussels: Energy Charter Secretariat Knowledge Centre.

Holz, F., C. Hirschhausen, C. Kemfert. 2006. A Strategic Model of European Gas Supply (GASMOD). Fourth Conference of Applied Infrastructure Research, Technical University Berlin, Germany, 8 October.

Hu, B. 2014. Oil and Gas Cooperation between China and Central Asia in an Environment of Political and Resource Competition. *Petroleum Science* 11: 596–605.

Kubicek, P. 2013. Energy Politics and Geopolitical Competition in the Caspian Basin. *Journal of Eurasian Studies* 4: 171–180.

Mantel, R. 2015. EU-Central Asia Relations in the Energy Sector with a Special Focus on Kazakhstan. *Centre International de Formation Europeenne* 1(375): 55–71.

Mathiesen, L. 2010. On modeling the European Market for Natural Gas. In *Energy, Natural Resources and Environmental Economics, Energy Systems* edited by E. Bjorndal et al., pp. 83–100. Berlin: Springer-Verlag.

Pirani, S. 2012. *Central Asian and Caspian Gas Production and the Constraints on Export.* OIES Paper: NG 69. Oxford: The Oxford Institute for Energy Studies.

Pirani, S. 2019. *Central Asian Gas: Prospects for the 2020s.* OIES Paper: NG 155. Oxford: The Oxford Institute for Energy Studies.

Rowse, J. 1986. Allocation of Canadian Natural Gas to Domestic and Export Markets. *Canadian Journal of Economics* 19(3): 417–442.

5 Financing Infrastructure in Central Asia

The Water Sector

Iskandar Abdullaev and Shakhboz Akhmedov

5.1 Introduction

During almost three decades since they gained independence in 1991, Central Asian economies have undergone varying degrees of reforms and changes. Despite having chosen different development paths, they have one feature in common—a Soviet legacy. This applies to almost every sector, and primarily to the water sector.

Outdated infrastructure, aging roads and rail networks, central planning of the economy, cross-border issues on energy, communication and complicated transboundary water resources are a few elements of that legacy (Adelphi & CAREC 2017). These complications have strongly affected the relationships among Central Asian countries.

Water is arguably one of the most constrained and valuable resources in Central Asia sustaining the bedrock of its socioeconomic development. The availability of water determines economic performance, social coherence, and even political stability. Water is also an important resource for food, energy production, environmental safety, and livelihood security. The region is driven by a growing population, where there is a pressing need for efficient management of water resources and upgrade of infrastructure. Yet, this government-dominated sector has a relatively low profile compared to other sectors such as energy, transport, telecommunications, etc., which limits investment flows.

The water sector in Central Asian countries has been the least reformed, keeping Soviet time-planning and management approaches until the mid-2000s. Limited funding for operating and maintaining infrastructure undermined the efforts to make changes in the water systems. In the early 2000s, countries started to exercise Integrated Water Management with the support of international partners (Abdullaev and Atabaeva 2012; Abdullaev and Rakhmatullaev 2015).

Currently, the countries of Central Asia have state-led water governance and management systems, with only limited space for non-governmental actors. Despite small-scale reforms, the water sector is still confined to the countries' leading water consumers (energy for upstream and irrigation for downstream). Therefore, the intersectoral nature of water resources is a major problem at both the national and regional levels (EU 2018). The water sector contributes 5%–28%

DOI: 10.4324/9781003228790-7

of countries' gross domestic product (GDP) through irrigated agriculture and almost 30% of total energy in the region via hydro-energy production. Currently, the region is utilizing almost 95% of available water resources of the Aral Sea basin (CA-Water Info 2019).

Hence, water is a precious, limited, and non-renewable resource and the issue of investment in water infrastructure is critical. Access to water resources is a key economic, social, and political priority of each riparian state of the region. The augmenting impact of climate change, increasing economic development, and a growing population will further increase the demand and the competition for water resources (CAREC Institute 2020a).

This chapter reviews infrastructure financing in Central Asia and argues that it is an important factor in sustaining economic growth and stability in the region. As the region's economies continue their reforms toward a more market-oriented development, the need for reliable and effective water infrastructure remains crucial.

5.2 Infrastructure Financing in Central Asia

Central Asia is one of the least economically integrated regions of the world due to, inter alia, infrastructure bottlenecks (Figure 5.1). Infrastructure can improve communities and societies through better connectivity, mobility, and business opportunities, yet its construction and maintenance requires substantial financial

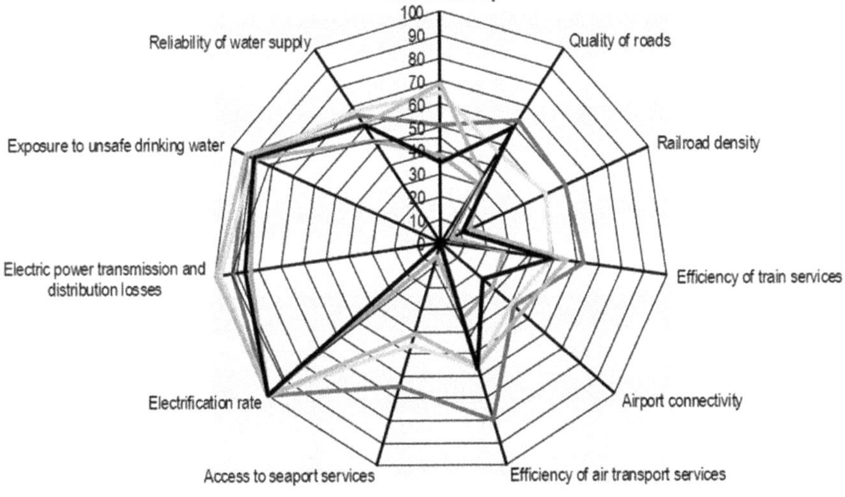

Figure 5.1 Quality of Infrastructure in Selected Countries Central Asia and the Caucasus. Source: OECD (2019).

resources and it is an enormous financial burden on the public sector. This, in turn, is impeding the development of economic cooperation and trade in the region.

Central Asian states, as with many other countries of the Central Asia Economic Cooperation (CAREC) region, are facing serious challenges on infrastructure financing (CAREC 2018). Demand for infrastructure investment in the region is around 5%–7% of GDP of the countries. This can increase if climate conditions are to be considered (ADB 2017). The major reason for the infrastructure conundrum in the region is the decline in financing from 1990–2010. During these years, infrastructure spending in Central Asia was around 0.5% of GDP (Fay et al., 2019). This is significantly below international trends, particularly for rapidly growing economies. As the former Soviet countries of the CAREC region underwent economic transition, infrastructure investments were not prioritized.

Central Asia currently spends around 4% of GDP on infrastructure investments (OECD 2019), with estimates reaching 6.8% until 2030, and even 7.8% for climate-proof infrastructure (ADB 2017). The region should invest $492 billion until 2030 or $33 billion annually in infrastructure (Table 5.1). As the region is one of the most vulnerable to climate change (CAREC Institute 2020a), its climate-adjusted spending equals $565 billion until 2030 or $38 billion annually (Table 5.1). The data also addressed population growth, which is projected to hit 96 million by 2030, exacerbating the pressure on natural resources, particularly water. If the present economic and demographic growth persists, the region will be exposed to worse climate change than predicted and the financing gap will further increase.

Recent economic growth and expanding trade highlight the region's attraction for investment. However, economic growth may be limited due to infrastructure bottlenecks. Public debt levels greater than 40% of GDP on average are a serious concern for potential investors (World Bank 2019). Therefore, inflow of infrastructure investments should go hand in hand with structural and sectoral reforms.

Table 5.1 Estimated Infrastructure Investment Needs of Central Asia, 2016–2030, ($ billion in 2015 prices)

Projected Annual GDP growth (%)	*2030 UN Population Projection (million)*	*Baseline Estimates*			*Climate-Adjusted Estimates*		
		Investment Needs	*Annual Average*	*Investment Needs as % of GDP*	*Investment Needs*	*Annual Average*	*Investment Needs as % of GDP*
3.1	96	492	33	6.8	565	38	7.8

Source: ADB (2017).

Major areas of infrastructure investments are transport (44%), power generation (38%) and water sanitation (6%). Most of the infrastructure investment needs are emerging from the rehabilitation or extension of existing outdated ones. However, the growing economy and positive demographics are demanding new infrastructure development (Figure 5.2).

International finance institutions (IFIs) play a major role in financing Central Asia's infrastructure needs. Since the early 2000s, CAREC invested $34 billion; the Asian Development Bank, $12.5 billion; the World Bank, $7.4 billion; the Islamic Development Bank, $1.4 billion; and the European Bank for Reconstruction and Development, $1.6 billion, to support the CAREC region, which covers all five Central Asian countries (World Bank 2020). Most of the infrastructure financing in the region is currently directed to the extractive industries such as oil, gas, and mining, while the water sector enjoys only 3%–5% of international infrastructure financing (Abdullaev et al. 2020).

Private capital in infrastructure in the Central Asian region is not yet developed (Table 5.2) and most of the existing funding comes from the public sector or, as mentioned, from bi- and multilateral IFIs. Yet the region is developing and needs modernized infrastructure. Currently, public financing covers only 50% of existing infrastructure financing need. Infrastructure investment should be diversified through financing mechanisms such as public-private partnerships.

The People's Republic of China's Belt and Road Initiative (BRI) has started to fund infrastructure in the region. Although the coronavirus may reduce BRI investment, the initiative has become a source for significant infrastructure funding for Central Asian countries (WB 2019). Currently, 261 different projects related to BRI, with total budget of $136 billion, are being implemented in Central Asia (Vakulchuk et al. 2019).

Yet, while BRI has easier and more attractive financing, vulnerable Central Asian financial systems may not be able to manage the terms. Levels of public debt are a serious concern; for example, in the Kyrgyz Republic, total government debt is 62% of GDP, while, in Tajikistan, it is 45% (Hurley, Morris, and Portelance 2018). Another serious issue is the absence of long-term infrastructure development strategies. Although all Central Asian states by now have developed their long-term visons 2030 to 2050, infrastructure development strategies are not clearly stipulated in these documents.

The transboundary nature of water resources requires a more careful and collaborative approach to infrastructure financing in Central Asia. Investments in water infrastructure from BRI or other financing mechanisms may provoke political tensions both between individual Central Asian countries and between recipient and donor countries, as investments in the water sector, especially in the transboundary systems, are highly politicized. Central Asian countries share water resources of transboundary systems; therefore, any intervention into the water sector will affect riparian countries. Hence, financing water infrastructure requires regional consensus among riparian states.

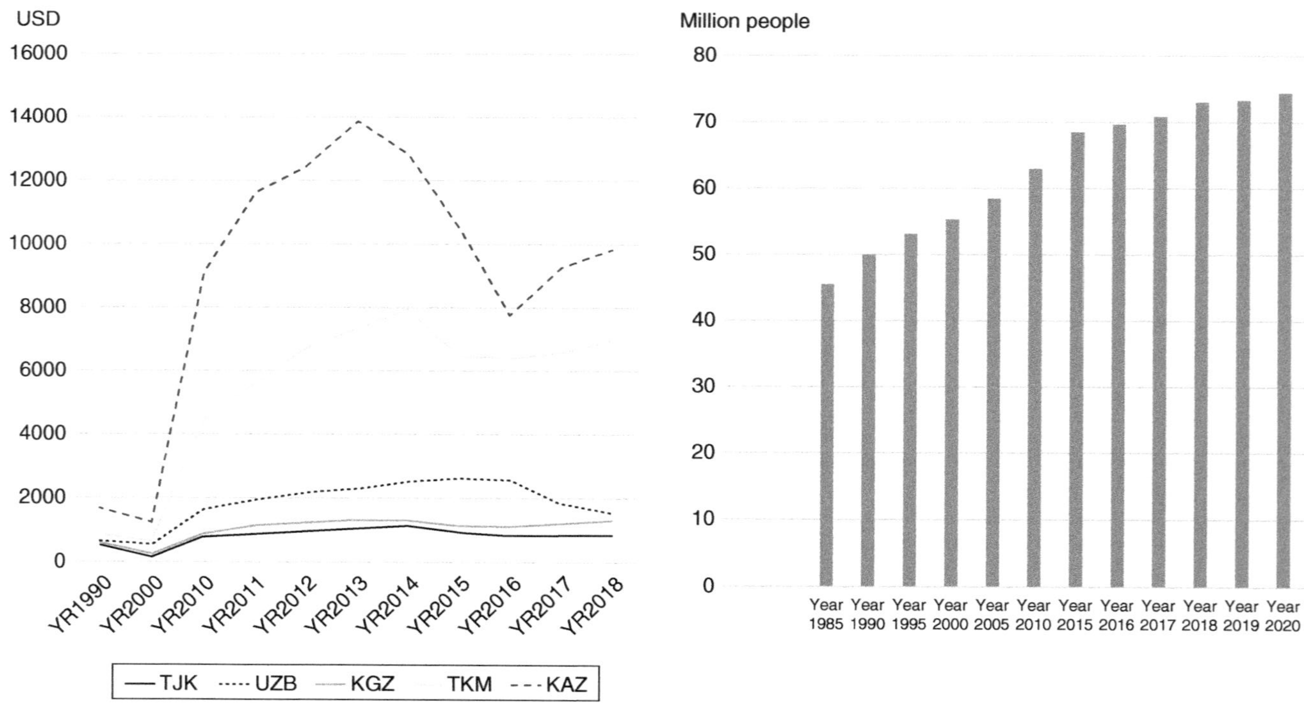

Figure 5.2 Change in GDP Per Capita and Population in Central Asia.
Source: World Bank (2020).

Table 5.2 Infrastructure Projects with Private Investment Participation in Central Asia, 1990–2019

Countries	*Number of projects*	*Total investment (in millions of dollars)*
Kazakhstan	45	5,371
Kyrgyz Republic	6	140
Tajikistan	5	961
Uzbekistan	7	370

Source: Private Participation in Infrastructure – World Bank Group (https://ppi.worldbank.org/en/ppi).

Note
Turkmenistan omitted due to lack of data.

5.3 Water Sector Financing: Review of the Current Situation in Central Asia

Infrastructure is critical to convey water resources to areas and sectors with high demand and economic value. Water systems of Central Asia include large-scale water delivery canals, water storage facilities and irrigated areas. The region's annual total water resources are around 116 km^3, 90% of which is formed in the two large river systems, namely the Amu Darya and Syr Darya (ICWC 2019). The groundwater resources of the region are 43.49 km^3 (Dukhovniy and de Schutter 2011). Almost 80% of water resources are used for agriculture, around 7%–8% for industries, and the rest for households, services, etc.

The current irrigated area in the region is around 8 million hectares, a figure that has doubled since the 1960s. The local population is 72 million, and is expected to reach 96 million by 2030 (WB 2017). The largest water consumer of the region is Uzbekistan, which has the largest population in the region, and which consumes around 56 km^3 of water per annum. The highest per capita water use is in Turkmenistan, reaching almost 6,000 m^3 per annum (Figure 5.3).

While the region consumes a great deal of water, it is increasingly exposed to environmental risks and water scarcity. Especially, the last three years were dry and water scarcity levels have been much higher than earlier observed levels. Environmental consequences of water mismanagement in the region are well known. Long-ignored environmental needs during the Soviet period led to the desiccation of the Aral Sea, the world's fourth-largest lake, creating a new, 5-million-hectare desert—Aral Kum. Millions of tons of dust and salt from the dried seabed pollute irrigated lands, compromise the health of the populace, and threaten ice caps in the mountains. Moreover, salinization, land and water degradation, and biodiversity losses are common problems in the region, threatening the sustainability of national economies. As a result, more than half of the land is exposed to desertification.

Until recently, transboundary water management in the region has been highly politicized and the cost of insufficient water cooperation is about $4.5 billion

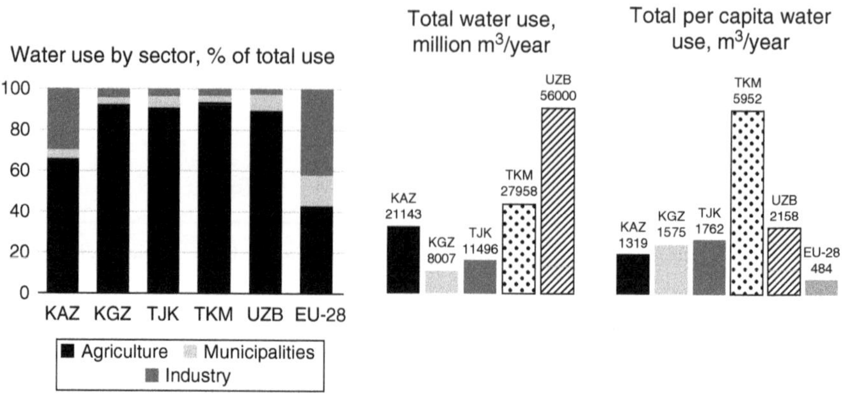

Figure 5.3 Water Use by Sectors, Total Water Use and Per Capita Water Use in Central Asia. Note: EU = European Union, KAZ = Kazakhstan, KGZ = Kyrgyz Republic, TJK = Tajikistan, TKM = Turkmenistan, UZB = Uzbekistan.

Source: www.faostate.org.

annually (Adelphi & CAREC 2017). Limited cooperation not only undermined the potential benefits that more integrated economies can offer, but also negatively affected the access to international finance for water infrastructure in the region.

One month before the collapse of the Soviet Union, the Central Asian states' Ministers of Water Management set up the first regional water management institution, i.e., the Interstate Commission on Water Coordination, to coordinate transboundary water management. Since then, states of Central Asia have taken several attempts to reform their water governance and management systems. In the early 1990s, immediately after the collapse of the Soviet Union, the countries of Central Asia tried to preserve the Soviet-like water systems as much as possible. The only changes started at the lower levels—interfirm and on-farm water management, due to de-collectivization. Reintegration of the economies and reduced growth due to collapse of the economic ties affected the water sector. Financing of the water system was reduced considerably; downsizing of the water ministries happened in the mid-1990s. This could be seen as an initial phase of the changes in the water systems of Central Asian countries.

Since 2016, the political situation has improved, and the heads of the Central Asian states meet regularly. The water and energy issues have become a regular agenda for such meetings, with water the subject of cooperation and dialogue. In 2018, the heads of Central Asian countries met in Ashgabat,[1] the first time since 2009 that the heads of the founding states of the International Fund for Saving the Aral Sea convened. This was a landmark event to reinvigorate regional water cooperation. The joint communiqué of the summit highlights the willingness of the parties to improve integrated use and protection of water resources, transboundary watercourses, water management, energy, and socio-economic development. Infrastructure is crucial for realizing these intentions.

In Central Asia, water sector financing is still mostly public, although user fees have been introduced for each use: irrigation, drinking, and industrial uses. However, user fees are covering only a fraction of water delivery costs of different sectors. The major problem of the sector is both low public financing and low collection rates of user fees. According to World Bank estimates, water sector financing receives only 50% of required funding. Accordingly, the sector has suffered from chronic underinvestment.

Rehabilitation of dilapidated infrastructure and reconfiguration of water systems into individualized agricultural land units are current challenges for the Central Asian countries. Currently, almost 60% of the water withdrawn for agriculture is lost before reaching the irrigated plots. Costs for operation, management, and development of water infrastructure in Central Asia are huge (World Bank 2020). Sustainable and long-term financing of the sector remains a crucial challenge for water governance in the region.

A minimum of \$20–\$25 billion is required to upgrade water infrastructure in Central Asia (World Bank 2018). Private investment in infrastructure in the region is not yet developed. National budgets cannot provide enough financing for water infrastructure. Starting from the 2010s, national financing to the water sector started improving, covering 40%–69% of required funding in Central Asian states (Abdullaev et al. 2020). However, no states were able to provide an acceptable and long-term solution to water financing. Most of the funding for the water sector still comes from state budgets. Public and private financing schemes are used for water sector financing in many parts of the world. However, neither of these two schemes has been considered successful (Water Alternatives 2019).

The financing of water systems is critical for both governance and management of the water sector. To ensure that capital investments in infrastructure translate into sustainable water services delivery, they also need to be supported by institutional strengthening and management improvement. The water sector in Central Asian countries is state-led, and both financing and operation of water systems are conducted by state or semi-state organizations. However, the above analysis shows that the states are not able to fully finance the water sector, nor to efficiently manage it. Therefore, infrastructure, human, transport, and technological needs of the water sector are currently inadequately supported and funded in this region.

Water reforms conducted since the collapse of the Soviet system have led to the changes in rights on land and water infrastructure. The states of Central Asia have changed the water service delivery system from Soviet times and developed a new set of rules. The ownership rights for irrigation systems for the large infrastructure were left in state hands, while only on-farm canals were transferred to the temporary ownership of the farmers.

The countries of Central Asia tried to develop sustainable mechanisms for financing the operations and management (O&M) costs for irrigation systems. For example, the introduction of irrigation service fees (ISFs), despite the long-term (20 years) experimentation, generated funds to cover only 20% of actual costs of infrastructure expenditure in Central Asian countries. In the Kyrgyz Republic and Tajikistan, ISF collection on the farm level reaches up to 80%–90% (Strikeleva 2020).

Service fees charged by state water organizations are not fully collected, with water users reluctant to pay for an unreliable supply. However, lately, household water supply fee collection has been improved due to better metering and infrastructure improvements. In irrigation water supply, service fee collection rates are insufficient even to cover O&M costs.

One of the reasons for the low ISF collection rate could be weak mechanisms of public involvement in the development of water sector reforms. Therefore, a change in the system and the introduction of ISF in many places were not welcomed. As a result, the collection rate was about 30%–40% (Sehring 2009). This led to a decline in water services and conditions of irrigation systems. Countries are trying to improve service collection rates by introducing water metering (Uzbekistan), giving more of a role to users (Kyrgyz Republic) and management organizations (Tajikistan) and a right to keep part of the fees, and a more commercial model of water supply (Kazakhstan) (Table 5.3).

Deregulation and privatization, concessions, or any other private engagement in the water sector are not common in Central Asian countries. Both ownership of and investing in the water sector by private finances are very limited in the region. Only construction works in the water sector are tendered out for private companies. Yet, in most cases, they are quasi-state private companies. No private companies are engaged in water delivery services for the irrigation sector. All water infrastructure is owned by the state, with only fishing, recreation, and sports rights rented out to the private sector.

The main obstacle to private sector engagement in water infrastructure is the high level of regulation and unclear ownership rules. Although water agencies operate and maintain the water infrastructure, ownership rights are not clearly defined. Water infrastructure may belong to municipalities, in some cases belonging to different line ministries or agencies, e.g., energy, water supply, etc. Therefore, interagency coordination failure (governance issue) results both in failure of water services performance and reduced attractiveness for private financing. None of the water sector infrastructures in Central Asian countries have been privatized. Highly subsidized by state budgets, the region's water systems are not attractive to private investors. Annually, Central Asian countries are subsidizing the water sector for more than $300 million (Abdullaev et al. 2020).

One more reason for limited private engagement in the water sector is agriculture policies and land ownership issues. Although land reforms in Central Asian countries have abolished collective ownership, they have not been able to produce full, private ownership in any of the countries. State intervention in land issues spans from total control of agriculture production to removing land ownership. No markets for land trading exist in Central Asian countries. Although the land rights in Kazakhstan, the Kyrgyz Republic, and Tajikistan are private, none of the countries has competitive land markets. Mostly, the region's agriculture

Table 5.3 Water Sector Reforms and the Role of Different Stakeholders

Countries	*Financing*	*Decision making- planning*	*Implementation- control*
Kazakhstan	• Funding major O&M needs, new	• State sets long-term vision and strategies infrastructure development	• State controls water sector policy implementation through Committee for Water Resources
	• Local governments contribute to smaller infrastructure and O&M costs	• Shorter -term decisions are made by local governments, basin organizations	
Kyrgyz Republic	• State provides major needs of the water sector	State makes major decisions on sectoral water allocations	• State is engaged in water sector policy implementation partially, most of the control is done by local-rural councils
	• Contributions from water users — fees are sensible part of the water sector financing	• Local governments are responsible for large infrastructure under their jurisdiction	
Tajikistan	• State funds major costs	• Water planning is centralized	• Control on implementation of decisions in water sector is centralized and conducted by ministry of Energy & Water
	• Users fees are sensible for covering operational costs	• Local level decisions by local branches of government and water agencies	
Turkmenistan	• State fully finances water sector costs at all levels	• Water planning is prerogative of central government	• State controls implementation of water decisions; water committee is responsible for implementation control
Uzbekistan	• State fully finances water sector costs at all levels	• Water planning is prerogative of central government	• State controls implementation of water decisions, water ministry is responsible for implementation control and operation

Source: Based on authors' compilations.

markets are overregulated. Therefore, water pricing is not market-based, but rather regulated by the state.

Moreover, in all Central Asian countries, agriculture water supply is considered as a social function of the state, which causes the tight regulation of water services. In this context, the state is neither using a full market system into agriculture, nor charging a full price for water delivery.

5.4 Rethinking Water Financing in Central Asia

Investment in water infrastructure can be unleashed provided business opportunities are easy to notice and the water sector's complexities are widely recognized and understood by both citizens and policymakers. These complexities include, irrigation, or water for food, quality of water, increasingly diminishing mountain snowcaps and melting icecaps, increasing number of floods and other hazards, to name a few. These complex water related environmental problems and natural disaster issues listed above are regulated by different government agencies. The wide recognition of these social, environmental and governance complexities of the water sector can help integrate water efficiency and infrastructure issues into decision making rather sooner than later.

There is already plenty of evidence how water scarcity and climate change risks can influence the sustainability of Central Asian economies causing social and environmental implications. The CAREC Institute analysis (CAREC Institute 2020b) shows the positive correlation between high water footprint of economy of Central Asian countries and their high vulnerability to projected climate change in the region (Figure 5.4). Indeed, the high dependence on water resources is the main reason behind the high susceptibility of Central Asian countries to climate change impacts. This dependence roots in low economic productivity of water use (CAREC Institute 2020b), which is to a large extent caused by outdated infrastructure. To prepare for the anticipated water stress, manage risks of climate change and reduce sensitivity, governments will have to improve water use efficiency and thus rethink water infrastructure financing in the region.

One option for sustainable water infrastructure financing could be changes in the agriculture sector. If agriculture production were made more market-oriented, private companies would have an incentive to invest in water services. In this context, the authors are suggesting a more careful approach because, in the Central Asian state system, this is the least feasible option. Currently, agriculture, land, and water reforms in Central Asia are unfinished business. While the levels of regulation in agriculture and land ownership are reduced in comparison with the Soviet period, the state in Central Asian countries still plays an enormous role in production quotas, land distribution, and agriculture pricing. The state in Central Asia is practicing the role of social stabilizer by providing food and water security to the population. However, the downside of this tightly regulated system is reduced incentive for private sector financing, especially infrastructure.

Globally, this scheme is already facing serious socioeconomic resistance from both users and governments (Water Alternatives 2019). Yet, a more realistic

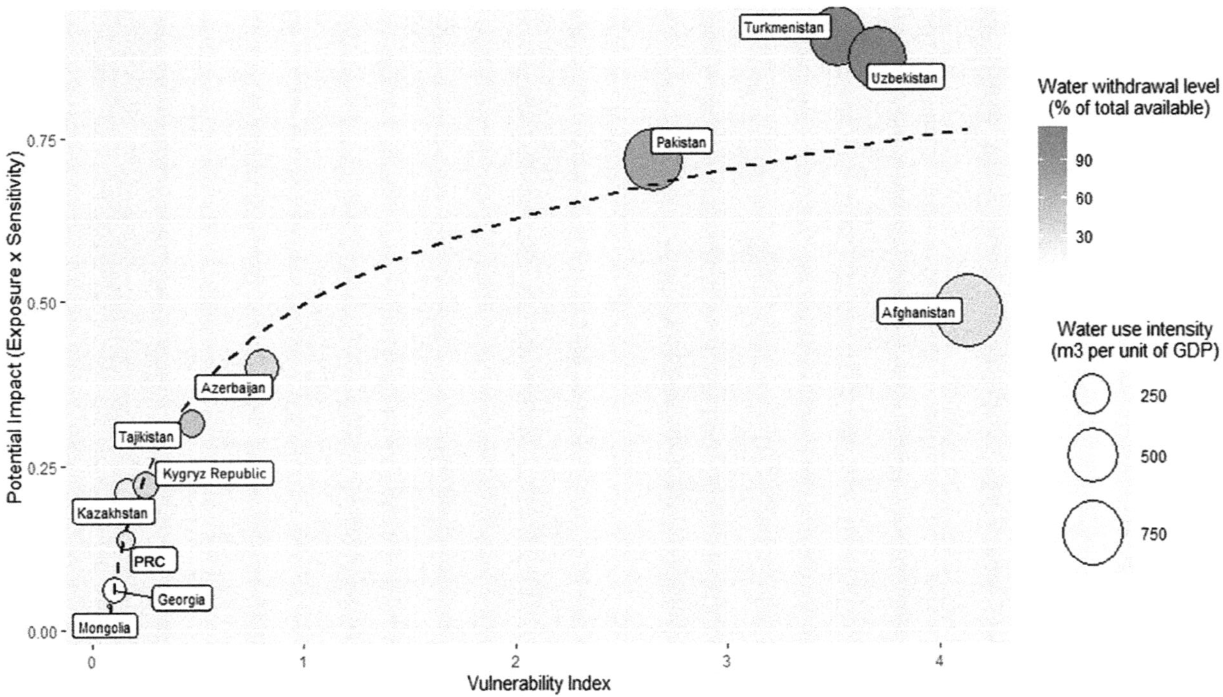

Figure 5.4 Relationship of the Estimated Vulnerability of the CAREC Region Countries to Climate Induced Water Stress.

approach for Central Asia would be introducing public-private partnership schemes into irrigation services. The state currently allows private companies to oversee only water service delivery and O&M functions, while keeping the infrastructure as state assets. Agriculture and national administrative reforms have had a greater influence on the water sector, which, even before Soviet rule in Central Asia, has always been a state affair (Abdullaev et al. 2019). Although new states in Central Asia provided some level of deregulation after the collapse of the Soviet system, almost all countries have kept both central planning and a strong state role in the water sector.

Water sector management and policymaking in the region have long been dominated by traditional stakeholders such as public sector agencies and non-governmental organizations. To effectively manage water, the role of the private sector should be increased. To stimulate this, governments should provide private sector stakeholders with the opportunity to make legitimate inputs into the policymaking process and management of water resources. Hence, a public-private-partnership can by itself stimulate the involvement of the private sector, as it will reduce risks for private investors with technical support from public capital.

Another way to increase the role of the private sector can be incentivizing efficiency among large water users. To minimize the water footprint, water consumers can consider the application of efficiency technologies that also will provide a ground for private sector involvement.

Paradoxically, at the same time, the lack of financing from or limited involvement of business in the water sector is one of the main reasons for the limited application of the latest technologies. Management of water resources can be improved by using the latest technologies, but to bring those technologies and use them effectively can be realized if policymakers and businesses collaborate closely.

Beyond that, utilizing multipurpose schemes for water use to cover supply costs could improve private financing of the water sector. The concessions of irrigation infrastructure and the surrounding land and renting out facilities to private users will bring more finances to the sector.

In the above contexts, the state could play a role of social regulator, ensuring that each water user receives a fair share of water resources on time. However, in this scheme, more financial control and regulations are required to avoid corrupt schemes and substandard water supply systems.

Hence, diversification of investment in infrastructure should become a priority for Central Asian countries. Otherwise, infrastructure deterioration, combined with increasing impact of climate change, land degradation, and demographic growth, would give rise to long-term economic, social, and environmental risks.

5.5 Conclusions

Policy reforms to increase productivity of water demand and expand supply and minimize industry's water footprint are still underway in Central Asia. To meet the increasing water consumption implied by economic and population growth, and augmenting impact of climate change, water management policies and practices, both at national and regional levels, need to be optimized. The role of governments in setting up production quotas, land distribution, and agriculture pricing are still strong. Consequently, private sector financing is obstructed, and infrastructure continues decaying, with low water productivity commonplace due to the high inefficiency in delivery and distribution.

Delayed water sector investments from the late 1990s on led to dilapidation of water infrastructure. These problems persist due to inadequate funding. Attempts to develop sustainable financing of the water sector have not generated expected results.

Shrinking financing has been a major obstacle for sustainable and reliable water supply for all sectors in almost all Central Asian countries. Irregular financing also prevents long-term planning, and leads to serious delays in O&M. Almost 70% of the irrigation infrastructure and 50% of the water supply systems are outdated and need rehabilitation or replacement. Such scale makes the water sector investment-hungry.

The region's need for investments to rehabilitate and build new infrastructure is around 7%–8% of GDP annually or $38 billion (ADB 2017). The region's current economic profile requires buildup of the infrastructure. Although economic growth in the region is attractive for FDI, growing public debt and structural problems makes infrastructure financing very risky.

Certainly, it is difficult to expect a revolutionary approach to how water resources are managed, and infrastructure building is intensified in the region. However, there are indicators of change triggering financing for water infrastructure, such as increasing susceptibility of the countries to water stress, and potentially, the changing dynamics of intraregional cooperation. As the ongoing global pandemic has brought health matters to the forefront, the quality of potable water and food security has moved to the strategic limelight, which in turn questions water infrastructure.

Similarly, since the political and economic reforms commenced in Uzbekistan in 2016 under the new administration, whose mandate has got extended to another five-year term recently, intraregional trade and regional economic cooperation have undergone tremendous growth. By enhancing regional cooperation and connectivity, the Central Asian region seems now to be heading to greater integration ahead. This can positively affect the overall intraregional cooperation and unlock more potential for financing joint regional infrastructure, including water ones. Yet, better to keep in mind, growing water scarcity, energy deficit may also lead to a gridlock in regional cooperation. Lack of due consideration of these aspects in sustaining regional collaboration on these matters might create irrevocable headwinds for the water sector in the region.

5.6 Policy Recommendations

Incentives for diversifying financing, and, particularly, for mobilizing private capital must be found through creating a favorable business climate that would be possible by implementing robust public policies. Governments in Central Asia should change their agriculture policies to be more market-oriented, with policies that may generate private sector interest in investing in water services and infrastructure. The introduction of private or semi-private water supply companies operating and maintaining irrigation infrastructure may be a solution to water sector financing.

Increasing returns to private investors through integrating technologies can unlock upfront capital for water infrastructure. Lack of private capital in infrastructure is often explained by poor governance, failed institutions, and limited understanding of investors' needs. A deep understanding of investors' expectations, behavior, and motives is therefore a precondition for private investment. The level of commercial appeal of infrastructure projects to private investors is a key element for successful PPPs. The mobilization of private investment can happen provided both governments and private investors increase their focus on infrastructure, while the former securing investment environment by providing reasonably respected property rights and predictable factors affecting return on infrastructure (Walter 2016).

However, ill-coordinated water sector planning and investment in Central Asian countries will not aid infrastructure financing. Rather, economic frameworks that promote cooperation and integrated planning among sectors could be a solution. The approach should help to leverage possible synergies for decreasing costs, assessing trade-offs, demand-side interventions, and decentralized services to ensure sustainability of infrastructure. In this context, the state could play a role of social regulator, ensuring that each water user receives a fair share of water resources.

At the regional level, a major focus should be given to renewed discussions on setting up a water-energy consortium for the Syr Darya and Amu Darya projects. Joint operation of transboundary infrastructure, benefit-sharing schemes, joint O&M of the water infrastructure could be the focus areas of the project. In current small basins, PPP schemes for operating small and medium infrastructure could be tested. At the national level, the focus could be on provision of both legal basis and financial instruments for financing from private sources.

In view of current dynamics of regional collaboration in Central Asia, the region seems to have created the most favorable ever momentum for unlocking finance for regional infrastructure development that should be seized immediately.

Note

1 https://kazaral.org/en/2018/08/ (accessed 12 June 2021).

References

Abdullaev, I., and S. Rakhmatullaev. 2015. Transformation of Water Management in Central Asia: From State-Centric, Hydraulic Mission to Socio-Political Control. *Environmental Earth Science* 73: 849–861.

Abdullaev, I., and S. Atabaeva. 2012. Water Sector in Central Asia: Slow Transformation and Potential for Cooperation. *International Journal of Sustainable Society.* 4(1/2): 103–112.

Abdullaev, I., E. Strikeleva, and S. Rakhmatullaev. 2020. *Water Sector Development in Central Asia and Afghanistan. Smart Waters Project.* Almaty: USAID.

ADB. 2017. *Meeting Asia's Infrastructure Needs.* Manila: Asian Development Bank.

Adelphi & CAREC. 2017. *Rethinking Water in Central Asia. The Costs of Inaction and Benefits of Water Cooperation.* Berlin: Laserline Druckzentrum.

Aldaya, M.M., G. Munoz, and A.Y. Hoekstra. 2010. *Water Footprint of Cotton, Wheat and Rice Production in Central Asia. Value of Water Research Report Series 41.* Delft: UNESCO-IHE.

CAREC. 2015. *Central Asia Regional Economic Cooperation Program Development Effectiveness Review 2015.* CAREC Secretariat. Manila: ADB.

CAREC Institute. 2020a. *Climate Vulnerability, Infrastructure, Finance and Governance in CAREC Region.* Research Report. Urumqi: CAREC Institute.

CAREC Institute. 2020b. *Determinants of Vulnerability to Climate-Induced Water Stress in CAREC. Policy Brief.* Urumqi: CAREC Institute.

CA-WATER. 2019. Info. http://cawater-info.net/news/index_e.htm (accessed 21 August 2020).

Dukhovniy, V. and J. de Schutter. 2011. *Water in Central Asia: Past, Present and Future.* London: Taylor and Francis.

Elliott, R. J. R., E. Strobl, and P. Sun. 2015. The Local Impact of Typhoons on Economic Activity in China: A View from Outer Space. *Journal of Urban Economics* 88: 50–66.

European Union. 2018. EPRS | European Parliamentary Research Service Author: Martin Russell. Water in Central Asia: An Increasingly Scarce Resource. www.europarl.europa.eu/RegData/etudes/BRIE/2018/625181/EPRS_BRI(2018)625181_EN.pdf (accessed 21 August 2020).

FAO. 2018. *Policy Analysis of Nationally Determined Contributions (NDC) in Europe and Central Asia.* Budapest: Food and Agriculture Organization of the United Nations.

FAO. 2011. *The State of the World's Land and Water Resources for Food and Agriculture (SOLAW) – Managing Systems at Risk.* Rome: Food and Agriculture Organization of the United Nations; and London: Earthscan.

Fay, M. et al. 2019. *Hitting the Trillion Mark: A Look at How Much Countries Are Spending on Infrastructure.* No. 8730. Washington, DC: World Bank Group. http://documents.worldbank.org/curated/en/970571549037261080/pdf/WPS8730.pdf (accessed on 4 August 2020).

Hurley, J., S. Morris, and G. Portelance. 2018. Examining the Debt Implications of the Belt and Road Initiative from a Policy Perspective. CGD Policy Paper 121. www.cgddev.org/publication/examining-debt-implications-belt-and-road-initiative-policy-perspective (accessed 26 June 20201).

IPCC. 2015. Climate Change 2014: Synthesis Report. Contribution of Working Groups I, II and III to the Fifth Assessment Report of the Intergovernmental Panel on Climate Change [Core Writing Team, R.K. Pachauri and L.A. Meyer (eds.)]. Geneva: IPCC.

Liu, B. et al. 2016. Similar Estimates of Temperature Impacts on Global Wheat Yield by Three Independent Methods. *Nature Climate Change* 6: 1130–1136.

McDonald, D.A. and E. Swyngedouw, eds. 2019. Remunicipalization: The Future of Water Services? Special Themed Section: *Water Alternatives* 12(2).

Mekonnen, M.M., and A.Y. Hoekstra. 2010. The Green, Blue and Grey Water Footprint of Crops and Derived Crop Products. Value of Water Research Report Series No. 47. Delft: UNESCO-IHE.

OECD. 2019. Sustainable Infrastructure for Low-Carbon Development in Central Asia and the Caucasus: Hotspot Analysis and Needs Assessment, Green Finance and Investment. Paris: OECD Publishing. https://doi.org/10.1787/d1aa6ae9-en.

Rakhmatullaev S., I. Abdullaev. 2014. Central Asian Irrigation Sector in a Climate Change Context: Some Reflections. *Journal of Water and Climate Change* 5(3): 341–356.

Rakhmatullaev, S., F. Huneau, H. Celle-Jeanton, P. Le Cousumer, M. Motelica-Heino, M. Bakiev. 2013. Water Reservoirs, Irrigation and Sedimentation in Central Asia: A First-Cut Assessment for Uzbekistan. *Environmental Earth Sciences* 68: 985–998. doi: 10.1007/s12665-012-1802-0

Sehring, J. 2009. Path Dependencies and Institutional Bricolage in Post-Soviet Water Governance. *Water Alternatives* 2(1): 61–81.

Sommer, R., et al. 2013. Impact of Climate Change on Wheat Productivity in Central Asia. *Agriculture, Ecosystems & Environment* 178: 78–99.

Strikeleva, E. 2020. Irrigation Service Fee as a Financial Instrument for Effective Water Use: Case Study from Kyrgyzstan and Tajikistan. Unpublished report.

UNESCAP. 2015. *Statistical Yearbook for Asia and the Pacific 2015: Facts and Trends at the Outset of the 2030 Development Agenda*. Bangkok: United Nations Economic and Social Commission for Asia and the Pacific.

Vakulchuk, R., F. Aminjonov, I. Overland, B. Eshchanov, A. Abylkasymova, and D. Moldokanov. 2019. BRI in Central Asia: Overview of Chinese Projects. 10.13140/RG.2.2.13032.52488/1.

Walter, I. 2016. Infrastructure, Performance and Economic Growth. Stern School of Business, and New York University. Open Book Publishers.

World Bank. 2019. Quality Unknown: The Invisible Water Crisis. *International Bank for Reconstruction and Development/The World Bank*. Washington, DC: World Bank.

World Bank. 2020. *Central Asia: Towards Water-Secure Sustainable Economies*. Washington, DC: World Bank Group.

WRI. 2019. *Creating a Sustainable Food Future: A Menu of Solutions to Feed Nearly 10 Billion People by 2050*. Washington, DC: World Resources Report.

WWAP (United Nations World Water Assessment Programme). 2014. *The United Nations World Water Development Report 2014: Water and Energy*. Paris: UNESCO.

6 Does Infrastructure Investment Lead to Economic Growth?

Evidence from Central Asian Countries

K. P. Prabheesh, Farhad Taghizadeh-Hesary, and Rakesh Padhan

6.1 Introduction

This chapter explores the relationship between infrastructure investment and economic growth in Kazakhstan, Tajikistan, Uzbekistan, the Kyrgyz Republic, and Uzbekistan. The countries are rich in natural and human resources but quite diverse in terms of their stages of development despite their shared history as a part of the Soviet Union. Following independence, Kazakhstan and Turkmenistan moved to the upper-middle-income group, while the Kyrgyz Republic, Tajikistan, and Uzbekistan remained in the lower-middle income category. One of the obstacles faced by these landlocked countries is the lack of well-developed infrastructure. Since these countries are landlocked, intra-regional trade is a significant challenge due to various cross-border regulations, with limited transportation connections inside and outside the region. Despite some infrastructure investment in the last quarter-century, the lack of connectivity between Central Asia and the outside world remains a significant obstacle to trade and economic development (Batsaikhan and Dabrowski 2017). Similarly, as these economies are primarily dependent on the exports of oil, natural gas, metals, and agricultural raw materials, the development of infrastructure is crucial to obtain higher economic growth.

The trends in investment in infrastructure and the number of related projects show a high variation during the last two decades (Figure 6.1). One of the major bottlenecks for infrastructure investment is higher fiscal deficits and other budgetary constraints. The Asian Development Bank estimates that the countries of Central Asia require the investment of $33 billion for infrastructure development by 2030 to meet their domestic and international demand (ADB 2019). In this scenario, it is important to know how infrastructure investment affects regional economic growth.

Infrastructure reduces the cost of transportation and facilitates the mobility of goods and labor and the realization of economies of scale. It also enhances productivity and generates employment opportunities (Javid 2019). Further, increased public investment in infrastructure improves the business environment

DOI: 10.4324/9781003228790-8

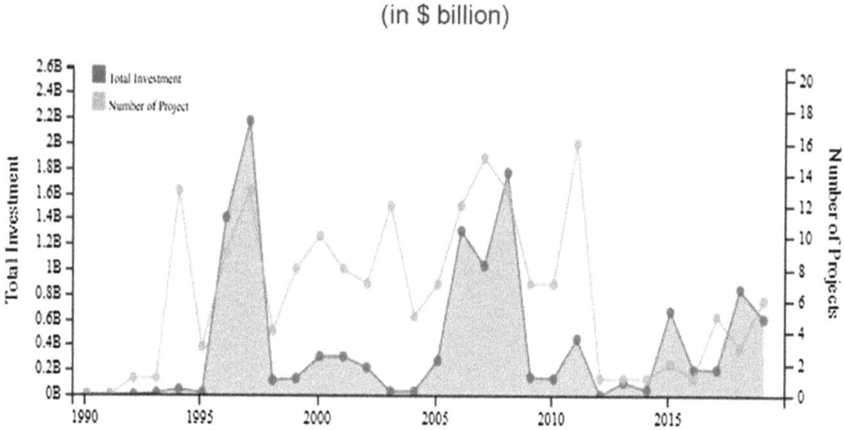

Figure 6.1 Trends in Central Asian Investment in Infrastructure and Number of Projects, 1990–2018 (in $ billion).

Source: World Bank.

of a country and thereby encourages the private sector to expand their economic activity (Aschauer 1989; Abiad et al. 2016). However, the impact of infrastructure investment on economic growth can vary across economies as well as different sectors of the economy. The empirical findings of the existing studies do not reveal any consistent patterns. For instance, a positive relationship is established between public infrastructure investment and economic growth by Aaron (1990) and Nourzad and Vriese (1995), whereas Pritchett (1999) finds that public investment in infrastructure may not produce a positive impact and can even adversely affect economic growth if these investments are inefficiently managed and crowd out private investment due to higher fiscal deficits. Some studies show a non-linear relationship between these two, stating the actual economic benefits of infrastructure investment may be observed after a certain level of threshold (Sutherland et al. 2009). Some studies even established a strong relationship running in reverse, from economic growth to infrastructure investment (Munnell 1992). It might well be the case that high gross domestic product (GDP) and high infrastructure investments are correlated without a causal relationship, which has important implications for public policy. Given these inconclusive findings from the existing literature, the present study repositions the infrastructure investment and economic growth relationship using Central Asian economies as an underexplored example. More specifically, the study addresses the following questions: 1) does higher investment in infrastructure lead to higher economic growth? and 2) is there any by-directional relationship between these two?

Our approach toward examining the above issues is as follows. We use quarterly data from 1990 to 2018 and the Autoregressive Distributed Lagged

(ARDL) approach to cointegration to test the long-run relationship between output and infrastructure investment. Our findings suggest that infrastructure investment has helped to achieve economic growth in Kazakhstan, Tajikistan, and Uzbekistan, while in the case of the Kyrgyz Republic, economic growth drives the infrastructure investment. Our findings also suggest that there is a bi-directional relationship between economic growth and infrastructure investment in the case of Uzbekistan.

The rest of the chapter is organized as follows. Section 6.2 presents the definition of infrastructure and its measurement issues. Section 6.3 and 6.4 provides a brief snapshot of infrastructure in Central Asia and a review of literature, respectively. Section 6.5 presents the empirical model and data, and section 6.6 presents the econometric methodology. Empirical findings and conclusions are given in sections 6.7 and 6.8.

6.2 Infrastructure: Definition and Measurement Issues

In both the theoretical and empirical literature, there is no universally accepted definition of infrastructure. Hasan (2017) states that "there is no single way or international best practice to measure infrastructure investment" due to the lack of aggregate data. Thus, infrastructure is often considered a specific type of capital asset that is used to produce services fundamental to sectors like transport, energy, water, telecommunications, education, or healthcare. It is argued that the development of these types of capital assets can influence economic growth directly and factor productivity indirectly (Feng and Wu 2018). Therefore, the lack of infrastructure could create several obstacles for an economy, and hence an accurate measurement is crucial for policy action. Nevertheless, the lack of a widely accepted definition could yield more difficulty in measuring infrastructure accurately. A detailed explanation of the various challenges in measuring infrastructure was provided by Välilä (2020).

Table 6.1 broadly classified the measurement problem into a definitional issue and appropriateness of data. The first classification is associated with "a lack of an unambiguous definition," i.e., what exactly infrastructure covers, which forces researchers to quantify it using various proxies. For instance, "public investment" is commonly used to measure infrastructure due to the easy availability of data. Public investment refers to the capital expenditure on physical infrastructure (roads, government buildings, etc.) and soft infrastructure (human capital development, innovation support, research, and development, etc.) with a productive use that extends beyond a year and comprises both direct and indirect investment. Direct investment is defined as gross capital formation and acquisitions, less disposals of non-financial, non-produced assets during a given period, whereas indirect investment is defined as capital transfers, i.e., investment grants and subsidies in cash or in-kind made by subnational governments to other institutional units. While public investment measurements vary across countries, gross fixed capital formation is often used as the best available proxy for direct public investment (OECD 2014).

Table 6.1 Challenges in Measuring Infrastructure

Measurement Problems	*Proposed Solutions*	*Problems with Proposed Solutions*
Lack of unambiguous definition	a) Government investment or public capital as a proxy b) Consider a subset of individual sectors	a) Only part of government investment or public capital comprises infrastructure; exclude non-government infrastructure b) Conclusions limited to the sectors considered
Lack of appropriate data	c) Estimate aggregate-level stocks from investment flows d) Use physical (sectoral) measures e) Use project-level data	c) Extensive assumptions required d) Do not measure quality or value e) No centralized source; commercial confidentiality

Source: Välilä (2020).

The use of public investment is associated with implicit assumptions such as: first, a large amount of infrastructure originates from the government; and second, government investment mostly includes support (Välilä 2020). However, the lack of accuracy of these implicit assumptions makes it difficult to differentiate between government investment and government infrastructure investment. Further, the terms "public investment" and "public capital" are used interchangeably in the empirical literature, which should not be automatically considered as a good proxy for infrastructure development. The exclusive focus on government infrastructure and capital also leaves out private infrastructure investment and capital, a major omission in the infrastructure basket. To overcome this problem, many researchers have looked into the infrastructure sub-sectors, such as transport, energy, telecommunications, water, and sanitation. However, this approach is associated with the consistent availability of data, which subsequently leads to the second classification, i.e., lack of appropriate data. These sub-sectoral data are often limited and less accurate for both developed and developing economies. Finally, due to the above issues, another option is to utilize the project-level data related to infrastructure. However, as most of the project-specific information is sensitive to commercial consideration, the complete details are not publicly available to maintain confidentiality (Välilä 2020).

6.3 A Brief Snapshot of Infrastructure of Central Asia

Though the Central Asian countries, rich in resources and human capital, have adopted various reforms to alleviate poverty, they are still unable to attain higher economic growth. The average growth rate of Kazakhstan, the Kyrgyz Republic, Tajikistan, Turkmenistan, and Uzbekistan over three decades is 2.162%, 2.953%, 1.923%, 5.599%, and 4.338%, respectively. The growth rate of Turkmenistan is the

Table 6.2 Key Macroeconomic Indicators for Central Asian, Emerging Asian, and Developed Countries, 1997–2019

Indicators	*GDP growth rate (%)*	*Per capita GDP (in $)*	*Current account balance (% of GDP)*
Central Asian Countries			
Kazakhstan	2.953	7,096.69	-1.414
Kyrgyz Republic	1.720	816.462	-7.245
Tajikistan	1.854	701.392	-7.594
Turkmenistan	5.752	3,838.084	-3.566
Uzbekistan	4.215	1,379.754	2.214
Emerging Asian Countries			
PRC	9.432	3,256.01	3.377
India	6.333	1,105.193	-1.350
Indonesia	4.940	2,723.897	0.408
Advanced Countries			
Japan	1.135	43,327.93	2.879
UK	2.033	36,782.55	-3.073
US	2.467	45,197.56	-3.319

Source: Authors' calculation from World Economic Outlook, International Financial Statistics, and Balance of Payment Data. https://data.imf.org (accessed 18 March 2020).

Note
The GDP growth rate is expressed in terms of percent change to the previous year, whereas the current account is expressed in terms of percent of GDP. The per capita GDP is expressed in terms of US dollars.

GDP = gross domestic product, PRC = People's Republic of China, UK = United Kingdom, US = United States.

highest, whereas Tajikistan's remains low. The economic growth rate of Kazakhstan, the Kyrgyz Republic, and Tajikistan is small in comparison to Turkmenistan and Uzbekistan. Although the economic growth rate has increased for all these economies during 2010–2018, the growth rates of Kazakhstan (4.466%), and the Kyrgyz Republic (4.064%) are low in comparison to Tajikistan (7.034%), Turkmenistan (8.988%), and Uzbekistan (6.738%). Asymmetric infrastructure development may have resulted in growth difference across these countries.

Table 6.2 depicts the key macroeconomic indicators of these five countries, such as GDP growth, per capita income, current account balance, and international reserves. Kazakhstan and Turkmenistan's per capita GDP ($7,096.90 and $ 3,838.00, respectively) are much higher than the emerging Asian economies. By contrast, the Kyrgyz Republic and Tajikistan have the lowest per capita income in the region. More interestingly, most of these economies experienced high current account deficits except for Uzbekistan during 1997–2019, as compared to selected emerging economies (People's Republic of China [PRC], India, and Indonesia) and advanced economies (Japan, the United Kingdom [UK], and the United States [US]). The Kyrgyz Republic and Tajikistan incurred current account deficit of more than 7% of GDP, which needs to be financed using

Table 6.3 Net Official Development Assistance Received, Central Asian and Selected Emerging Asian Countries, 1993–2018

Variables	*Net official development assistance (% of GNI)*
Central Asian Countries	
Kazakhstan	0.392
Kyrgyz Republic	9.481
Tajikistan	7.293
Turkmenistan	0.584
Uzbekistan	0.850
Emerging Asian Countries	
PRC	0.133
India	0.254
Indonesia	0.473

Source: Authors' calculation from World Development Indicators Data. https://databank.worldbank.org/source/world-development-indicators (accessed 18 March 2020).

Note
GNI = gross national income, PRC = People's Republic of China.

domestic or foreign savings, and which restrict the government from undertaking any long-term infrastructure investment.

Table 6.3 shows the net official development assistance (ODA) for these five countries, with the Kyrgyz Republic (9.5%) and Tajikistan (7.3%) being the highest recipients of gross national income (GNI). The net ODA received by Kazakhstan, Turkmenistan, and Uzbekistan is low in comparison to the Kyrgyz Republic and Tajikistan, but high in comparison to other emerging countries. Moreover, Figure 6.2 shows that during 1999, the Kyrgyz Republic and Tajikistan received ODA of more than 17% and 10%, respectively, of GNI. As the purpose of ODA is mostly infrastructure development, these economies' infrastructure investment may be highly dependent on it. By contrast, Kazakhstan, Turkmenistan, and Uzbekistan are far behind receiving the assistance, indicating higher dependence on public infrastructure.

Table 6.4 details private participation in infrastructure (PPI), showing the number of projects and sectors that receive the highest investment in these five countries as compared with emerging ones such as the PRC, India, Indonesia, which receive much more. Among the Central Asian economies, Kazakhstan is associated with the highest number of projects (42) and the highest total investment ($5.12 billion). In contrast, the Kyrgyz Republic has the lowest total investment ($140 million), with six projects only. We can see that electricity occupied major investments in most cases, indicating that the power sector is the primary attraction for private investment in most countries. Further, the PRC has attracted high PPI in the road transport sector. From a policy perspective, Central Asian countries should improve PPI in all sectors to promote infrastructure.

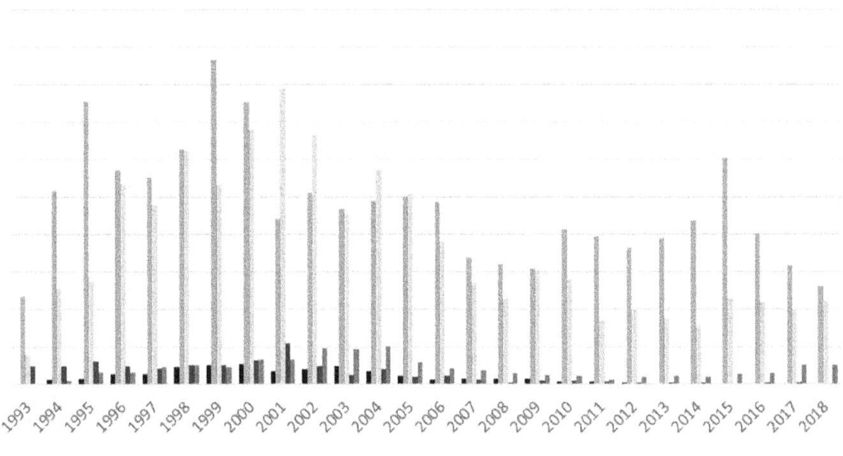

Figure 6.2 Net Official Development Assistance Received by Central Asian Countries, 1993–2018 (% of GNI).

Note: GNI = gross national income.

Source: World Development Indicators.

Table 6.4 Private Participation in Infrastructure, Central Asian and Selected Emerging Asian Countries, 1990–2019

Countries	*Total Number of Projects*	*Total Investment (in US$ billions)*	*Sector with Higher Investment*
Central Asian Countries			
Kazakhstan	42	5.12	Electricity
Kyrgyz Republic	6	.140	ICT
Tajikistan	5	.961	Electricity
Uzbekistan	7	.370	ICT
Emerging Asian Countries			
PRC	1,768	226.7	Roads
India	1,086	270.5	Electricity
Indonesia	141	67.5	Electricity

Source: World Bank-Private Participation in Infrastructure Database. https://ppi.worldbank.org/en/ppi (accessed 18 March 2020).

Note

ICT = Information and Communications Technology, PRC = People's Republic of China.

Table 6.5 World Bank Logistic Performance Index (Infrastructure) Score and Rank for Central Asian, Selected Emerging Asian, and Advanced Countries

Year	*2010*		*2014*		*2016*		*2018*	
Countries	*Score*	*Rank*	*Score*	*Rank*	*Score*	*Rank*	*Score*	*Rank*
Central Asian Countries								
Kazakhstan	2.66	57	2.38	106	2.72	68	2.55	81
Kyrgyz Republic	2.09	118	2.05	147	1.96	150	2.38	103
Tajikistan	2.00	127	2.36	108	2.13	130	2.17	127
Turkmenistan	2.24	101	2.06	146	2.34	103	2.23	117
Uzbekistan	2.54	70	2.01	148	2.45	91	2.57	77
Emerging Asian Countries								
PRC	3.54	27	3.67	23	3.75	23	3.75	20
India	2.91	47	2.88	58	3.34	36	2.91	52
Indonesia	2.54	69	2.92	56	2.65	73	2.90	54
Advanced Countries								
Japan	4.19	5	4.16	7	4.10	11	4.25	2
UK	3.95	16	4.16	6	4.21	5	4.03	8
US	4.15	7	4.18	5	4.15	8	4.05	7

Source: World Bank Logistic Performance Index. https://lpi.worldbank.org/ (accessed 18 March 2020).

Note
This index covers the 160 economies, which are ranked based on their score. Here, the high score (1=Low to 5=High) indicates a higher infrastructural facility, which enables the economies to face challenges to improve their trade logistics and performance.

PRC = People's Republic of China, UK = United Kingdom, US = United States.

Table 6.5 summarizes the infrastructure score and rank in the logistics performance index for Central Asian countries, emerging Asian countries (the PRC, India, and Indonesia), and advanced countries (Japan, the UK, and the US). The infrastructure score of Central Asian countries is very low in comparison to emerging Asian and advanced countries, and the Kyrgyz Republic, Turkmenistan, and Tajikistan rank more than 100. For this reason, developing infrastructure for utilizing Central Asia's rich natural and human resources can play an important role in promoting higher economic growth. As per Forbes' 2018 global 2,000 rankings, Kazakhstan provides 3.3% of the world's total oil exports and needs transport infrastructure like road, railways, and ports to obtain higher economic growth.

Table 6.6 shows the infrastructural capability of Central Asian countries compared to the emerging Asian countries and advanced countries. Various details can be observed as follows:

(1) Central Asian countries are relatively better compared with emerging Asian countries in terms of access to electricity and energy use, whereas they are far behind in infrastructure development compared to advanced countries except for access to electricity, which is nearly 100% of the population.

Table 6.6 Comparison of Infrastructure: Central Asian Countries Versus Selected Benchmark Emerging and Advanced Countries (average 2000–2018)

Infrastructure Variables	*Access to electricity (% of Population)*	*Railways, passenger carried (Millions of passengers-km)*	*Fixed telephone subscription (per 100 People)*	*Energy use (kg of oil equipment per capita)*
Central Asian Countries				
Kazakhstan	99.646	14,744.030	20.300	3,749.149
Kyrgyz Republic	99.654	62.040	7.995	550.776
Tajikistan	98.846	37.778	4.521	327.802
Turkmenistan	99.826	1,675.067	9.818	4,191.581
Uzbekistan	99.811	2,878.407	7.541	1,798.835
Emerging Asian Countries				
PRC	98.977	666,416.700	19.560	1,589.094
India	74.351	804,833.900	2.900	503.128
Indonesia	92.686	18,365.170	8.029	807.851
Advanced Countries				
Japan	100	243,069.100	47.738	3,830.645
UK	100	44,690.390	53.743	3,355.698
US	100	9,794.420	50.751	7,436.558

Source: Authors' calculation from World Development Indicators Data. https://databank.worldbank.org/source/world-development-indicators (accessed 18 March 2020).

Note
PRC = People's Republic of China, UK = United Kingdom, US = United States.

(2) Passenger railway density is far behind in comparison to other emerging economies and advanced economies. Indeed, it is very low in the case of the Kyrgyz Republic and Tajikistan.
(3) Information and communication technology (ICT), as proxied by fixed telephone subscriptions, is lagging Japan, the UK, and the US, but is more or less similar to Indonesia. This indicates a crucial area for policy action in Central Asia to enhance productivity, skill, and development.
(4) In the case of energy use, Kazakhstan and Turkmenistan are comparable to advanced economies, whereas the Kyrgyz Republic, Tajikistan, and Uzbekistan use much less in comparison to Japan, the UK, and the US. Except for Tajikistan, they are better than the PRC, India, and Indonesia. This comparative analysis indicates that Central Asian countries should cover the infrastructure needed to enhance economic growth.

From the above tables and graphs, it can be concluded that the highest-growing countries in Central Asia, such as Kazakhstan, attracted higher PPI. In contrast, the lowest-growing countries, such as the Kyrgyz Republic and Tajikistan, depend on official development assistance. Further, these two low-growth countries have a higher infrastructure gap and lower infrastructure score and experienced a higher current account deficit. These facts induce us to examine whether infrastructure investment plays any role in determining the economic performance of these countries. Is there any by-directional relationship between these two?

6.4 Infrastructure Investment and Economic Growth: A Brief Review

The literature on the economic importance of infrastructure can be classified into three major strands. The first strand focuses on the micro aspect of an infrastructure project by analyzing its social cost-benefit (Aschauer 1989; Gramlich 1994; Marcelo et al. 2016), i.e., its negative externalities. The second strand deals with the demand side of the infrastructure, thereby measuring the infrastructure investment gap (Fay 2000; Gill and Kharas 2007; Kennedy and Corfee-Morlot 2013; McKinsey 2013; OECD 2006; Ruiz-Nuñez and Wei 2015). The third strand investigated the role of infrastructure in promoting economic growth through productivity and trade (Bougheas et al. 1999; Cavallo and Daude 2011; Vijil and Wagner 2012). As the present study mainly focuses on infrastructure investment and economic growth, the research papers related to this issue are reviewed.

The effect of infrastructure on aggregate economic growth or output has been a long debate in the literature. The initial work related to the role of infrastructure by Rosenstein-Rodan (1943) and Hirschman (1957) indicated the importance of capital in enhancing growth. Theoretical attempts by Romer (1986), Lucas (1988), and Barro (1990) included public capital into the production function to capture the effect of infrastructure on output. Investment in infrastructure can enhance productivity and competitiveness through trade facilitation, reduce transportation costs, and create employment, thereby improving economic development and reducing poverty (Démurger 2001; Estache and Limi 2008). It is argued that the marginal productivity of public infrastructure spending is more than twice that of private capital (Aschauer 1989).

The empirical studies of infrastructure primarily focused on transportation and electricity and their link to economic growth. For instance, better transport leads to increased market access and thereby affects growth in Kenya (Jedwab and Moradi 2016). It is also found that rail and road infrastructure helped to increase the real income of colonial India by reducing the trade cost, interregional price differences, and increasing trade (Donaldson 2018). Similar findings have also been found in the case of the US at the end of the nineteenth century (Donaldson and Hornbeck 2016).

Equally, there have been many attempts to analyze how electricity consumption affects economic growth, with evidence suggesting that higher consumption leads to higher economic growth, as in the cases of Indonesia (Chen et al. 2007), Fiji (Narayan and Singh 2007), and Australia (Narayan and Prasad 2008). On the other hand, it is also found that higher economic growth leads to electricity consumption in Australia (Narayan and Smyth 2005), Bangladesh (Mozumder and Marathe 2007), and the United Arab Emirates (Shahbaz et al. 2014). Likewise, telecommunication infrastructure is found to have a positive impact on the economic growth of the Organization for Economic Co-operation and Development (OECD) countries (Röller and Waverman 2001). Similarly, Mitra et al. (2002) found that infrastructure investment has a strong positive effect on the total factor productivity of the Indian manufacturing sector. Likewise, Fedderke and Bogetić (2009) observed a strong positive effect of infrastructure investment on economic growth in South Africa.

It is also argued that infrastructure investment, especially in the case of publicly financed projects, may not produce a positive effect on economic growth due to corruption, poor maintenance, and cost overruns (Arezki et al. 2017; Warner 2013). Roy (2018) found that infrastructure investment negatively impacts economic growth and contributed to large cost overruns of Indian projects during 1980–2014. As the existing literature did not give enough attention to the Central Asian countries, the present study attempts to find their relationship between infrastructure investment and economic growth.

6.5 Empirical Model and Data

We propose the following econometric model to examine the relationship between infrastructure investment and economic growth.

$$Y_t = \beta_0 + \beta_1 Infra_t + \varepsilon_t \tag{1}$$

$$Infra_t = \alpha_0 + \alpha_1 Y_t + \varepsilon_t \tag{2}$$

where Y represents the output and *Infra* represents infrastructure investment. Equation 1 shows the effect of infrastructure investment on economic growth, whereas equation 2 shows the effect of economic growth on infrastructure investment. β_1 and α_1 are the parameters to be estimated. β_0 and α_0 are the intercepts and t stands for time, while ε_t indicates the error term. All variables are measured in logarithmic form. We expect a positive relationship between infrastructure investment and output as higher investment in infrastructure enhances economic growth. So, we expect $\beta_1 > 0$. Similarly, higher economic growth can lead to higher investment in infrastructure, thus the expected relationship is positive, $\alpha_1 > 0$. The above equations are estimated using ARDL co-integration technique to find the long-run relationship of these variables. Economic growth is proxied by real GDP, whereas infrastructure investment is proxied by Gross Fixed Capital Formation due to the paucity of infrastructure investment data for these countries. Annual data related to the above variables covering the period 1990 to 2018 were collected and interpolated into the quarterly series due to the unavailability of related long time-series data. Moreover, data are largely available from 1990 onwards, and using annual data with fewer than 30 observations significantly reduces freedom. Therefore, the linear interpolation method is adopted to convert the annual data series into quarterly series.

Thus, the above equations are estimated using quarterly data from 1990Q1 to 2018Q4, drawn from the World Bank and International Monetary Fund. Moreover, because the continuous time-series data related to the above variables for Turkmenistan are not available, this country is excluded from the analysis.

6.6 Econometric Methodology

The ARDL approach to cointegration by Pesaran and Shin (1999) and Pesaran, Shin, and Smith (2001) is employed to estimate equations 1 and 2. This test can be performed irrespective of whether variables in the model are purely stationary, i.e., I(0), purely non-stationary, i.e., I(1), or mutually cointegrated. This test is widely applied when the macroeconomic variables are mixed in order (Prabheesh and Laila 2020; Prabheesh and Vidya 2018; Vidya and Prabheesh 2019). There are two steps involved in this test. The first step is to identify whether any cointegrating or long-run relationship exists between the variables in the model. If yes, the next step is to estimate the coefficients associated with long-run and short-run models using the error correction model. The error correction model of the ARDL model of equation (1), which can be written as:

$$\Delta \Upsilon_t = \lambda_0 + \lambda_1 \Upsilon_{t-1} + \lambda_2 Infra_{t-1} + \sum_{j=1}^{n} \varnothing_j \Delta \Upsilon_{t-j} + \sum_{j=1}^{n} \gamma_j \Delta Infra_{t-j} + \varepsilon_t \tag{3}$$

where parameter λs represents the long-run relationship, and $\varnothing_j$ and γ_j represent the short-run dynamics of the model. F-test procedure is followed to examine the long-run relationship between variables by testing the joint significance of the coefficients of the lagged levels of the variables, i.e., $H_1 : \lambda_1 = \lambda_2 = 0$ against $H_2 : \lambda_1 \neq \lambda_2 \neq 0$. A rejection of the null hypothesis indicates the evidence of cointegration. A lower and upper bound critical value for the F-statistic is proposed by Pesaran et al. (2001) by assuming all variables are I(0) for the lower bound and I(1) for the upper bound. The null of no cointegration can be rejected if the calculated F-statistic exceeds the upper critical value, irrespective of the order of integration. Contrariwise, the null of no cointegration cannot be rejected if the F-statistic is less than the lower critical bound. The result is inconclusive if the F-statistic lies between the lower and upper critical values. The present study follows the critical values suggested by Narayan (2005) for the small sample size.

6.7 Empirical Findings

6.7.1 Findings from Unit Root Tests

Augmented Dickey-Fuller (ADF) and Phillips–Perron (PP) tests are employed to examine the stationarity of the variables, before estimating the empirical models. The results reported in Table 6.7 show that the null hypothesis of the unit root (non-stationarity) cannot be rejected at the level for both variables for

Table 6.7 Results of Unit Root Test

Variables	*ADF Test Statistic*		*PP Test Statistic*	
	Levels	*First Difference*	*Levels*	*First Difference*
Kazakhstan				
Y	2.597 (0.991)	-1.850 (0.092)***	-1.329(0.613)	-1.730 (0.062)***
Infra	0.499 (0.818)	-3.473 (0.000)*	-0.192 (0.624)	-2.463(0.019)**
Kyrgyz Republic				
Y	1.430 (0.976)	-3.167 (0.000)*	0.831(0.885)	-2.179 (0.030)**
Infra	0.724 (0.865)	-3.714 (0.000)*	0.437 (0.801)	-3.703 (0.000)*
Tajikistan				
Y	-1.043 (0.721)	-3.593 (0.000)*	0.061(0.694)	-1.668 (0.089)***
Infra	-0.703 (0.400)	-2.437 (0.017)**	-0.969 (0.287)	-6.981 (0.000)*
Uzbekistan				
Y	1.626 (0.971)	-1.266 (0.183)	2.883 (0.998)	-3.051(0.000)*
Infra	1.586 (0.969)	-4.797 (0.000)*	1.990 (0.986)	-3.222 (0.000)**

Source: Authors' calculation.

Note

The table shows the results of the stationary test of the variables based on Augmented Dickey-Fuller (ADF) and Phillips–Perron (PP). The null hypothesis is the variable is non-stationary and the alternative hypotheses series is stationary. Where, *, ** and *** denotes rejection of unit root at 1%, 5%, and 10% level respectively.

all countries, whereas, in the case of first-difference, the null can be rejected in all cases, implying the variables are non-stationary at levels I(1). As all these two variables are non-stationary, it is possible to check for long-run relationships by following the cointegration framework.

6.7.2 *Findings from ARDL Analysis*

The findings from the F-test are reported in Table 6.8. In the case of Kazakhstan, when the output becomes the dependent variable, i.e., equation 1, the calculated F statistic is found to be 9.238, which is higher than the upper bound critical value of 4.428. This indicates that the null hypothesis of no cointegration can be rejected, and there exists a unique cointegration relationship between output and infrastructure investment. Whereas in the case of equation 2, where the dependent variable is infrastructure investment, the null of no cointegration cannot be rejected, indicating economic growth does not drive infrastructure investment in the long-run in the case of Kazakhstan. Interestingly, in the case of the Kyrgyz Republic, the finding suggests the calculated F statistic, 0.931 is smaller than the lower bound critical value of 3.538, which implies no cointegration relationship. However, the long-run relationship is established from output to infrastructure investment (Equation 2). This finding suggests that output is the long-run driving force of infrastructure investment. Similarly, it can be seen that, in the

Table 6.8 Results of F-Test

Models		*Optimum lag (SBC)*	*Calculated F-statistic*	*Critical values (95% level)*		*Conclusion*
				I(0)	*I(1)*	
Kazakhstan						
Equation 1	$Y = f(Infra)$	4	9.238*	3.538	4.428	Co-integration
Equation 2	$Infra = f(y)$	4	3.469	3.538	4.428	No Co-integration
Kyrgyz Republic						
Equation 1	$Y = f(Infra)$	4	0.931	3.538	4.428	No Co-integration
Equation 2	$Infra = f(y)$	4	7.314*	3.538	4.428	Co-integration
Tajikistan						
Equation 1	$Y = f(Infra)$	4	5.993*	3.538	4.428	Co-integration
Equation 2	$Infra = f(y)$	4	3.120	3.538	4.428	No Co-integration
Uzbekistan						
Equation 1	$Y = f(Infra)$	4	13.639*	3.538	4.428	Co-integration
Equation 2	$Infra = f(y)$	4	4.999**	3.538	4.428	Co-integration

Source: Authors' calculation.

Note

The table presents the Auto Regressive Distributed Lag (ARDL) cointegration test developed by Pesaran and Shin (1999) and Pesaran et al. (2001). The null hypothesis of no integration is tested against an alternative of integration. The critical values for the lower and upper bound of I (0) and I (1) for the F statistic with constant and trend are obtained from (Narayan 2005). Where, *, ** and *** denotes rejection of null of cointegration at 1%, 5% and 10% level respectively. SBC = Schwarz lag selection criteria.

case of Tajikistan, whereas the evidence of cointegration is established from infrastructure investment to output but not from output to infrastructure investment, in the case of Uzbekistan, the cointegration is established in both ways, i.e., bi-directional. Table 6.9 reports the long-run coefficients of ARDL models suggested by Schwarz lag selection criteria (SBC).

Table 6.9 shows the long-run effect of infrastructure investment on output in the three economies, where the cointegration is found based on Equation 1. As we measured the variables in the model in natural logarithmic form, the coefficients associated with the variables can be interpreted as the elasticity of the dependent variable in response to the changes in the independent variable. In all cases, the sign of the coefficient of *Infra* is found to be positive and statistically significant, implying that higher investment in infrastructure leads to higher output. The highest positive impact is found in Uzbekistan, where a 1% increase in investment in infrastructure leads to 0.6% increase in output. Similarly, in Kazakhstan and Tajikistan, the impact is found to be 0.54 and 0.39, respectively. The high sensitivity of output to infrastructure investment in Kazakhstan and Uzbekistan is clear evidence of fixed assets, such as infrastructure, promoting

Table 6.9 Long-run Coefficient Estimates by the ARDL Approach (Equation 1) (Dependent variable, Y)

Regressor	*Kazakhstan*	*Tajikistan*	*Uzbekistan*
Infra	0.542 (3.027)*	0.396 (3.401)*	0.688 (2.98)*
Constant	3.467 (0.819)	-0.043 (-0.022)	0.459 (0.082)

Source: Authors' calculation.

Note
The table reports the long-run coefficients estimated by Auto-Regressive Distributed Lag (ARDL) after the long-run relationship is established for model 1. Here, *, ** and *** denote statistical significance at 1%, 5 % and 10% levels, respectively and values in parenthesis indicate t values.

Table 6.10 Long-run Coefficient Estimates by the ARDL Approach (Equation 2) (Dependent variable, *Infra*)

Regressor	*Kyrgyz Republic*	*Uzbekistan*
Infra	0.544 (4.911)*	0.799 (18.163)*
Constant	-1.233 (-2.703)*	-3.931 (-14.268)*

Source: Authors' calculation.

Note
The table reports the long-run coefficients estimated by Auto-Regressive Distributed Lag (ARDL) after the long-run relationship is established for model 2. Here, *, ** and *** denote statistical significance at 1%, 5 % and 10% levels, respectively and values in parenthesis indicate t values.

growth. The higher infrastructure score and ranking in the logistic performance discussed in the previous section could be the reason for the higher impact of infrastructure investment on output.

Similarly, Table 6.10 shows the long-run effect output on infrastructure investment in the case of the Kyrgyz Republic and Uzbekistan. The findings suggest that the variable *Infra* is positive and statistically significant in determining the output. The impact is found to be 0.54 and 0.79 for the Kyrgyz Republic and Uzbekistan, respectively. It can be observed that the coefficient of *Infra* (0.79) is higher than the coefficient associated with Y(0.54) in the case of Uzbekistan. This is a clear indication of a strong relationship that runs from economic growth to infrastructure investment, as compared to the other way around.

The short-run dynamics estimated by error correction representation of the ARDL associated with Equation 1 is reported in Table 6.11. In the case of Kazakhstan, the coefficient of Δ is found to be positive and statistically significant. It is important to see that the coefficient of these variables is small, i.e., 0.04, indicating a low impact of infrastructure investment on output in the short run. Similarly, a positive and low impact can be seen in the case of Uzbekistan as well, whereas, in the case of Tajikistan, the short-term impact

Table 6.11 Error Correction Representation for the ARDL Model (Equation 1) (Dependent variable, Y)

Variables	*Kazakhstan*	*Tajikistan*	*Uzbekistan*
	ARDL (4,1)	*ARDL (2,2)*	*ARDL (3,2)*
ΔY_{t-1}	0.826 (4.121)*	0.627(5.351)*	0.341
ΔY_{t-2}	0.716 (4.104)*		0.326
ΔY_{t-3}	0.531 (5.163)*		
$\Delta Infra_t$	0.045 (3.134)*	-0.045(-2.655)*	0.021 (2.655)*
$\Delta Infra_{t-1}$		-0.078 (-3.189)*	
Ecm (-1)	-0.255 (-4.353)*	-0.130 (-3.971)*	-0.192 (-7.314)*
Adjusted R^2	0.329	0.239	0.323
χ^2_{AC}	0.965 [0.456]	1.553(0.244)	1.846[0.169]
χ^2_{Arch}	0.152 [0.958]	0.125 [0.970]	0.910[0.479]
χ^2_{Norm}	2.128 [0.541]	13.900[0.000]	0.026[0.986]
CUSUM	Stable	Not stable	Stable
CUSUMQ	Stable	Not stable	Stable

Source: Authors' calculation.

Note

Where Δ and Ecm (-1) denote the first difference and the error correction term, respectively. χ^2_{AC} and χ^2_{Arch} and χ^2_{Norm} are LM statistics for serial correlation, ARCH effect and normality in residuals respectively. *.**and***are statistically significantly different from zero at 1, 5 and 10% levels respectively. Figures in parenthesis show t- statistics.

of the infrastructure variable is found to be negative and statistically significant. This finding indicates that higher investment in infrastructure leads to a reduction in output. This could be due to the crowding out of private investment in the short run due to higher public investment in the fixed capital. It is important to note that, in both models, the error correction terms are statistically significant at 1% level and expected negative sign. The error correction term varies from -0.13 to -0.25, indicating around 13%, and 25% of the deviation from equilibrium is eliminated within a quarter. Further, diagnostic statistics indicate no serial correlation and autoregressive conditional heteroscedasticity (ARCH) effect in the residuals. Likewise, the models confirm the residuals are normal. The cumulative sum (CUSUM) and cumulative sum of squares (CUSUMQ) on the recursive residuals indicate the coefficients' stability across sample periods.

Similarly, the error correction representation of the ARDL associated with Equation 2 for the Kyrgyz Republic and Uzbekistan is reported in Table 6.12. It can be observed that the short-run effect of output on infrastructure investment is positive for both quarters. The coefficient is found to be more than one in the case of Uzbekistan, indicating a higher impact of output on public spending. The statistics reported in the bottom part of the table show that the model passes all diagnostics tests.

Table 6.12 Error Correction Representation for the ARDL Model (Equation 2) (Dependent variable, *Infra*)

Variables	*Kyrgyz Republic*	*Uzbekistan*
	ARDL (2,2)	ARDL (2,4)
$\Delta Infra_{t-1}$	0.647 (2.897)*	0.826 (4.531)*
ΔY_t	0.411 (2.911)*	1.200 (1.672)
ΔY_{t-1}	0.674 (2.162)*	1.774 (1.940)***
ΔY_{t-2}		1.163 (3.079)*
ΔY_{t-3}		1.054 (2.542)**
Ecm (-1)	-0.362 (-4.241)	-0.488 (-4.365)
Adjusted R^2	0.487	0.840
χ^2_{AC}	1.183[0.346]	1.491[0.26]
χ^2_{Arch}	0.700[0.410]	0.266[0.890]
χ^2_{Norm}	0.557[0.753]	0.158[0.924]
CUSUM	Stable	Stable
CUSUMQ	Stable	Stable

Source: Authors' calculation.

Note
Where Δ and Ecm (-1) denote the first difference and the error correction term, respectively. χ^2_{AC} and χ^2_{Arch} and χ^2_{Norm} are LM statistics for serial correlation, ARCH effect and normality in residuals respectively. *, **and***are statistically significantly different from zero at 1, 5 and 10% levels respectively. Figures in parenthesis show t- statistics.

6.8 Conclusion

The countries of Central Asia are rich in natural and human resources but quite diverse in their stages of development. One of the obstacles to their economic transformation is the lack of well-developed infrastructure. Kazakhstan, the highest-growing country, attracted higher PPI, while the Kyrgyz Republic and Tajikistan, the lowest-growing countries, depend upon official development assistance. Further, the low-growing countries have a higher infrastructure gap and lower infrastructure score and a higher current account deficit. Hence this study addressed the role of infrastructure investment and economic growth in these economies. Using quarterly data from 1990 to 2018 and ARDL approach cointegration, the study finds that the economic growth in Kazakhstan, Tajikistan, and Uzbekistan is significantly driven by infrastructure investment, while, in the case of the Kyrgyz Republic, economic growth drives infrastructure investment. Similarly, in the case of Uzbekistan, a bi-directional relationship between infrastructure investment and economic growth is observed, which may stem from efficient use of infrastructure with the help of private participation, along with strong macroeconomic fundamentals. Thus, attracting more private participation can accelerate growth and thereby maintain a sustainable infrastructure investment in Uzbekistan. Lastly, certain interventions such as efficient use of official development assistance and increased private participation may bring the positive effect of infrastructure investment on economic growth, especially in the case of the Kyrgyz Republic and Tajikistan.

References

Aaron, H.J. 1990. Discussion of "Why Is Infrastructure Important?" in *Is There Any Shortfall in Public Capital Investment?* edited by A.H. Munnel. Federal Reserve Bank of Boston: 51–63.

ADB. 2019. Asian Development Bank Member Fact Sheet. Manila: Asian Development Bank. www.adb.org/publications/series/fact-sheets (accessed 18 March 2020).

Abiad, A., D. Furceri, T. Petia. 2016. The Macroeconomic Effects of Public Investment: Evidence from Advanced Economies. *Journal of Macroeconomics* 50: 224–240.

Arezki, R., P. Bolton, S. Peters, F. Samama, J. Stiglitz. 2017. From Global Savings Glut to Financing Infrastructure. *American Economic Journal: Economic Policy* 32: 221–261.

Aschauer, D.A. 1989. Is Public Expenditure Productive?. *Journal of Monetary Economics* 23: 177–200.

Barro, R.J. 1990. Government Spending in a Simple Model of Endogenous Growth. *Journal of Political Economy* 98: 103–125.

Batsaikhan, U., M. Dabrowski. 2017. Central Asia—Twenty-Five Years After the Breakup of the USSR. *Russian Journal of Economics* 3: 296–320.

Bougheas, S., P.O. Demetriades, E.L. Morgenroth. 1999. Infrastructure, Transport Costs and Trade. *Journal of International Economics* 47: 169–189.

Cavallo, E., C. Daude. 2011. Public Investment in Developing Countries: A Blessing or a Curse? *Journal of Comparative Economics* 39: 65–81.

Chen, S.T., H.I. Kuo, C.C. Chen. 2007. The Relationship between GDP and Electricity Consumption in 10 Asian Countries. *Energy Policy* 35: 2611–2621.

Démurger, S. 2001. Infrastructure Development and Economic Growth: An Explanation for Regional Disparities in China? *Journal of Comparative Economics* 29: 95–117.

Donaldson, D. 2018. Railroads of the Raj: Estimating the Impact of Transportation Infrastructure. *American Economic Review* 108: 899–934.

Donaldson, D., R. Hornbeck. 2016. Railroads and American Economic Growth: A "Market Access" Approach. *The Quarterly Journal of Economics* 131: 799–858.

Estache, A., A. Iimi. 2008. *Procurement Efficiency for Infrastructure Development and Financial Needs Reassessed.* Washington, DC: World Bank.https://elibrary.worldbank.org/doi/pdf/10.1596/1813-9450-4662 (accessed 18 March 2020).

Fay, M. 2000. Financing The Future: Infrastructure Needs in Latin America, 2000-05. Washington, DC: World Bank. https://elibrary.worldbank.org (accessed 18 March 2020).

Fedderke, J.W., Z. Bogetic. 2006. Infrastructure and Growth in South Africa: Direct and Indirect Productivity Impacts of 19 Infrastructure Measures. Washington, DC: World Bank. https://elibrary.worldbank.org (accessed 18 March 2020).

Feng, Q., G.L. Wu. 2018. On the Reverse Causality between Output and Infrastructure: The Case of China. *Economic Modelling* 74: 97–104.

Gill, I.S., H. Kharas. Eds. 2007. *An East Asian Renaissance: Ideas For Economic Growth.* Washington, DC: World Bank.

Gramlich, E.M. 1994. Infrastructure Investment: A Review Essay. *Journal of Economic Literature* 32: 1176–1196.

Hasan, R. 2017. *Meeting Asia's Infrastructure Needs.* Manila: Asian Development Bank www.adb.org/sites/default/files/publication/227496/special-report-infrastructure.pdf (accessed 21 November 2018).

Hirschman, A.O. 1957. Investment Policies and "Dualism" in Underdeveloped Countries. *The American Economic Review* 47: 550–570.

Javid, M. 2019. Public and Private Infrastructure Investment and Economic Growth in Pakistan: An Aggregate and Disaggregate Analysis. *Sustainability* 11: 3359.

Jedwab, R., A. Moradi. 2016. The Permanent Effects of Transportation Revolutions in Poor Countries: Evidence from Africa. *Review of Economics and Statistics* 98: 268–284.

Kennedy, C., and J. Corfee-Morlot. 2013. Past Performance and Future Needs For Low Carbon Climate Resilient Infrastructure–An Investment Perspective. *Energy Policy* 59: 773–783.

Lucas, R.E. 1998. On the Mechanics of Economic Development. *Econometric Society Monographs* 29: 61–70.

Marcelo, D., C. Mandri-Perrott, S. House, J. Schwartz. 2016. Prioritizing Infrastructure Investment: A Framework For Government Decision Making. Washington, DC: World Bank. https://openknowledge.worldbank.org/handle/10986/24511 (accessed 18 March 2020).

Mitra, A., A. Varoudakis, M.A. Veganzones-Varoudakis. 2002. Productivity and Technical Efficiency in Indian States' Manufacturing: The Role of Infrastructure. *Economic Development and Cultural Change* 50: 395–426.

Mozumder, P., A. Marathe. 2007. Causality Relationship Between Electricity Consumption and GDP in Bangladesh. *Energy Policy* 35: 395–402.

Munnell, A.H. 1992. Policy Watch, Infrastructure and Economic Growth. *Journal of Economic Perspectives* 6: 189–198.

Narayan, P.K. 2005. The Saving and Investment Nexus for China: Evidence from Cointegration Tests. *Applied Economics* 37: 1979–1990.

Narayan, P.K., A. Prasad. 2008. Electricity Consumption–Real GDP Causality Nexus: Evidence from A Bootstrapped Causality Test for 30 OECD Countries. *Energy Policy* 36: 910–918.

Narayan, P.K., B. Singh. 2007. The Electricity Consumption and GDP Nexus for the Fiji Islands. *Energy Economics* 29: 1141–1150.

Narayan, P.K., R. Smyth. 2005. Electricity Consumption, Employment and Real Income in Australia Evidence from Multivariate Granger Causality Tests. *Energy Policy* 33: 1109–1116.

Nourzad, F., M.D. Vrieze. 1995. Public Capital Formation and Productivity Growth: Some International Evidence. *Journal of Productivity Analysis* 6: 283–295.

OECD. 2006. Infrastructure to 2030: Telecom, Land Transport, Water and Electricity. Paris: Organisation for Economic Co-operation and Development. www.oecd-ilibrary.org/economics/infrastructure-to-2030_9789264023994-en (accessed 18 March 2020).

OECD. 2014. Recommendation of the Council on Effective Public Investment Across Level of Government. Paris: Organisation for Economic Co-operation and Development www.oecd.org/effective-public-investment-toolkit/recommendation-effective-public-investment-across-levels-of-government.htm (accessed 18 March 2020).

Pesaran, M.H., Y. Shin. 1999. An Autoregressive Distributed-Lag Modelling Approach to Cointegration Analysis. *Econometric Society Monographs* 31: 371–413.

Pesaran, M.H., Y. Shin, R.J. Smith. 2001. Bounds Testing Approaches to the Analysis of Level Relationships. *Journal of Applied Econometrics* 16: 289–326.

Prabheesh, K.P., N. Laila. 2020. Asymmetric Effect of Crude Oil and Palm Oil Prices on Indonesia's Output. *Bulletin of Monetary Economics and Banking* 23: 253–268.

Vidya, C.T., K.P. Prabheesh. 2019. Intra-Industry Trade Between India and Indonesia. *Bulletin of Monetary Economics and Banking* 21: 511–530.

Prabheesh, K.P., C.T. Vidya. 2018. Do Business Cycles, Investment-Specific Technology Shocks Matter for Stock Returns? *Economic Modelling* 70: 511–524.

Pritchett, L. 1999. Mind Your P's and Q's: The Cost of Public Investment Is Not the Value of Public Capital. Washington, DC: World Bank https://elibrary.worldbank.org (accessed 18 March 2020).

Röller, L.H., L. Waverman. 2001. Telecommunications Infrastructure and Economic Development: A Simultaneous Approach. *American Economic Review* 91: 909–923.

Romer, P.M. 1986. Increasing Returns and Long-Run Growth. *Journal of Political Economy* 94: 1102–1037.

Rosenstein-Rodan, P.N. 1943. Problems of Industrialization of Eastern and South-Eastern Europe. *The Economic Journal* 53: 202–211.

Roy, A.G. 2018. Infrastructure Investment and the Indian Economy. *Bulletin of Applied Economics* 5: 29–38.

Ruiz-Nuñez, F., Z. Wei. 2015. Infrastructure Investment Demands in Emerging Markets and Developing Economies. Washington, DC: World Bank. https://elibrary.worldbank.org/doi/abs/10.1596/1813-9450-7414 (accessed 18 March 2020).

Shahbaz, M., R. Sbia, H. Hamdi, I. Ozturk. 2014. Economic Growth, Electricity Consumption, Urbanization and Environmental Degradation Relationship in United Arab Emirates. *Ecological Indicators* 45: 622–631.

Sutherland, D., S. Araujo, B. Égert, T.J. Kozluk. 2009. *Infrastructure Investment: Links to Growth and the Role of Public Policies.* Paris: Organisation for Economic Co-operation and Development. www.oecd-ilibrary.org/economics/infrastructure-investment_225678178357 (accessed 18 March 2020).

Välilä, T. 2020. Infrastructure and Growth: A Survey of Macro-Econometric Research. *Structural Change and Economic Dynamics* 53: 39–49.

Vijil, M., L. Wagner. 2012. Does Aid for Trade Enhance Export Performance? Investigating the Infrastructure Channel. *World Economy* 35: 838–868.

Warner, M.E. 2013. Private Finance for Public Goods: Social Impact Bonds. *Journal of Economic Policy Reform* 16: 303–319.

7 Three Models of Local Public Financing for Infrastructure Investment in the People's Republic of China[1]

Minquan Liu

7.1 Introduction

An emerging consensus in theoretical and policy analysis of development recognizes that investment in physical infrastructures (typically roads and railways, water and waterway management, irrigation and farmland consolidation, access to electricity and other energy sources, as well as access to mass communications) can play a critical and catalytic role in economic development (World Bank 1994; Wu et al. 2005; Sahoo et al. 2012; Ouattara et al. 2019). In late-industrializing countries, however, large-scale physical infrastructure investments have been carried out not by the private sector, but by the state, including various local governments, and this is certainly true of the People's Republic of China (PRC) (Gerschenkron 1962; Wade 1990; Oi 1995; Bateman 2017).[2]

This chapter compares three contrasting models of local public financing for infrastructural investments in the PRC, ranging from the radical to the mainstream. Rather than being hypothetical, these models are widely practiced, currently or in the past, or are likely to be practiced in the future. The first was premised on the PRC's former agricultural collectives from four decades ago, while the second is in wide practice in the country today. The third derives from the British local council tax system. Although not yet in extensive practice in the PRC today, it may well represent the direction in which its local public financing will move. The chapter also argues that the most effective model of local public financing at any one time in a country would depend on its current socio-economic conditions. When these conditions change, the choice of the right model will also need to change.

Below, Section 7.2 introduces the past model, while Section 7.3 presents the model that is now widely practiced in the country. The model mostly likely to be adopted in the future is discussed in Section 7.4. Section 7.5 concludes with general comments on the conditions that shaped the models.

DOI: 10.4324/9781003228790-9

7.2 Local Infrastructure Investment on the PRC's Agricultural Collectives

The PRC's agricultural collectives proper started around 1958. They went through tumultuous initial "commune" phases, until, in 1962, it become a three-tier system involving the commune, the brigade, and the team.[3] Being a full agricultural collective in the best sense of the word, the team, i.e., the bottom tier, typically had 30–50 rural households, usually from the same village settlement, with their land cultivated together and collectively "owned." The latter means that the land that each household brought into the collective—the team—when it was first formed no longer entitled it to a dividend, as it did formerly, and that all remuneration (monetary or in-kind) from the collective entirely depended on the labor contributions from that household's members, in what is called a workpoint payment system.

The basic construct of the workpoint payment system was as follows: Each member of a team would contribute to team work and thereby earn workpoints based on an accounting system such as an hourly-rate or piece-rate system, or a mix of both. Each member would accumulate workpoints in this fashion over the course of a year. At the end of the year, the team would calculate a dividend rate by dividing the team's distributable income by the total number of workpoints earned by all the members over the year. The annual remuneration to a member (or household) would then be this dividend rate multiplied by the annual total number of workpoints the member (or household) had earned.[4]

Two points are worth noting: First, team work would, of course, typically include time and effort spent on agricultural production such as crop planting, management and harvesting, but not just these. Team work also usually included time and effort spent on such things as irrigation improvement, farmland consolidation, road building, etc. Each year during the rural commune period in the PRC, every team member expended significant labor on these projects in exchange for workpoints. Second, before distributing a team's yearly income to members, two portions were set aside, first as the team's accumulation fund, and second as the team's welfare fund. While the latter was used for team members' social welfare, the former was specifically designed to improve the team's production facilities and promote production (Table 7.1).

The earmarking of part of a team's income for the accumulation fund, and the fact that members expend labor on team work other than for direct production (current crop planting, management and harvesting, etc.), represented two extremely important sources of local infrastructural investment financing during the PRC commune period. The first source covered the material cost of such investments (e.g., the cost of cement and sand to build roads and irrigation systems), while the second was used to take care of their labor input (Table 7.1).

Indeed, in the second case, something intricate was in fact at work. Each member would earn workpoints for labor expended on infrastructural investment projects that did not produce an output for the current period and, therefore, did not add to current year's collective income. But these members received

Table 7.1 Local Public Financing on Communes in the PRC, 1960s–1970s

	Items of Infrastructure Investment	*Funding Source*	
		Material and running costs (non-labor)	*Labor and running costs (labor)*
Physical Infrastructure Investment	Rural and farm roads Irrigation stations and canals Farm drainage ditches Farmland consolidation (plot reconfiguration and leveling) Farm machinery Other	Accumulation Fund	Workpoints
Social Sector Investment	Building, manning and running schools Building, manning and running village clinics Providing basic social protections Other	Welfare Fund	Workpoints

Source: Liu (1994a).

Note
PRC = People's Republic of China.

remuneration, nonetheless, for such labor in current year income. It turns out that the workpoint payment system acted as a surrogate income tax in proportion to the size of the income each member would have received had there been no infrastructural investment labor whatsoever in the team. It should be recognized that there should have been a dividend rate before any workpoints earned for infrastructural investment labor inputs were included. Adding these workpoints would cause the dividend rate to fall (because these labor inputs did not add to current-year output and income). This difference in the dividend rate times the total original number of workpoints in the team is the total payment for infrastructural investment labor. This was shared by all the members in proportion to their *original* share of the labor inputs and income.

Extensive rural infrastructure investments such as those mentioned above took place during the PRC's agricultural collective period. Unfortunately, no matching documentation of this investment has survived, so its true scale is not known. However, judging by the numerous reports at the time, and the accounts of many contemporary observers, the scale was truly great, so much so that, even today, PRC agriculture is still reaping the benefit of this earlier investment.[5]

Some outside observers at the time even disparaged such scenes of PRC peasants working on infrastructure as "working like ants."[6] Worse, it was sometimes implied that these people were forced to work. Available accounts disprove this and explain it in terms of individual team members voluntarily making choices to advance their personal welfare.[7]

The second tier—the brigade—was typically composed of 15–20 teams, with the largest tier—the commune—further consisting of 20–30 brigades. While not as important as the team, these two tiers also contributed to rural infrastructure by mobilizing resources they had at their command (many brigades and communes at the time engaged in various non-agricultural activities such as rural sidelines and industries—a relatively lucrative activity at the time). Organizationally, they enabled projects to encompass several teams or even brigades. They also often played an exhortation role, pushing and motivating local teams and brigades to undertake such investment.[8]

7.3 Land Financing

7.3.1 Rural Reform in the PRC

The PRC's rural reform in the late 1970s and early 1980s abolished practically all agricultural collectives in the country, and, in effect, restored private farming by distributing the land use rights to individual farmers. The collapse of agricultural collectives was followed by the disappearance of the workpoint payment system and the demise of the old, and, one might argue, successful, model of local public finance for infrastructure investment.[9] This, of course, had an immediate effect; new rural infrastructure was no longer built, and that which remained gradually collapsed due to a lack of maintenance.

The situation became so serious that, by the mid-1980s, the government, led by the Ministry of Finance, had to set aside from its very tight budget a large sum for the upkeep and renewal of rural infrastructure in what has been known as the Comprehensive Agricultural Development program (Liu 2002; Wu et al. 2015). This program, while important, is *not* the second model of local infrastructure investment financing addressed in this chapter. It is critical to realize that the above-mentioned rural reform, while restoring de facto private farming to rural PRC, did not actually abolish collective ownership of rural land. That is, even though each farmer was now cultivating their land as if it were their own, legally all rural land remained collectively owned. One might think that this "legal" collective ownership is only in name; in fact, in times of need, a local government (typically at the township or county level) could claim whatever land it wanted from the farmers, often with only modest compensation. Here lies the origin of a new, extremely important local public financing model that was going to emerge in the PRC, and which has been known as "land financing." Here also lies the key to an explanation of the relative ease with which the PRC government (central and local) has been able to acquire almost any land it needs for public investments.[10]

7.3.2 Land Financing

"Land financing" is a practice whereby a local government leases out the land it owns to an economic agent for a fee. The local government then uses the proceeds to finance its various activities, including investments in various local infrastructure, just as it would use any other part of its revenue. It is worth noting that a closely related term is "land investment" or "land management," whereby a local government makes certain necessary prior investments in the land it has set aside for lease, prior to actually leasing it. In the case of a green field site, this would typically include building necessary road and communication networks, providing access to electricity, water and sewage, etc. Where the land has existing residents or economic units on it, the investment would include relocating and resettling the incumbent users, compensating them, etc.

To the extent that land financing has itself usually meant certain prior investments in infrastructures in the form of "land investment" or "land management," it necessarily contributes to local development. However, land financing represents an important model of this in the PRC because it has been responsible for the financing of a great portion of physical infrastructural investments at the local levels by the land leasing proceeds it entitles local governments to collect.[11]

Available data indicate the scale of this financing, with some estimates reporting that it has accounted for over a third of all local government revenue in the PRC in recent years (Figure 7.1). Note that this estimate is only a national average—it hides the fact that, in some places, where the practice has been especially extensive, the share could go as high as over 70% of all local public revenue.

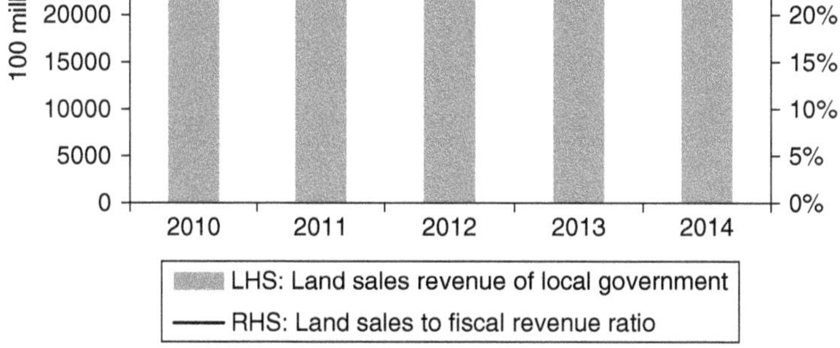

Figure 7.1 Shares of Land Lease Revenue in Total Local Government Revenue in the People's Republic of China.

Note: PRC = People's Republic of China.

Source: Huang (2016), based on CEIC data.

7.3.3 The 1993–94 Fiscal Reform

With public ownership of land in place, two other things that subsequently set land financing in motion in PRC were the fiscal reform in 1993–94, and the introduction of a *Zhaopaigua* mechanism. We address the former first.

The PRC fiscal system has undergone several major changes since 1949 (see Figure 7.2). In the years immediately preceding 1993–94, the division of fiscal revenue and spending responsibilities between the central and local governments had been very much in favor of the latter, leaving the central government severely short of resources. The reform sharply reversed that, leaving less than half of the total fiscal revenue in the country to the local governments, which had to shoulder over 70% of regular spending responsibilities (Figure 7.3).[12] While the ratios may have fluctuated a bit since then, the basic situation has remained the same: a severe mismatch of the level of revenue and spending responsibilities for local governments.[13]

While the central government thus regained the greater proportion of fiscal revenues from regular sources, it did, as part of the 1993–94 fiscal system reform,

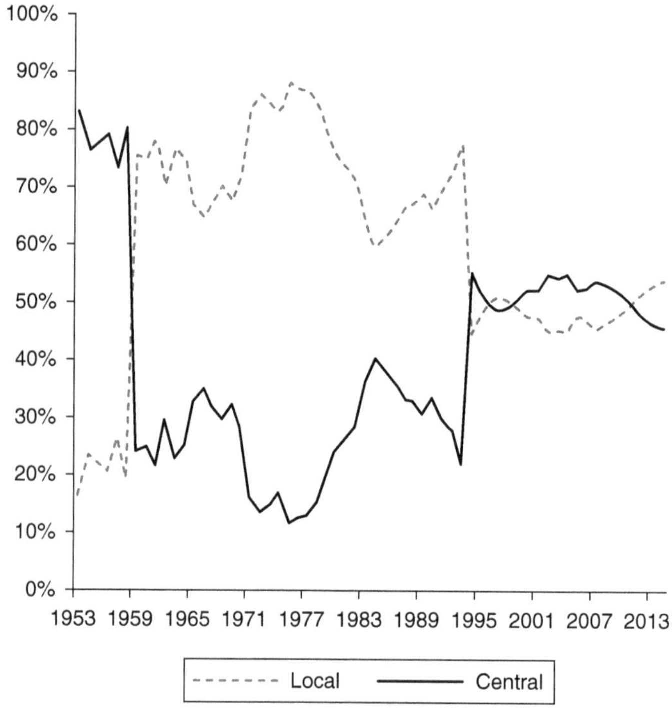

Figure 7.2 Shares of Central and Local Governments of Total Fiscal Revenue in the People's Republic of China, 1953–2014.

Source: Huang (2016) based on CEIC data.

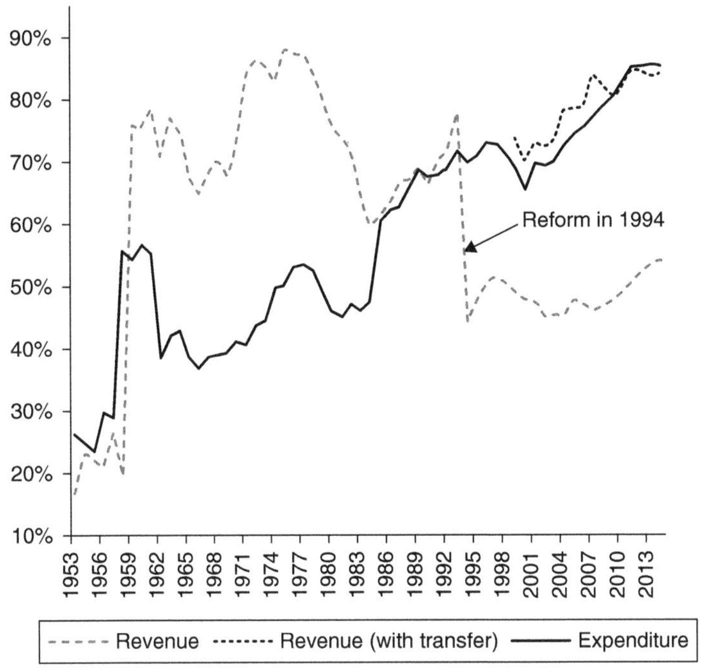

Figure 7.3 Shares of Local Government Revenue and Expenditure with and without Central Transfer, 1953–2014.

Source: Huang (2016) based on CEIC data.

give way to local governments by allowing them to engage in land financing. Indeed, to encourage local governments to do so, the central government even gave up all its claims to land transfer proceeds. These proceeds had previously been shared between central and local governments; following the reform, they were entirely for local governments to keep.

Beginning in 1994, PRC local governments were under both heavy fiscal pressures and strong incentives to engage in land financing, and presumably also to push for higher land (and house) prices.[14] However, in the next decade, land financing had actually remained only a meager source of revenue for local governments, and land and house prices had been stable. This has to do with a lack of a transparent market value revealing mechanism for the land. Without such a mechanism, public land transfers failed to generate many proceeds for local governments, but easily degenerated into cases of personal favor, bribery, and kickbacks involving public officials.[15] It is also for this reason that land and house prices in the PRC, although beginning to move up, did not undergo any sharp rise in the following decade.

7.3.3.1 Land Transfer in the PRC and the Zhaopaigua Process

Before 1979 in the PRC, the state (central or local government) had only transferred or allocated land to a user entirely for free—there was no land use or lease fee to be paid by any user. The first introduction of a user fee took place in 1979, when public land needed to be allocated to the newly permitted foreign-funded enterprises then mushrooming in the country. However, in this very first phase, after obtaining the use right of a given piece of land, the new acquirer could not then transfer that right to any other user with compensation. Thus, there was not any "market for land transfer" in any true sense of the term. The situation changed in 1987, when a revision to the PRC's constitution legalized such transfers. Soon thereafter, various rules and regulations were put in place that governed all aspects of land transfer, from initial primary transfers (i.e., from the public to private agents) to subsequent secondary transfers (among economic agents, including when the land changes hands only as collateral), and finally to cessions of the lease (Liu et al. 2009).

Much of the policy making had been focused on the governance of the initial process of primary transfer. Until 2002, that process was non-transparent, and was sometimes entirely at the discretion of the local government in question or, indeed, the officials in charge. Understandably, that provided enormous scope for favoritism, bribery, and kickbacks, which undermined public land leases as an effective source of public revenue.

Beginning in 2002, several key regulations were passed that required local governments to adopt a process of public bidding, auction or listing when leasing public land. In the Chinese language, these are called *zhaobiao*, *paimai*, and *guapai*, respectively, which have been shortened to *zhaopaigua*. As part of these processes, local governments were also instructed to follow certain procedures in land leasing (Liu et al. 2009). All other forms of public land leasing were completely phased out by 31 August 2004. At the same time, all geographical or jurisdictional restrictions were removed to allow real estate developers to expand on a national scale, that is, they could now pay to lease land anywhere in the country. A competitive national market for land leasing and land transfer had thus sprung up in the PRC.

The institution of the *zhaopaigua* processes/mechanisms for public land leasing had a major effect on land prices. It meant that, by and large, whoever offered the highest land transfer price could claim the land, and that, consequently, the local governments in question could receive the highest level of proceeds per unit of land leased. Indeed, it was no coincidence that only shortly after the institution of this process, both land and house prices in many parts of the country began to soar, and that this trend has continued without major interruption until today. Now, the same trend has spread to the entire country.[16]

By the time the *zhaopaigua* process was installed in 2004, all the necessary pieces were in place, causing local governments to extensively engage in land financing and push for ever-rising land and house prices. Liu et al. (2009) explored the compelling linkages that mutually reinforced sharp house and land

Table 7.2 Real Estate Sector Boom and Bust: People's Republic of China and Comparisons with Other Economies

	Boom Period and Cumulative Price Rise		*Period of Adjustment and Cumulative Price Fall*	
	Boom Period	*Cumulative Price Rise (%)*	*Period of Adjustment*	*Cumulative Price Fall (%)*
Japan	1978–1991	145	1991–2009	46
United States	1993–2006	159	2006–2011	30
Hong Kong, China	1985–1997	759	1997–2003	62
United Kingdom	1994–2007	226	2007–2009	9
Rep. of Korea	1975–1991	881	1991–1995	11
Switzerland	1979–1990	114	1990–1999	21
Canada	1985–1994	96	1994–1996	4
France	1998–2011	153	2011–2015	5
Denmark	1994–2007	216	2007–2009	17
Spain	1994–2007	235	2007–2013	35
PRC	1994–	383		

Source: Xingye Security Institute.

Note
PRC = People's Republic of China.

price rises in the PRC, and identified both the fiscal pressures and incentives for local governments to practice land financing and the *zhaopaigua* process as two key factors that had shaped the long-run trends in the post-2004 PRC land and housing markets.

Table 7.2 shows rises in the average nominal land and house prices in the PRC since 1994, compared with several other cases. Note, first, that the sharpest rise in fact took place after 2004, a whole decade after the 1993–94 fiscal reform but immediately after the institution of the *zhaopaigua* process. Second, while other economies' cases showed both ups and downs in the prices, there have been only price rises in the PRC. Third, the indicated extent of the rise is only in terms of the PRC's average. In cities such as Beijing, Shanghai, and Shenzhen, the size of the rise was easily many times greater than the average, and could outperform any international comparator. It is important to bear in mind the sheer size of the economy when using the PRC average in this and other contexts. The sheer scale of land price rises has naturally helped to make land lease proceeds a key source of revenue for local governments.

7.3.4 Local Government Financing Vehicles (LGFVs)

Still further, fuel was added to the already rapidly expanding and sharply rising land and house markets and prices, when, in 2008, a massive CNY4 trillion fiscal stimulus package was launched to shield the PRC from the impact of the international financial crisis (Wong 2011). Of this, only CNY1.18 trillion actually

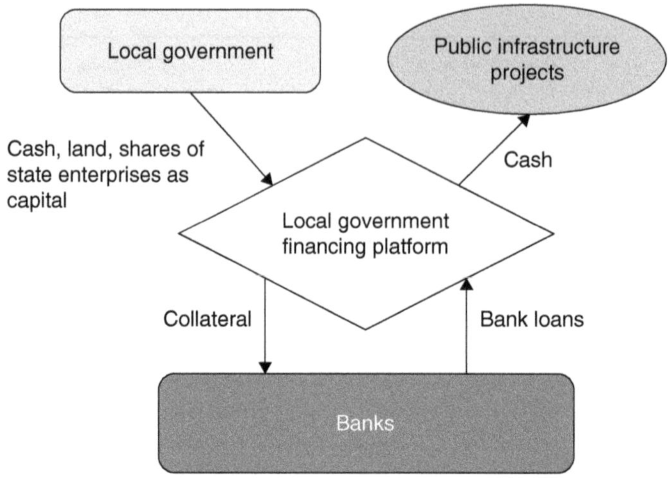

Figure 7.4 The People's Republic of China's LGFV, a Conceptual Illustration.
Note: PRC = People's Republic of China, LGFV = local government financing vehicle.
Source: Lu and Sun (2013).

came from the central government; the remainder was to be financed by local governments. But most local governments were already in a difficult fiscal position, as noted earlier, and the PRC's budget law also prohibited local governments from borrowing directly from financial markets, whether in the form of bank loans or through direct issuance of local municipal bonds. A practice was soon widely adopted, with the approval from the central government, to circumvent this Budget Law, whereby local governments would set up purposely designed financing platforms in the form of a local state-owned enterprise, and these would then borrow from the financial markets on behalf of the local governments. For this to work, local governments would first have to inject sufficient capital into these entities, and one way to do so was to transfer the use rights of some public land. With this and other assets as capital, the purposely designed local state-owned enterprises could then borrow from the banks on behalf of their local governments. Figure 7.4 illustrates a typical LGFV.

Similar LGFVs had existed in the PRC before 2008, but had not been widespread. They were used by only a few local governments with a strong financing need and a healthy long-term fiscal position, which meant only those local governments from economically relatively active and developed areas. They subsequently mushroomed and became widespread after 2008, as a result of the mounting financing needs placed by the central government on local governments. One major consequence of this has been the rapid accumulation of local government debts. In most cases, it was the local governments which bore the direct responsibility of repaying them; in others, local governments had acted only as guarantors of repayment. In recent years, the rising local government public debt in the PRC has become a major international concern. However, the truth may well be that, although they have grown rapidly to worrying proportions, the total amount of the debt is nevertheless still manageable.[17]

7.4 A Future Local Public Financing Model for the PRC

7.4.1 Need for an Alternative Model of Local Public Financing in the PRC

In a country with very high person-to-land ratios, or at least in those parts where most of the population has settled, sooner or later a time will come when there is no longer any significant land left for lease in a locality. To an extent, this is already happening in some suburban districts around certain major metropolises (e.g., Shanghai, Shenzhen, etc.) along the PRC's eastern coast. In other places, that time has not arrived but is expected to come soon, as the available land pool in the hands of local governments is drying up. In still other places, land is still abundant for lease. Whichever may be the case, eventually, more and more localities will join the former group. Once a locality (township, county, or prefecture-level city) no longer has any significant amount of land left for lease, how will its local government manage to raise the revenue it needs to fulfill its spending responsibilities, including making adequate infrastructural investments in its jurisdiction?

To answer this, much attention has been paid among the PRC's policy circle to some form of local residential property (primarily house) tax as the succeeding model of local public financing. To be sure, the country has been levying a form of property tax at least since 1986, but its scale has been very limited, only being applicable to various businesses and, when it comes to domestic dwellings, foreign nationals.[18] The vast and fast-expanding sweep of residential houses belonging to local residents had all been left out of this taxation until 2011, when two municipalities, Shanghai and Chongqing, began to experiment with collecting a modest property tax. At that time, a nationwide rollout of the tax for local residents was expected to take place shortly thereafter, but for various reasons, that has not happened in the country until today.[19] There has been, however, much research, discussion and debate of the need for, appropriate extent and likely size of the additional revenue that could be raised for local governments from such a tax. For example, according to a macro-level study carried out by the Chinese Academy of Social Sciences in 2015, a tax on local residents' domestic dwellings at 1% of the rentable value could raise CNY1.6 trillion for local governments in that year, while the total value of land leasing proceeds in the country would rapidly fall to around CNY1.5 trillion in 2017 because of dwindling land sources.[20] Note that this is only the national calculation made for the country as a whole. No doubt, some localities in the country will be facing up to the challenge of plummeting local public revenues on existing sources much sooner and in much graver ways than others.

In view of the fact that a nationwide local property tax on residents' domestic dwellings is still only under deliberation in the PRC, the rest of this section shall review a typical case of property taxes on residents that have been in use for a long time as a main source of local government revenue—the case of the UK, to illustrate some of the key issues involved, and to underline the sheer logic for such a tax. Looking at the UK's case is especially appropriate since it has been used very frequently as a reference in the PRC in the relevant policy discussions and debates.

7.4.2 Property Tax in the UK

In the UK, local governments raise revenue mostly through a "council tax" on local residents, based on the properties (dwellings) a person or household owns or uses (even if a person does not own a house but rents it, s/he may have to pay the tax, in place of the landlord—a common practice in the UK).

In recent years, local government revenues in the UK have come from four sources: central government grants, business rates, council taxes, and fees and charges. Table 7.3 gives a detailed breakdown of these sources, including their sub-items. As can be seen, the single largest source is central government grants. Before the 2013–14 financial year, this included business rates which were collected by local (typically district) councils but were handed over to the central treasury, which then reallocated them to local councils. Since 2013–14, however, local authorities have been able to retain up to 50% of the business rates. This change in policy was intended to give incentives to local governments to be more business-friendly and to attract more business investments to their jurisdiction. Businesses rates have been a traditional source of local government financing in the UK, by taxing non-domestic properties according to their rentable value, which in recent years have ranged from a third to half of that value.

Before the introduction of the Council Tax, the UK government under Margaret Thatcher had experimented with using other taxable base, namely the poll tax or Community Charge introduced in the 1989–91 financial year in Scotland and a year later in England. This imposed a flat tax on each adult resident. However, the practical difficulty of collecting the tax and, more importantly, the sheer unfair nature of the tax as seen by the general public soon ended it only two years after its introduction.

In general, a local government may raise its tax revenue from residents in three ways: according to a person's income, according to his/her property, or on a per-capita basis. In many countries, the right to levy an income tax is the privilege of the central government, meaning a local government may raise its tax revenue on the basis of the other two. After the fiasco with the poll tax, the UK government eventually opted for a property-based tax—the council tax, which is a revised version of its former system of domestic rates. Table 7.4 gives an example of UK council tax in action.

Table 7.3 Local Authority Incomes 2010/11–2014/15, England

£ million

	2010–11	*2011–12*	*2012–13*	*2013–14*	*2014–15*
Grant Income:					
Revenue Support Grant [(a)]	3,122	5,873	448	15,175	12,675
Redistributed non-domestic rates [(a)]	21,517	19,017	23, 129	-	-
Police Grant [(a)]	4,374	4,546	4,224	7,565	7,784
Specific and special grants inside Aggregate External Finance (AEF)	45,750	45,502	41,820	41,760	40,805
Area Based Grant	4,363	-	-	-	-
Local Services Support Grant (LSSG) [(b)]	-	253	223	77	48
General GLA Grant	48	63	50	-	-
Grants outside AEF [(c)]	19,069	18,614	18,850	18,417	18,655
Housing subsidy [(d)]	-494	-704	-791	-795	-692
Grants towards capital expenditure	9,592	8,637	9,739	8,782	9,996
Total grant income	**107,341**	**101,800**	**97,692**	**90,982**	**89,271**
Locally-funded Income:					
Council tax [(e)]	26,254	26,451	26,715	23,371	23,964
Retained Income from Rate Retention Scheme [(a)]	-	-	-	10,719	11,331
External interest receipts	663	860	815	839	865
Capital receipts [(f)]	1,498	2,013	2,124	2,481	2,996
Sales, fees and charges [(g)]	12,597	11,991	12,201	12,695	11,741
Council rents	6,317	6,583	6,916	7,215	7,439
Total locally-funded income	47,328	47,899	48,771	57,319	58,335
Other income and adjustments [(h)]	10,535	9,995	8,842	9,253	18,469
Total income	**165,204**	**159,694**	**155,306**	**157,554**	**166,075**
Grants as a percentage of total income	65%	64%	63%	157,554	54%

Source: Department for Communities and Local Government 2016, p.7.

Notes

Revenue Outturn (RO) returns and Capital Outturn Returns (COR), 2010–11 to 2014–15.
Comparisons across years may not be valid owing to changing local authority responsibilities and methods of funding.

(a) Since 2013–14 there were changes to the Department's Local Government Finance Settlement. This affects the figures for Revenue Support Grant, Police Grant and Non-domestics rates.
(b) From 2011–12, Local Services Support Grant (LSSG), an unringfenced grant paid under section 31 of the Local Government Act 2003, was introduced to support local government functions.
(c) Excludes council tax benefit subsidy and rent rebates granted to HRA tenants.
(d) Housing Subsidy includes Government grants and assistance (including downward adjustments)' less Transfers to the General Fund Revenue Account (GFRA) and Major Repairs Reserve (MRR). These are all recorded in the Housing Revenue Account (HRA) in RO4.

(*continued*)

Table 7.3 Cont.

(e) Includes council taxes financed from Council Tax Benefit Grant but excludes council taxes financed from local authority contributions to council tax benefit.
(f) Capital receipts for 2011–12 exclude the One-off HRA self-financing determination & premium.
(g) Since 2014–15, Sales, Fees and Charges from the Trading account are no longer recorded. For 2014–15 onwards this figure excludes any sales, fees and charges from the trading account.
(h) Other income and adjustments include Other Income from the Services areas, Other Items (surpluses/deficits from the collection fund), Inter-authority reorganization recoupment, lease-holder charges and other contributions toward expenditure in the Housing Revenue Account. Prior to 2014–15 this also included other income in the Trading Accounts; this was not recorded for 2014–15 onwards.

To avoid double counting, levies and recharges from other accounts recorded in the RO6 are removed from this. Before 2014–15, receipts from other authorities were also excluded but this figure is no longer regularly collected as part of the SAR return.

Table 7.4 Local Council Tax Bands and Charges in Bristol, United Kingdom, 2020–2021 Each Property in Bristol is in one of these council tax bands

Council tax band	*Property value range*	*Property value charge*
A	Up to and including €40,000	€1,374.01
B	€40,001 – €52,000	€1,603.04
C	€52,001 – €68,000	€1,832.02
D	€68,001 – €88,000	€2,061.03
E	€88,001 – €120,000	€2,519.04
F	€120,001 – €160,000	€2,977.05
G	€160,001 – €320,000	€3,435.04
H	Over €320,000	€4,122.04

Source: www.bristol.gov.uk/council-tax/council-tax-charges-and-bands; visited on 30 March 2020.

Note
In England, these bands have been based on their value on 1 April 1991.

7.4.3 A Necessary Step for the PRC

The reason that a property-based local tax system is more socially equitable than a poll tax is that it recognizes the differences in people's ability to pay, and in the level of benefits that the spending of the tax will bring to people of different levels of property. One would typically expect that the more property a person has, the more that benefits of spending the tax are likely to accrue to him/her, and the more able s/he will be able to pay the tax.

In the case of the PRC, differences in the level of property which people own in a given locality have become enormous, and these differences are further accentuated each time the local real estate price rises. It would seem only socially fair, and, enforcement-wise, more effective, to make those who own more local properties to pay more tax towards local government revenue.

A form of property tax has existed in the PRC since 1986, but only in respect of non-domestic buildings. The question facing the government and the tax authority in the PRC today is whether, when, and how to levy a similar tax on domestic dwellings. Discussions and debates over the issues have gone on throughout the last decade, and city-level experiments have been conducted in Shanghai and Chongqing. Yet there has been no firm decision on nationwide implementation from the government. Much opposition has come from the better-propertied sections of the population, and it is not clear when the government will eventually take the decisive step. It is likely that this dithering will continue for a while, but eventually the government will have to take the inevitable step.

7.5 Conclusion

An emerging consensus in theoretical and policy analysis of development recognizes that investment in physical infrastructures can play a critical and catalytic role in promoting economic development. Large-scale historical and present-day physical infrastructural investments have, in fact, often been financed locally, through local public financing. This has certainly been true in the PRC. This chapter discusses and compares three contrasting models of local public financing for infrastructural investments in the country, ranging from the most radical to the mainstream. The first came from the country's recent past and was premised on the former agricultural collectives, while the second has been on-going and is centered on the leasing of land, which is still all publicly owned across the country. The third one is not yet in wide practice but is expected to gain importance in the future.

The PRC's local governments, at various levels, played an extremely important role in driving forward the country's rapid economic development. Indeed, most of the country's impressive recent economic progress, whether in the form of rapid industrialization, radical modernization of its physical infrastructures such as the road and rail systems, water and waterway management, and agricultural infrastructures including irrigations and farmland consolidation, and speedy development of public utilities such as electricity and information technology, as well as fast urbanization—all owe much of their dynamism to the country's local governments. Naturally, these local governments were able to play such a critical role only because they were able to mobilize the necessary resources, and were also able, broadly speaking, to use these resources effectively to benefit local development. A principal way to mobilize such resources has been through local public financing.

Taking the country as a whole, the PRC's local public financing model has thus far undergone two distinct phases: the early dependence on the collective model, and the subsequent reliance on land financing. Both provided huge amounts of resources at the hands of the PRC's local government—in addition to those standard sources which a typical local government from any other country would have access to. In a real sense, these additional resources provided a critical extra engine of growth for the PRC, which would help explain the country's extraordinarily rapid growth in recent times.

This change-over from the early dependence on the collective model to subsequent reliance on land financing was entirely due a fundamental change in the larger social and economic institutions of the country—it is this larger change that conditioned the evolution of the PRC's local public financing model. Judging by all the signs, quite imminently, the PRC's model of local public financing will undergo yet another major change, to one that principally relies on property taxes. Will this remove the "extra engine" of growth that has benefited the PRC so much, and slow down its growth? It remains to be seen.

Notes

1 The author wishes to thank two anonymous referees for their detailed helpful comments. All remaining errors are the author's responsibility.
2 Bateman (2017) provides a good coverage of the current thinking behind the concept of a "local development state," with extensive references.
3 See Minquan Liu, "Work Incentives and Labour Allocation on China's Communes," D.Phil. thesis, University of Oxford 1991, for a fuller account of the three-tier structure and other features of the commune system in PRC in the 1960s–1970s, and their implication.
4 For a fuller account of the workpoint payment system and its incentive effects, see Liu (1994a).
5 See Liu (1994b, 2002, 2015) and the references therein.
6 See Riskin (1973) and the references therein.
7 See Liu (1994a) and the references therein.
8 While not part of the subject matter of this study, it is worth pointing out that the local public financing model in use at the time was also responsible for funding most of rural social sector investments (certainly those at the brigade and team levels), including building and running most rural schools and health clinics, and remunerating some of the rural teachers and doctors (in workpoints). It also provided some basic level of social protection for the needy. See Table 7.1 for more detail.
9 As a system of accounting for each member's labor contribution to the team, i.e., when all members pooled their labor, workpoints became obsolete when team work collapsed. With its disappearance went the financing mechanism for infrastructural investment characteristic of the collective period.
10 Many other countries have, of course, faced much greater challenges in land acquisition for their public investments. See, for example, some of the country reports in this study.
11 On the scale of urban build-up in recent years in PRC, see Ye et al. (2014). Subsequently, there also emerged what has been known as local government financing vehicles (LGFVs) responsible for much of the PRC's local government debt, using land as collateral. We will discuss LGFVs later.
12 Principally among local governments' spending responsibilities are spending on health, education, various social protection schemes, central government approved infrastructure projects, and other projects and programs.
13 A provision existed in the new fiscal system, under which the central government would transfer back part of its revenue to local governments to help them meet their spending needs. However, this happened usually on a project-by-project or

program-by-program (i.e., earmarked) basis. Non-earmarked central–local transfers do exist but have usually been very limited in scale. In either case, these transfers can only be secured after intense negotiations with the central government. All in all, the transfers in question did nothing to significantly reverse the imbalance (see the faint dotted line in Figure 3).

14 For higher land prices to be sustainable, house prices would of course also have to rise correspondingly, as real estate developers would otherwise not be able to reap any profit.

15 In 2004, the China Daily wrote: "China's Ministry of Lands and Resources announced new measures to crack down on corruption and inefficiency in the land sector… . It is estimated that in 2003, the country faced 168,000 violations of its Land Law." Quoted from Cai et al. (2009), p.2.

16 It needs to be pointed out, however, that although the introduction of the *zhaopaiguo* mechanism did limit the extent of land lease-related corruption, it did not entirely stamp it out. See Cai et al. (2009).

17 See Jin and Rial (2016) for some recent estimates and analyses.

18 See the Provisional Regulations of the People's Republic of China on Real Estate Tax, issued by the State Council and effective from 1 October 1986, available on www.lawinfochina.com/display.aspx?lib=law&id=1269&CGid=, visited on 20 October 2020.

19 A Baidu search (https://baike.baidu.com/item/%E6%88%BF%E4%BA%A7%E7%A8%8E) could provide much further information on the planned tax and its delayed rollout in the country over time.

20 PRC Global Net, "CASS Forecasts of 1.6 Trillion CNY Tax Income on Domestic Dwellings," 15 December 2015, Beijing. https://china.huanqiu.com/article/9CaKrnJSjm0, visited on 13 September 2020.

References

Bateman, M. 2017. *Bringing the Local State Back into Development: The 'Local Developmental State' and the Promotion of Sustainable Economic Development and Growth from the Bottom-Up.* Paper presented at the 29th Annual Conference of the European Association for Evolutionary Political Economy (EAEPE), Corvinus University of Budapest, Budapest, Hungary 19–21 October.

Cai, H., J.V. Henderson, Q. Zhang 2009. China's Land Market Auctions: Evidence of corruption, NBER Working Paper Series 15067. Cambridge, MA: National Bureau of Economic Research.

Gerschenkron, A. 1962. *Economic Backwardness in Historical Perspective: A Book of Essays.* Cambridge, MA: Belknap Press of Harvard University Press.

Huang, Z. 2016. *Enhancing Responsibility of Local Government Borrowings in the PRC.* Master's Dissertation. Cambridge, MA: Harvard Kennedy School.

Jin, H. and I. Rial 2016. *Regulating Local Government Financing Vehicles and Public-Private Partnerships in the PRC.* IMF Working Paper WP/16/187. Washington, DC: IMF.

Liu, M. 1994a. Work Incentives on China's Communes: A Dichotomy. *Journal of International Trade and Economic Development* 3(2): 103–128.

Liu, M. 1994b. Commune, Responsibility System, and China's Agriculture, in *China's Economic Reform: The Costs and Benefits of Incrementalism,* edited by P. Nolan and Q. Fan (eds.), 104–136. London: Macmillan Press.

Liu, M. 2002. Sustained Agricultural Growth and Economic Structural Change (in Chinese), *China Economic Quarterly* 1 (2): 455–484.

Liu, M. 2011. *Understanding the Pattern of Growth and Equity in the People's Republic of China*. ADBI Working Paper Series No. 331. Tokyo: Asian Development Bank Institute.

Liu, M. 2015. Objectively Assessing the Achievements and Failures of the Rural Commune System. *Open Times* 2015 (1) (in Chinese).

Liu, M. and B. Sun. 2009. Land Price Formation, Real Estate Bubbles, and Policy Responses. *Journal of Financial Research* 2009 (10): 22–37 (in Chinese).

Lu, Y. and T. Sun. 2013. *Local Government Financing Platforms in the PRC: A Fortune or Misfortune*. IMF Working Paper WP/13/243. Washington, DC: IMF.

Oi, J. 1995. The Role of the Local State in China's Transitional Economy, *The China Quarterly* 144: 1132–1149.

Ouattara, B., and Y.-F. Zhang. 2019. Infrastructure and Long-Run Economic Growth: Evidence from Chinese Provinces. *Empirical Economics* 57: 263–284.

Riskin, C. 1973. Maoism and Motivation: Work Incentives in China, *Bulletin of Concerned Asian Scholars* 5(1): 10–24.

Sahoo, P., R.K. Dash, and G. Nataraj. 2012. China's Growth Story: The Role Of Physical And Social Infrastructure, *Journal of Economic Development* 37(1): 53–75.

UK Department for Communities and Local Government. 2016. Local Government Financial Statistics England, No.26, London. https://assets.publishing.service.gov.uk/government/uploads/system/uploads/attachment_data/file/539179/2905557_LGF_Accessible.pdf (accessed 25 June 2021).

Wade, R. 1990. *Governing the Market: Economic Theory and the Role of Government in East Asian Industrialization*. Princeton: Princeton University Press.

Wong, C. 2011. The Fiscal Stimulus Program and Problems of Macroeconomic Management in China. 32nd Annual Meeting of OECD Senior Budget Officials, Luxembourg, 6–7 June.

World Bank. 1994. *World Development Report 1994: Infrastructure for Development*. New York: Oxford University Press.

Wu, Z., M. Liu, and J. Davis. 2005. Land Consolidation and Productivity in Chinese Household Crop Production, *Chinese Economic Review* 16(1): 28–49.

Ye, L. and A.M. Wu. 2014. Urbanization, Land Development, and Land Financing: Evidence from Chinese Cities, *Journal of Urban Affairs* 36(1): 1–15.

8 Impacts of the Patterns of Financing on Logistic Infrastructure in CAREC Member Countries

Muhammad Ayub Mehar

8.1 Introduction and Scope of the Study

The role of sustainable infrastructure development in economic growth is strongly supported by economic theory. Infrastructure can generate a variety of economic activities in construction, utility services, chemicals, cement, steel, banking, transportation, energy, agriculture, and services; however, its main role is to catalyze development of other sectors. There are several examples in the literature that explain how development of various kinds of infrastructure improves household income, employment, and living standards. A study carried out in Pakistan by the World Bank concluded that per capita income (PCI) at purchasing power parity is improved by sustainable infrastructure development (World Bank 2017). According to this study, spending PRs1 billion ($600 million) on roads can permanently increase PCI by PRs371 ($2.30). This mechanism is stronger than subsidies and transfer payments because it provides a sustainable poverty elimination solution.

The linkages between economic growth and infrastructure in the context of developing countries have been established by various studies, some of which have explained how various types of infrastructure affect gross domestic product (GDP). The direction of causality was tested in those studies (Mehar 2020). Hussain and Zhang (2018) estimated that net annual income loss from lack of reliable access to electricity for households in Pakistan is $4.5 billion, about 1.7% of GDP.

The impact of various types of infrastructure (i.e., provision of electricity, road transport, railways, and water and sanitation) on the growth of per capita income has been estimated by the World Economic Forum (2012) and the Organisation for Economic Co-operation and Development (2012). Mehar (2018) has ascertained a causal relation between deterioration in infrastructure and the level of poverty. The World Bank (2017) and the Organisation for Economic Co-operation and Development (2012) have also estimated the required investment in infrastructure to achieve the United Nations' Sustainable Development Goals (SDGs) targets. Lack of sustainable infrastructure, declining business activities, lack of competitiveness, lower rate of growth, and economic distresses are the

DOI: 10.4324/9781003228790-10

interconnected variables. Government institutions are undercut by insufficient tax collection and low economic growth, leading to the common phenomenon of cutbacks in investment in public sector infrastructure.

The required investment for sustainable infrastructure development has been estimated by various studies. According to the Asian Development Bank, developing Asia will need US$1.5 trillion per year in infrastructure through 2030 to maintain its economic growth momentum and tackle poverty (Asian Development Bank 2017). Total infrastructure financing as a percentage of GDP should increase from around 3.8% to 5.6% by 2020 worldwide. In this scenario, declining government expenditures and the negligible role of the private sector in infrastructure development indicates an alarming situation.

Hussain and Zhang (2018), Inderst (2018), and Mehar (2017) have discussed the determinants of sustainable infrastructure and their relation to income. The role and determinants of various types of infrastructure have also been examined by Yoshino, Helble, and Abidhadjaev (2018) and the World Bank (2017).

According to the Asian Development Bank (2017), developing Asia will need $26 trillion in infrastructure investment over the next decade to maintain growth, which includes $14.7 trillion for power, $8.4 trillion for transport, $2.3 trillion for telecommunications, and $800 billion for water and sanitation. In the present global financial environment, with the world facing the COVID-19 pandemic and complexity in prevailing financial markets and instruments, there is a need for innovative measures to attract private sector capital to the region's infrastructure financing shortfall. Improved public-private participation (PPP), financial guarantees, and utilizing spillover tax revenues are possible ways to finance infrastructure in Asian countries. Investment banks, venture capital companies, insurance companies, and pension fund management companies also may provide the long-term funding for large-scale infrastructure projects. By contrast, commercial banks and money market instruments, which are considered a means of financing for working capital to manage liquidity, are not suitable for long-term projects.

Despite its importance, spending on sustainable infrastructure has become the lowest priority in developing countries. Most governments in those countries have prioritized their recurring expenditures such as general administration, law and order, defense, and debt servicing. Because existing hard infrastructure goes unmaintained, these countries face limited energy supplies, water shortages, damaged sanitation systems, and outdated transportation. This harms business competitiveness rankings, resulting in a situation where industries cannot utilize their available production capacity. Thus, weak, hard infrastructure becomes the primary cause of lower GDP and PCI in those countries.

The private sector investment can improve the physical infrastructure, it is obvious that inducing private sector investment—foreign and domestic—requires visible improvement in public goods infrastructure. However, the lack of sufficient funds for the infrastructure development is the problematic area, which is the basic concern of this study. The core objective of this study is to determine the financial options to develop the logistic infrastructure in Central Asian Regional Economic Cooperation (CAREC) member countries.

Table 8.1 Annual Required Global Investment in Infrastructure, 2016–2040

Type of Infrastructure	*Required ($ billion at 2015 prices)*	*Required (% of GDP)*	*Current Trend (% of GDP)*
Road	7.2	1.30	0.90
Rails	0.2	0.09	0.08
Airports	0.4	0.10	0.05
Ports	0.3	0.10	0.02
Telecom	6.1	1.10	0.85
Electricity	2.4	0.40	0.30
Water	2.6	0.50	0.25

Source: GI-Hub/Oxford Economics (2016).

Note
GDP = gross domestic product.

Table 8.2 Cumulative Global Infrastructure Investment (in $ billion, 2015 prices)

Type of Infrastructure	*Current Trend (2016–40)*	*Requirement (2016–40)*	*Gap (2016–40)*	*SDG Requirement (2016–30)*
Road	137	180	43	--
Rails	5	5	0	--
Airports	6	9	3	--
Ports	3	9	6	--
Telecom	116	153	37	--
Electricity	50	59	9	137
Water	39	64	26	28
Total:	**356**	**479**	**124**	--

Source: GI-Hub/ Oxford Economics (2016).

Note
SDG = Sustainable Development Goal.

One of the objectives of this study is to identify the most effective mode of financing sustainable logistics infrastructure development. It is hypothesized that, since the political and economic history of the Central Asian Regional Economic Cooperation member countries plays an important role in the determination of their infrastructure financing, private sector financing will differ as compared to the West. To determine the factors of infrastructure development, this study is limited to the magnitude and quality of logistic infrastructure only. The study also tests the effects of the quality and magnitude of logistic infrastructure on economic development. For this purpose, economic development has been defined by PCI.

The study has been divided into seven sections. The next section discusses the global financing patterns for sustainable infrastructure development. It indicates how public and private sectors are contributing to infrastructure-related development. Section 8.3 discusses the various modes of private sector financing and their effectiveness for infrastructure development. It also describes some innovative modes for private sector investment inducement. The impacts of the various modes of financing on logistic infrastructure and its role in economic development will be analyzed in sections 8.4 and 8.5. The results of estimated equations have been explained in section 8.6, while section 8.7 discusses the conclusions and policy recommendations.

8.2 Changing in Global Patterns of Infrastructure Financing

Development projects in low- and middle-income countries have typically been associated with supply-side constraints. The nature and size of the infrastructure projects were determined by grants from international financial institutions and advanced countries, and long-term public sector debts. Even within the countries, it is common practice that the development funds are distributed on the basis of regional or political sharing formulas. Even today, the use of development funds in developing countries is not based on demand-derived mechanisms, but rather to enhance the vote banks of ruling parties or to show developmental activities in the region or to compete with neighboring countries. Even some projects in those countries are launched only for entertainment purposes. It is obvious that such decisions are not based on economic feasibility (Mehar 2020). Such macro-financing activities may negatively affect the patterns of public expenditures and debt burdens, while higher taxes may be required. All such expenditures are considered over-investment in infrastructure development, as when, for example, the size of a project is larger than required. Such over-investments inflate the cost of capital, which will negatively affect the national income.

Another dimension of the excessive use of public financing is the borrowing from commercial banks to finance the development activities. No doubt, this is an easy option for the government, and, from the bankers' point of view, it provides a handsome, risk-free rate of return. These infrastructure projects provide economic benefits to some people and commercial organizations, but the higher burden of external debts which were not utilized for creating the earning assets leads to deficits. The result is that private investment becomes the only option to develop costly infrastructure (Mehar 2021). The diversion of the inflow of FDI is a possible alternative means to develop sustainable infrastructure, as are equity participation infrastructure bonds. A combination of these options is usually applied for infrastructure-related projects.

Based on long-term trends (comparison from 1995 to 2017), a growth in investment in infrastructure projects with PPP can be observed worldwide (World Bank 2017). The private sector participates in energy, transportation and water and sanitation sectors in developing countries, as in high-income countries, and the telecommunications sector has been deregulated all over the world. During 2012–2017, the decline in government support to infrastructure projects correlated with the decline in investment levels. The growth of investment in

2017 indicates the significance of government support in encouraging private participation in infrastructure development projects. Capital and revenue subsidies, free land, various kinds of contingent liabilities, government liabilities that directly cover project costs (either in cash or in kind) and guarantees (such as the exchange rate, payment, revenue, debt, and tax breaks etc.) are included in the government support.

However, in 2017, a declining trend in private sector investment was observed. According to the World Bank (2017), the magnitude of private investment commitments in energy, transport, telecommunications, and water infrastructure in low- and middle-income countries was US$93.3 billion in 2017, which was the second-lowest level of investment in the previous 10 years, and 15% below the average for the previous five years. The increase over 2016 levels can be attributed to a few megaprojects in the People's Republic of China (PRC) like the Belt and Road Initiative, and in Indonesia, as well as a recovery in South Asia, led by Pakistan. The PRC received US$17.5 billion, Indonesia US$15.4 billion, Mexico US$8.6 billion, Brazil US$7.3 billion, and Pakistan US$5.9 billion (World Bank 2017). These five countries attracted US$54.5 billion, which was 58% of global investment in 2017. The share of commercial financing was 63% in Mexico, 23% in Indonesia, 7% in Pakistan, and 4% in Brazil, while PRC projects are known to be mostly publicly financed. It is notable that debt was the most popular source of financing in 2017. The share of debt financing in infrastructure projects with private participation was 70%, while 26% came from equities and 4% in the form of public subsidies. Out of 26% equities, 23% was from the private sector and 3% from the public sector. The 70% debt financing was divided between international and local (commercial) participants: 55% financed by international and 15% by local participants. Out of the 55% international debt financing, 30% belongs to development finance institutions (DFIs) (6% multilateral and 24% bilateral). Of non-DFI debt financing, 18% was contributed by the public sector and the remaining from the private (commercial) sector. This shows how long-term private sector debt is the main source of infrastructure financing, though it has been previously discussed that the share of short-term financing is declining globally.

The patterns of public and private financing, logistics infrastructure and economic development are summarized in Tables 8.3 to 8.5. The tables also reflect the contribution of various types of debt in public and private sector financing.

8.3 Unlocking Private Investment in Sustainable Infrastructure Financing: Innovations and Strategies

Michael (2018) has described several options for financing infrastructure projects. These include the following:

- reordering budget appropriations;
- raising taxes;
- privatization;
- initial public offerings (IPOs);

Table 8.3 Logistic Infrastructure and Economic Development

Country/ Region/ Group	*GDP Per Capita ($)*	*Exports ($ billion)*	*Transport & Trade Related Logistic Index (1 to 5; 5 is best)*	*Investment in Transport Infrastructure with Private Participation ($ billion)*
2007				
Afghanistan	366	.	1.10	
Azerbaijan		22.4	2.00	
PRC	2,695	1,257.1	3.20	4.49
Georgia	2,635	3.2		0.06
Kazakhstan	6,771	51.8	1.86	0.03
Kyrgyz Republic	722	2.0	2.06	
Mongolia	1,634	2.5	1.92	
Pakistan	950	21.9	2.37	0.58
Tajikistan	520	1.7	2.00	
Turkmenistan	2,600			
Uzbekistan	830		2.00	
For Comparison				
Low-Income Countries	501	81.9	1.98	
Middle-Income Countries	2,826	4,339.6	2.30	27.88
High-Income Countries	37,287	12,981.3	3.41	
European Union	35,602	6,755.0	3.34	
World	8,674	17,396.3	2.58	
2016				
Afghanistan	550	1.1	1.84	
Azerbaijan	3,881	17.6		
PRC	8,117	2,197.9	3.75	3.47
Georgia	3,857	6.2	2.17	
Kazakhstan	7,715	43.6	2.76	
Kyrgyz Republic	1,121	2.4	1.96	
Mongolia	3,695	5.6	2.05	
Pakistan	1,442	26.8	2.70	
Tajikistan	796	0.9	2.13	
Turkmenistan	6,389		2.34	
Uzbekistan	2,118		2.45	
For Comparison				
Low-Income Countries	758	115.5	2.14	
Middle-Income Countries	4,775	5,978.0	2.46	21.25
High-Income Countries	39,791	14,777.1	3.54	
European Union	32,367	7,279.6	3.56	
World	10,229	20,868.0	2.75	

Source: World Bank, World Development Indicators (Various Issues).

Note
PRC = People's Republic of China, GDP = gross domestic product.

Table 8.4 Domestic and External Leverage Financing

Country/ Region/ Group	*Domestic Credit to Private Sector (% of GDP)*	*Total Outstanding Debt ($ billion)*	*Public Sector Long-term Debt ($ billion)*	*Private Sector Long-term Debt ($ billion)*	*Short-term Debt (% of Total Outstanding Debt)*
2007					
Afghanistan	6.8	2.0	1.9	0.0	1.07
Azerbaijan	14.4	3.9	2.3		28.99
PRC	105.7	373.5	86.9	82.5	54.54
Georgia	27.9	3.0	1.6	0.2	22.22
Kazakhstan	58.9	96.2	1.7	82.5	11.98
Kyrgyz Republic	6.4	2.9	1.9	0.4	11.09
Mongolia	41.6	1.7	1.6	0.0	3.34
Pakistan	27.8	42.0	36.9	1.2	5.30
Tajikistan	13.2	1.3	1.1	0.0	5.37
Turkmenistan		0.9	0.6	0.0	10.74
Uzbekistan		4.7	3.2	0.9	4.26
For Comparison					
Low-Income Countries	12.6	77.1	62.1	1.1	13.43
Middle-Income Countries	59.7	3,014.9	1,178.0	1,082.8	23.81
2016					
Afghanistan	3.6	2.4	1.9	2.36	8.48
Azerbaijan	32.9	15.0	11.0	442.27	9.73
PRC	156.8	1,415.8	162.7	7.44	56.60
Georgia	61.9	15.8	5.7	134.87	14.88
Kazakhstan	33.0	163.7	21.4	3.66	4.25
Kyrgyz Republic	20.6	7.9	3.6	17.97	4.43
Mongolia	56.9	25.7	5.1	6.15	10.06
Pakistan	16.5	72.2	51.6	1.98	9.87
Tajikistan	19.2	5.3	2.3	0.03	15.35
Turkmenistan		0.5	0.2		29.64
Uzbekistan		16.3	7.4	0.00	2.13
For Comparison					
Low-Income Countries	20.7	139.9	109.1	10.3	8.19
Middle-Income Countries	99.2	6,295.0	2,233.3	2,431.7	24.28

Source: World Bank, World Development Indicators (Various Issues).

Note
The World and High-Income Countries average of domestic credit to private sector as a percentage of GDP is always greater than 100.

PRC = People's Republic of China, GDP = gross domestic product.

Table 8.5 External Financing by Market Mechanism

Country/ Region/ Group	*Bonds Issued by Private Sector, Non-Guaranteed ($ billion)*	*Bonds (Amount Disbursed) by Private Sector, Non-Guaranteed ($ billion)*	*Bonds Issued by Public Sector, Guaranteed ($ billion)*	*Bonds (Amount Disbursed) by Public Sector, Guaranteed ($ billion)*	*Net Inflow of Foreign Direct Investment (FDI) ($ billion)*
2007					
Afghanistan	0.0	0.0	0.0	0.0	
Azerbaijan	0.0	0.0	0.0	0.0	5.0
PRC	0.0	0.7	0.0	1.5	-139.1
Georgia	0.0	0.0	0.0	0.0	-1.7
Kazakhstan	0.4	11.0	0.4	0.0	-8.0
Kyrgyz Republic	0.0	0.0	0.0	0.0	-0.2
Mongolia	0.0	0.0	0.0	0.1	-0.4
Pakistan	0.0	0.0	0.0	0.8	-5.5
Tajikistan	0.0	0.0	0.0	0.0	-0.4
Turkmenistan	0.0	0.0	0.0	0.0	
Uzbekistan	0.0	0.0	0.0	0.0	
For Comparison					
Low-Income Countries	0.0	0.0	0.0	0.0	
Middle-Income Countries	16.6	59.6	40.5	64.4	
2016					
Afghanistan	0.0	0.0	0.0	0.0	-0.1
Azerbaijan	0.0	0.0	0.0	1.0	-1.9
PRC	0.0	27.6	6.9	9.5	41.7
Georgia	7.9	0.4	0.0	0.3	-1.2
Kazakhstan	0.10	1.0	0.0	0.0	-13.4
Kyrgyz Republic	1.5	0.0	0.0	0.0	-0.6
Mongolia	0.0	0.0	0.0	0.5	4.2
Pakistan	0.0	0.0	0.5	1.0	-2.4
Tajikistan	0.0	0.0	0.0	0.0	-0.2
Turkmenistan	0.0	0.0	0.0	0.0	
Uzbekistan	0.0	0.0	0.0	0.0	
For Comparison					
Low-Income Countries	0.0	0.0	0.0	0.0	
Middle-Income Countries	53.7	76.2	56.9	119.8	

Source: World Bank, World Development Indicators (Various Issues).

Note

PRC = People's Republic of China.

- capital recycling of brownfield assets;
- public borrowings and budget deficits;
- tax exempted bonds;
- green bonds for sustainable infrastructure;
- revenue bonds;
- municipal bonds;
- government enterprises;
- bank borrowing;
- corporate bonds;
- use of pension funds;
- loans from multilateral agencies;
- international banks securitization; and
- public-private partnerships.

Michael examined these options in the context of post-2008 market conditions, when global infrastructure financing was experiencing difficulties. Such innovative modes of financing for infrastructure have been used in the past. However, Yoshino, Helble, and Abidhadjaev (2018) have noted that many daunting engineering works have been successfully completed by relying upon imaginative and innovative approaches to attract private finance to projects for the greater public good. The first transcontinental railroads across North America, the US Highway Trust Fund, the Suez Canal, and the Tokyo Metropolitan Rail Network are the successful projects that had innovative infrastructure financing methods.

It is obvious that more prudence is required in decision making regarding infrastructure financing. The variations in the prices of goods and services produced by supporting industries (steel, wood, construction materials, electricity, gas, water and other utilities, banking, insurance, and other overheads) may disturb the initial estimates. Higher initial cash outflows, longer projects, high political uncertainty, and barriers to exit are factors that clearly distinguish infrastructure from other types of business ventures. As a result, the demand for a higher return on investment or internal rate of return is a natural condition for infrastructure. Freeriding, particularly in construction of highways and land development, is another type of infrastructure investment risk. Some beneficiaries, including residents, commercial enterprises, and transporters in the neighboring areas of such development projects, do not contribute to the cost of these projects. Here, government support is required to ensure the participation of all beneficiaries through additional taxes, user charges, and fees. This is one of the main reasons that public finance is always required in infrastructure development despite the role of private investment.

There are several requirements for government support in the financing of PPP projects, some which will be discussed here:

- Funded products: Government support through cash or kind (land, assets, and major maintenance), subsidies, grants, equity participation and debt constitute funded products. Such products are useful if some specific risks are not manageable by the private investors or lenders. Without government support, such risks may affect the bankability or financial viability of the projects. Some payments which are usually paid by the private sector companies to the public sector entities are waived, which is an example of the funded products. Similarly, the loans (including mezzanine debt) or equity investment (including viability gap funding) are also included in these funded projects. The incremental tariffs that will be paid by the beneficiaries of the projects (in water and electricity, etc.) are also included in funded products.

- Contingent products: Several instruments are included in this category. The hedging of risk due to weather, currency exchange rates, interest rates or commodity pricing is one of its sub-categories. The provision of a contingent debt when required is also included in this category. To provide guarantees for a certain exchange rate, convertibility of local currency, a certain rate of interest, purchaser obligations, rate of tariff, rate and level of demand for services, termination compensation, and indemnities against non-payment by state entities are also included. (World Bank Legal Resource Center 2018).
- Financial intermediaries: As defined by the World Bank (2018), this implies the intermediation of debt from commercial financial markets by creating an intermediary. In this case, the government uses its support to mobilize private financing from local financial markets. Otherwise, financing cannot be available for infrastructure projects for several reasons. Lack of experience and risk management are included in these reasons.
- Project development funds: In this category, the government establishes an independent fund for the cost of advisers and other related costs of the project. For instance, the cost of documentation, standardization, monitoring of the implementation, preparing of feasibility studies and designing the financial and commercial structure for the project are paid from the project development fund.

According to Mehar (2021), PPP infrastructure can be financed through several mechanisms. One of the most important is government funding through national or subnational budgets. The other option is corporate financing, which is also known as on-balance-sheet financing. In this case, it is financed by the companies' debt and equity. This option depends on the opportunity costs of other available alternative projects. The third option is project financing, which creates a special purpose vehicle (SPV). The SPV is based on the revenues and earnings after completion of the project. This mechanism is considered the most efficient, and also the most common, method to finance the large projects. However, it is risky because lenders require extensive due diligence on potential viability and bankability of the projects. It is a good characteristic of this mechanism that it ensures that public money will not be used in unviable projects because the SPV company will be responsible for collecting money from the users.

Another benefit of project financing is that it allows off-balance-sheet financing. This implies that leverage position of the shareholders or the government contracting authority will not be adversely affected. Obviously, some of the project risk is shifted to the lenders in this way. As a result, lenders require a relatively higher return than normal on lending. The impact on the cost of capital is also reduced through off-balance-sheet financing, while the shareholders can use their equity for other ventures. However, this treatment requires careful application of international financial reporting standards and accountancy rules. In fact, such a mechanism does not reduce actual liabilities. If the SPV fails to pay the required payments, the lenders will then have recourse to the assets and revenue of the shareholders, with no limitation. The several key issues are involved in the project financing agreements. The certainty of revenue stream, financial ratios, and covenants (debt-equity ratio,[1] loan life cover ratio,[2] debt service cover ratio,[3] rate of return,[4] weighted average cost of capital[5]), lender protection (including warranties and undertakings, step-in rights, direct agreements and taking security), and compensation on termination are included in these key issues. These issues are covered in the agreements and compliance with the laws and lands and legal system (Mehar 2021).

Domestic and foreign commercial banks, bond markets, equity markets, export credit agencies, and DFIs are the investors of infrastructure projects. If equity shares are issued particularly for infrastructure projects, these are known as an infrastructure fund that provides mezzanine financing, taking more risk than traditional lenders, but less than the sponsors. Bilateral agencies and multilateral development banks are some of the infrastructure investors. The "sovereign wealth fund" is another important category of investment, which allows the exports of surplus savings or capital to other countries. These state-owned funds are created when governments have budgetary surplus and have little or no international debt. The state-owned properties, precious metals, financial assets (stocks and bonds) and other financial instruments are included in these investable funds.

The nexus of contracts among the various types of investors governs the patterns of financing and distribution of the yield of the projects. Inter-creditor agreements, syndication, mezzanine financing and subordinated financing are the important ingredients in the project financing. The distribution of yield depends on the initial contracts; however, it is related to the level of risk associated with the various types of investment. To minimize the risks, some supports are provided to the sponsors. Market price purchase guarantees (to purchase a minimum quantity of product at market) for compensating losses due to taxes, technical support (warranties and maintenance arrangements) and contingent equity or subordinated debt commitments are included in these supports.

8.4 Impacts of Private Investment: Alternative Models

It is proposed that the underlying objective of the sustainable logistics infrastructure development is to improve incomes; in this study, PCI in US dollars is the chosen measure. The research is based on an econometric model consisting of four equations. Equation (1) explains the determinants of the magnitude of logistic infrastructure in a country, which has been measured by the capacity of

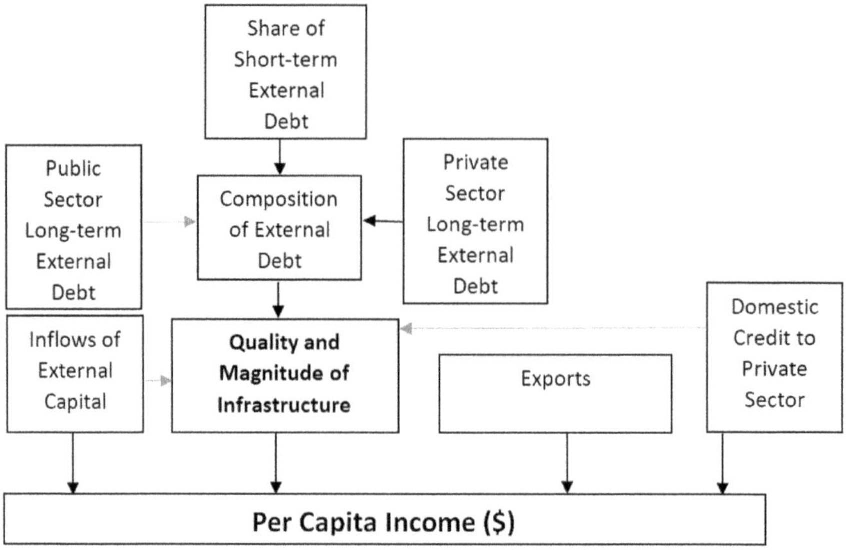

Figure 8.1 Simultaneity in the Model Determinants and Impact of Logistic Infrastructure on Income.

Source: Author.

transport infrastructure; equation (2) measures the quality of logistic infrastructure, which has been measured through the quality of logistics infrastructure indices constructed by the World Bank (2019); and equations (3) and (4) determine the factors of PCI.

Figure 8.1 shows the simultaneity in the model. It explains that how different modes of financing are transformed into logistics infrastructure development and national economy.

8.5 Estimation Techniques

For estimation purposes, the above-mentioned model can be mathematically expressed in the following equations:

$$LGSTALL_{it} = \propto_i + \beta_1 DBTLT_{it} + \beta_2 DBTLTPB_{it} + \beta_3 * DBTLTPV_{it} + \beta_4 BNDPN_{it} + \beta_5 FDI_{it} + \beta_6 DBTST_{it} + \beta_7 DPS_{it} \quad (1)$$

$$LGSQLTY_{it} = \propto_i + \beta_1 DBTLT_{it} + \beta_2 DBTLTPB_{it} + \beta_3 * DBTLTPV_{it} + \beta_4 BNDPN_{it} + \beta_5 FDI_{it} + \beta_6 DBTST_{it} + \beta_7 DPS_{it} \quad (2)$$

$$PCI\$_{it} = \propto_i + \beta_1 DBTTOT_{it} + \beta_2 DCPSGDP_{it} + \beta_3 * DBTST_{it} + \beta_4 LGSTALL_{it} \quad (3)$$

$$PCI\$_{it} = \propto_i + \beta_1 DBTTOT_{it} + \beta_2 DCPSGDP_{it} + \beta_3 * DBTST_{it} + \beta_4 LGSTQLTY_{it} \quad (4)$$

These variables have been described in Table 8.6. To explain the factors of logistic infrastructure development, two alternative models have been established. In the first model, it is hypothesized that the development of logistic infrastructure development (LGSTALL) depends on the various types and components of financing. We included the long-term external debt (DBTLT), long-term external debt to public sector (DBTLTPB), long-term external debt to the private sector (DBTLTPV), bonds issued by the private sector in international markets (BNDPN), foreign direct investment (FDI), share of short-term debt in total external debt (DBTST) and domestic credit to private sector as percentage of

Table 8.6 Technical Glossary

Name of Variable	*Abbreviation*	*Description*
Bonds issued by Private Sector	BNDPN	Bonds issued by private sector in international markets in different currencies. The amount is reported after conversion in US dollars.
CAREC Countries	CAREC	Member countries of Central Asia Regional Economic Cooperation Program
Long-term Debt	DBTLT	External long-term debt stocks in current US dollars
Long-term Public Debt	DBTLTPB	External public and publicly guaranteed debt stock in current US dollars
Long-term Private Debt	DBTLTPV	External private nonguaranteed debt stock in current US dollars
Short-term Debt	DBTST	External short-term debt stocks in current US dollars
Total External Debt	DBTTOT	Total external debt stocks (all kind of debts) in current US dollars
Domestic Credit to Private Sector	DCPS	Domestic credit to private sector equivalence in US dollars
Domestic Credit as % of gross domestic product	DCPSGDP	Domestic credit to private sector (% of gross domestic product)
Exports	EXPR	Exports of goods and services in current US dollars
Net Foreign Direct Investment	FDI$	Net foreign direct investment in current US dollars
Inflow of Foreign Direct Investment	FDIINF	Net Inflow of foreign direct investment in current US dollars
Logistic Index	LGSTALL	Logistics performance index: Overall (1=low to 5=high)
Logistic Quality Index	LGSTQLTY	Logistics performance index: Competence and quality of logistics services (1=low to 5= high)
Per Capita Income	PCI$	GDP per capita (current US dollars)

Source: Author.

GDP (DCPS) as explanatory variables to explain the LGSTALL. To measure the quality and capacity of transport infrastructure we applied the logistic infrastructure index constructed by World Bank (2019). This index ranged from 1 to 5, with "1" indicating the lowest and "5" the highest quality of logistic infrastructure. The second model explains the causal factors of the quality of logistic infrastructure (LGSTQLTY) and the same explanatory variables have been included in the second model.

Equation (4) identifies the determinants of the per capita income based on the quality of logistic infrastructure (LGSTQLTY). To determine the per capita income of a country (PCI$), we included the foreign direct investment (FDI) in billion US dollars, domestic credit to private sector (DCPS) as percentage of GDP, share of short-term debt (DBTST) as percentage of total external debt and logistic infrastructure index (LGSTALL) as explanatory variables.

To measure the specific effects of the CAREC member countries on logistic infrastructure development, we introduced a dummy variable in the first and second equations, which is equal to "1" if country belong to CAREC and "0" otherwise.

For this study, we extracted the data from the World Development Indicators' Data Bank (World Bank 2019). The data consist of 219 countries for nine years (from 2007 to 2016). The last two years (2017 and 2018) could not be included in the model because of data unavailability on some indicators included in the analysis. It provides 2,190 observations. However, data were not consistent for some countries and some observations were missing for some years. As a result, an unbalanced panel least square (PLS) technique to estimate the parameters was applied.

8.6 Estimated Results

Tables 8.7, 8.8, 8.9, and 8.10 present the regression analysis results. The impacts of explanatory variables have been measured by the estimated parameters. The robustness of estimated parameters has also been shown in these tables. The effects of explanatory variables have been estimated through the PLS techniques. It has been shown in the results that parameters are statistically significant. The models show overall fitness of good. Some control variables in the regression analysis have been introduced in the model for falsification tests. There are some surprising results, which are counterintuitive.

It is concluded that external debt to public sector (DBTPB) is a significant determinant of the magnitude and quality of the logistic infrastructure (LGSTALL and LGSTQLTY), while the share of short-term debt in total external debt also affects the logistic infrastructure positively. The positive and significant effects of the exports on per capita income have also been confirmed.

Other than domestic credit to private sector, the most important significant determinant of logistic infrastructure development is the long-term public sector external debt (DBTLTPB), which is an indicator of the government participation in infrastructure projects. It is envisaged in Table 8.3 that the indices of logistic

Table 8.7 Dependent Variable: Logistic Infrastructure- Overall Index (LGSTALL)

Panel Least Squares
Periods included: 5; Cross-sections included: 109;
Total (Unbalanced) observations: 486
Sample: 2007–2016

Explanatory Variable	*Option: I*		*Option: II*		*Option: III*		*Option: IV*	
	B	*T*	*β*	*T*	*β*	*T*	*β*	*T*
Constant	2.312	114.400***	2.325	118.143***	2.311	119.023***	2.299	112.142**
CAREC	-0.125	-2.981***	-0.090	-2.072**	-0.106	-2.462**	-0.1069	-2.532**
DCPSGDP	0.005	9.563***	0.006	13.321***	0.006	13.736***	0.005	9.853***
DBTLT	1.56E-12	9.855***					0.003	2.948***
DBTST	0.004	3.240***						
BNDPN			-2.06E-11	-1.876*	-2.18E-11	-1.951*	-2.73E-11	-2.334**
DBTLTPB			3.93E-12	7.213***	4.03E-12	7.318***	3.58E-12	6.370***
DBTLTPV			3.26E-13	0.759	4.04E-13	0.943	7.32E-13	1.691*
FDI$			-5.07E-13	-0.616				
Adjusted R^2	0.4634		0.4982		0.4955		0.4783	
F-statistic	102.4676		77.9586		96.2682		72.8094	
AIC	0.1384		0.1136		0.15258		0.1145	
Schwarz Crit.	0.1825		0.1759		0.2043		0.1762	
H-Q Criterion	0.1558		0.1381		0.1729		0.1388	
D-W Statistic	0.9157		0.9413		0.91406		0.9108	

Source: Author's estimations.

Note
'β' indicates Coefficient; 'T' indicates t-Statistics.
*p < 0.1; **p < 0.05; ***p < 0.01.

Table 8.8 Dependent Variable: Quality of Logistic Infrastructure (LGSTQLTY)

Panel Least Squares
Periods included: 5; Cross-sections included: 109;
Total (Unbalanced) observations: 486
Sample: 2007–2016

Explanatory Variable	*Option: I*		*Option: II*		*Option: III*		*Option: IV*	
	β	*T*	*B*	*T*	*β*	*T*	*β*	*T*
Constant	2.245	96.123***	2.260	98.995***	2.248	101.090***	2.236	93.877***
CAREC	-0.166	-3.408***	-0.134	-2.650***	-0.145	-2.937***	-0.147	-2.989***
DCPS	0.004	7.8122***	0.005	10.653***	0.005	11.274***	0.005	8.046***
DBTLT	1.87E-12	10.235***						
DBTST	0.003	2.666***					0.003	2.397**
BNDPN			-2.17E-11	-1.709*	-2.30E-11	-1.794*	-2.79E-11	-2.052**
DBTLTPB			4.29E-12	6.792***	4.39E-12	6.964***	3.97E-12	6.091***
DBTLTPV			6.09E-13	1.223	7.10E-13	1.447	1.00E-12	1.993**
FDI$			-9.04E-13	-0.946212				
Adjusted R^2	0.4189		0.4490		0.4504		0.4313	
F-statistic	85.7083		64.1651		80.4815		60.4159	
AIC	0.4321		0.41065		0.4239		0.4147	
Schwarz Crit.	0.4762		0.4729		0.4756		0.4764	
H-Q Criterion	0.4494		0.4352		0.4442		0.4390	
D-W Statistic	0.8881		0.9056		0.8806		0.8811	

Source: Author's estimations.

Note
'β' indicates Coefficient; 'T' indicates t-Statistics.
*p < 0.1; **p < 0.05; ***p < 0.01.

Table 8.9 Dependent Variable: Per Capita Income

Panel Least Squares
Periods included: 5; Cross-sections included: 163;
Total (Unbalanced) observations: 745
Sample: 2007–2016

Explanatory Variable	*Option: I*		*Option: II*		*Option: III*		*Option: IV*	
	β	*T*	*B*	*T*	*β*	*T*	*β*	*T*
Constant	-59,250.370	-26.032***	-53,604.930	-18.474***	-3,939.615	-3.548***	-3,902.896	-3.503***
LGSTALL	24,006.820	28.721***	20,937.440	17.147***	2,143.801	4.744***	2,119.086	4.654***
EXPR	98.649	5.932***	101.429	6.027***	36.950	4.725***	36.319	4.572***
FDIINF	71.781	2.305**	58.339	1.850*	-19.374	-1.243	-19.255	-1.234
DCPS			52.365	3.568***	12.451	2.239**	11.885	2.086**
DBTTOT					4.42E-09	4.544***	4.30E-09	4.279***
DBTST							5.468	0.466
Adjusted R^2	0.6195		0.6215		0.2818		0.2806	
F-statistic	404.7174		293.2161		36.5539		30.4445	
AIC	21.6765		21.6874		18.5596		18.5635	
Schwarz Crit.	21.7012		21.7195		18.6140		18.6270	
H-Q Criterion	21.6860		21.6998		18.5810		18.5885	
D-W Statistic	1.0333		1.0374		1.0848		1.0852	

Source: Author's estimations.

Note
'β' indicates Coefficient; 'T' indicates t-Statistics.
*p < 0.1; **p < 0.05; ***p < 0.01.

Table 8.10 Dependent Variable: Per Capita Income

Panel Least Squares
Periods included: 5; Cross-sections included: 163;
Total (Unbalanced) observations: 745 S
ample: 2007–2016

Explanatory Variable	*Option: I*		*Option: II*		*Option: III*		*Option: IV*	
	β	*T*	*B*	*T*	*β*	*T*	*β*	*T*
Constant	-52,602.890	-24.574***	-45,841.790	-17.668***	-3,068.259	-3.203***	-3,045.596	-3.174***
LGSTQLTY	21,770.890	27.559***	17,962.350	16.274***	1,796.445	4.616***	1,775.058	4.538***
EXPR	123.801	7.407***	121.481	7.210***	38.913	4.949***	38.103	4.769***
FDIINF	65.238	2.051**	48.345	1.513	-19.568	-1.253	-19.403	-1.242
DCPS			71.070	4.944***	14.387	2.657***	13.622	2.444**
DBTTOT					4.51E-09	4.650***	4.36E-09	4.337***
DBTST							6.865	0.586
Adjusted R^2	0.6029		0.6101		0.2800		0.2789	
F-statistic	377.4923		279.5182		36.2320		30.2063	
AIC	21.7191		21.7170		18.5621		18.5658	
Schwarz Crit.	21.7439		21.7490		18.6165		18.6293	
H-Q Criterion	21.7287		21.7294		18.5836		18.5908	
D-W Statistic	1.0211		1.0337		1.0761		1.0766	

Source: Author's estimations.

Note
'β' indicates Coefficient; 'T' indicates t-Statistics.
*p < 0.1; **p < 0.05; ***p < 0.01.

infrastructure are much lower in CAREC member countries (except the PRC), which indicates the demand for investment in infrastructure development.

Based on the statistical analysis in Tables 8.9 and 8.10, it has also been concluded that FDI was a significant determinant of PCI; however, the presence of external debt falsifies the impact of FDI on per capita income and logistic infrastructure development. It is the external financing which supports the infrastructure development. The role of FDI is insignificant in determination of PCI.

The results envisage that share of short-term debt in total external debts affects the quality of infrastructure positively. The effects of short-term debt are robust and significant. The effect of external long-term debt to public sector is also positive, which indicates that utilization of public sector external long-term debt plays an important role in the improvement of infrastructure. The effects of domestic credit to private sector in determination of logistic infrastructure is also positive.

Surprisingly, no significant impact of the private sector external debt (DBTLTPV) on infrastructure development has been proved. Several reasons are possible; for instance, private investors may avoid investing in politically motivated long-term projects or they require guarantees for sustainable returns on their investment. The requirement of public sector financial support to make infrastructure projects financially viable and guarantees for collection of user charges to minimize the risk of free-riding may be other reasons for insignificant role of private investment. All these issues have been discussed in detail in the previous section. Similarly, the private sector bonds for long-term financing, private sector long-term debts and FDI have not been recognized as significant determinants of the magnitude or quality of the logistic infrastructure, which indicates that long-term external financing to private sector does not have a significant role in determination of infrastructure.

In light of these results and statistical tests, the role of the various types of the modes of financing has been identified. The higher share of short-term borrowing in total external debt and long-term public sector debt have been identified as good options for the infrastructure development and growth in per capita income. The role of domestic credit to the private sector is also important in determination of the infrastructure development and per capita income. It was concluded that a higher share of short-term borrowing in the total external borrowing will improve the growth and logistic infrastructure development. Similarly, the long-term public debt will also lead the growth and development. The domestic debt to the private sector also plays an important role in the economic growth and development. However, private sector long-term external debts have not been identified as a significant determinant of economic growth and development.

The quality and magnitude of the logistic infrastructure have been proved important factors of the per capita income. This finding is concerned with the core area of this study. The results emphasize the causal relations between infrastructure and economic growth. It has been shown in earlier sections that there are no significant changes in the logistic infrastructure indices in CAREC member countries during the period included in this analysis. The infrastructure has been identified as these countries' weakest area. The region is far behind the developed countries in the world.

The results provide several insights, the most important of which is the identification of short-term external borrowing as the most effective mode of financing. The results show the significant and robust effects of short-term external borrowing on growth and development. The study does not recommend long-term external borrowing to the private sector for infrastructure development. The strong, significant, and robust impact of the share of short-term borrowing in total external debt on income and infrastructure development indicates the pressure on policy makers and economic managers for effective and efficient utilization of resources. The effects of short-term debt seem positive for growth, which indicates that such financings are used to manage immediate economic requirements. Because these activities must generate funds for repayment of short-term debt, in most cases, long-term borrowing is spent through public entities. Not only is this conclusion against common sense, it also contradicts the famous pioneer studies in the literature. For instance, the famous theorem of Miller and Modigliani (1966) favors long-term debt financing for the corporate sector from the wealth maximization point of view. The theorem supports the superiority of debt in the presence of taxes on corporate income. This overemphasis on debt superiority has been determining the monetary policies whereby the prime interest rate, as determined by the central bank, has always been considered an effective tool to balance the economy.

8.7 Conclusions and Policy Implications

Some conclusions of this study contradict the recommendations in some previous studies. For example, Tobin (1998) has inferred that banks and businesses need to be prevented from incurring net short-term debt positions in hard currency. Similarly, Sing and Hamid (1992) noted that developing countries' corporations rely very heavily on external funds to finance their growth of net assets, though Williamson (1988) has pointed out that debt and equity are alternative "Governance Structures" rather than just "Financial Structures." According to Mehar (2005), debt is not a perfect substitute for equity. The debts and equity are determined independently based on given circumstances, though debt financing is considered a favorite option worldwide. It was estimated that the largest 500 multinational corporations have raised 80% of their capital through debts. The imbalance between debt and equity is even more marked in aggregate global data, which estimates that only 7% of the money raised in the international capital markets belong to equities (Mehar 2005).

To differentiate the impacts of various modes of financing on the magnitude and quality of infrastructure, we introduced various variables (domestic credit to private sector, short-term borrowing, long-term borrowing by private sector, long-term borrowing by public sector and foreign direct investment etc.). Based on the statistical analysis in Tables 8.7, 8.8, 8.9, and 8.10, it was observed that magnitudes and levels of significance of the modes of financing are varied, while the magnitude and quality of infrastructure significantly affect the per capita income.

In the presence of short-term loans, the managers must show their success in the short-term. They cannot transfer the burden of repayments and their policies on the forthcoming governments. In fact, short-term borrowing is not a source of financing for long-term development; it is a part of operational activities. It invites the attention of policy makers. A global change in the lending and investment policies of the industrialized countries and lending institutions is required. To provide lending facilities to the governments and public sector organizations is a *modus operandi* for development financing by international financial institutions. In this way, the risk of failure is transferred to the governments of developing countries, which enhance usually indirect taxes for payment of interest and repayment of these loans. Unfortunately, the history of public finance in various developing countries shows the misuse of external borrowing for politically motivated and popular projects. It is obvious that this is a bias mechanism against the lower middle class in developing countries. The global financial architecture should focus on the provision of short-term lending facility to improve the efficiency of developing projects.

It is important for CAREC countries that they should focus on improving their sustainable logistic infrastructure because it improves PCI. A significant positive effect of the logistic infrastructure on income has been identified, while it has been noted that quality of logistic infrastructure in the CAREC member countries (except the PRC) is at or below the world average. So, it is the basic requirement to improve the logistic infrastructure for PCI growth. The growth in exports is another significant determinant of PCI, while growth in exports is directly linked with the logistic infrastructure. A trade-led growth model is proved in this study. Thus, CAREC member countries can use the infrastructure development for enhancing their exports, which will further increase their PCI.

An important recommendation for unlocking private investment in CAREC countries pertains to the role of monetary policy. The CAREC countries should enhance credit to the private sector. It is obvious that monetary policy can play an important role to enhance the credit to private sector by tuning into interest rates and quantitative easing. The qualitative easing for banks and financial institutions may also play a role in enhancing private sector credit. The enhancement in credit to private sector will improve per capita income and logistic infrastructure. In consideration of external borrowing, CAREC countries should also concentrate on short-term borrowing. The higher share of short-term borrowing in total external borrowing indicates the efficient utilization of funds for infrastructure. The logistic infrastructure can be improved by external long-term borrowing by the public sector; however, to make private sector external borrowing effective and efficient, policy makers must identify the incentives for the private sector. The creation of a viability fund to support the private sector projects, provision of guarantees for collection of user charges, tax exemptions, subsidized credit and tax incentives may be the possible incentives for private sector investment in sustainable development projects. Such policy measures can play an important role in unlocking private sector investment in sustainable infrastructure projects.

Notes

1 Debt-equity Ratio: Long-term debts divided by owners' equity. This ratio is used to assess the leverage position of a company.
2 Loan Life Coverage Ratio: Used to estimate the solvency of a firm, or the ability of a borrowing company to repay an outstanding loan. It is calculated by dividing the net present value of the money available for debt repayment by the amount of outstanding debt.
3 Debt Service Cover Ratio: A measurement of a firm's available cash flow to pay current debt obligations. It shows investors whether a company has enough income to pay its debts.
4 Rate of Return: The annual income from an investment expressed as a proportion (usually a percentage) of the original investment.
5 Weighted Average Cost of Capital: The weighted average cost of capital is the rate that a company is expected to pay on average to all its security holders to finance its assets.

References

Asian Development Bank. 2017. *Country Partnership Strategy: Pakistan, 2015–2019.* Manila: ADB.

Asian Development Bank. 2017. *Meeting Asia's Infrastructure Needs.* Manila: Asian Development Bank.

Bhattacharyay, B.N. 2012. Estimating Demand for Infrastructure 2010–2020. In *Infrastructure for Asian Connectivity*, edited by B.N. Bhattacharyay, M. Kawai, and R. Nag. 19–79. Cheltenham: Edward Elgar, and Tokyo: Asian Development Bank Institute.

Budina, N., H.P. Brixi, T. Irwin 2007. Public Private Partnerships in the New EU Member States – Managing Fiscal Risks. World Bank Working paper 114. Washington, DC: World Bank.

Conley, T., and C. Taber. 2005. Inference with Difference in Differences with a Small Number of Policy Changes. NBER Technical Working Paper No. 312. Cambridge, MA: National Bureau of Economic Research.

Delmon, J. 2005. *Implementing Social Policy into Contracts for the Provision of Utility Services.* Washington, DC:World Bank.

Farole, T. 2011. *Special Economic Zones in Africa: Comparing Performance and Learning from Global Experience.* Washinton, DC: World Bank.

Federation Pakistan Chamber of Commerce and Industry (FPCCI). 2016. *FPCCI Stance on China Pakistan Economic Corridor: Farsightedness, Apprehensions and Background.* Karachi: FPCCI.

Federation Pakistan Chamber of Commerce and Industry (FPCCI); 2015. *Revival of the Economy of Pakistan: Historical Evidences and Future Prospects.* Karachi: FPPCI.

Global Infrastructure Hub Ltd- GI Hub. 2016. *Global Infrastructure Outlook.* Oxford: GI Hub.

Global Infrastructure Hub Ltd- GI Hub. 2016. *Economic Outlook: Country Profile-Pakistan.* Oxford: GI Hub.

Global Infrastructure Hub Ltd- GI Hub. 2016. *Allocating Risks in Public-Private Partnerships*. Oxford: GI Hub.

Government of Pakistan. 2010. *Pakistan Policy on Public Private Partnership: Private Participation in Infrastructure for Better Public Services*. Islamabad: Economic Coordination Committee (ECC) of the Cabinet.

Government of Pakistan. 2010. *Pakistan's PPP Program: Presentation to UNESCAP Expert Group Meeting on Infrastructure Public Private Partnership for Sustainable Development*, 11–13 November. Islamabad: Ministry of Finance/Infrastructure Project Development Facility.

Government of Pakistan. 2014. *China-Pakistan Economic Corridor*. Islamabad: Planning Commission.

Government of Pakistan. 2017. *The Public Private Partnership Authority Act*. The Gazette of Pakistan, 31 March. Islamabad: National Assembly Secretariat.

Government of Pakistan. 2017. *Households Integrated Economic Survey (HIES)- 2015–16*. Islamabad: Statistics Division, Pakistan Bureau of Statistics.

Government of Pakistan. 2018. *Budget in Brief*. Islamabad: Ministry of Finance.

Government of Pakistan. 2018. *Economic Survey of Pakistan*. Islamabad: Ministry of Finance.

Havard, H., J.J. Beardsworth, B.C. Land, and J.A. Schmidt. 2014. Resource Financed Infrastructure: A Discussion on a New Form of Infrastructure Financing. Washington, DC: World Bank/ Public-Private Infrastructure Facility.

Hussain, S. and F. Zhang. 2018. Electrification and Household Welfare Evidence from Pakistan. Policy Research Working Paper 8582. Washington, DC: The World Bank Group, South Asia Region.

Husted, S. 1992. The Emerging U.S. Current Account Deficit in the 1980s: A Cointegration Analysis. *The Review of Economics and Statistics* February:159–166.

Imran, M. and J. Niazi. 2011. Infrastructure and Growth. *Pakistan Development Review* 50(4): 355–364.

Inderst, G. 2013. Private Infrastructure Finance and Investment in Europe. European Investment Bank Working Paper 2. Luxembourg: EIB.

Inderst, G. 2018. Infrastructure Investment, Private Finance, and Institutional Investors: Asia from a Global Perspective in *Financing Infrastructure in Asia and the Pacific Capturing Impacts and New Sources*. Tokyo: Asian Development Bank Institute.

International Monetary Fund. 2005. *Government Guarantees and Fiscal Risk*. Washington, DC: IMF.

Khan, K. and A. Saba. 2017. *Special Economic Zones (SEZs) and CPEC: Background, Challenges and Strategies*. Islamabad: Pakistan Institute of Development Economics.

Kindleberger, C.P. 1970. *Power and Money: The Economics of International Politics and the Politics of International Economics*. New York: Basic Books.

Mehar, A. 1995. Impacts of Households' Income on Demand for Means of Transportation and Communications. *Pakistan Economic and Social Review* 33(1): 117–136.

Mehar, A. 2002. Stock Market Consequences of Macro Economic Fundamentals. *Pakistan Business Review*; 2002: 1–17.

Mehar, A. 2005. Is Debt a Substitute of Equity? Relevancy of Financial Policy in New Economic Scenarios. *Applied Financial Economics* March.

Mehar, A. 2010. *Impact of Privatization Policy on Socioeconomic Development of Pakistan*. Islamabad: Economic Freedom Network.

Mehar, A. 2015. *Infrastructure Development by Liberalizing Economic Policies: The Straight Path of Economic Prosperity*. Islamabad: Economic Freedom Network.

Mehar, A. 2017. Infrastructure Development, CPEC and FDI in Pakistan: Is There any Connection? *Transnational Corporation Review* September: 2–10.

Mehar, A. 2018. Impact of Monetary Policy on Growth and Poverty: Drastic Consequences of Government Intervention. *Journal of Modern Economy* 1:1.

Mehar, A. 2020. *Measuring Impacts and Financing Infrastructure in Pakistan: Role of Public Private Partnership.* Tokyo: Asian Development Bank Institute.

Mehar, A. 2021. Bridge Financing during Covid-19 Pandemics: Nexus of FDI, External Borrowing and Fiscal Policy. *Transnational Corporation Review* 13(1): 1–13.

Michael, R. 2018. *Infrastructure Financing Modalities in Asia and the Pacific Region: Strengths and Limitations in Financing Infrastructure in Asia and the Pacific Capturing Impacts and New Sources.* Tokyo: Asian Development Bank Institute.

Miller, M. and F. Modigliani. 1966. Some Estimates of the Cost of Capital to Electric Utility Industry, *American Economic Review* June: 333–391.

Morag, B. 2016. *Global Infrastructure Hub: Promoting Quality Infrastructure for Long Term Investment.* Oxford: GI Hub.

Naoyuki, Y., M. Helble, and U. Abidhadjaev. 2018. *Financing Infrastructure in Asia and the Pacific Capturing Impacts and New Sources.* Tokyo: Asian Development Bank Institute.

Naoyuki, Y., P.J. Morgan, and P.B. Rana. 2018. *Global Shocks and the New Global and Regional Financial Architecture: Asian Perspectives.* Tokyo: Asian Development Bank Institute; and S. Rajaratnam School of International Studies.

Naoyuki, Y., S. Paul, V. Sarma and S. Lakhia. 2018. *Land Trust Laws as a Solution to the Land Acquisition Dilemma for Infrastructure Development in Asia.* Tokyo: Asian Development Bank Institute.

Organisation for Economic Co-operation and Development (OECD). 2010. *Infrastructure to 2030, Volume 2: Mapping Policy for Electricity, Water and Transport.* Paris: OECD.

Organisation for Economic Co-operation and Development (OECD). 2012. *Strategic Transport Infrastructure Needs to 2030.* Paris: OECD Publishing.

Organisation for Economic Co-operation and Development (OECD). 2018. *Infrastructure to 2030: Telecom, Land Transport, Water and Electricity.* Paris: OECD Publishing.

Peterson, G.E. and P.C. Annez. 2007. *Financing Cities: Fiscal Responsibility and Urban Infrastructure in Brazil, China, India, Poland and South Africa.* Washington, DC: World Bank.

Sarkar, A. 2007. Development and Displacement: Land Acquisition in West Bengal. *Economic and Political Weekly* 42(16): 1435–1442.

Serageldin, I. 1996. Sustainability and the Wealth of Nations First Steps in an Ongoing Journey. Environmentally Sustainable Development Studies and Monographs Series No. 5. Washington, DC: The World Bank.

Singh, A. and J. Hamid. 1992. Corporate Financial Structures in Developing Economies; IFC Technical Paper No.1. Washington, DC: IFC.

State Bank of Pakistan. 2016. *Balance Sheet Analysis.* Karachi: State Bank of Pakistan.

State Bank of Pakistan. 2017. *Annual Report: Part I.* Karachi: State Bank of Pakistan.

Tobin, J. 1998. Financial Globalization: Can National Currencies Survive? Cowles Foundation Discussion Papers 1188, Cowles Foundation for Research in Economics. New Haven: Yale University.

UNU-IHDP and UNEP. 2012. *Inclusive Wealth Report 2012; Measuring Progress toward Sustainability.* Cambridge: Cambridge University Press.

US Department of Transportation, Federal Highway Administration- FHWA. 2010. Project Finance Primer – Update to the Innovative Finance Brochure FHWA: 2010.

Williamson, O.E. 1988. Corporate Finance and Corporate Governance. *Journal of Finance* 43(3): 567–591.

World Bank. 2007. *Government Guarantees: Allocating and Valuing Risk in Privately Financed Infrastructure Projects.* Washington, DC: The World Bank Group.

World Bank. 2017. *Private Participation in Infrastructure (PPI)- Annual Report 2017.* Washington, DC: The World Bank Group.

World Bank. 2018. *Global Financial Development Report: Bankers without Borders.* Washington, DC: The World Bank Group.

World Bank. 2018. *International Debt Statistics.* Washington, DC: The World Bank Group.

World Bank. 2018. *Procuring Infrastructure Public-Private Partnerships Report 2018: Assessing Government Capability to Prepare, Procure, and Manage PPPs.* Washington, DC: The World Bank.

World Bank. 2018. *Procuring PPP Pakistan.* Washington, DC: The World Bank.

World Bank 2018. *Public-Private Partnership; World Bank Legal Resource Center.* Washington, DC: The World Bank.

World Bank. 2018. *World Development Indicators.* Washington: The World Bank Group.

World Economic Forum. 2011. *World Competitiveness Report: 2009.* Geneva: World Economic Forum.

World Economic Forum. 2018. *World Competitiveness Report: 2016.* Geneva: World Economic Forum.

World Economic Forum. 2012. *Strategic Infrastructure: The Green Investment Report.* Geneva: World Economic Forum.

Yoshino, N., and U. Abidhadjaev. 2017. An Impact Evaluation of Investment in Infrastructure: The Case of a Railway Connection in Uzbekistan. *Journal of Asian Economics* 49: 1–11.

Part II

The Role of Governments and New Models for Unlocking Private Investment in Sustainable Infrastructure

9 Private Financing for Water Infrastructure in Central Asia

Naoyuki Yoshino, Nella Hendriyetty, Derek Hondo, and Misuzu Nakamura

9.1 Introduction

As cities grow and economic development increases, clean water becomes scarcer. Further, as a result of climate change, water shortages and lack of proper sanitation could become even more serious, especially for developing countries. Therefore, the United Nations has made access to clean water and sanitation as one of the Sustainable Development Goals (SDGs): SDG 6. A large part of achieving SDG 6 relies on expanding and upgrading water infrastructure.

In Central Asia, climate change, geographical landscape, and poor supply management make water infrastructure a crucial issue. Much of the water infrastructure has not been upgraded since the Soviet era. Water systems are still being managed by the government, which lacks sufficient funds to address infrastructure problems. Since the dissolution of the Soviet Union, there have been transboundary water management and allocation issues, in part due to the lack of reliable data shared throughout the region. Moreover, water availability tends to decrease in the medium to long term due to temperature increase. While improved regional cooperation is necessary, financing water infrastructure without the help of the private sector remains an obstacle.

This chapter reviews key factors, challenges, and opportunities facing water infrastructure in Central Asia. The relevant concepts are identified in the literature by scholars and policy makers. There are three main objectives of this chapter. First, it emphasizes the importance of developing high-quality water infrastructure in the region, as measured by how much economic and social value can be created, values that could address the financing gap. Second, it discusses the challenges of developing water infrastructure in the region. Third, it proposes some policy responses and new concepts for governments to maintain water infrastructure development. The recommendations range from utilizing a portion of spillover tax revenue to compensating for risk and financing further expenditures for supporting small and medium-sized enterprises. Additionally, these spillover effects can support secondary markets, technology advancements, and environmental protection in future infrastructure development.

DOI: 10.4324/9781003228790-12

9.2 The Role of Water Infrastructure in Central Asia Development

Water is one of the key precursors of sustainable development—economically, socially, and environmentally. However, as the effects of climate change become more apparent each year, providing adequate water remains a challenge. Now more than ever, it is important that governments begin to realize the urgency of this issue and implement strategies to ensure a water supply for their citizens, especially in Central Asia, which already has severe shortages and insufficient water infrastructure.

As one of the core SDG concepts, water resources provide a wide range of services that can help to alleviate poverty, contribute to economic growth, and maintain a healthy environment. Moreover, water is essential for food and energy security, human and environmental health, and building resilient communities in the face of climate change. Guaranteeing the supply of water is one issue, but it is also important to ensure that the clean, drinkable water can reach everyone through adequate infrastructure. With urbanization occurring at rapid rates, it is projected that Asia's urban population will grow from 1.8 billion in 2017 to nearly 3 billion by 2050. While Central Asia is just a small piece in the larger picture, urbanization rates are also expected to maintain its growth. This will increase the demand for clean water and the need for water infrastructure to ensure its provision. On the other hand, by-products of urbanization, such as liquid and solid waste, if not managed well, will compromise the water quality and supply in the future (McDonald, et al. 2014). For many years, Central Asia has struggled to address this key issue, which will not only jeopardize food and energy security but also sustainable economic growth in the years to come.

Water is a major driver of economic activity in Central Asia, in particular in the agriculture sector, which, as the largest consumer of the resource per capita, much higher than in European countries, relies on heavily. The cultivation of cotton and other water-intensive crops puts considerable stress on the region's water resources. In addition, because of little rainfall, there is a heavy reliance on irrigation systems, with the total areas estimated at 100,000 km^2 (Russell 2018). Despite a steep downward trend in recent years, agriculture still accounts for a significant portion of gross domestic product (GDP) in countries such as Uzbekistan, the Kyrgyz Republic, and Tajikistan (Gharleghi 2018). It also provides employment to 15%–30% of the labor force, varying between countries (Rakhmatullaev, Abdullaev and Kazbekov 2017).

Energy production is also another major consumer of water resources and some upstream countries such as the Kyrgyz Republic and Tajikistan rely heavily on hydropower plants. Both of these countries produce over 90% of their electricity from hydropower, lacking the fossil fuel reserves of downstream countries like Kazakhstan, Turkmenistan, and Uzbekistan (Russell 2018). The unbalanced distribution of water among these countries has long presented challenges surrounding governance and international relations. Such issues will be addressed in more detail in later sections of this chapter.

9.3 Supplying Water to Central Asia

Water infrastructure has long been a limiting factor of sustainable development in Central Asia. While regional policymakers have recognized the development benefits of expanding and upgrading infrastructure, there are many challenges that have inhibited the growth of this sector. This section will examine some of the barriers to supplying water to Central Asia, ranging from climate change impacts on water resources to geographical limitations, financing, and cross-border regional issues. The following section will then address sustainable ways of overcoming such challenges.

9.3.1 Climate Change and its Impacts in Central Asia

Central Asia is particularly vulnerable to climate change, with many reports projecting temperature increases greater than the global mean. Known for its arid to semi-arid conditions, the region is also plagued by severe droughts, with the exception of mountainous areas in the Kyrgyz Republic. Increased temperatures and changes in precipitation patterns will have adverse environmental, social, and economic impacts.

Large-scale studies have all shown a consistent increase in temperature since the beginning of the last century. According to Haag et al., Central Asia has seen an annual temperature increase of 0.39°C per decade between 1950 and 2016 (Haag, Jones and Samimi 2019). It is projected that, in 2071–2099, the average temperatures in boreal regions could see an increase of 2.5°C and 6.5°C in summers compared to 1951–1980. This is different from the global average, which is projected to see an increase of 2°C and 4°C (Reyer, et al. 2015). Temperature increases will have detrimental effects on agriculture, a major economic driver. Farmers will need to adapt to climate change, possibly adjusting the harvest cycles, and adopting climate-smart agriculture technologies or types of crops since they may not be so tolerant of extreme heat, especially during summer months (Mirzabev 2018).

The effects of climate change could impact annual precipitation; however, recent studies showing conflicting outlooks make it unclear the extent to which this may happen. The latest outputs from the Phase 6 of the Coupled Model Intercomparison Project[1] have offered improved possible scenarios based on the climate projections under different levels of greenhouse gas emissions. The changes in the annual cycles of precipitation associated with climate change may lead to increased precipitation in the spring followed by dryer conditions in the summer. Additionally, taking into consideration thermodynamic effects linked to changes in humidity, this could contribute to increased evaporation and drying as temperatures increase throughout the region. Furthermore, in response to precipitation, an increase in temperature could lead to extreme seasons (Jiang, et al. 2020).

Considering precipitation itself may not pose as serious a threat as the increase in temperature, water availability also needs to be considered. Although, in the short term, water availability may not be a problem due to the rapid melting of glaciers and snow, this will eventually lead to a decrease in water availability in the medium to long term (Reyer, et al. 2015). Such impacts could have significant consequences on agriculture and hydropower. Moreover, dryer summers coupled with higher temperatures will likely lead to a rise in the number of droughts and expansion of deserts. In such conditions, without the presence of thriving plant life, the probability of natural disasters such as mudflows and avalanches may rise, ultimately affecting the surrounding communities.

The impacts of climate change are becoming more evident, especially for the agriculture and energy sectors. Water is already scarce as Central Asia has depleted its natural resources, i.e., the Aral Sea and the Amu Darya and Syr Darya rivers. It is important that measures are taken to protect the environment and ensure inclusive growth throughout the region.

9.3.2 Water Stress and Limitations of Geographical Landscape and Financing for Water Infrastructure in Central Asia

Traditionally, infrastructure investments have been financed publicly. Consequently, this paradigm also remains the largest barrier to expanding and upgrading infrastructure in developing countries because of the lack of adequate public finances. In recent years, public deficits have also been increasing and public debt-to-GDP ratios have decreased the availability of finances for infrastructure. Moreover, a large portion of public funds have historically been allocated for agriculture, while water infrastructure that is not explicitly used for irrigation purposes, including provision of potable water for communities, sanitation, and energy, has not been as highly prioritized.

Equitable access to clean water through adequate infrastructure is a precursor to development. However, diminishing water supply coupled with inadequate infrastructure to address climate change and other sustainable development issues will continually put an increasing amount of pressure on the region. Improving water infrastructure will alleviate some of them and it is important to first assess the different types. Three general categories include: 1) hydropower infrastructure; 2) water resources for irrigation; and 3) urban water infrastructure (clean water and sanitation). Hydropower infrastructure involves a complicated business model and rapid technological advancements. Therefore, this category usually attracts more private investment (Briscoe 1999). Water resources for irrigation (dams or reservoirs) are usually subsidized or financed by public funding, especially in the dryland areas, commonly found throughout Central Asia. This type of infrastructure is usually poorly maintained because governments are reluctant to allocate funding after construction is completed (Ward 2010). Often, water infrastructure issues are controversial, encouraging governments to privatize this sector and create market mechanisms for scarce water supplies. Urban water infrastructure is usually financed through a combination of central and local governments together with the private sector (Hendriyetty, et al. 2020).

According to McDonald, et al. (2014), geographical and financial limitations are important in determining the needs for water in the area. In terms of geographical limitations, coordination is needed among the cities; if they are within the same country, the national government can design a system to have a water transfer mechanism among them. However, if the limitations involve many countries, collective actions should be taken, and the region should convene a regional water management solution. This transboundary issue has been a major barrier in the region and is discussed in more detail in the following section. For cities with limited financing, increased private investment will be needed to upgrade and expand water infrastructure.

Though water plays important roles in their economies, Kazakhstan, Turkmenistan, and Uzbekistan lack reliable access to water since they are downstream of the major sources. The main source of water comes from Aral Sea Basin, which is shared among countries in Central Asia. However, due to regional mismanagement and subsequent failure to maintain adequate infrastructure, enormous stress has been put on the Aral Sea Basin, leaving it depleted in recent years. Since the 1970s, the area of the lake is now 25% of its original size, holding just 10% of its original volume of water (Dunbar 2012). As previously mentioned, these water demands are essential for mountainous countries like the Kyrgyz Republic and Tajikistan, which rely on water for energy, and cotton-producing countries like Uzbekistan and Turkmenistan need river water for agriculture (Russell 2018). These water demands call on improved cooperative sharing and expansion of water infrastructure in the region.

Infrastructure and sufficient operational and maintenance support are key to solving the water crisis in developing countries. However, in the past, these types of infrastructure have not attracted a lot of private investment, particularly due to the high operational and maintenance costs. It is important to recognize the contribution that the private sector can have in this situation. In addition to introducing well-designed and cost-effective business models, it can help to drive development through capital injection; moreover, it can introduce new technology and improved governance and efficiency (Kerr 1995).

9.3.3 Regional Issues Affecting Water Infrastructure

Historical transboundary issues present challenges for other countries in the region that are unable to utilize water to fulfill energy needs. Dating to when the countries were republics of the Soviet Union, major dams and reservoirs were constructed in the Kyrgyz Republic and Tajikistan. During that time, the primary function of water stored in reservoirs was irrigation in the other three downstream countries during summer months. Since energy was cheap, hydropower generation only served as a secondary objective (Pohl, et al. 2017).

With the dissolution of the Soviet Union came growing tensions over the water availability for the downstream countries. Lack of regional cooperation divided upstream countries who were more interested in hydropower than use of reservoirs for water storage, which is of growing importance, especially with the frequent droughts in the downstream countries. The failure of the regional water management institutions set up after the dissolution of the Soviet Union is only part of the problem as the issues lie much deeper in the interlinked national and regional water governance challenges. If the region wants to improve the situation and find common ground, they will need to unilaterally invest in constructing high-quality infrastructure to increase self-sufficiency in regards to water, energy, and agriculture industries (Pohl, et al. 2017). Together with updating and expanding water infrastructure, regional tensions need immediate attention in order to achieve sustainable development.

9.3.4 Challenges of Attracting Private Financing on Water Infrastructure

Water privatization started in the 1980s and was expected to be a solution for the low performance of public utilities. While privatization worked well in other sectors, such as telecommunications, electricity, and transportation, it did not work well in water supply and sanitation, and became a monopolistic business due to the limited competitiveness and disregard of investors and the quality of their services. It also became difficult to estimate the volume of underground water, and very low user charges posed additional obstacles for the sector with social and cultural issues (Marin 2009). Furthermore, the market for water infrastructure is very small, with only 5.4% of the total investment commitment coming from the private sector. The Asian Development Bank's *Meeting Asia's Infrastructure Needs* 2017 report noted that the internal rate of return (IRR) for water infrastructure, especially for supply, has been around 18.1% since 1966 (ADB 2017). The IRR is relatively low compared to that of power and transport sectors.

Since 1990, public-private partnerships (PPPs) have been used to finance water infrastructure, and, in 2001–06, there was an increase in private participation in PPPs for water infrastructure, in both developed and developing countries. Along with population growth and urbanization, by 2007, private operators were serving more than 67 million people globally in water supply or around 40% of the market. Despite PPPs' success in water infrastructure development, around one-third of projects in developing countries returned to public management due to PPPs' complexity and risky nature. Moreover, water infrastructure and the private companies that manage them struggle with generating revenue solely based on user charges.

There are additional challenges to securing PPPs and, as explained by Kacaribu et al. (Chapter 13), PPPs still need fiscal support through a Viability Gap Fund (VGF), up to 49% of the project cost, to mitigate uncertainty in water infrastructure. Private investors also face other risks and uncertainties associated with the cross-border investment, especially amid the transboundary challenges surrounding the distribution of water in Central Asia. Since water is a politicized commodity, such kinds of investment are often perceived as a liability. It also involves a lengthy implementation that private investors become subject to. During this lengthy process, there is the possibility that future water policies and tariff levels could change; thus, with the high upfront costs required, plus the delayed repayment period, it is not seen as an attractive opportunity for private investors.

Finally, land acquisition poses another major obstacle for infrastructure projects. Prior to the dissolution of the Soviet Union, state institutions were responsible for the water management. By contrast, each country now has its own agricultural, land tenure, and water allocation policies. In some cases, such as in Kazakhstan and Tajikistan, land was transferred to companies or farmers via long-term leases and private ownership. Such institutional changes have made it difficult for smaller private farms who lack the capacity to pump and irrigate on their own (Rakhmatullaev, et al. 2009). With much of the land in these areas being privately owned, it poses challenges for land acquisition.

The Asian Development Bank projects that the Asia and the Pacific region will require $22.55 trillion in infrastructure investment between 2016 and 2030 and Central Asia alone will need $492 billion or $33 billion per year (ADB 2017). The cost will amount to 6.8% of countries' GDP per year. However, infrastructure financing from the public sector and multinational development banks is very limited, accounting for 45% of this amount (Yoshino, Hendriyetty, Lakhia 2019). Water infrastructure, excluding water's role in transportation and power generation, is 3.5% of the total needs.

Based on the above, the failure to fill the financing gaps has compromised water infrastructure in the region. It is clear that water infrastructure cannot attract full private investment, while the PPP concept also brings great risk to countries' fiscal sustainability. Therefore, alternative financing that brings private and public finding together without creating fiscal risk should be considered. The following section proposes innovative means to compensate the private sector, using the spillover effects or increases in economic and social value from infrastructure projects through the concept of spillover effects.

9.4 Spillover Effects of Water Infrastructure Projects

Water projects create economic opportunities, long-term productivity savings to customers, and reliability of water services. Since water supply and sanitation are necessary goods and services for everyone, operation companies or local governments cannot charge high prices for services. Consequently, operation of water supply and sanitation does not produce enough revenue to cover maintenance costs. However, these costs are necessary in order to continue supplying quality water.

Yoshino, Hendriyetty, and Lakhia explained the concept of infrastructure project spillover effects, i.e., that the effects are both direct and indirect. Using production function, the direct effects of infrastructure can be reflected from the input into infrastructure projects, such as private and public capital and labor (Yoshino, Hendriyetty and Lakhia 2019). In water infrastructure, direct effects can involve design, engineering, construction, and employment opportunities created during the construction. The indirect impacts are generated by spending from construction company firms and employees. An example is when the construction company buys machinery, equipment, and other supplies for water infrastructure. Additionally, employees will also purchase personal goods, health amenities, and other services. These sequences occur several times and create multiplier effects in the region along the infrastructure project. This creates new businesses and employment opportunities. According to a report published in 2020 by the American Society of Civil Engineers and the Value of Water Campaign, for every $1 million invested in water infrastructure, at least 15 jobs are created in many sectors of the US economy. The report also emphasizes that if the US government invests $123 billion every year in water infrastructure for the next 10 years, the economy will generate over $220 billion every year, including 1.26 million jobs per year (American Society of Civil Engineers and Value of Water Campaign 2020).

Economic impacts of water supply and sanitation can vary. First, in the case of dams or reservoirs, they will improve productivity in the region and invite people to develop residential areas. Second, new businesses can open along the water lines. Third, manufacturing industries will come to the region. Furthermore, agriculture could benefit from this new water supply. Lastly, water supply and sanitation will improve health conditions in the region. Therefore, in production function, capital stock will be created while simultaneously improving quality of labor, which will increase overall regional development.

As a result of economic development, corporate and individual tax revenues will rise. These large spillover effects can increase corporate tax revenues, individual income tax revenues, property tax revenues, sales tax revenues and so on. In the past, all these increased tax revenues went to the government.

However, in this chapter, we propose to quantify the economic benefits of water infrastructure in the form of the increase of tax revenue. If the increase of the tax revenue (the incremental amount of tax revenue) is shared with private investors to compensate their return of investment, then the private sector will be more likely to invest as opposed to receiving the revenue brought in from user charges and tariffs. To quantify the economic benefits of water infrastructure, we propose using the difference-in-differences (DiD) method.

9.4.1 Difference-in-Differences Method

In the past, DiD, which is a statistical technique used in social sciences and econometrics to quantify the value of a differential effect of a treatment group, has measured the economic benefits of road and railway infrastructure projects. This concept can also be applied to water infrastructure with the adjustment to specific components of multiplier effect.

Yoshino and Abidhadjaev (2018) explained that infrastructure affects economic activities in at least three ways. One of these is the supply of infrastructure in the area, measured qualitatively and quantitatively. This is one consideration made by investors to decide whether starting a business is worthwhile. Since technology infrastructure will eliminate information asymmetry, such conditions will also

Figure 9.1 Spillover Effects of Infrastructure.
Source: Yoshino, N., U. Abidhadjaev, and M. Nakahigashi (2019).

improve the business environment. Finally, basic infrastructure, which includes paved roads and railways, will create new opportunities for new businesses and expand markets for the local products as seen in Figure 9.1. These activities can be measured or quantified using the DiD method.

To better explain how DiD was applied, this chapter will refer to the calculation of Yoshino and Abidhadjaev (2017), which measured the economic impact of the Kyushu high-speed rail line in Japan. The chapter uses total tax revenue as a measurement of the economic impacts. It includes all types of taxes, such as personal income, corporate income, property, etc. Furthermore, in their estimation, the authors divided the areas based on geographical focus and categorized them as either regional effects or spillover effects. From there, the authors can estimate the net difference between the observed actual outcome and an alternative counterfactual outcome for the region in the specific time frame.

Based on this explanation, the economic value of infrastructure development is reflected in the increased growth rate and the increase in total tax revenue. The growth is reflected in the total GDP, including value added from industries impacted by the projects in surrounding areas. The total tax revenue could be in the form of personal and corporate income taxes or property and sales taxes. Yoshino and Abidhadjaev (2017; 2016) use DiD to quantify the additional economic value of infrastructure projects in Kyushu, Japan, and Uzbekistan using tax revenue and growth rate, respectively. Their studies found that growth and tax revenue in the regions rise in line with the economic development of the areas.

9.4.2 Applying DiD to Water Infrastructure

Similarly, development of a region through the provision of quality water supply, sanitation, and electricity will attract new residential areas and commercial businesses. Consequently, property values will increase as these new businesses open. This will then lead to a rise in taxes from property, corporate income, sales, and individual income due to the opening of businesses and jobs created. All these effects are the result of the newly constructed water infrastructure; without it, it would be difficult for such regional economies to develop since water is an essential resource. While private water operators usually bring in revenue through user charges, these amounts are minimal and insufficient to cover maintenance and operation costs. Furthermore, when spillover tax revenues are generated from water infrastructure, it is normally returned to the government as opposed to private companies.

As Yoshino and Abidhadjaev (2017a; 2017b) propose, DiD can identify the amount of tax revenue created by each infrastructure investment made. Generally, tax revenue following provision of water supply is compared to tax revenue in conditions without the water supply. Figure 9.2 shows the difference between the two scenarios. Then we can identify how much water supply can create new tax revenues compared to the region that is far away from water supply. Water supply and sanitation will in a sense have a multiplier effect, as shown above. Noting that significant spillover tax revenue is created by constructing water and other utility infrastructure, it confirms that private investments in infrastructure is worthwhile. It must, however, be emphasized that the tax revenue must be shared with the infrastructure operators and not be solely absorbed by the government's finances. Furthermore, it is recommended that some of this spillover tax revenue be allocated for annual maintenance costs that operators incur over time. This will ensure that the infrastructure is properly maintained and upgraded when necessary to avoid the current situation in Central Asia, where much of the infrastructure is outdated. It will also allow these operating companies to expand

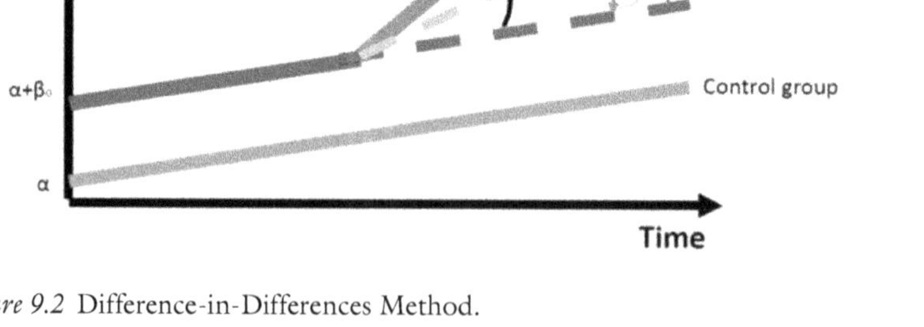

Figure 9.2 Difference-in-Differences Method.
Source: Yoshino, N. and N. Hendriyetty (2020).

their water supply to much larger regions, which can generate even greater tax revenues and spillover effects, ultimately promoting regional sustainable development. Likewise, these spillover effects will increase tax revenues again and the new tax revenues can be shared by the government and water supply operating companies.

Traditionally, it has been difficult for water supply and sanitation to receive enough revenue. However, incremental tax revenues and spillover tax revenues, as demonstrated by DiD, allow us to identify how much increased tax revenue can be attributed to the new water supply and sanitation infrastructure. Another incentive for these companies would be their ability to expand their water supply through construction of new pipelines, reaching much larger regions and more customers. Such kinds of spillover effects will be very crucial in addressing sustainable development issues, especially in densely populated regions, such as Southeast Asia and South Asia.

9.5 Beyond Water Supply: Additional Recommendations through the Utilization of Infrastructure Spillover Effects

In developing infrastructure, we cannot investigate projects in isolation. There are many areas that require careful design in order to build quality infrastructure projects and maximize the positive spillover effects resulting from the investment and construction. In order to positively impact productivity and tax revenue while maintaining sustainable and inclusive growth, it is imperative that reforms be implemented in infrastructure development. Creating an institutional framework with poor implementation may lead to more problems than solutions. In addition to the revenue returned to private operating companies, there are five areas that should be considered when allocating additional funds generated from the spillover effects of water infrastructure. In the last section of this chapter, additional suggestions are proposed to facilitate better implementation of the private investments in infrastructure and how different development needs can share the spillover revenue from those projects.

9.5.1 City Infrastructure

When city planners, i.e., policymakers, contractors, and builders plan infrastructure, they often overlook certain aspects such as its layout. City planning is a crucial initial step that must be properly assessed before moving forward, especially when considering sustainable infrastructure. Proper planning will ensure the maximum amount of spillover effects generated from infrastructure investments. However, traditionally, this has not always been the case as many times infrastructure planning is considered only from a construction perspective. It is imperative to address the capability of the intended infrastructure to be developed in a given region and how the benefits from the project will provide a cascading effect on multiple communities. Infrastructure projects should also designate specific zones for essential services and commercial businesses such as markets, shopping districts, residential areas, and industries (e.g., manufacturing). Proper zoning will allow city planners to ensure the maximum benefits of the infrastructure, developing a better designed city.

9.5.2 Hometown Trust Funds to Promote Smes and Start-Up Businesses

Policymakers need to think beyond the construction of infrastructure. Governments should also focus on attracting businesses to come to the region with a new water supply, but the infrastructure itself will not be enough of an incentive to encourage these businesses to come because most small and medium-sized enterprises (SMEs) encounter difficulties when seeking financial support. Since startups pose an inherent risk to investors and lenders, banks and other financial institutions are usually reluctant to lend funds to these types of businesses. This is where the "hometown investment trust" (HIT) funds can play an integral role. The basic objective of HIT funds is to connect local investors with projects in their own locality in which they have personal knowledge and interest (Yoshino and Taghizadeh-Hesary 2017). Moreover, HIT funds can also help a region to become more inclusive by providing an opportunity for greater female participation in labor markets through start-ups.

9.5.3 Enabling Digital Literacy for Better Education

Another area where spillover effects can help is education. Education is often regarded as one of the barriers to development, where its level among stakeholders determines the limits of economic value coming from the infrastructure spill-over effects. Stakeholders can include the government, investors, farmers, and landowners who benefit from the infrastructure. Using data collected from 40 countries, Yoshino and Abidhadjaev (2016) illustrate that secondary school education and university education could lead to a higher GDP in a region that has improved infrastructure.

A more modern approach to education uses the internet and smartphones. An important aspect of an improved education system, especially in STEM education, is technological advancements and innovative learning tools. In developing Asia, for students to receive a higher quality of education, they were expected to attend private schools, which often requires a rigorous and competitive application process. However, as technology expands and becomes more accessible, it has become more convenient for students to further their education and obtain information, which previously had not been possible. With e-learning on the rise, students are able to listen to lectures given by professors from around the world regardless of their geographical location, so long as they have access to a computer or a smartphone and the internet. In this regard, it is imperative that governments continue to invest in providing facilities with quality technology, encouraging students and those who drop out to take advantage of these tools for personal growth.

The relationship between technology, education, and a region's economic growth is expressed in the production function as: Y= A F(Kp, L, Kg) where Y= regional GDP, A= technological progress, Kp= private capital, L= Labor, and Kg= infrastructure (Yoshino, Hendriyetty and Lakhia 2019). As a region makes technological advancements (A), the regional output generated from investments in infrastructure will also increase. By continuing to build and develop human capital (L), regional output will also increase from the spillover effects. Therefore, it is important to recognize the potential benefits associated with reinvesting spill-over effects into improving education, especially through digital technology.

9.5.4 Land Trust for Water Infrastructure Development

Land acquisition is one of the difficulties in infrastructure investment. When the construction of a dam or reservoir is planned, city officials must negotiate with landowners. This process takes time and money, adding to the amount to finance the construction of infrastructure itself. Several practices have been implemented to solve the problem. For example, in Japan, the government designed a land trust system. The country experienced major problems constructing commercial buildings and condominiums. They introduced and extensively used this land trust system where landowners could keep the land as their own and lease it to commercial and condominium developers. Landowners still maintained ownership of the land while also receiving annual rent from the developers.

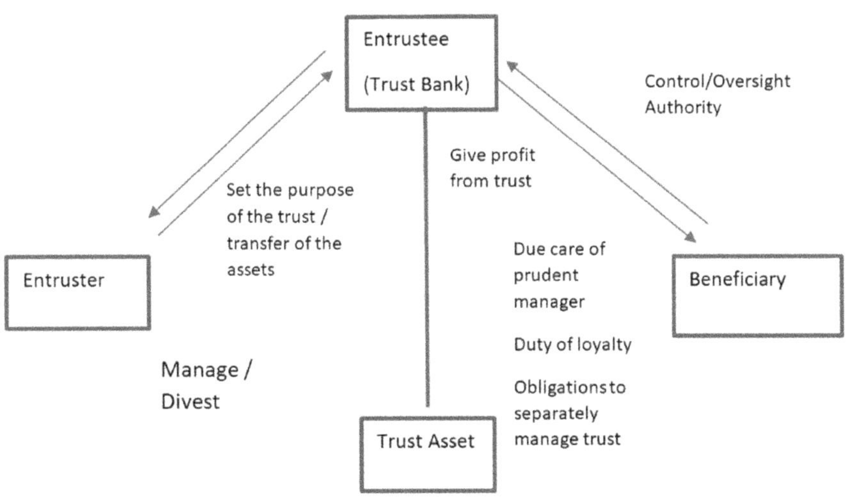

Figure 9.3 Trust Contract/Will.
Source: Authors.

In line with the concept of quality infrastructure, the implementation of the land trust system can be expanded by utilizing the increase of productivity generated by quality infrastructure for future sustainability payments to landowners. The land trust acts as an intermediary between government and the landowners. In order to do that, the increase in productivity, called the spillover effects, should be measured and the role of land trust should be clear.

9.5.5 Regional Collaboration and Sharing Tax Revenues Among Countries

Central Asia is not as densely populated as South Asia and Southeast Asia. Therefore, spillover effects might not be as big as other regions in Central Asia. It is better to think about the contributions of the water supply not only to the population, but also how Central Asia will be able to invite more tourists and foreign companies to come to the region. Then Central Asia can be developed by bringing those overseas businesses into the region, later supplying and expanding them to other countries. In this way, Central Asia could become a hub for tourism, manufacturing, and services. This is all possible with development of sustainable water infrastructure. This will contribute to sustainable growth and regional development, by improving health conditions and the quality of life for its people.

Note

1 The Coupled Model Intercomparison Project provides the latest outputs of nearly 30 models developed by institutions from around the world for ScenarioMIP, which is designed to provide climate projections under different emission scenarios. It involves improved climate modeling groups to yield more reliable projections (Jiang, et al. 2020).

References

ADB. 2017. *Meeting Asia's Infrastructure Needs.* Manila: Asian Development Bank. doi: http://dx.doi.org/10.22617/FLS168388-2 (accessed 1 November 2020).

ADB. 2003. *Water for All: The Water Policy of Asian Development Bank.* Manila: Asian Development Bank.

American Society of Civil Engineers and Value of Water Campaign. 2020. *The Economic Benefits of Investing in Water Infrastructure.* Value of Water Campaign.

Briscoe, J. 1999. The Financing of Hydropower, Irrigation and Water Supply Infrastructure in Developing Countries. *Water Resources Development* 14(4): 459–491.

Dunbar, B. 2012. *Landsat Top Ten – A Shrinking Sea, Aral Sea.* July 23. www.nasa.gov/mission_pages/landsat/news/40th-top10-aralsea.html (accessed 1 November 2020).

Gharleghi, B. 2018. *Farewell to Agriculture? Productivity Trends and the Competitiveness of Agriculture in Central Asia.* October 11. https://doc-research.org/2018/10/farewell-agriculture-productivity-trends-competitiveness-agriculture-central-asia/ (accessed 1 November 2020).

Haag, I., P.D. Jones, and C. Samimi. 2019. Central Asia's Changing Climate: How Temperature and Precipitation Have Changed Across Time, Space, and Altitude. *Climate* 7(10): 1–19.

Hendriyetty, N., P.D. Dey, C.J. Kim, and N. Buchoud. 2020. Urban Sanitation and Waste Management for All. *U20 Saudi Arabia White Paper Task Force 3: Nature-Based Urban Solutions.* www.urban20riyadh.org/sites/default/files/2020-09/Urban%20Sanitat (accessed 1 November 2020).

Jiang, J., T. Zhou, X. Chen, and L. Zhang. 2020. Future Changes in Precipitation over Central Asia Based on CMIP6 Projections. *Environmental Research Letters.*

Kerr, T.M. 1995. Supplying Water Infrastructure to Developing Countries via Private Sector Project Financing. *The Georgetown International Environmental Law Review* 8: 91–108.

Marin, P. 2009. Public-Private Partnerships for Urban Water Utilities: A Review of Experiences in Developing Countries. *Trends and Policy Options.* http://documents1.worldbank.org/curated/en/984921468182666780/pdf/Public-private-partnerships-for-urban-water-utilities-a-review-of-experiences-in-developing-countries.pdf (accessed 15 November 2020).

McDonald, R.I., et al. 2014. Water on an Urban Planet: Urbanization and the Reach of Urban Water Infrastructure. *Global Environmental Change* 27: 96–105.

Mirzabev, A. 2018. Improving the Resilience of Central Asian Agriculture to Weather Variability and Climate Change. In *Climate Smart Agriculture: Building Resilience to Climate Change*, edited by L. Lipper, N. McCarthy, D. Zilberman, S. Asfaw and G. Branca. Cham: Springer.

Patel, A. 2014. *Infrastructure for Agriculture & Rural Development in India: Need for a Comprehensive Program & Adequate Investment.* www.findevgateway.org/sites/default/files/publications/files/mfg-en-paper-infrastructure-for-agriculture-rural-development-in-india-need-for-a-comprehensive-program-adequate-investment-sep-2010.pdf (accessed 15 November 2020).

Pohl, B., et al. 2017. *Rethinking Water in Central Asia: The Costs of Inaction and Benefits of Water Cooperation.* Adelphi and CAREC, Swiss Agency for Development and Cooperation SDC.

Rakhmatullaev, S., et al. 2009. Groundwater Resources Use and Management in the Amu Darya River Basin (Central Asia). *Environmental Geology* (article in press).

Rakhmatullaev, S., I. Abdullaev, and J. Kazbekov. 2017. Water-Energy-Food-Environmental Nexus in Central Asia: Transition to Transformation. In *Water Resources in Central Asia: International Context*, edited by S.S. Zhiltsov, et al. Almaty: Springer International Publishing.

Reyer, C.P.O., et al. 2015. Climate Change Impacts in Central Asia and their Implications for Development. *Regional Environmental Change* 15(8).

Russell, M. 2018. *Water in Central Asia: An Increasingly Scarce Resource.* European Parliamentary Research Service.

Wang, Y., and B. Wu. 2015. Railways and the Local Economy: Evidence from Qingzang Railway. *Economic Development and Cultural Change* 63(3): 551–588.

Ward, F.A. 2010. Financing Irrigation Water Management and Infrastructure: A Review. *International Journal of Water Resources Development* 26(3): 321–349.

Yoshino, N., and U. Abidhadjaev. 2018. An Impact Evaluation of Infrastructure Investment: The Case of the Tashguzar–Boysun–Kumkurgon Railway in Uzbekistan. In *Financing Infrastructure in Asia and the Pacific: Capturing Impacts and New Sources*, edited by N. Yoshino, M. Helble and U. Abidhadjaev, 13–46. Tokyo: Asian Development Bank Institute (ADBI).

Yoshino, N., and U. Abidhadjaev. 2017. Impact of Infrastructure on Tax Revenue: Case Study of High-Speed Train in Japan. *Journal of Infrastructure, Policy and Development* 1(2). doi: 10.24294/jipd.v1i2.69 (accessed 15 November 2020).

Yoshino, N., U. Abidhadjaev, and M. Nakahigashi. 2019. Inducing Private 996. Finance to Water Supply and Inland Water Transport Using Spillover Tax Revenues. ADBI Working Paper Tokyo: Asian Development Bank Institute. www.adb.org/publications/inducing-private-finance-water-supply-inland-watertransport-using-spillover-tax (accessed 30 November 2020).

Yoshino, N., and N. Hendriyetty. 2020. Quality Infrastructure Investment and Land Trust in the face of COVID19 crisis. G20 Insights. www.g20-insights.org/wp-content/uploads/2020/05/quality-infrastructure-investment-and-land-trust-in-the-face-of-covid19-crisis-1590753397.pdf (accessed 15 November 2020).

Yoshino, N., N. Hendriyetty, and S. Lakhia. 2019. Quality Infrastructure Investment: Ways to Increase the Rate of Return for Infrastructure investments. *T20 Japan Task Force 4: Economic Effects of Infrastructure Investment and its Financing*.

Yoshino, N., U. Abidhadjaev, and N. Hendriyetty. 2019. Quality Infrastructure Investment and Land Trust. *Global Solutions Journal* (4).

10 The Role of Government in Attracting Private Investment in Sustainable Infrastructure

Case of Foreign Direct Investment Inflows in Central Asia

Keun Jung Lee and Chul Ju Kim

10.1 Introduction

Developing countries must overcome the financial constraints of their undeveloped financial markets to increase essential investments in infrastructure. The government can seek financing from foreign investors to solve this problem through public-private partnerships (PPPs). This chapter investigates the determinants of foreign direct investment (FDI) inflow in five Central Asian countries: Kazakhstan, the Kyrgyz Republic, Tajikistan, Turkmenistan, and Uzbekistan. FDI plays a significant development role because it is one of the main influences on technological and other types of knowledge transfer to a country's economy. Given that FDI is now more competitive, countries need to assess their attractiveness as it has become vital to implement various foreign policy reforms and projects.

The following research questions were also considered: do FDI determinants impact inflows to the host country? Furthermore, which variables have the most influence on a country's attractiveness to FDI?

10.2 Literature Review and Hypotheses

This section discusses the existing literature on private investment in infrastructure and the determinants of inflowing FDI. The studies differ in the scope of analysis (countries and time-period in consideration) and the methodologies used. More importantly, they differ in conclusions drawn from several comments.

10.2.1 Private Investment in Infrastructure and FDI

PPPs are commonly used to increase infrastructure demand when state funds are constrained (Babatunde and Perera 2017; Osei-Kyei, et al. 2019; Kuru and Ilter 2020). Governments favor PPPs for several reasons, including preventing initial investment costs, securing an integrated solution that involves building and operations, minimizing administrative costs, serving effective methods,

DOI: 10.4324/9781003228790-13

risk-sharing, and ensuring policy benefits (Osei-Kyei, et al. 2014). However, challenges for PPPs include political and social environments, macroeconomic and financial factors, legal aspects and inter-party disputes, and those related to operating duration (Ameyaw and Chan 2013; Osei-Kyei and Chan 2017; Osei-Kyei, et al. 2019).

Furthermore, Kuru and Ilter (2020) use the Business Canvas framework to build a pre-assessment canvas for risk management and success estimation, a new dimension to the PPP literature. The normalized weights of all classes of factors are displayed as PPP hazards (Kuru and Ilter 2020; 12). In the PPP project, Kuru and Ilter (2020) showed "Stability Economic Situation," "Government Interventions," "Political Support," and "Business Climate" as significant risk factors. Therefore, risk management and success prediction would be more reliable with more precise weights. Though insufficient infrastructure is a significant constraint in many low-income countries, FDI can be attracted for its construction when host governments allow foreign investor involvement.

Well-developed infrastructure enhances efficiency and stimulates FDI inflows (Jordaan 2004). Infrastructure and FDI inflows aid developing countries, as it provides financial resources; an opportunity to transfer technical, organizational, and management practices and skills; and access to international markets (Alfaro et al. 2004).

The establishment of international arbitration to refuse to implement contracts obtained by corrupt means, including agreements with the People's Republic of China (PRC), the Russian Federation, and other non-Organisation for Economic Co-operation and Development investors, must be sponsored. The new administration should extend the Extractive Industries Transparency Program to include other industries, set credible enforcement timetables, and finance capacity building monitoring to improve transparency and accountability. These risks are multiplied due to many stakeholders having conflicting objectives, the complex contractual relations between the parties, lengthy project durations, broader definitions of scope, and more massive amounts of investment in PPP projects (Zou et al. 2014).

10.2.2 Review of Determinants of FDI in Transition Economy

Frenkel, Funke, and Stadtmann (2004) looked at the factors that affect FDI flows between five home countries and 22 emerging economies in Asia, Latin America, and Central and Eastern Europe. According to their findings, economic growth and trade openness have a positive impact on FDI inflow to host countries. Further, FDI inflows are affected by market size, and are harmed by inflation. FDI flow is inversely proportional to the distance between the host and home countries.

Using panel data on 25 countries with transition economies from 1990 to 1998, Campos and Kinoshita (2003) found that institutions, accumulation, and trade openness are the key determinants of FDI attractiveness. Johnson (2006) also analyzed the FDI determinants in transition economies by separating the chosen countries into Central and Eastern Europe and the Commonwealth of Independent States. Central and Eastern Europe economies maintain higher gross domestic product (GDP) per capita compared to the Commonwealth of Independent States. Johnson suggested that FDI flows to Central and Eastern Europe economies are driven by a market-seeking motive, while resource-seeking factors drive FDI flows to the Commonwealth of Independent States.

Barauskaite (2012) studied the determinants of inward FDI in the Nordic and Baltic countries. Using Ownership, Location, and Internalization theories as a foundation, Barauskaite selected the following independent variables: FDI inflows, GDP, inflation rate, exports, tax burden, competition index, number of granted patents, economic freedom index, market size, workforce, labor costs, and expenditures for research and development (R&D). The most important relationships were discovered between FDI inflows and labor costs, the number of issued patents, the active population, and R&D expenses. In Estonia, the economic, political, and business environment had the most significant positive effect on attracting FDI, while demographic factors are the most critical in Latvia and Lithuania.

Raudonen and Freytag (2013) analyzed FDI inflows into Baltic countries using a gravity approach, scrutinizing the difference in corporate tax rates, GDP, geographical and cultural distance, and economic freedom index between host and investor countries. The results showed that the corporate tax rate differences are statistically significant. The greater geographical distance between the countries reduces FDI flows, and the economic freedom index has a significant positive impact in the Baltics. Simionescu (2017) found that GDP has a positive effect on attracting FDI flows into Baltic countries.

Ulzii-Ochir (2019) found that a higher return on capital, openness, and good infrastructure promote FDI in Central Asia. The corporate tax rate, and inflation rate have a positive impact on FDI.

Azam (2010) researched significant determinants of FDI in post-Soviet countries, including Armenia, the Kyrgyz Republic, and Turkmenistan. Notably, Azam reveals similarities in FDI determinants' characteristics and suggests the possible neighboring effect of observed countries. The author also considers the importance of market size and governmental support in facilitating the environment to create all conditions for FDI. This result suggests the insignificant role of government assistance in the case of Armenia and the Kyrgyz Republic. Azam (2013) later analyzed the determinants of FDI in Azerbaijan and Kazakhstan, with variables including the inflation rate, trade openness, market size, and government support, representing economic and political factors. Trade openness in both countries was insignificant, as was market size, while government assistance played an important positive role.

Jungwan, Baimukhamedova, and Akhmetova (2009) investigated the relationship between FDI inflows, exchange rates, and economic growth in developing countries and their effects on the country's main economic activities. In particular, from 1997 to 2006, they discovered that FDI had a negligible or statistically insignificant effect on Kazakhstan's GDP. They claim that resource-seeking

FDI has only a small impact on developed countries' economic development in transition.

Ni and Xu (2012) analyzed the dependence of FDI on the Gross Domestic Growth rate per capita in panel data of 88 countries across the world from 1965 to 2005. The results show that economic development in the observed countries had a positive relationship with FDI in the long term, which implies that it can slightly increase GDP per capita.

FDI has also shown an interrelationship with GDP growth. This notion explains emerging economies' motivation to attract more FDI to boost growth and overall GDP output through developing specific sectors of the economy. Lee, Fariz, and Sharipova (2015) investigate the relationship between FDI and economic development as it pertains to the diversification of Kazakhstan's natural resource-oriented economy. They found that FDI inflows affected both the natural resource and manufacturing sectors from 1994 to 2013.

Previous empirical research on the determinants of FDI in Eastern Europe and Central Asia yielded mixed results that differed depending on the countries and periods studied. Therefore, this study investigates the main factors in attracting FDI using representative data of its main determinants in developing and transition economies as follows.

Economic conditions. GDP could show a general understanding of how well a country's economy is doing. Various studies pointed out the positive relation between FDI and GDP (Pantulu and Poon 2003; Liu, Wang, and Wei 2001).

Reliability. We use the stock of FDI in a host country (in millions of US dollars, at 2019 value) as a proxy for reliability since its accumulation represents the investment climate. The amount of funds, reserves, retained earnings, and net indebtedness of FDI enterprises' affiliates are all included in FDI stocks. The investments that the country has already earned would have a positive effect on future investors (Frawsen and Josefsson 2004).

Exports. Exports are one of the critical factors that can influence the level of FDI in a host country. Exports may have differing effects on FDI, which may vary from country to country (Eaton and Tamura 1994; Hsiao and Hsiao 2006).

Imports. Imports sometimes can be measured as a substitute for FDI. Changes in the number of implications can affect FDI in a country, according to Liu, Wang, and Wei (2001). Import growth, in particular, resulted in an increase in inward FDI from the home country.

Economic stability. Inflation is one of the most relevant variables affecting FDI inflows. When inflation is unstable and fluctuates regularly, investors are more likely to avoid such countries because they fear losing money (Azam 2013).

Fiscal freedom. The fiscal freedom variable is a composite of marginal tax rates and total taxation levels, including direct and indirect taxes levied by all levels of government, as a percentage of GDP. The component score is derived from three quantitative subfactors (Mudenda 2015): the personal income top marginal tax rate, the company's top marginal tax rate, and the overall tax burden as a percentage of GDP. For this study's purpose, the level of taxation, the annual budget surplus or deficit, and the size of public debt reflect the degree of fiscal freedom (Raudonen and Freytag 2013).

Economic freedom. A person's constitutional right to manage his or her labor and property is known as economic freedom. As a result, the economic freedom index is often referred to as one of the most significant factors affecting a country's attractiveness to FDI. A higher index value suggests more economic and political independence. Individuals can work, create, consume, and invest freely. As a result, the economic freedom index can be used as a proxy for economic and political liberty.

Market size. A small market size in a developing country is associated with non-market-seeking FDI activities. In the eclectic theory, the number of people in the host country is one factor that affects the amount of FDI inflow (Dunning 1979). Therefore, we consider the total population in a country as a proxy of market size (Azam 2013; Barauskaite 2012).

Labor force. The total labor force comprises people ages 15 to 64 who are economically active. Many empirical papers in the literature review considered the labor force as a significant driver of FDI inflow (Labes 2015).

Infrastructure. Infrastructure resources must be available in sufficient quantities to ensure efficiency and growth. A region's economy cannot survive with major infrastructure distortions (Frawsen and Josefsson 2004). Therefore, the infrastructure of a country is another crucial factor for FDI inflows. We apply the percentage of internet users in the total population as a proxy for infrastructure (Baibekova and Hoang 2010).

Trade openness. The trade openness of a host country is defined by its export capabilities and access to foreign markets. This is a key factor in improving the investment climate, especially for export-oriented FDI (Azam 2013). An index of trade openness [(EXP+IMP)/GDP] is a proxy for trade openness (Demirhan and Masca 2008).

10.2.3 Hypotheses

This study hypothesizes relationships between FDI and 11 variables representing the determinants vis-à-vis Central Asia as determined by the literature review. The hypotheses are presented below:

H1: Good economic conditions, as reflected by GDP growth rate, will positively correlate with FDI inflow in the host country.

H2: A larger stock of FDI attracts more foreign investment. Thus, FDI stock affects inflow positively in the host country.

H3: A positive relationship between exports and inward FDI is expected in the host country.

H4: A positive relationship between imports and inward FDI is expected in the host country.

H5: Economic stability affects FDI inflow positively. Since high inflation or higher Consumer Price Index (CPI) represents greater instability in the host country, higher CPI is expected to affect FDI inflow negatively.

H6: A higher score on the economic freedom index is positively associated with FDI inflow in the host country.

H7: There is a positive relationship between fiscal freedom and inward FDI in the host country.

H8: Market size is positively related to FDI attractiveness; therefore, it is expected that a country's population would be positively related to its attractiveness to FDI.

H9: A larger labor force is positively associated with FDI inflow in the host country.

H10: There is a positive relationship between infrastructure and inward FDI in the host country.

H11: Trade openness represented by an index [(export + import)/GDP] affects the FDI inflow positively in the host country.

10.3 Methodology and Data

10.3.1 Data

Time series analysis (Keller 2012) was used to familiarize ourselves with basic FDI inflow fluctuations and to compare selected countries based on the amount of FDI they attracted to their economies. This study looked at FDI inflows from 1998 to 2018. The data for GDP growth rate, exports, imports, inflation (consumer price index, percentage), trade openness, population, labor force and infrastructure were obtained from the World Bank Database. The stock of FDI data came from the UNCTAD database (United Nations Conference on Trade and Development). The data for fiscal freedom and the index of economic freedom were collected from the Heritage Foundation.

10.3.2 Methodology

Eleven determinants have been chosen as independent variables of FDI inflow in Central Asian countries (see Table 10.1).

According to Hair, Anderson, Tatham, and Black (1998) and Keller and Yeaple (2009), the statistical form of the model is:

$$\begin{aligned} IFDI = {} & \alpha_0 + \alpha_1 GDP_{i,t} + \alpha_2 FDIS_{i,t} + \alpha_3 EXP_{i,t} + \alpha_4 IMP_{i,t} + \alpha_5 CPI_{i,t} \\ & + \alpha_6 FISF_{i,t} + \alpha_7 ECOF_{1,t} + \alpha_8 POP_{i,t} + \alpha_9 EMP_{i,t} + \alpha_{10} INF_{i,t} \\ & + \alpha_{11} OPEN_{i,t} + \varepsilon i \end{aligned} \tag{1}$$

Table 10.1 Descriptions of the Variables

Variable	*Abbreviation*	*Description*
Economic condition	GDP	Gross domestic product
Reliability	FDIS	Inflow of foreign direct investment stock ($ millions)
Exports	EXP	Total exports ($ millions)
Imports	IMP	Total imports ($ millions)
Economic stability	CPI	Inflation rate (percentage)
Fiscal freedom	FSF	A composite measure of the burden of taxes (percentage)
Economic freedom	ECOF	Economic freedom (index)
Market size	POP	Population of the country
Labor force	EMP	Number of actively employed people
Infrastructure	INF	Percentage of population with Internet access
Trade openness	OPEN	Index calculated as [(EXP + IMP) / GDP]

Source: World Bank Database. The stock of FDI data came from the UNCTAD database (United Nations Conference on Trade and Development). The data for fiscal freedom and the index of economic freedom were collected from the Heritage Foundation.

$$
\begin{aligned}
IFDI = {} & \alpha_0 + \alpha_1 GDP_{i,t} + \alpha_2 FDIS_{i,t} + \alpha_3 EXP_{i,t} + \alpha_4 IMP_{i,t} + \alpha_5 CPI_{i,t} \\
& + \alpha_6 FISF_{i,t} + \alpha_7 ECOF_{1,t} + \alpha_8 POP_{i,t} + \alpha_9 EMP_{i,t} + \alpha_{10} INF_{i,t} \\
& + \alpha_{11} OPEN_{i,t} + \alpha_{12} YEAR + \alpha_{13} Country + \varepsilon i \qquad (2)
\end{aligned}
$$

We use two different econometric regression methodologies, namely, ordinary least squares (OLS) in model (1) and two-stage least squares (2SLS) with fixed effect in model (2), including year and country variables to find which of the independent variables are crucial in determining the dependent variable.

10.4. Analysis and Findings

10.4.1 Descriptive Statistics

The first analysis includes descriptive statistics. The results for minimum, maximum, and mean values are presented separately for each of the Central Asian countries in this study in Table 10.2.

Of the Central Asian economies, Kazakhstan has the highest FDI inflow, FDI stock, exports, imports, economic freedom, and infrastructure.

In the case of the Kyrgyz Republic, during the chosen period, the minimum variable for FDI inflow was reported as -$2.36 million. A negative FDI inflow means that foreign investors removed their investment from the Kyrgyz Republic, which exports and imports goods and services comparatively less than other Central Asian countries.

The lowest amount of FDI stock is in Tajikistan ($18 million). The growth of GDP and fiscal freedom index were high in Turkmenistan for 21 years. The

Table 10.2 Descriptive Statistics (Minimum, Mean and Maximum)

Country	*Variables*	*Min*	*Mean*	*Max*
Kazakhstan	FDI inflow ($ millions)	1,370	8,051	16,975
	GDP growth (%)	1.1	6.7	13.5
	FDI stock ($ millions)	7,977	63,227	132,574
	Export ($ millions)	7,163	47,017	91,747
	Import ($ millions)	6,768	34,626	63,395
	Inflation (%)	5.1	8.6	17.2
	Fiscal freedom (index)	73.7	84.1	93.2
	Economic freedom (index)	47.3	57.7	63.7
	Population (unit)	14,858,335	15,916,109	17,794,397
	Active people (unit)	7,655,067	8,343,328	9,172,348
	Internet users (% of total people)	0.5	25.9	74.6
	Trade openness (index)	53.0	82.2	105.7
Kyrgyz Republic	FDI inflow ($ millions)	-24	29.4	1,139.3
	GDP growth (%)	-0.47	4.4	10.9
	FDI stock ($ millions)	427	1,747	5,102
	Export ($ millions)	527.1	1,826.5	3,380.2
	Import ($ millions)	564.6	3,234.9	6,731.8
	Inflation (%)	0.4	9	37
	Fiscal freedom (index)	68.7	86.4	94.8
	Economic freedom (index)	52	58.6	61
	Population (unit)	4,840,400	5,351,955	6,079,500
	Active people (unit)	2,001,039	2,341,521	2,565,487
	Internet users (% of total people)	0.2	14.1	34.5
	Trade openness (index)	73.7	113.5	146.1
Tajikistan	FDI inflow ($ millions)	6.7	178.3	426.1
	GDP growth (%)	3.7	7.5	11
	FDI stock ($ millions)	18	880	2,399
	Export ($ millions)	601	934.5	1,644.2
	Import ($ millions)	733.5	2,592.6	5,812.8
	Inflation (%)	5.0	13.3	38.6
	Fiscal freedom (index)	57.6	81.9	92.8

	Economic freedom (index)	41	50.6	55
	Population (unit)	6,114,886	7,303,449	8,734,951
	Active people (unit)	2,024,243	2,684,106	3,351,954
	Internet users (% of total people)	0.03	7.91	20.47
	Trade openness (index)	82.7	99.3	199.6
Turkmenistan	FDI inflow ($ millions)	125	1,997	4,553
	GDP growth (%)	0.26	8.83	16.50
	FDI stock ($ millions)	818	11,199	36,241
	Export ($ millions)	1,375.8	13,769.9	32,311
	Import ($ millions)	2,046.2	8,498.1	19,159
	Inflation (%)	-2.67	7.7	23.47
	Fiscal freedom (index)	57.5	89.2	98.4
	Economic freedom (index)	36	43	51
	Population (unit)	4,466,132	4,971,307	5,662,544
	Active people (unit)	1,779,209	2,172,570	2,565,153
	Internet users (% of total people)	0.05	4.40	17.99
	Trade openness (index)	104	123	176
Uzbekistan	FDI inflow ($ millions)	65.3	469.7	1,636.4
	GDP growth (%)	3.8	7.0	9.9
	FDI stock ($ millions)	624	3,963	8,957
	Export ($ millions)	2,985	9,170	1,5340
	Import ($ millions)	2,843	12,359	17,819
	Inflation (%)	7.3	14.6	29.1
	Fiscal freedom (index)	57.9	78.5	94.4
	Economic freedom (index)	39	44.4	52
	Population (unit)	24,311,650	27,613,766	31,847,900
	Active people (unit)	9,470,322	12,127,101	15,030,626
	Internet users (% of total people)	0.03	14.16	46.79
	Trade openness (index)	36.55	59.42	79.70

Source: World Bank Database. The stock of FDI data came from the UNCTAD database (United Nations Conference on Trade and Development). The data for fiscal freedom and the index of economic freedom were collected from the Heritage Foundation.

Note
FDI = foreign direct investment, GDP = gross domestic product.

highest amount of inflation is similar in Tajikistan and the Kyrgyz Republic, with 37% and 38.5%, respectively. Tajikistan's trade openness index is the maximum amount, at almost 200. However, it is arguable to say that a high trade openness index results in better economic growth.

In the case of Turkmenistan, the population and number of actively employed are comparatively low. The minimum percentage of internet users are similar to the five Central Asian countries. Turkmenistan experienced inflation of 45%, whereas the other countries' lowest inflation rate was positive.

In the case of Uzbekistan, the minimum fiscal and economic freedom indexes are similar to the other four countries. Uzbekistan's minimum GDP growth and inflation rate is higher than other Central Asian countries. Uzbekistan dominates population in Central Asia.

10.4.2 Analysis of Autocorrelation, Heteroscedasticity and ANOVA Test

OLS regression assumes that there is a linear relationship between dependent and independent variables. Before conducting OLS regression tests for autocorrelation, heteroscedasticity would apply. First, the autocorrelation outputs are presented in Table 10.3. We can see that the Durbin-Watson statistic for all five Central Asian countries is close to 2, suggesting no autocorrelation in the time series.

Further, by using the Glejser Test, the presence of heteroscedasticity in the data set is examined and the results are presented in Table 10.4. For the countries other than Uzbekistan, the value of Sig. FDI inflow > 0.05. This indicates that there is no heteroscedasticity problem for these countries, but there is a problem of heteroscedasticity in the Uzbekistan case. The significance level of all independent variables for all Central Asian countries except Uzbekistan is larger than 0.05. However, for Uzbekistan, the sig. values of FDI stock, import, population, active population, and internet users are less than 0.05, suggesting that there is a heteroscedasticity problem for the Uzbekistan model.

In the ANOVA test reported in Table 10.5, The p-values are compared to significance level 0.05. The p-value of the ANOVA test for the Tajikistani model is more than 0.05. (0.145 > 0.05), and the value of the F-test is 2.508 < 4.03; therefore, the null hypothesis is accepted. The null hypothesis rejects the case of

Table 10.3 Autocorrelation Analysis (Durbin-Watson)

Kazakhstan	*Kyrgyz Republic*	*Tajikistan*	*Turkmenistan*	*Uzbekistan*
DW = 2.275	DW = 2.284	DW = 2.737	DW = 2.632	DW = 2.957

Source: Authors.

Note
DW = Durbin-Watson.

Table 10.4 Heteroscedasticity

Model	*Kazakhstan*	*Kyrgyz Republic*	*Tajikistan*	*Turkmenistan*	*Uzbekistan*
	Sig.				
(Constant)	.581	.521	.373	.534	.002
GDP growth (%)	.854	.387	.370	.692	.932
FDI stock ($ millions)	.723	.357	.550	.128	.005
Export ($ millions)	.500	.289	.280	.706	.460
Import ($ millions)	.645	.456	.873	.682	.021
Inflation (%)	.520	.539	.965	.358	.326
Fiscal freedom (index)	.917	.767	.745	.653	.125
Economic freedom (index)	.345	.476	.236	.920	.054
Population (unit)	.365	.477	.428	.347	.004
Active employed people (unit)	.394	.684	.472	.145	.017
Internet users (%)	.571	.652	.682	.581	.001
Trade openness (index)	.971	.590	.581	.518	.091

Source: Authors.

Note
FDI = foreign direct investment, GDP = gross domestic product.

Table 10.5 ANOVA Test

Model		*Sum of Squares*	*df*	*Mean Square*	*F*	*Sig.*
Kazakhstan	Regression	487,516,162	11	43,410,560	15.749	.003b
	Residual	16,538,343	6	2,736,390		
	Total	494,054,805	17			
The Kyrgyz Republic	Regression	1,386,360	11	126,033	4.916	.031b
	Residual	153,816	6	25,638		
	Total	1,540,181	17			
Tajikistan	Regression	325,407	11	30582	2.808	.145b
	Residual	69,831	6	14,521		
	Total	394,543	17			
Turkmenistan	Regression	45,858,458	10	5,585,845	42.500	.003b
	Residual	840,877	7	123,125		
	Total	56,699,435	17			
Uzbekistan	Regression	4,133,093	11	373,008	9.075	.030b
	Residual	246,611	6	42,101		
	Total	4,329,705	17			

Source: Authors.

Kazakhstan, the Kyrgyz Republic, Turkmenistan, and Uzbekistan, as *p*-values are 0.003, 0.031, 0.003, 0.030, respectively, and all of these values are less than 0.05.

10.4.3 Findings in OLS and 2SLS Results

In Table 10.6, as mentioned, the variable "FDI inflow" is the dependent variable and GDP growth, FDI stock, export, import, inflation rate, fiscal freedom, economic freedom, unit of total population, labor force, percentage of internet users out of total people are independent variables in OLS regression analysis.

In the case of Kazakhstan, FDI stock is a significant factor for the model, meaning that reliability is an essential factor for inflows. Exports are significantly associated with FDI inflows in Kazakhstan, while inflation is positively associated. However, fiscal freedom of Kazakhstan has a negative correlation and statistically

Table 10.6 OLS Test Results

Model	*Kazakhstan*	*Kyrgyz Republic*	*Tajikistan*	*Turkmenistan*	*Uzbekistan*
GDP growth (%)	19.198 (0.745)	22.853 (1.127)	39.691* (1.758)	-22.19 (-0.488)	37.122 (-0.483)
FDI stock ($ millions)	0.448** (2.616)	0.103 (0.157)	-0.019 (-0.067)	0.031 (0.242)	0.524 (1.575)
Export ($ millions)	0.443*** (3.373)	-0.13 (-0.564)	-0.121 (-0.42)	-0.23 (-1.132)	0.295** (2.722)
Import ($ millions)	0.404* (2.252)	-0.033 (-0.336)	0.033 (0.385)	0.378 (1.151)	-0.315*** (-3.984)
Inflation (%)	8.391** (2.581)	21.746 (1.333)	-1.365 (-0.203)	-13.62* (-2.663)	39.935 (1.247)
Fiscal freedom (index)	-12.532** (-3.202)	-8.573 (-0.234)	30.366*** (3.426)	-27.809 (-2.291)	13.323 (0.562)
Economic freedom (index)	28.502 (0.793)	-34.472 (-0.64)	25.615* (0.813)	-71.235* (-0.795)	-38.755 (-0.876)
Population (unit)	-0.027** (-2.343)	0.002 (0.339)	0.002* (1.818)	0.002* (1.218)	-0.002 (-1.5)
Employment (unit)	0.03* (2.111)	0.004** (2.413)	0.007* (2.138)	0.010* (2.163)	0.002 (1.481)
Internet users (% of total people)	19.861 (1.068)	-88.955 (-1.502)	73.166* (1.402)	-13.358 (-0.902)	-2.268 (-0.047)
Trade openness (index)	8.169 (0.518)	-1.87* (-0.164)	-1.419* (-0.522)	-1.419* (-0.522)	8.677* (0.511)
R^2	0.767	0,600	0.525	0.685	0.543

Source: Authors.

Note

***, ** and * denote significance at 1%, 5% and 10% level, respectively.

FDI = foreign direct investment, GDP = gross domestic product, OLS = ordinary least squares.

significant. Kazakhstan has a negative correlation between population and FDI; we found that, as the population decreased from 1995 to 2000, FDI sharply increased for this period and increased from 2001 to 2019. The number of employed people (EMP) as a proxy for the labor force has a statistically significant positive effect on FDI in Kazakhstan, the Kyrgyz Republic, Tajikistan, and Turkmenistan.

In the Kyrgyz Republic, the inflation coefficient is negative; however, it is not statistically significant, meaning that the country's economic stability is not a substantial factor in FDI inflows. EMP has a statistically significant positive effect on FDI.

The relationship between FDI and GDP is positive for all Central Asian countries, Tajikistan in particular. Fiscal freedom is statistically significant and correlates strongly with FDI, while economic freedom also has a positive correlation and is statistically significant. Population as market size shows a statistically positive effect on FDI into Tajikistan, while EMP also has a statistically significant positive effect.

In the case of Turkmenistan, inflation is negatively associated with FDI. We can assume that high inflation and deflation are not especially harmful to FDI because we used it as a proxy for economic stability. We presume that Turkmenistan's poor economic stability, coupled with high inflation, has a major negative impact on FDI inflows. Turkmenistan's economic independence has a statistically important negative correlation. The economic freedom of Turkmenistan has a negative correlation and a statistically significant one. Economic freedom and fiscal freedom are indicators of a non-interventionist government.

Similarly, a higher fiscal freedom score connotes a smaller, less interventionist, and more efficient government. The population shows a statistically positive effect on FDI into Turkmenistan, while EMP also has a statistically significant positive effect.

Exports are significantly associated with FDI inflows only in Kazakhstan and Uzbekistan. Imports have a statistically significant positive effect on FDI in Uzbekistan but are insignificant in the other countries. The coefficient of inflation is positive in Uzbekistan; however, it is not statistically significant. The market size of Uzbekistan has a negative correlation between population and FDI.

In the case of infrastructure (INF), a positive sign was hypothesized, but the coefficient is negative or positive and statistically insignificant. However, Tajikistan has a positive correlation and is statistically significant. An insignificant result of INF may be related to our variable (internet users of the total population); using a different variable (e.g., road, electricity, and transportation,) as a proxy for infrastructure might have produced significant results.

Finally, the coefficient of trade openness (OPEN) was expected to be positive. The coefficient of OPEN in Uzbekistan shows a statistically significant positive sign, suggesting that its trade openness is one of the main determinants of FDI inflows. However, the coefficient of OPEN shows a statistically significant negative sign in the Kyrgyz Republic, Tajikistan, and Turkmenistan.

We used the 2SLS methodology to estimate the model (2) simultaneously for the five countries in Central Asia. This economic model addresses whether the FDI inflows function as endogenous rather than exogenous variables. Table 10.7 presents the results and compares how the signs of the coefficients differ compared to the OLS results in Table 10.6.

Table 10.7 Results of 2SLS test for Central Asia Countries

Model	*Kazakhstan*	*Kyrgyz Republic*	*Tajikistan*	*Turkmenistan*	*Uzbekistan*
GDP growth (%)	4.198 (1.745)	2.853 (1.127)	3.901* (1.858)	-2.191 (-0.488)	2.122* (1.103)
FDI stock ($ millions)	1.047*** (2.916)	0.203 (0.187)	-0.041 (-0.168)	0.031 (0.242)	0.926* (2.978)
Export ($ millions)	0.873*** (3.703)	-0.13 (-0.564)	-0.121 (-0.42)	-0.23 (-1.132)	0.505** (2.802)
Import ($ millions)	0.825* (2.650)	-0.133 (-0.382)	0.303 (0.782)	0.392 (1.101)	-0.910*** (-4.083)
Inflation (%)	5.391** (2.581)	2.746* (1.333)	-1.365 (-0.203)	-0.672* (-2.663)	1.935* (1.042)
Fiscal freedom (index)	2.532 (0.402)	-1.573 (-0.234)	3.366*** (3.426)	-1.712 (-0.291)	1.323 (0.562)
Economic freedom (index)	2.502 (0.793)	-3.472 (-0.64)	5.615* (0.813)	-1.235* (-0.795)	3.755 (0.876)
Population (unit)	0.027* (0. 843)	0.002 (0.339)	0.002* (1.818)	0.002* (1.218)	-0.002 (-1.5)
Employment (unit)	0.03* (2.111)	0.004** (2.413)	0.007* (2.138)	0.010* (2.163)	0.002 (1.481)
Internet users (% of total people)	1.861 (1.068)	-8.955 (-1.502)	7.166* (1.402)	-3.358 (-0.902)	-2.268 (-0.047)
Trade openness (index)	0.709 (0.308)	-1.97 (-0.594)	-1.419 (-0.522)	-0.807 (-0.122)	3.607* (1.518)
Year (fixed effect)	Yes	Yes	Yes	Yes	Yes
Country (fixed effect)	Yes	Yes	Yes	Yes	Yes
R^2	0.695	0.556	0.545	0.654	0.532

Source: Authors.

Note
***, ** and * denote significance at 1%, 5% and 10% level, respectively.
FDI = foreign direct investment, GDP = gross domestic product, 2SLS = two-square least squares.

The variables have higher levels of importance, according to the 2SLS model's findings. The coefficient of GDP, in particular, has a statistically significant value for both Tajikistan and Uzbekistan, meaning that economic conditions are an important factor in FDI inflows to these countries.

FDI stock is a significant factor for Kazakhstan and Uzbekistan's model, meaning that reliability is an important factor for FDI inflows there. The export and import factors for determinants of FDI inflows impact on Kazakhstan and Uzbekistan. However, imports in Uzbekistan have a statistically significant negative effect on FDI inflows. This result implies that investors consider a market-seeking FDI and efficiency-seeking FDI in Uzbekistan.

Inflation as a proxy for economic stability is positively significant in Kazakhstan and Uzbekistan and negatively significant in Turkmenistan. These results are different from those of the previous analysis, which found a meaningful positive relationship in Kazakhstan and a negatively significant relationship in Turkmenistan. Therefore, we can suggest that the economic stability is an essential factor for FDI inflows.

Further, the inflation coefficient is negative in the Kyrgyz Republic and positive in Uzbekistan. Still, it is not statistically significant, meaning that the country's economic stability is not a significant factor in FDI inflows. We can assume that high inflation and deflation are not especially harmful to FDI investors because we used inflation as a proxy for economic stability. We can suggest that weak economic stability (associated with high inflation) has a significant negative effect on FDI inflows in Turkmenistan.

Fiscal freedom is statistically significant in Tajikistan. However, in the case of Kazakhstan, fiscal freedom has a positive sign but is statistically insignificant.

The population shows a statistically positive effect on FDI in Kazakhstan, Tajikistan, and Turkmenistan. Therefore, we can suggest that market size becomes an important factor for FDI inflows in these countries.

As in the OLS results, the number of employed individuals as a proxy of labor force has a positive effect and is statistically significant on FDI in Kazakhstan, the Kyrgyz Republic, Tajikistan, and Turkmenistan. This suggests that human capital is an essential factor for FDI inflows in Central Asia.

Further, the coefficient of INF is statistically insignificant in Kazakhstan, the Kyrgyz Republic, Turkmenistan, and Uzbekistan. However, Tajikistan has a strongly positive effect on FDI. We argue once more that the variable we used as a proxy for infrastructure (i.e., internet users or mobile cellular subscriptions) is inadequate to describe a country's infrastructure.

Finally, for Uzbekistan, the coefficient of OPEN is highly significant, implying that trade openness is one of the most critical factors affecting FDI inflows. The findings in Kazakhstan, the Kyrgyz Republic, Tajikistan, and Turkmenistan, on the other hand, suggest that trade openness is not a major factor in FDI inflows to Central Asia. The result implies that state-owned enterprises operate most large businesses in Central Asia, and FDI inflows in the business environment depend on government policy rather than trade open (Lee 2020).

10.5 Conclusion and Discussion

In this chapter, for the period 1999–2019, the determinants of attracting FDI in five developing Central Asian countries were examined. To assess which of the independent variables were critical factors in evaluating the dependent variable, OLS and 2SLS regression methodologies were used. When compared to OLS, the 2SLS results appeared to be more effective. As a result, these findings were chosen as the base for economic interpretation. We can analyze each country in terms of the variables' effects on FDI inflow.

Kazakhstan ranks first for attracting FDI inflow during 1999–2016, receiving most of it from the Netherlands, the US, Switzerland, and France. The oil and mining sectors, which receive more than half of the FDI, are still the most attractive for investors. 2SLS analysis shows that reliability, exports, imports, economic stability, and labor force are significant determinants for the model.

Turkmenistan ranks second for average FDI inflow. Hydrocarbons and petrochemicals are increasingly attracting more foreign investors, who recently showed interest in the manufacturing sector. The leading investors in Turkmenistan are Germany, the Russian Federation, and Austria. The regression analysis showed that economic factors (economic condition, economic freedom, market size, and labor force) are significant for the model.

Uzbekistan ranks third, with an average FDI inflow of $470 million due to its sizable interior market (more than 30 million people), diversified economy, personnel resource base, and political stability in the wake of a recent political transition. Uzbekistan's leading investors are the PRC, which is interested in the gas pipeline industry, Republic of Korea, and Japan. Findings from the 2SLS regression analysis showed that economic condition, reliability, exports and imports, and trade openness are statistically significant.

The Kyrgyz Republic ranks fourth in average FDI inflow. Most inflows have been driven toward mining-related activities and other sectors such as finance and manufacture of petroleum products, but overall non-mining FDI remains low. The Kyrgyz Republic's prominent investors are Canada, the PRC, the UK, Russian Federation, and Kazakhstan. Regression analyses (OLS and 2SLS) showed that none of the independent variables is statistically significant in the model. An explanation for this result may be the small size of the economy and fewer natural resources, suggesting government policy's effectiveness to increase the FDI inflows.

Tajikistan attracted the lowest amount of FDI among all Central Asian countries. The industries that draw the most foreign investment are aluminum, cotton, and energy. Tourism is also demonstrating its value. Tajikistan provides an ideal setting for regional and cross-border investment. The PRC, Russian Federation, Kazakhstan, the UK, and the US are the top five investing nations, in that order. Regression analysis showed that economic condition, market size, and government policy (fiscal freedom, economic freedom, human capital, and infrastructure) are significant determinants of FDI inflow.

FDI flows in Central Asia are unpredictable and do not tend to obey economic cycles; instead, major investment projects' timing dictates their dynamics. Most investments are made in the Central Asian economies' natural resource industries, especially in the mining, refining, and transportation of hydrocarbons and metals.

The rise in international oil prices and other primary products has been a major driver of these investments. Non-tradable service sectors, such as real estate growth, trade, finance, and communications, are also popular and growing destinations for FDI. Central Asia will be affected by geography, infrastructure, trade facilitation, and government policies.

Because of the variations between oil exporters and non-oil exporters and their dependency on various export commodities, a one-size-fits-all solution might not be sufficient for Central Asia's transition economies. Given that natural resources will inevitably be depleted and global commodity prices will remain unpredictable, depending on favorable world commodity prices and concentrating only on a few export products could prove problematic in the future. Central Asia must consider diversifying into new products and markets to ensure its long-term growth. A stable political environment, reliable institutions, and infrastructure all help to increase FDI flows. Free trade is another critical factor in increasing FDI, given that trade and FDI are complementary. Opening up trade increases FDI flows, and a higher FDI stock in a country leads to a higher trade volume. This research has implications for policymakers about the role of government in attracting private investment for sustainable infrastructure. This research has implications for policymakers about the role of government in attracting private investment for sustainable infrastructure.

References

Alfaro, L., A. Chanda, S. Kalemli-Ozcan, and S. Sayek. 2004. FDI and Economic Growth: The Role of Local Financial Markets. *Journal of International Economics* 64(1): 89–112.

Ameyaw, E.E., and A.P.C. Chan. 2013. Identifying Public-Private Partnership (PPP) Risks in Managing Water Supply Projects in Ghana. *Journal of Facilities Management* 11(2): 152–182.

Azam, M. 2010. Economic Determinants of Foreign Direct Investment in Armenia, Kyrgyz Republic and Turkmenistan: Theory and Evidence. *Eurasian Journal of Business and Economics* 3(6): 27–40.

Azam, M. 2013. Foreign Direct Investment, Financial Deepening and Economic Growth in Azerbaijan and Kazakhstan: A Comparative Empirical Study. *The Empirical Economics Letters* 12(6): 5–9.

Babatunde, S.O., and S. Perera. 2017. Analysis of Financial Close Delay in PPP Infrastructure Projects in Developing Countries. *Benchmarking* 24(6):1690–1708.

Baibekova, K., and T.N.A. Hoang. 2010. *Determinant of Foreign Direct Investment in Ireland.* Bachelor's Thesis. Jönköping, Sweden: Jönköping international Business School.

Barauskaite, L. 2012. *An Analysis of Foreign Direct Investments: Inflows and Determinants.* Master's Thesis, University of Agder. https://uia.brage.unit.no/uia-xmlui/bitstream/handle/11250/135808/oppgave%20laura%20barauskaite.pdf?sequence=1&isallowed=y (accessed 21 June 2021).

Campos, F., and Y. Kinoshita. 2003. *Why Does FDI Go Where It Goes? New Evidence from the Transition Economies.* IMF Working Paper, WP/03/228. Washington, DC: International Monetary Fund.

Demirhan, E., and M. Masca. 2008. "Determinants of Foreign Direct investment Flows to Developing Countries: A Cross-Sectional Analysis." *Prague Economic Papers, University of Economics*, Issue 4: 356–369.

Eaton, J., and A. Tamura. 1994. Japanese and U.S. Exports and investment As Conduits of Growth. In *Financial Deregulation and Integration in East Asia*, T. Ito and A. O. Krueger (eds.), 51–75. Chicago: University of Chicago Press.

Frawsen, G., and H. Josefsson. 2004. *Foreign Direct Investment and Developing Countries: How to Attract Transnational Corporations.* Bachelor's Thesis. Lund, Sweden: Lund University.

Frenkel, M., K. Funke, and G. Stadtmann. 2004. A Panel Analysis of Bilateral FDI Flows to Emerging Economies. *Economic Systems* 28(3): 281–300.

Hair, J.F., R.E. Anderson, R.L. Tatham and W.C. Black. 1998. *Multivariate Data Analysis* (5th ed.). New Jersey: Prentice-Hall.

Hsiao, F.S.T. and M.C.W. Hsiao. 2006. FDI, Exports, and GDP in East and Southeast Asia – Panel Data Versus Time-Series Causality Analysis. *Journal of Asian Economics* 17: 1082–1106.

Jordaan, J.C. 2004. Foreign Direct Investment and Neighbouring Influences. Unpublished Doctoral Thesis. Pretoria: University of Pretoria.

Johnson, A. 2006. *FDI Inflows to the Transition Economies in Eastern Europe: Magnitude and Determinants.* CESIS Electronic Working Paper Series, No. 59. https://static.sys.kth.se/itm/wp/cesis/cesiswp59.pdf (accessed 21 June 2021).

Jungwan, L., G. Baimukhamedova, and S. Akhmetova. 2009. The Effects of Foreign Direct investment on Economic Growth of a Developing Country: From Kazakhstan. Allied Academies International Conference. *Academy for Economics and Economic Education* 12(2): 22–27.

Keller, W., and S.R. Yeaple. 2009. Multinational Enterprises, International Trade, and Productivity Growth: Firm-Level Evidence from the United States. *The Review of Economics and Statistics* 91(4): 821–831.

Kuru, K. and D.A. Ilter. 2020. A Canvas Model for Risk Assessment and Performance Estimation in Public-Private Partnerships, *International Journal of Construction Management* 20(3):1–16.

Labes, S.-A. 2015. FDI Determinants in BRICS. *CES Working Papers* 7(2): 296–308.

Lee, K.J., B. Fariz, and Z. Sharipova. 2015. The Relationship Between FDI, Diversification and Economic Growth in Natural Resource-Oriented Countries: Case of Kazakhstan. *Journal of International Business and Economics* 3(2): 51–62.

Lee, K.J. 2020. The Effects of Privatization and Corporate Governance of SOES in Transition Economy: The Case of Kazakhstan. Working Paper Series No. 1127, Asian Development Bank Institute. Tokyo: ADBI.

Liu, X., C. Wang, and Y. Wei. 2001. Causal Links Between Foreign Direct Investment and Trade in China. *China Economic Review* 12(2–3): 190–202.

Moran, T. 2008. Foreign Direct Investment and Development. In *The White House and the World: A Global Development Agenda for the Next U.S. President*, edited by Nancy Birdsall. Center for Global Development, Washington, DC, 121–140.

Mudenda, L.D. 2015. *Corporate Income Tax Rate and Foreign Direct Investment: The Case of Southern African Economies.* Master's Thesis. Umeå, Sweden: Umeå University.

Ni, D., and C. Xu. 2012. FDI and Economic Growth. www.coursehero.com/file/13624102/fdi-and-economic-growth/

Osei–Kyei, R., D. Ayirebi, J.K. Ofori–Kuragu. 2014. Reasons for Adopting Public–Private Partnership (PPP) for Construction Projects in Ghana. *International Journal of Construction Management* 14(4): 227–238.

Osei-Kyei, R., and A. Chan. 2017. Risk Assessment in Public-Private Partnership infrastructure Projects: Empirical Comparison Between Ghana and Hong Kong. *Construction Innovation* 17(2): 204–223.

Osei-Kyei, R., A.P.C. Chan, Y. Yao, and K.M. Mazher. 2019. Conflict Prevention Measures for Public-Private Partnerships in Developing Countries. *Journal of Financial Management Property and Construction* 24(1): 39–57.

Pantulu, J., and J.P.H. Poon. 2003. Foreign Direct Investment and International Trade: Evidence from the US and Japan. *Journal of Economic Geography* 3(3): 241–259.

Raudonen, S., and A. Freytag. 2013. Determinants of FDI Inflows into the Baltic Countries: Empirical Evidence from a Gravity Model. *Journal of Business and Economics* 4(2): 180–194.

Simionescu, M. 2017. The Relationship Between Foreign Direct Investment and Economic Growth in Bulgaria, Romania and Croatia During the Recent Economic Crisis. *Internal Auditing and Risk Management* 42(1): 149–158.

Ulzii-Ochir, N. 2019. The Determinants of FDI in Landlocked Developing Countries in Central Asia. In *Trade Logistics in Landlocked and Resource Cursed Asian Countries*, edited by K. Jayanthakumaran, N. Shukla, C. Harvie, & O. Erdenetsogt, 94–101. Singapore: Palgrave Macmillan.

United Nations Conference on Trade and Development (UNCTAD). 2017. *Global and Regional FDI Trends in 2016*. UNCTAD Global investment Trends Monitor.

World Bank Data. 2020. World Bank National Account Data. https://data.worldbank.org/indicator/ny.gdp.mktp.cd

Zou, W., M. Kumaraswamy, J. Chung, and J. Wong. 2014. Identifying the Critical Success Factors for Relationship Management in PPP Projects. *International Journal of Project Management* 32(2): 265–274.

11 Private-Public Partnerships in the Association of Southeast Asian Nations and CAREC and their Scope for Renewable Energy Projects

Dharish David and Amar Causevic

11.1 Introduction

Currently, approximately 70% of greenhouse gas (GHG) emissions come from infrastructure such as electricity generation, transportation, industry, and buildings, making it central to how societies adapt to climate change. Carbon-intensive infrastructure is not sustainable in the long run as it increases air pollution, exacerbates urban congestion, and degrades the environment. At the same time, an estimated $93 trillion will be needed until 2030 to meet global infrastructure needs across transport, energy, telecommunications, and other infrastructure (New Climate Economy 2016). Simultaneously, the net costs of building low-carbon and climate-resilient (LCR) infrastructure are relatively low, while the benefits are net positive. There remain significant financing challenges as there is the real challenge of financing the upfront $13.5 trillion in additional LCR infrastructure investment—approximately $900 billion per annum (Bhattacharya, Oppenheim, and Stern 2015). Other challenges that need to be addressed are public sector coordination, greening the financial sector, making clean energy prices competitive vis-à-vis fossil fuels, the high cost of domestic debt capital, high perceived risk due to lack of knowledge within the domestic banking sector about innovative clean energy technologies, and off-taker and currency risks for foreign investors (Bayliss and Van Waeyenberge 2018).

Whatever infrastructure is built until 2030 will determine the carbon footprints of individual nations. However, the real challenge is to mobilize these infrastructure investments before they are committed, as, typically, these fund projects and facilities with long lifespans and decisions made today about such investments can lock in future emissions levels (Consortium of Multilateral Development Banks 2015). The considerable size of the LCR infrastructure investments and current constraints that the public sector balance sheets are reeling under mean that private capital will be essential in financing such investments. In the long run, it is expected that private capital could provide up to half of the finance needed to build the LCR infrastructure (Organisation for Economic Co-operation and Development 2017).

DOI: 10.4324/9781003228790-14

While the public sector faces climate finance shortages, the private sector has enough capital to finance the global sustainable transition. However, private investors are still reluctant to scale up LCR investments since they are not mainstreamed in the global financial markets (Urban and Wójcik 2019). With the large surplus of available capital, governments' challenge is to ensure that public policies and investment conditions facilitate a re-allocation of investment from carbon-intensive projects to LCR alternatives. To promote the re-allocation and scaling up of investment in LCR infrastructure, governments can use available public capital to mobilize much larger pools of private capital. According to the Climate Policy Initiative (2018), private sector investment has taken the largest share in climate finance. Project developers have been consistently driving the most substantial volume of private funding. While the share of more traditional lenders in the climate financing mix signals a maturing technology market, more commercial financial institutions are taking a more significant role with institutional investment.

Rapid economic growth in several Association of Southeast Asian Nations (ASEAN) member states, and in the Central Asia Regional Economic Cooperation (CAREC) region has caused a significant increase in energy consumption in industry, transportation, residential, and commercial sectors, among others. With demand sometimes outstripping supply, these countries are increasing their energy production and electricity generation capacity. While most of their energy supply comes from fossil fuels, there has been a rapid shift to renewables due to the voluntary commitments to reduce their carbon emissions through the Nationally Determined Contributions (NDCs). According to a report by REN21 (2016), the Asian sub-regions with the highest penetrations of renewables in the energy mix are Southeast Asia (45.7% on average) and South Asia (42% on average), in contrast to sub-regions where renewables constitute a smaller share of the total (Central Asia, at 16.2% on average, Northeast Asia, at 11.7% on average).

Interestingly, ASEAN has taken a regional approach to renewable energy policy with an ambitious 23% target for member countries' energy mix by 2025 and reducing energy intensity 30% by 2025. This was agreed upon in the 2015 ASEAN Plan of Action for Energy Cooperation 2016–2025. While CAREC does not have a regional renewables policy, there is a great emphasis on regional cooperation by integrating energy markets and grids to overcome the uneven distribution of resources. By 2018, CAREC had invested around $7.1 billion in 47 projects to develop a regional power transmission network (REN 21 2016).

However, challenges remain. In the case of ASEAN and CAREC countries, there is a shortage of climate finance needed to address decarbonization goals outlined in the respective NDCs of these two regions. This work will provide an overview of the World Bank's data on private-public partnerships (PPPs), especially in the energy sector, by analyzing information on ways they are being used for ASEAN and CAREC renewable energy projects. The latter part of the work will look at the qualitative information on the largest PPPs in the sector, the trends, and existing arrangements in emerging Asian economies, especially looking at the ASEAN and CAREC cases.

11.2 The Challenge of Financing Future Energy Demand in the ASEAN and CAREC Countries and the Role of PPPs

With the rapidly growing demand for electricity in ASEAN due to economic growth and demography, many countries in the region are re-evaluating their energy policy to account for risks from non-renewable fuel sources, exploit falling prices of renewables, and avoid subsidies to fossil fuels. For example, Cambodia, with approximately 5.8 hours of peak sunlight a day (Hasan and Lin 2018), very high electricity prices, and an ever-growing demand for electricity is well suited for solar energy. Malaysia is leading an ambitious campaign to increase renewables' share in the country's energy mix by adopting a Renewable Energy Act and feed-in-tariffs (FITs) for solar, wind, biomass, biogas, and mini-hydro (Abdullah, et al. 2019). Myanmar has abundant biomass and hydro potential, and is also targeting a 15%–20% renewables share in the total national installed capacity by 2030. The Philippines is a pioneer in adopting proactive renewables-related policies in ASEAN through its National Renewable Energy Program, approved in 2011 to accelerate renewable energy infrastructure development.

PPPs have been a critical financing approach in ASEAN, where hydropower, followed by solar power, is the preferred renewable energy projects. Simultaneously, rapid urbanization and a growing middle class in Southeast Asia are expected to see an 80% growth in demand for energy between 2013 and 2035, roughly Japan's demand (International Energy Agency 2013).

CAREC members are planning to develop an integrated electricity market that is reliable, affordable, and clean to address energy poverty and meet growing demand in the region, according to the CAREC Energy Strategy 2030 (ADB 2019). This might be easier said than done as developing a renewable energy mix will be somewhat gradual as existing fossil fuel plants, mainly coal and gas, will take time to be phased out. New renewable plants will similarly take time, and transition fuels may also be required. With lower carbon emissions on combustion per unit of energy delivered than both coal and oil, gas, which is already very abundant in the CAREC region, may act as a bridge fuel (ADB 2019).

The Asian Development Bank (ADB) (2019) estimates the energy infrastructure investment needs of the CAREC region (excluding the People's Republic of China) between 2020–2030 are $400 billion. The current trend in investments is only a quarter of the required levels, and is heavily dependent on the public sector (about 70% of investment. Like other regions globally with constrained public funding, crowding in private funding and creating regulations favorable to PPPs are crucial to meet renewable energy funding needs. With much of the investment to be financed by private investors in CAREC, reports have warned that attracting private financing in power generation and transmission will require improvements in the still-nascent legal and regulatory environment for PPPs (Central Asia Regional Economic Cooperation Program 2015).

PPPs in CAREC are less prevalent than in ASEAN because, until the early 1990s, most of this region was within the Soviet Union. In the former Soviet republics in Central Asia and the Caucasus, the government's role as a traditional financier of hard infrastructure is still dominant. In the case of fossil fuel-exporting CAREC member states (i.e., Azerbaijan, Kazakhstan, Turkmenistan, and Uzbekistan), a drop in the global oil price has diminished their capacity to finance new hard infrastructure projects, renewables infrastructure included (Huseynov 2016). The Economist Intelligence Unit's Infrascope report (2014) reviewed the PPP state of affairs in Georgia, Kazakhstan, the Kyrgyz Republic, and Tajikistan and concluded that, in general, these countries lack proper legal frameworks. Additionally, they have low utility bill collection rates, sometimes operate with non-transparent tariff-setting mechanisms, and do not have capable (or even any) promotion for PPPs (Economist Intelligence Unit 2014).

Kazakhstan adopted a new PPP law in 2015, creating a standard regulating framework (Economist Intelligence Unit 2020). The Kyrgyz Republic has gone one step further; in 2016, its PPP law, first implemented in 2012, was amended to build a suitable regulatory environment for projects by facilitating interaction between state bodies and international investors (Economist Intelligence Unit 2020). In Tajikistan, the PPP field remains underdeveloped, although the country has implemented PPP-themed projects, including an energy transmission line (Economist Intelligence Unit 2020). In Pakistan's case, PPPs are regulated on both federal and provincial levels, while the energy sector has attracted the most PPPs (Economist Intelligence Unit 2020).

Application of PPPs to financing renewables projects in ASEAN has presented many challenges, including with public sector coordination, greening the financial sector, making clean energy prices competitive vis-à-vis fossil fuels, contractual flexibility, bidding, and private players' debt and project costs. Besides lack of enough affordable domestic debt capital to finance infrastructure, the high perceived risk due to lack of knowledge within the domestic banking sector about innovative clean energy technologies, and off-taker and currency risks for foreign investors, need to be addressed (Zen 2018).

For CAREC countries, including its fossil fuel-rich Central Asian members and Azerbaijan, PPPs remain mostly unexplored, and renewables development remains threatened by domestically subsidized fossil fuel energy alternatives (Huseynov 2016). Though PPPs have not been used widely so far, there have been promising developments with many more countries passing or having passed PPP laws and regulations. Among renewable energy projects, large hydro is more common in hydrocarbon-poor countries (e.g., the Kyrgyz Republic and Tajikistan) as they have to rely more on renewable energy than their fossil fuel-rich neighbors (e.g., Kazakhstan, Turkmenistan, and Uzbekistan) (Shadrina 2019).

Nevertheless, CAREC countries have set future renewables transition targets. Kazakhstan plans to cut carbon dioxide emissions in the electric power industry by 50% until 2050 against a 2012 baseline and Mongolia's NDC includes increasing renewables' share of total electricity generation capacity share to 30% by 2030 (London School of Economics and Political Science 2020). Georgia has been promoting PPPs in the electricity sector, primarily through applying power purchase agreements (Economist Intelligence Unit 2020). Due to sporadic armed conflict, Afghanistan could not implement significant PPP projects (Barrow and

Table 11.1 Renewable Energy Targets and Renewable Energy Installed in the Power Sector in ASEAN

Country	*Renewable energy electricity generation (TWh, 2019)*	*Renewables (% electricity, 2019)*	*Renewable energy technology preference*
Brunei Darussalam	-	0.05%	Solar Energy
Cambodia	Hydro (3)	39.89%	Hydropower
Indonesia	Hydro (18), Biomass/waste (1)	11.80%	Hydropower
Lao PDR	Hydro (20)	62.85%	Small hydro
Malaysia	Hydro (27), Solar (1), Biomass/waste (1)	16.80%	Solar Energy
Myanmar	Hydro (14)	57.04%	Small hydro
Singapore	Biomass/waste (1)	1.76%	Solar Energy
Philippines	Hydro(7), Wind (1), Solar(1), Biomass/waste (1)	22.61%	Hydropower
Thailand	Hydro (13), Wind (3), Solar (6), Biomass/waste (21)	14.86%	Solar Energy and Biomass
Viet Nam	Hydro (65), Wind (1), Solar(6)	30.92%	Solar and Hydropower

Source: BP (2020); Ember (2020); Pranadi (2016).

Note
Lao PDR = Lao People's Democratic Republic.

Tornberg 2007; Crisis Group 2016), though it is located strategically in between Central and South Asia and it wants to deploy 4,500–5,000 MW of renewables by 2032.

ASEAN and CAREC, both of which are set to increase their renewable energy capacity and also implement more PPPs to scale investments, present interesting cases that can be used to study and implement renewable energy in other regions. This work will look into the growing number of PPPs in renewable energy, the regional and subsector (e.g., hydro, solar, and wind) trends while documenting the active policy settings, incentive structures, and the resulting challenges in scaling up PPPs.

Table 11.1 highlights the level at which ASEAN members have achieved their respective targets by comparing them with their latest installed capacities in 2019 and their preference in renewables technologies.

Table 11.2 highlights the renewables generation technology for selected countries, where the current renewables adoption is quite low at 1% of the total energy capacity produced in the region.

11.3 Public-private Partnerships in Renewables and Data Sources

Renewables projects require a high up-front investment. Private sector capital, technology, and innovation have often been cultivated through PPPs to

Table 11.2 Renewable Energy Target and Renewable Energy Installed in the Power Sector in CAREC[3]

Country	*Electricity generation by renewables technology (TWh 2019)*	*Renewables (% electricity 2019)*	*Renewables technology potential*
Afghanistan	Hydro (1)	86.29%	Solar and wind
Azerbaijan	Hydro (2)	6.93%	Solar and wind
Kazakhstan	Hydro (11), Wind (1)	9.95%	Solar and wind
Mongolia	Negligible	7.76%	Solar and wind
Pakistan	Hydro (36), Wind (2), Solar (2), Biomass/waste (3)	31.16%	Solar and small hydro
Tajikistan	Hydro (17)	93.52%	Solar and small hydro
Uzbekistan	Hydro (9)	10.34%	Solar, small hydro, and wind

Source: BP (2020); Ember (2020); International Energy Agency (2020); London School of Economics and Political Science (2020); United Nations Development Programme (2014).

supplement limited public sector funding. PPPs provide countries with limited public finance to crowd in private finance to fast-track green investments. In effect, PPPs allow for the transfer of traditionally public sector investment projects to the private sector. This works for developing and emerging countries with stable medium- to long-term demand for green investments; nevertheless, they are limited in making these investments due to their creditworthiness. Since these countries have a lower infrastructure base due to their citizens' limited ability to pay for their services, the government cannot raise the needed funds through taxation. Hence, governments will benefit from private sector participation through PPPs.

The study will start by looking at whether worldwide trends in PPPs in renewables have been gaining prominence compared with other energy sources (e.g., coal), considering that many emerging countries are actively trying to meet their NDCs. The proliferation of PPP project financing will further enable public sector green projects to become viable, improving the policy environment and coordination. The work will look at how governments that wish to mobilize private capital need to understand its barriers, as well as the channels through which it flows. The data analysis was carried out, and plots, heatmaps, and tables were generated, using the R programming language. The findings furnish these two regions' experiences and challenge the basis for relevant practices and suggest future research to improve areas of interest in sustainable PPP.

This work uses the World Bank Group's Private Participation in Infrastructure (PPI) database, with the updated methodology changes in 2019, other secondary sources, and case studies of the most significant renewables projects implemented through PPPs in ASEAN and CAREC, with a focus on the five core Central Asian countries. The database essentially covers the contractual arrangements for public infrastructure projects in low- and middle-income countries (as classified by the World Bank) that have reached financial closure. Private parties assume operating risks (World Bank Group 2019). As the database only contains data for low- and middle-income countries, the study includes the following ASEAN members: Cambodia, Indonesia, Lao PDR, Malaysia, Myanmar, the Philippines, Thailand, and Viet Nam. The high-income countries Singapore and Brunei Darussalam are not listed in the database, and will, therefore, be omitted. CAREC was established in 1997 by ADB to encourage economic cooperation among Central Asian countries. The CAREC partnership includes 11 countries.[1] A particular focus will be provided to the five Central Asian countries. Nevertheless, it is to be noted that there were no data available for some countries.[2]

The PPI database consists of 9,135 project cases with 45 variables worldwide for 1995–2020 (as of November 2020), including details on the region and country, as well as project information such as the name, sector, technology used (particularly for energy projects), total investment, etc. The database includes both privately owned, financed, or operated projects and ones that also include public participation. The total investment component represents the project entity's commitments at the contract signing or the beginning of the project and is not the annual investment. In this work, we also include PPP data on large hydro projects for our analysis as many projects that have already been built benefit from this renewable source and will provide a provide a bigger picture of renewables investments. However, we do acknowledge that they may not be categorized as renewables if a stricter definition is used due to their adverse environmental impacts and security due to the water-energy nexus (Shadrina 2019).

11.4 Financing Infrastructure and Private-Public Partnership Trends in ASEAN and CAREC since 2000

11.4.1 Worldwide, Private-Public Partnership Investments Dominate in the Energy Sector, Especially in Electricity

With most of the infrastructure investments in Asia going to the energy sector, especially electricity generation, it is no surprise that energy has also attracted the most interest in private investment in green projects, and more recently, in renewables projects. Estimates in 2009 (Table 11.3) for infrastructure investments suggested that half will be for energy projects (mostly electricity) with 30% of the remainder going to transport, and the rest split among telecommunications, and water and sanitation. According to ADB and ADB Institute (2009), the bulk of financing is needed for new capacity, but about 30% must finance existing facilities' replacement. Because infrastructure is considered a public good, its provision falls to the public sector. Though these figures have been updated, with climate mitigation costs estimated at $200 billion annually, the share in these sectors roughly stays the same (ADB 2017).

The power sector is considered essential regarding carbon emissions and, therefore, the need to invest heavily in renewables, smart grids, and energy efficiency (ADB 2017). The transport sector is the next most crucial sector for mitigating

Table 11.3 Established Infrastructure Investment Needs for 45 Developing Member Countries, 2016–2030

Sector	*Baseline est. ($ billion 2015 prices)*	*Climate-adjusted est. ($ billion 2015 prices)*
Power	11,689	14,731
Transport	7,796	8,353
Telecommunications	2,279	2,279
Water and Sanitation	787	802
Total	**22,551**	**26,166**
Region		
Central Asia	492	565
East Asia	13,781	16,062
South Asia	5,477	6,347
Southeast Asia	2,751	3,147
Total	**22,551**	**26,166**

Source: Asian Development Bank (2017).

climate change through shifts from more carbon-intensive modes of travel to less carbon-intensive modes such as public transit and railways. In the longer term, these shifts will need to come through policy.

It is no surprise that $888.4 billion has cumulatively gone to the electricity sector worldwide through PPPs between 1995 and 2020 (Table 11.4), as well as ASEAN and CAREC. The road transport subsector follows with a cumulative investment of $330.6 billion.

11.4.2 Private-public Partnerships Investments in the Energy Sector, Especially in Electricity, Dominate in ASEAN and CAREC

In ASEAN, the situation is no different, with most PPP investments ending up in the electricity subsector, with an even higher cumulative investment amount of $151.3 billion (Table 11.5). The electricity subsector got investments through PPP, eight times more than the second-largest subsector. The cumulative investment of $23 billion went to the road subsector. Though comparatively much smaller, PPP investments have also been made in the roads, railways, and water and sewerage sectors.

11.4.3 Worldwide Largest PPP Investments

Renewables PPPs have been gaining prominence in many regions, especially in the last five years (Figure 11.1). However, South Asia has received the largest share of PPP investments in coal-based electricity projects in the last 20 years, reaching $101.8 billion, followed by East Asia and the Pacific, which received $62.1 billion cumulatively, while Europe and Central Asia received only $27.4 billion.

Table 11.4 Number and Value of All Public–Private Partnerships Projects by Primary Sector and Subsector Worldwide, 1995–2020

Primary sector	*Subsector*	*Number*	*$ million*
Energy	Electricity	4,600	888,422
Transport	Roads	1,130	330,560
Transport	Railways	263	129,574
Transport	Airports	208	112,095
Information and communication technology (ICT)	ICT	328	105,063
Transport	Ports	506	83,462
Energy	Natural Gas	495	81,610
Water and sewerage	Water Utility	465	52,058
Water and sewerage	Treatment plant	667	26,900
Municipal Solid Waste	Treatment/ Disposal	286	21,930
Municipal Solid Waste	Collection and Transport	107	10,562
Municipal Solid Waste (MSW)	Integrated MSW	48	7,019
Energy	Electricity, Water Utility	10	5,107
Water and sewerage	Treatment plant, Water Utility	7	638
Energy	Electricity, Natural Gas	3	316
Energy	Electricity, Roads	1	205
Energy	Electricity, Treatment plant	1	78
Energy	Electricity, ICT	9	73
Transport	Ports, Railways	1	17

Source: Authors' tabulation from World Bank Group PPI Database utilizing 2020 data available till June 2020.

Table 11.5 Total Number and Value of PPP Projects by Sector and Subsector in ASEAN 2000–2020

Primary sector	*Subsector*	*Number*	*$ billion*
Energy	Electricity	510	151.266
Transport	Railways	16	22.884
Transport	Roads	53	18.484
Water and sewerage	Water Utility	54	15.896
Information and communication technology (ICT)	ICT	18	6.396
Transport	Ports	38	5.440
Transport	Airports	15	3.956
Energy	Natural Gas	11	3.731
Water and sewerage	Treatment plant	30	2.165
Municipal Solid Waste	Treatment/ Disposal	20	1.019
Energy	Electricity, Roads	1	0.205

Source: Authors' tabulation from World Bank Group PPI Database, utilizing 2020 data available till June 2020.

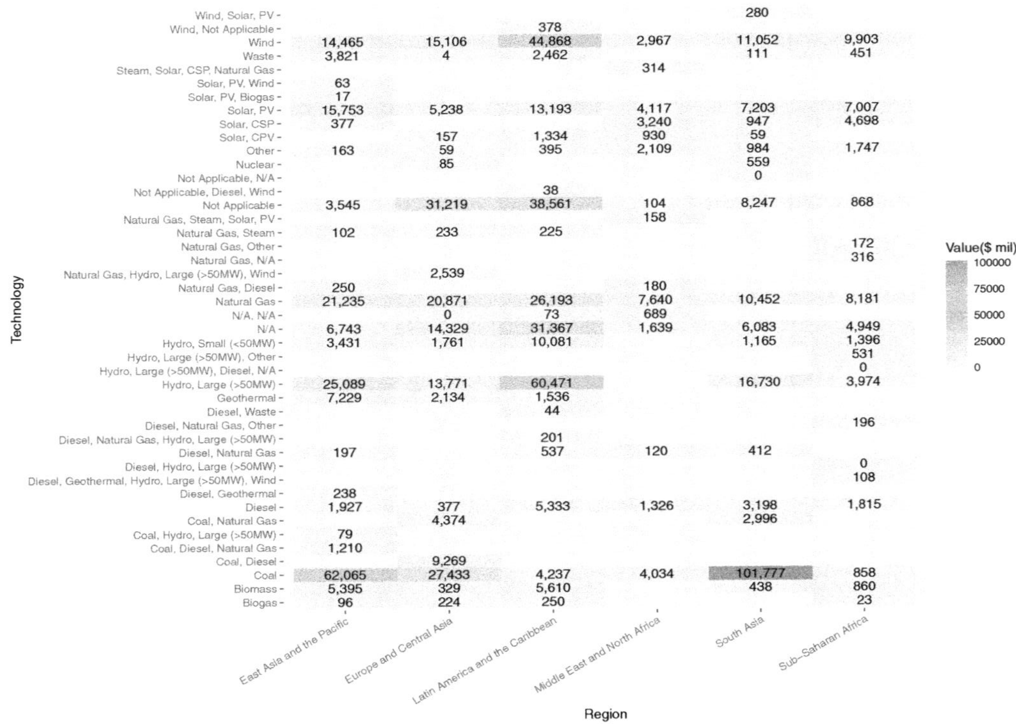

Figure 11.1 Worldwide Energy/Electricity PPP Projects by Technology Type, Cumulative Investment Between 2000 and 2020. ($ million)

Note: CPV = concentrator photovoltaics, CSP = concentrated solar power, PV = photovoltaics.

Source: Authors' tabulation from World Bank Group PPI Database, utilizing 2020 data available till June 2020.

11.4.4 In ASEAN, the Largest Private-Public Partnerships Investments Go To Coal, Hydro, and Natural Gas Technology-Based Electricity Generation Projects

ASEAN countries have also entered the renewables race, with governments providing policy support to investments and supply. For example, Viet Nam's government has raised the FITs paid for wind power exported to the grid and plans to introduce the same tariffs for solar energy projects (Ha 2019). However, in ASEAN countries, the ultimate leader in renewables technologies has been hydro (Table 11.6), followed by geothermal, solar, and wind.

Table 11.6 Number and Value of PPPs in Electricity Projects by the Technology Used in ASEAN, 2000–2020

Segment	*Technology*	*Number*	*Value $ billion*
Electricity generation	Coal	53	58.615
Electricity generation	Natural Gas	47	20.452
Electricity generation	Hydro, Large (>50MW)	57	20.426
Electricity generation	Geothermal	18	7.229
Electricity generation	Solar, PV	68	5.626
Electricity generation	Wind	43	5.248
Electricity transmission	Not Applicable	2	2.994
Natural gas transmission	N/A	4	2.363
Electricity generation	Hydro, Small (<50MW)	67	2.204
Electricity generation	Diesel	15	1.920
Electricity generation	Biomass	21	1.439
Electricity generation	Coal, Diesel, Natural Gas	1	1.210
Electricity generation and transmission	Hydro, Large (>50MW)	1	0.979
Natural gas distribution and transmission	N/A	5	0.718
Electricity generation	Waste	9	0.298
Electricity generation	Natural Gas, Diesel	1	0.250
Electricity generation and transmission	Coal	1	0.247
Electricity generation	Diesel, Geothermal	1	0.238
Electricity generation	Diesel, Natural Gas	1	0.197
Electricity transmission	Other	2	0.155
Electricity generation	Not Applicable	3	0.113
Electricity transmission	N/A	1	0.113
Electricity generation	Biogas	8	0.091
Electricity generation	Natural Gas, Steam	1	0.083
Electricity generation	Solar, CSP	1	0.072
Electricity generation	Solar, PV, Wind	1	0.063
Electricity generation	Solar, PV, Biogas	1	0.017
Electricity generation	Other	1	0.008

Source: Authors' tabulation from World Bank Group PPI Database, utilizing 2020 data available till June 2020.

Viet Nam, Thailand, and Malaysia have significantly increased their renewables capacities since 2009. Though traditionally it has been reliant on coal, Indonesia's energy generation sector has also been investing heavily in hydro and developing geothermal sources since it is in one of the world's most active volcanic regions (Kearney 2019). Thailand has also been actively developing renewable energy, establishing subsidies and tax incentives for various waste-to-energy power generation projects, including biomass and biogas.

In ASEAN, most of the investments in coal-based PPPs went to Indonesia, followed by the Philippines (Figure 11.2). Interestingly, Lao PDR received the most funding ($12.8 billion) for large hydro projects (>50 MW. In geothermal, Indonesia and the Philippines have received the most PPP investments with $4.5 billion and $2.6 billion, respectively.

Regarding ASEAN members' annual investments in PPPs, the electricity sector has dominated investments, including over coal projects, with wind investments, which started in 2004, peaking in 2017, and solar investments, which started in 2010, peaking in 2018 (Figure 11.3). Hydro, especially large hydro, has seen consistent investments since 2005, but came to a complete standstill in 2018.

11.4.5 In the CAREC Program, the Largest Private-Public Partnerships Investments Go To Hydro, Coal, and Wind Technology-Based Electricity Projects

In CAREC, the situation is no different, with most of the PPP investments occurring in the electricity subsector, with its $31.1 billion in cumulative investments (Table 11.7), being an amount three times greater than all the other sectors put together. The electricity subsector in the region got investments through PPP, almost 10 times more than the second-largest subsector— transport.

CAREC electricity subsector PPPs have surprisingly gone to hydro, which was even higher than coal till 2018, but coal projects have seen a comeback, especially in Pakistan in the last 2 years (Table 11.8 and Figure 11.4. Coal PPP projects in CAREC overtook hydro in 2018–2019, with just a billion-dollar difference currently, which could be a worrying trend. Though wind came in third, with PPP investments of $3.5 billion, it is quite clear that solar has yet to take off, with just $773 million in the last four years. The region with natural gas supplies has also used PPPs for electricity projects quite effectively, though it still has a long way to go to beat coal.

Despite the progress, it is worth mentioning that coal PPP projects have dominated, particularly in Pakistan. In context, as Figure 11.4 suggests, Pakistan has dominated electricity PPP projects investments across technologies, particularly in coal and large hydro, followed by wind and even natural gas. Georgia and Tajikistan have also had PPP investments in large hydro. Even wind PPPs have only been implemented in Pakistan, taking the lion's share, followed by Mongolia and Kazakhstan. Solar PPPs are only just taking off, with Kazakhstan leading ($532 million), followed by Pakistan ($124 million) and Mongolia ($72 million. Kazakhstan was the only other country in the region to receive PPP investments

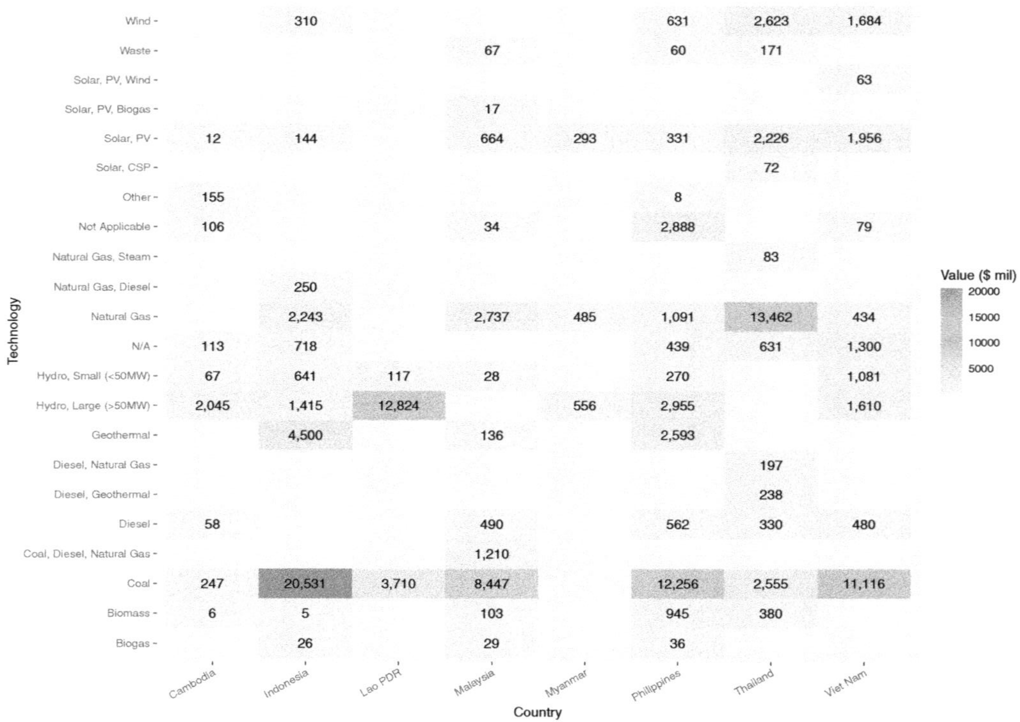

Figure 11.2 ASEAN Energy/Electricity PPP Technology Projects by Country, Cumulative Investment Between 2000 and 2020. ($ million)

Note: CSP = concentrated solar power, PV = photovoltaics.

Source: Authors' tabulation from World Bank Group PPI Database, utilizing 2020 data available till June 2020.

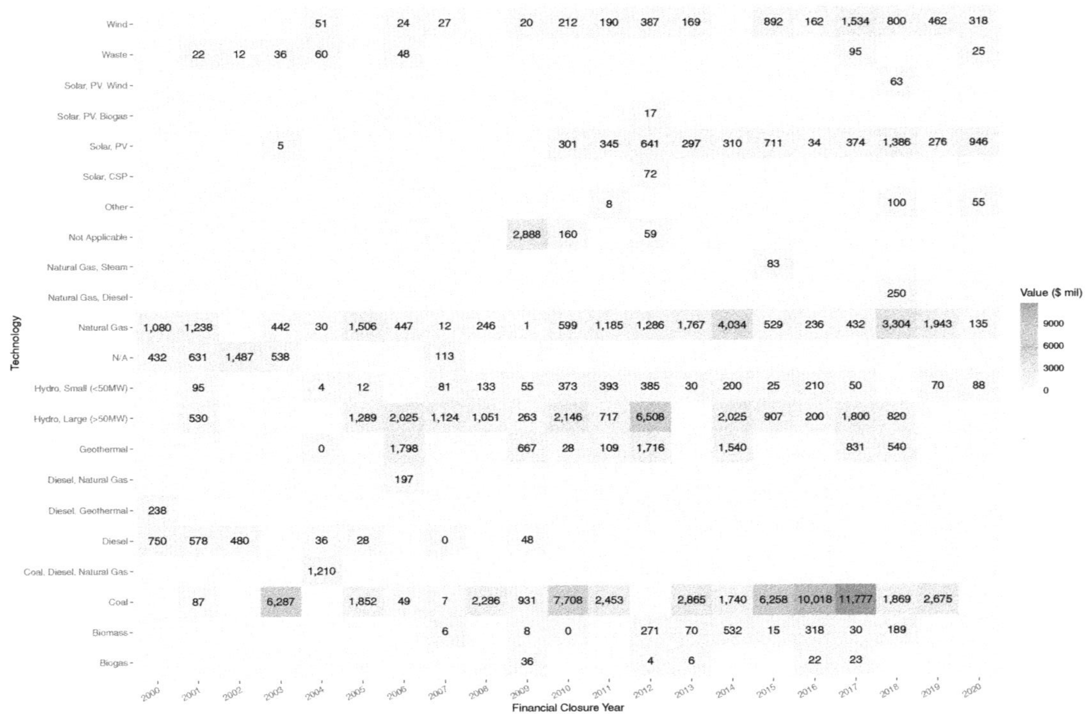

Figure 11.3 ASEAN Energy/Electricity PPP Technology Projects, Investment Between 2000 and 2020 by Year. ($ million)

Note: CSP = concentrated solar power, PV = photovoltaics.

Source: Authors' tabulation from World Bank Group PPI Database, utilizing 2020 data available till June 2020.

Table 11.7 Total Number and Value of Public–Private Partnership Projects by Sector and Subsector in CAREC, 2000–2020

Primary sector	*Subsector*	*Number*	*$ million*
Energy	Electricity	197	31,072
Transport	Ports	16	3,189
Information and communication technology (ICT)	ICT	17	2,981
Energy	Natural Gas	10	813
Transport	Roads	1	740
Water and sewerage	Water Utility	6	594
Transport	Railways	2	256
Transport	Airports	5	175
Municipal Solid Waste	Treatment/ Disposal	2	64
Water and sewerage	Treatment plant, Water Utility	1	25

Source: Authors' tabulation from World Bank Group PPI Database, utilizing 2020 data available till June 2020.

Table 11.8 Number and Value of PPPs in Electricity Projects by Technology Used in CAREC, 2000–2020

Segment	*Technology*	*Number*	*Value $ million*
Electricity generation	Coal	10	7,358
Electricity generation	Hydro, Large (>50MW)	16	6,321
Electricity generation	Wind	35	3,512
Electricity generation	Natural Gas	15	2,169
Electricity transmission	Not Applicable	1	1,658
Electricity distribution, generation, and transmission	N/A	6	1,300
Electricity generation	Diesel	11	1,095
Electricity generation	Solar, PV	15	777
Electricity generation	Nuclear	1	559
Electricity distribution	N/A	6	513
Electricity distribution	Not Applicable	1	450
Electricity generation	Other	2	439
Electricity generation and transmission	Hydro, Large (>50MW)	1	417
Electricity generation	Biomass	4	333
Electricity generation	Hydro, Small (<50MW)	6	139
Natural gas distribution	N/A	1	94
Natural gas distribution	Not Applicable	2	50
Natural gas distribution and transmission	Not Applicable	1	40
Natural gas distribution and transmission	N/A	1	29
Electricity distribution and generation	Hydro, Large (>50MW)	1	16
Electricity generation	Waste	1	7

Source: Authors tabulation from World Bank Group PPI Database, utilizing 2020 data available till June 2020.

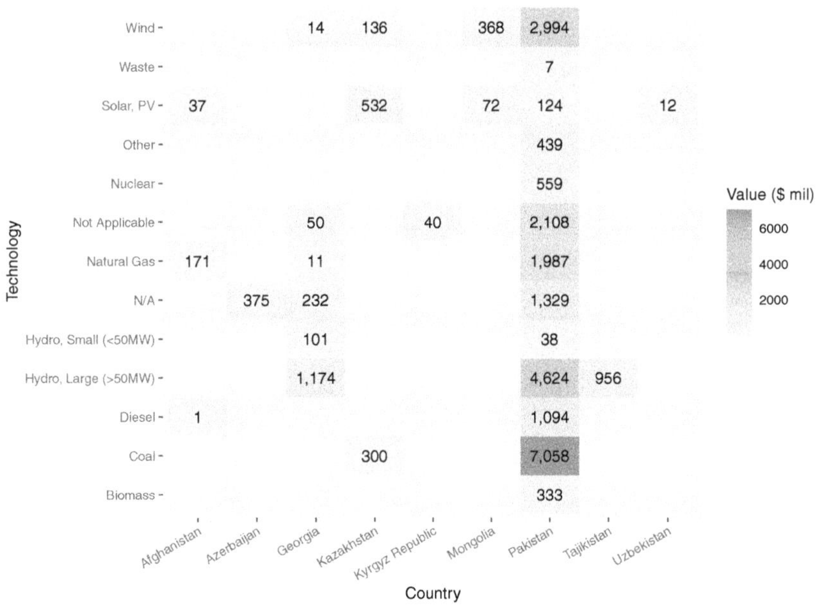

Figure 11.4 CAREC Energy/Electricity PPP Project by Country, Cumulative Between 2000 and 2020. ($ million)

Note: PV = photovoltaics.

Source: Authors' tabulation from World Bank Group PPI Database, utilizing 2020 data available till June 2020.

in coal-based electricity projects worth $300 million. Pakistan seems to be the region's leader in garnering PPP investments in electricity across the board which could also be explained by PRC investments through the Belt and Road Initiative, but its experience could serve as case study, especially regarding the development of PPP regulations and laws and how effective they are.

Hydro project PPP investments have been popular since 2006 but are still scant. A worrying trend is that coal-based PPP projects are receiving more investment since 2016, which is not good for renewables. As seen in Figure 11.4, most of this went to Pakistan. While wind-based PPP projects have been receiving investments since 2011, they have been entirely consistent with no investments in 2014 and 2018, possibly indicating a massive opportunity. As can be seen in Figure 11.5, solar has only begun to take off, with most of the investments only coming in 2019, $486 million.

11.4.5.1 Business Models of the PPP Projects for Solar, Wind, Hydro

The three most significant PPP projects by size for each technology for the two regions are listed with their details, followed by a short description. As the

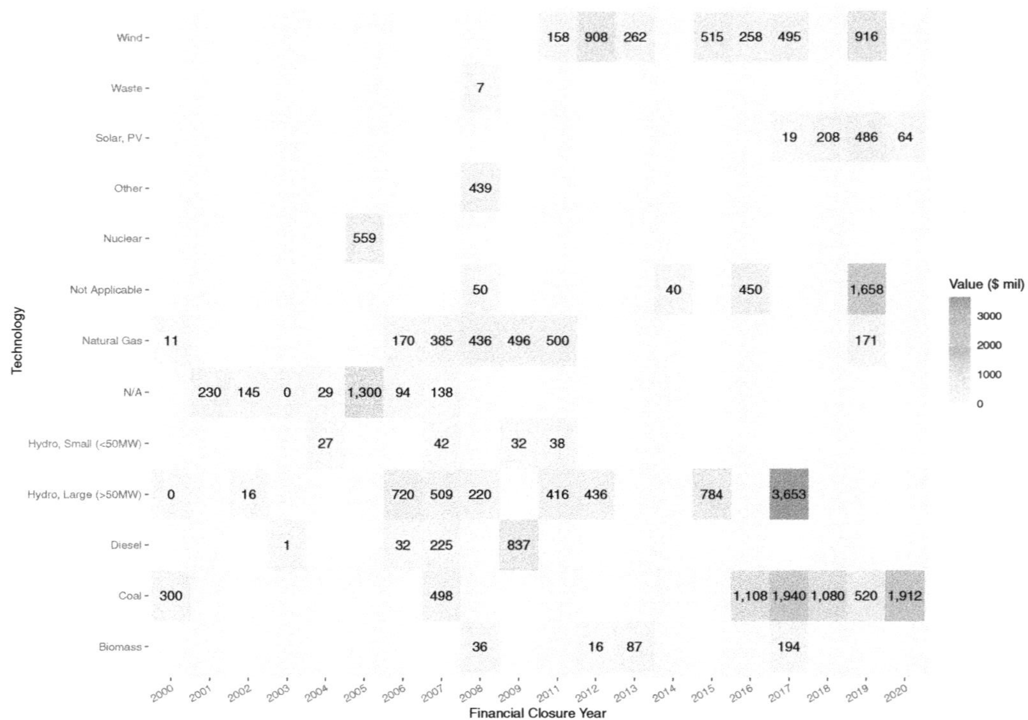

Figure 11.5 CAREC Energy/Electricity PPP Technology Project by Year, Investment Between 2000 and 2020 by Year. ($ million)

Note: PV = photovoltaics.

Source: Authors' tabulation from World Bank Group PPI Database, utilizing 2020 data available till June 2020.

business models were not always publicly available, it is difficult to understand whether there were challenges and other motives in implementing the projects. But the descriptions help understand the trends in renewable energy PPP projects, including the size of the investment, government granting contract, percentage of private participation, capacity in MW, etc.

Lao PDR has clearly been the largest recipient for hydro in ASEAN, including the Sinohydro Nam Ou 1-7 HPPs PPP project developed by the Lao PDR government and PRC hydropower developer Sinohydro. In this PPP, Sinohydro will own 85%, and the remaining 15% will be owned by the Lao PDR electricity utility (Vientiane Times 2014) (Table 11.9).

Ninh Thuan and Dau Tieng projects, both in Viet Nam, are the largest solar power plants in Southeast Asia. A leading private investor is Dau Tieng Tay Ninh Energy JSC, a joint venture of Bangkok-based multinational conglomerate B. Grimm Power Company and Xuan Cau Corporation Limited (Kenning 2018). Sinohydro Corporation Limited and Powerchina Huadong Engineering Corporation Limited, both subsidiaries of Powerchina Group, will implement it (Table 11.10).

Wind Energy Holding Portfolio is a leading renewable energy developer in Southeast Asia. It has already developed five onshore wind farms with a capacity of more than 700MW, obtaining loans from Siam Commercial Bank (The Business Times 2018) (Table 11.11).

The largest hydropower projects are in Pakistan, with significant investments of $1.9 billion and $1.7 billion, followed by the Sangtuda 1 hydropower project in Tajikistan. The Suki Kinari Hydropower Plant and Karot Hydropower Plant in Pakistan are parts of the PRC-Pakistan economic corridor. Sangtuda 1 is a $500 million plant, with construction financed by Russian electricity company Unified Energy Systems, which reached full capacity in 2008 (Table 11.12).

Interestingly, all the wind power projects are based in Pakistan, with ADB approving a $75 million loan with Tricon Boston Consulting Corporation to develop the country's largest wind farm. Tricon Boston Consulting Limited is a Special Purpose Vehicle set up by Sapphire Textile Mills Limited, a local energy developer, to develop, own and operate the wind farm (Table 11.13).

Though of all the solar power plants that reached financial closure in 2018 were in Pakistan, Mongolia, and Kazakhstan, 2019 saw the two of the largest solar projects in the region going to Kazakhstan. The 100-MW Nura solar farm was commissioned by Russian photovoltaic manufacturer Hevel Group, the first for the company outside the Russian Federation. The M-KAT Solar project is also a 100-MW solar plant and is being sponsored by the European Bank for Reconstruction and Development, with the rest of the funding coming from ADB. The Quaid-e-Azam Solar plant is a public sector for-profit company established by the Government of Punjab to operate solar energy power projects (Table 11.14).

Solar projects such as in Kazakhstan and Mongolia's Desert Solar Power One, the largest solar plant in Mongolia, are examples of cooperation between multilateral development financial institutions in sustainable infrastructure, such as between the European Bank for Reconstruction and Development and ADB.

Table 11.9 Largest Hydro PPPs in ASEAN, Large (>50MW)

Financial closure year	*Project name*	*Subtype of PPI*	*Contract Period*	*Govt Granting Contract*	*Percent Private*	*Total Investment $ million*	*Capacity MW*
2012	Sinohydro Nam Ou 1-7 HPPs, Lao PDR	Build, operate, and transfer	N/A	National	100	2,000	1,156
2017	Nam Theun I, Lao PDR	Build, operate, and transfer	27	National	85	1,300	650
2005	Nam Theun II Hydropower Project, Lao PDR	Build, operate, and transfer	25	National	75	1,250	1,075

Source: Authors' tabulation from World Bank Group PPI Database, June 2020.

Note
ASEAN = Association of Southeast Asian Nations, Lao PDR = Lao People's Democratic Republic, PPI = private participation in infrastructure, PPP = public-private partnership.

Table 11.10 Largest Solar PPPs in ASEAN

Financial closure year	*Project name*	*Subtype of PPI*	*Contract Period*	*Govt Granting Contract*	*Percent Private*	*Total Investment $ mill*	*Capacity MW*
2020	Ninh Thuan solar plant, Viet Nam	Not Available	N/A	National	100	593	450
2018	Dau Tieng 1 and Dau Tieng 2 solar PV power plants, Viet Nam	Build, own, and operate	20	National	100	397	350
2017	Merchang, Jasin and Gurun Solar Farms, Malaysia	Build, own, and operate	21	National	100	293	197
2018	Minbu Solar Power Plant, Myanmar	Build, operate, and transfer	N/A	National	100	293	220

Source: Authors' tabulation from World Bank Group PPI Database, June 2020.

Note

ASEAN = Association of Southeast Asian Nations, PV = photovoltaics, PPI = private participation in infrastructure, PPP = public-private partnership.

Table 11.11 Largest Wind PPPs in ASEAN

Financial closure year	*Project name*	*Subtype of PPI*	*Contract Period*	*Govt Granting Contract*	*Percent Private*	*Total Investment $ million*	*Capacity MW*
2017	Wind Energy Holding Portfolio, Thailand	Build, own, and operate	N/A	National	100	1,135	450
2018	Bac Lieu Wind Power Project (Phase 3), Viet Nam	Rehabilitate, operate, and transfer	N/A	National	100	390	142
2015	Wayu Windfarm, Thailand	Build, own, and operate	N/A	Not Available	100	353	60

Source: Authors' tabulation from World Bank Group PPI Database, June 2020.

Note
ASEAN = Association of Southeast Asian Nations, PPI = private participation in infrastructure, PPP = public-private partnership.

Table 11.12 Largest Hydro PPPs in CAREC, Large (>50MW)

Financial closure year	*Project name*	*Subtype of PPI*	*Contract Period*	*Govt Granting Contract*	*Percent Private*	*Total Investment $ million*	*Capacity MW*
2017	Suki Kinari Hydropower Plant Pakistan	Build, operate, and transfer	30	State/Provincial	63	1,888	870
2017	Karot Hydropower Plant Pakistan	Build, operate, and transfer	30	State/Provincial	100	1,700	720
2006	Sangtuda 1 Hydropower Plant Tajikistan	Build, operate, and transfer	N/A	National	100	720	670

Source: Authors' tabulation from World Bank Group PPI Database, June 2020.

Note
CAREC = Central Asia Regional Economic Cooperation, PPI = private participation in infrastructure, PPP = public-private partnership.

Table 11.13 Largest PPP Wind Electricity Generation Projects in CAREC

Financial closure year	*Project name*	*Subtype of PPI*	*Contract Period*	*Govt Granting Contract*	*Percent Private*	*Total Investment $ million*	*Capacity MW*
2017	Tricon Boston Consulting Limited Pakistan	Not Available	20	National	100	335	150
2011	Zorlu Sindh Wind Farm Pakistan	Build, own, and operate	20	National	100	158	56.4
2019	Zhanatas Wind Power Plant, Kazhakstan	Build, own, and operate	20	National	100	136	100

Source: Authors' tabulation from World Bank Group PPI Database, June 2020.

Note
CAREC = Central Asia Regional Economic Cooperation, PPI = private participation in infrastructure, PPP = public-private partnership.

Table 11.14 Largest PPP Solar PV Electricity Generation Projects in CAREC

Financial closure year	*Project name*	*Subtype of PPI*	*Contract Period*	*Govt Granting Contract*	*Percent Private*	*Total Investment $ million*	*Capacity MW*
2019	Nura solar plant, Kazakhstan	Build, own, and operate	15	National	100	158	100
2019	M-KAT Solar PV Power Plant	Build, own, and operate	15	National	100	118	100
2018	Quaid-e-Azam PV Solar Plant Pakistan	Build, own, and operate	25	National	100	102	100

Source: Authors' tabulation from World Bank Group PPI Database, June 2020.

Note

CAREC = Central Asia Regional Economic Cooperation, PV = photovoltaic, PPI = private participation in infrastructure, PPP = public-private partnership.

These institutions support their member states' efforts to meet their development and climate change-related goals by improving the investment climate, associated policies, and institutional capacities, and maximizing the use of PPPs to support infrastructure building and maintenance.

11.5 Policy Implications and Challenges to Private-Public Partnerships and Renewable Energy Financing in the ASEAN and CAREC

11.5.1 Policy Implications Renewable Energy Financing Through Private-Public Partnerships

It is not surprising that policy support for renewable energy in these two regions' power sectors will vary based on each country's economic and political situation. More precisely, this will relate to the country's energy security and meeting emissions reduction targets while continuing industrial competitiveness, and issues such as providing last-mile connectivity by expanding electrification to poorer and remote populations. In countries that have rapidly industrialized and are seeing concomitant economic growth such as Thailand, Indonesia, and the Philippines, policies are being implemented to reduce carbon intensity. Others, such as Myanmar, Lao PDR, Tajikistan, and the Kyrgyz Republic are geared to increase electricity generation and provide transmission for last-mile electrification to their citizens not connected to the grid.

Across ASEAN and CAREC, the renewable energy share is still focused heavily on hydropower (especially large-scale hydropower) and bioenergy (especially for cooking and electricity. As the PPP data suggest, other renewables such as solar and wind have only recently begun to grow and have a huge potential. In the region, too, especially in ASEAN, there is a lot of innovation. New technologies are being implemented, such as floating solar panels and distributed energy resources, especially for countries with limited land or geographies not located within the national grid. Renewables are expected to see even more rapid growth, especially with the electrification of transport, heating, and cooling, as a result of the changing technology landscape, and reduced costs for solar and wind technologies.

Governments in the region are also catching up with the latest market developments. They are actively announcing policies, plans, and investment pipelines to incorporate more renewables into their energy mix, especially in their power sector. For example, in ASEAN, Viet Nam has prioritized renewable energy through its Power Master Plan, with a new decree to encourage PPPs. In the Philippines, the Department of Energy in 2017 adopted renewables portfolio standards to increase their share to 35% by 2030, while in Central Asia, there is a conscious shift to renewable energy development, especially after 2015, focusing on wind and solar power, with assistance from development institutions and banks. Mongolia has amended its 2007 Renewable Energy Law, proposing to cap the tariffs for renewables, introduce auctions, and improve regulation for

Table 11.15 Renewable Energy Plans in the Power Sector in the Selected ASEAN and CAREC Countries

Country	*Plans related to achieving the targets*
Indonesia	Electricity Supply Business Plan 2019 (RUPTL 2019–2028)
Philippines	Renewable Energy Roadmap
	National Renewable Energy Program
Thailand	Power Development Plan (PDP, 2018–2037)
	2015 Alternative Energy Development Plan (with revision)
	New Energy Reform 2018–2022
Viet Nam	National Power Development Master Plan (with vision for 2030)
Georgia	First National Renewable Energy Action Plan (draft)
	New Energy Policy (2015)
Kazakhstan	Strategy Kazakhstan 2050: A New Political Course of the Established State
	Concept for the Republic of Kazakhstan's Transition to a Green Economy (2013)
Pakistan	Renewable Energy Policy 2019 (draft)
Uzbekistan	Action Program on Renewable Energy Development for 2017–2021

Source: REN 21 (2019).

Note
ASEAN = Association of Southeast Asian Nations, CAREC = Central Asia Regional Economic Cooperation.

power purchase agreements; this has led to a few projects financed by ADB and Japan. Table 11.15 outlines the renewable energy plans for selected countries in the two regions.

In most countries in Asia and these two regions, the most common government mechanisms to support renewable energy have been FITs, which are slowly being phased out in favor of auctions or tenders to reflect recent declines in solar costs and the resulting expiring subsidies (REN 21 2019). Successful auctions have already been held in Kazakhstan, Pakistan, Indonesia, the Philippines, Thailand, and Viet Nam. A few successful examples of reverse auctions for renewable energy projects make solar and wind generation costs at grid parity levels.

Quotas or mandated targets are not so common in the region, and net metering is also gradually introduced in some countries. Other public financing and fiscal incentives include capital subsidies, public loans and grants, investment tax credits, and customs duty exemptions (REN21 2019). In general, countries that are hydrocarbon poor, have low per capita incomes and are excessively reliant on hydro and international aid and non-commercial financing have been slow to articulate their renewable energy policy, including countries like Myanmar, Lao PDR, Kyrgyz Republic, Tajikistan, and Turkmenistan (Tablew 11.16 and 11.17).

The technology disruption in solar and wind is fundamentally changing the global energy landscape, especially via the rapidly falling cost of solar energy and battery storage (Heinberg 2016). Even though clean energy costs have come down significantly in recent years, risks and barriers remain in these countries and prevent investment. There are different risks associated with the successful

Table 11.16 Policy Instruments to Promote Renewable Energy in the Power Sector in ASEAN

Country	*Policy Instrument*	*Renewable energy target*	*Target year*
Brunei Darussalam	Not yet developed	10% in power generation	2035
Cambodia	Tax incentives and permits for renewable energy projects	2 GW of hydropower	2020
Indonesia	Feed-in-tariff	23% share in energy mix	2025
Lao PDR	Tax incentives and permit preparation for renewable energy projects	30% share of total energy consumptions	2025
Malaysia	Capital subsidies and feed-in-tariff	4 GW installed capacity	2030
Myanmar	Not yet developed	15%–20% share in installed capacity	2030
Singapore	Tax incentives, permits for renewable energy projects and feed-in-tariff	350 MW installed capacity of solar energy	2020
Philippines	Capital subsidies, tax incentives, feed-in-tariff, and renewable portfolio standard	15 GW installed capacity	2030
Thailand	Tax incentives, permits for renewable energy projects and feed-in-tariff	30% share in total energy consumption	2036
Viet Nam	Tax incentives, permits for renewable energy projects and feed-in-tariff	27 GW installed	2030

Source: ASEAN Centre for Energy (2017).

Note
ASEAN = Association of Southeast Asian Nations, Lao PDR = Lao People's Democratic Republic.

Table 11.17 Policy Instruments to Promote renewable energy in the Power Sector in CAREC

Country	*Policy Instrument*	*Renewable energy target*	*Target year*
Afghanistan	Feed-in-tariff	4,500–5,000 MW	2032
Azerbaijan	Feed-in-tariff	20% of electricity production	2020
Kazakhstan	Project-based tariffs, concessions, power-purchase agreements	50% of alternative and renewable energy in the energy mix	2050
Mongolia	Concessions and feed-in-tariff	30% share of total electricity generation capacity	2030
Pakistan	Feed-in-tariff	30% of total power generation	2030
Tajikistan	Tax incentives	20% of total power generation	2030
Uzbekistan	Feed-in-tariff and tax incentives	30% of electricity generation	2030

Source: International Energy Agency (2016, 2020); New Climate Institute (2020).

Note
CAREC = Central Asia Regional Economic Cooperation.

completion of renewable energy PPP projects. Those risks are an off-taker risk, barriers to financing, currency risk, policy risk, and liquidity and scale risks (Tonkonogy, et al. 2018).

Further, many of these countries' energy transitions could also be delayed due to stranded asset risk. The lock-in with uneconomical fossil fuel-based electricity generation plants to recover their investment costs could keep electricity prices high. Policy change risks affecting renewable energy projects' long-term profitability may lead private sector investors to require additional reassurance to protect their interests. For example, offered tax exemptions or lower tax regimes for renewable energy PPP projects for a particular period will encourage investments and make the projects more competitive when compared to carbon-intensive energy generation alternatives. More substantial policies that incentivize private finance in electricity are needed to boost investments in renewable energy PPPs. Simultaneously, they also must be complemented by measures such as the phasing-out of fossil-fuel subsidies.

The private sector has, for years, been recognized as a significant financing source for meeting developing country investment requirements in infrastructure. However, financial markets remain underdeveloped for this purpose and have yet to expand their potential (Wiek and Weber 2014). PPPs enable the pooling of public, private, and donor funds for clean energy investment in developing and emerging economies. Those economies are also eligible for support from international financial institutions, such as the World Bank Group and regional development banks. Lenders, including commercial investment banks, would too often hesitate to provide loans to infrastructure with long gestation periods and often under-tested technology projects because of uncertainty about whether the project company, whose income stream is at risk, can service its loans. Sponsors may also hesitate to provide equity capital. PPPs arose mainly to get the public and private sectors to share in investments, operations, and risks. Governments can crowd in private finance through PPPs locally and overseas to fill the financing and service delivery gap. However, there are issues in regulation and risk-sharing that governments need to implement and monitor to enable private sector involvement in infrastructure projects.

Since both ASEAN and CAREC are developing regions with low per capita energy consumption, they require reliable energy sources for future development. Governments need to play a role in creating a conducive environment for PPPs to develop and finance renewable energy projects. For example, in some cases, end-users' low purchasing power must be strengthened with subsidies. PPPs, in this regard, can also be viewed as a financial mechanism that directly supports sustainable development and, at the same time, provides private funding for infrastructure delivering public goods. In general, many countries also need to move away from purely state-owned utility companies to the vertically integrated system with unbundled and liberalized market structures served by the broader private sector to stimulate competition. This can attract investment and generate efficiency across the value chain.

In several ASEAN and CAREC countries, the energy sector is now undergoing critical structural adjustments. Many emerging Asian countries such as Indonesia, Pakistan, and Kazakhstan also subsidize and provide FDI allowances for coal projects. However, if governments are slow in pursuing the energy transition based on existing financing structures and markets, the cost of implementing renewable energy projects would end up exceeding the current rates. Fortunately, a growing list of financial institutions and central banks are putting restrictions on new investments in fossil fuel-based plant financing, including the three major banks in Singapore and the Philippine Central Bank. In contrast, renewable energy projects are not supported adequately.

For investors, PPPs are one of the safest formats to invest in developing countries. Infrastructure development policies should give due consideration to the robust regulatory frameworks for PPPs and even FDI in such projects. The frameworks will serve as a safety system that secures the interests of investors and fosters the cooperation between the public and private sectors. In addition to strengthening sectoral regulators, countries should consider a dedicated PPP unit that could work solely on implementing different PPP projects. Such a regulator and electricity development authority will also serve as a focal point and streamline administrative and communication procedures for investors. This will ensure that well-structured and carefully planned PPP projects can attract FDI from firms outside the country and tap low-interest rate funding from developed nations. However, an FDI strategy for PPPs in sustainable infrastructure will require clear policy frameworks, viable and sustainable infrastructure project pipelines, public-private discussions on the PPP market, risk allocations, and other enabling policies (Ministry of Foreign Affairs of the Netherlands 2013).

For the transition to renewable energy, new market incentives will also need to be developed with flexibility, such as for demand management and energy storage that balance the intermittency of wind or solar power. It is also essential to support particular generation technologies based on the country's natural endowment. For example, with its long coastline, Viet Nam is using offshore wind to supply power. Pakistan has similarly harnessed wind, while Lao PDR has used more of its sizeable hydropower capacity, and Indonesia has seen a growth in geothermal. Thailand has a growing experience with waste-to-energy and biomass technology projects. Financing has also come from overseas, with PRC and Thai investments playing a significant role in ASEAN. Simultaneously, the PRC has also provided large economic corridor investments in Pakistan's solar and wind projects.

Though it may seem counterintuitive, most of the investment involved in a low-carbon energy system is intrinsically less risky than current fossil fuel-related investments, especially in the long term. Public policies that lower the cost of financing renewable energy projects would also lower energy costs in the long term and benefit government coffers. Eventually, lower-carbon energy systems are more local and less dependent on globally traded commodities such as oil, coal, or gas. This is good for developing countries that must bear the import costs of oil, coal, and gas, adding to a large part of their fiscal deficits. Though the dynamics of energy use for electricity generation are different across each country, a shift to renewable energy in many of these countries will provide them with long-term energy security, whether it be, for example, reliance on oil imports for many ASEAN countries and natural gas exports for CAREC countries, or gas imports for Thailand, coal imports for Philippines, or coal exports for Indonesia.

The uneven distribution of energy resources and sometimes complementarities provides a strong need for regional collaboration to allow energy to flow smoothly between countries, reinforcing security and economic gains for all (ADB 2019). A regional investment strategy will also help suitable partner organizations (international financial institutions and multilateral development banks) to guide policymakers in creating effective enabling conditions for private investments.

For example, a regional network development, CAREC Energy Strategy 2030, proposes a new regional mechanism for identifying joint regional interest projects through a platform that brings together transmission system operators from all over the region under one umbrella—the Central Asia Transmission Cooperation Association. The five Central Asian countries have been a compelling case for the energy grid that remained since the Soviet Union; since then has disintegrated, leaving the Kyrgyz Republic and Tajikistan more dependent on coal. With all the new developments and ADB support, the likelihood of reconnecting the unified energy grid and expanding it is high again.

11.6 Conclusion

Policymakers can think of PPPs as key policy support schemes for renewables that do not necessarily address all the barriers to financing projects. In the early phase of a country deploying a given technology, FITs, for example, provide revenue certainty but do not necessarily address novelty risk and the need for a track record. Green investment policy frameworks, such as those of the OECD, provide useful guidelines such as removing fossil fuel subsidies, pricing carbon, setting clear, long-term policy goals, and giving time-bound, tailored incentives for renewable energy investment that correct for market failures. When governments make renewable energy a priority, they provide a supportive environment for PPP projects to thrive, and incentive policies encourage investment.

Though it is encouraging to see the reduction of ASEAN PPPs for coal, and more recently in CAREC, more PPP investments and plans are needed for solar, wind, and geothermal in both these regions. While the energy sector continues to receive the bulk of global investments, the share of renewables for electricity generation projects still needs to increase. Since 2017, solar and wind technologies have attracted the most renewable energy investments. Each country needs to develop relevant renewable energy technology projects based on its endowments and develop a supportive policy framework and environment to succeed in a low-carbon alternative.

Power tariffs are pressure points, especially for countries dependent on imports for their energy needs (as many countries rely heavily on coal and gas imports.

COVID-19 has highlighted the need for more secure, reliable, and flexible power generation. Power sector planners assumed that large system lock-ins such as coal would lead to a least-cost system. Unfortunately, that has led to inflexibility, price instability, and high prices or subsidies. Even with a drop in renewable energy prices, the transition will take time, as, many times, the lock-in with existing plants is charged a capacity fee. The uncertainty in demand for electricity due to COVID-19 will delay investments in PPPs in the energy sector, forcing many investors to re-evaluate their strategy and risk. Renewables projects will have the upper hand, opening up a reset for low-carbon investments. With more countries committing to net-zero emission pledges by 2050, decarbonizing long-lived power generation assets such as coal-fired power plants and promoting PPPs in clean energy infrastructure will be crucial in accelerating the energy transition.

Notes

1 Including Afghanistan, Azerbaijan, the PRC (the Xinjiang Uygur Autonomous Region, and the Inner Mongolia Autonomous Region), Georgia, Kazakhstan, the Kyrgyz Republic, Mongolia, Pakistan, Tajikistan, Turkmenistan, and Uzbekistan.

2 There were no data on Turkmenistan in the World Bank PPI Database. The data for the PRC (the Xinjiang Uygur Autonomous Region and the Inner Mongolia Autonomous Region) are also omitted for CAREC.

3 There was no available renewable energy target and renewable energy installed capacity information on Georgia, the Kyrgyz Republic, and Turkmenistan. The PRC is not included as CAREC only includes Xinjiang Uyghur Autonomous Region, People's Republic of China.

References

Abdullah, W.S.W., M. Osman, M.Z.A.A. Kadir, and R. Verayiah. 2019. The Potential and Status of Renewable Energy Development in Malaysia. *Energies*, 12(12). https://doi.org/10.3390/en12122437.

ASEAN Centre for Energy. 2017. *The 5th ASEAN Energy Outlook*. Jakarta: ASEAN Centre for Energy. https://aseanenergy.org/the-5th-asean-energy-outlook/. Accessed 15 June 2020.

Asian Development Bank (ADB). 2017. *Meeting Asia's Infrastructure Needs*. Manila: ADB. www.adb.org/sites/default/files/publication/227496/special-report-infrastructure.pdf. Accessed 10 June 2020.

Asian Development Bank (ADB). 2019. *CAREC Energy Strategy 2030*. Manila: ADB. www.adb.org/sites/default/files/institutional-document/536941/carec-energy-strategy-2030.pdf. Accessed 10 June 2020.

AT Kearney. 2019. *Indonesia's Energy Transition: A Case for Action*. www.atkearney.com/documents/20152/2789427/2019+-+Indonesia%27s+Energy+Transition+A+Case+for+Action.pdf/3eba51da-43d3-7756-ca31-b5b6dbcc5b5b?t=1558915028402. Accessed 15 June 2020.

Barrow, M., and M. Tornberg. 2007. Potential for Public Private Partnerships in Afghanistan. In *The Enabling Environment Conference*. Kabul. www.akdn.org/sites/akdn/files/media/documents/enabling_environment/2007_eec_background_paper_ppps_eng.pdf. Accessed 9 June 2020.

Bayliss, K., and E. Van Waeyenberge. 2018. Unpacking the Public Private Partnership Revival. *Journal of Development Studies*, 54(4): 577–593. https://doi.org/10.1080/00220388.2017.1303671.

Bhattacharya, A., J. Oppenheim, and N. Stern. 2015. *Driving Sustainable Development through Better Infrastructure: Key Elements of a Transformation Program.* Paper No. 91. Washington D.C. www.lse.ac.uk/GranthamInstitute/wp-content/uploads/2015/07/Bhattacharya-et-al.-2015.pdf. Accessed 5 August 2020.

BP. 2020. *Statistical Review of World Energy 2020.* London. www.bp.com/content/dam/bp/business-sites/en/global/corporate/pdfs/energy-economics/statistical-review/bp-stats-review-2020-full-report.pdf. Accessed 1 November 2020.

Central Asia Regional Economic Cooperation Program. 2015. *Strategy and Work Plan (2016–2020) for Regional Cooperation in the Energy Sector of CAREC Countries.* Manila. https://policy.asiapacificenergy.org/sites/default/files/Strategy and Work Plan %282016–2020%29 %28EN%29.pdf. Accessed 18 July 2020.

Climate Policy Initiative. 2018. *Global Climate Finance: An Updated View 2018.* London. https://climatepolicyinitiative.org/publication/global-climate-finance-an-updated-view-2018/. Accessed 10 August 2020.

Consortium of Multilateral Development Banks. 2015. *Tracking Climate Co-Finance: Approach Proposed by MDBs.* http://pubdocs.worldbank.org/en/260421452810381181/Briefing-MDB-Co-financing-final-04122015.pdf. Accessed 18 July 2020.

Crisis Group. 2016. The Economic Disaster Behind Afghanistan's Mounting Human Crisis. www.crisisgroup.org/asia/south-asia/afghanistan/economic-disaster-behind-afghanistan-s-mounting-human-crisis. Accessed 10 August 2020.

Economist Intelligence Unit. 2014. *Evaluating the Environment for Public Private Partnerships in Asia-Pacific.* London. www.adb.org/sites/default/files/publication/158409/2014-infrascope.pdf. Accessed 20 June 2020.

Economist Intelligence Unit. 2020. Infrascope Index. https://infrascope.eiu.com/. Accessed 1 November 2020.

Ember. 2020. The Global Electricity Review 2020. https://ember-climate.org/project/data-global-electricity-review/. Accessed 1 November 2020.

Ha, T. 2019, July 31. Power Play—Who's Winning Southeast Asia's Renewables Race? *Eco-Business.* www.eco-business.com/news/power-play-whos-winning-southeast-asias-renewables-race/. Accessed 1 November 2020.

Hasan, K., and Lin, K. 2018. Summary of Regulation on Solar PV in Cambodia. *Reed Smith.* www.reedsmith.com/en/perspectives/2018/03/summary-of-regulation-on-solar-pv-in-cambodia. Accessed 1 November 2020.

Heinberg, R. 2016. *Our Renewable Future: Laying the Path for One Hundred Percent Clean Energy.* Washington, D.C.: Island Press.

Huseynov, F. 2016. The Time Is Ripe for Public-Private Partnerships in Central Asia. *Kennedy School Review.* https://ksr.hkspublications.org/2016/06/17/the-time-is-ripe-for-public-private-partnerships-in-central-asia/. Accessed 20 June 2020.

International Energy Agency. 2013. *South East Asia Energy Outlook.* Paris. www.iea.org/publications/freepublications/publication/SoutheastAsiaEnergyOutlook_WEO2013SpecialReport.pdf. Accessed 20 June 2020.

International Energy Agency. 2016. *Energy Policies Beyond IEA Countries: Eastern Europe, Caucasus and Central Asia 2015.* Paris. www.iea.org/reports/energy-policies-beyond-iea-countries-eastern-europe-caucasus-and-central-asia-2015. Accessed 1 November 2020.

International Energy Agency. 2020. Policies database. www.iea.org/policies%0D. Accessed 11 March 2020.

Kenning, T. 2018. B.Grimm and Xuan Cau to develop Southeast Asia's largest solar project. *PV Tech.* www.pv-tech.org/news/b.grimm-adn-xuan-cau-to-develop-southeast-asias-largest-solar-project. Accessed 18 July 2020.

London School of Economics and Political Science. 2020. Climate Change Laws of the World. https://climate-laws.org/. Accessed 13 March 2020.

Ministry of Foreign Affairs of the Netherlands. 2013. *Public-Private Partnerships in Developing Countries* (IOB Study No. 378. The Hague. www.oecd.org/dac/evaluation/IOBstudy378publicprivatepartnershipsindevelopingcountries.pdf. Accessed 13 March 2020.

New Climate Economy. 2016. The Sustainable Infrastructure Imperative: Financing for Better Growth and Development. Washington, D.C. http://newclimateeconomy.report/2016/wp-content/uploads/sites/4/2014/08/NCE_2016Report.pdf. Accessed 27 March 2021.

New Climate Institute. 2020. Policy database. http://climatepolicydatabase.org/index.php/Browse_countries. Accessed 1 November 2020.

Organisation for Economic Co-operation and Development. 2017. *Investing in Climate, Investing in Growth.* Paris. https://read.oecd-ilibrary.org/economics/investing-in-climate-investing-in-growth_9789264273528-en#page3. Accessed 13 March 2020.

Pranadi, A. D. 2016. The Current Status of Renewable Energy and its Target in ASEAN Member States. *ASEAN Center for Energy.* https://aseanenergy.org/the-current-status-of-re-and-its-target-in-asean-member-states/. Accessed 18 July 2020.

REN 21. 2016. *Renewables Global Status Report 2016.* Paris. www.ren21.net/wp-content/uploads/2019/05/REN21_GSR2016_FullReport_en_11.pdf. Accessed 1 November 2020.

REN 21. 2019. *Asia and the Pacific Renewable Energy Status Report.* Paris. www.ren21.net/wp-content/uploads/2019/05/REN21_Asia_Report_2019_Web.pdf. Accessed 1 November 2020.

Shadrina, E. 2019. *Renewable Energy in Central Asian Economies: Role in Reducing Regional Energy Insecurity* (ADBI Working Papers No. 993. Manila. www.adb.org/publications/renewable-energy-central-asian-economies. Accessed 11 March 2020.

The Business Times. 2018, Thailand's biggest Wind Power Generator Plans Solar, Hydro Expansion. February 5. www.businesstimes.com.sg/energy-commodities/thailands-biggest-wind-power-generator-plans-solar-hydro-expansion. Accessed 1 November 2020.

Tonkonogy, B., J. Brown, V. Micale, X. Wang, and A. Clark. 2018. *Blended Finance in Clean Energy: Experiences and Opportunities.* Accessed 11 March 2020. www.climatepolicyinitiative.org/publication/blended-finance-clean-energy-experiences-opportunities/

United Nations Development Programme. 2014. *Renewable Energy Snapshots.* www.eurasia.undp.org/content/rbec/en/home/library/environment_energy/renewable-energy-snapshots.html. Accessed 18 July 2020.

Urban, M.A., and D. Wójcik. 2019. Dirty Banking: Probing the Gap in Sustainable Finance. *Sustainability,* 11(6). https://doi.org/10.3390/su11061745.

Vientiane Times. 2014. Hydropower Construction Continues on Nam Ou. https://wle-mekong.cgiar.org/hydropower-construction-continues-on-nam-ou/. Accessed 1 November 2020.

Wiek, A., and O. Weber, 2014. Sustainability Challenges and the Ambivalent Role of the Financial Sector. *Journal of Sustainable Finance and Investment*, 4(1): 9–20. https://doi.org/10.1080/20430795.2014.887349.

World Bank Group. 2019. PPI data. https://ppi.worldbank.org/en/ppidata. Accessed 19 August 2020.

Zen, F. 2018. *Public–Private Partnership Development in Southeast Asia*. ADB Economics Working Paper Series No. 553. Manila. www.adb.org/sites/default/files/publication/444631/ewp-553-ppp-development-southeast-asia.pdf. Accessed 18 July 2020.

12 An Evidence-Based Approach to Infrastructure Development in Uzbekistan

Umid Abidhadjaev and Feruzbek Davletov

12.1 Introduction

Economists and the political elite have discussed infrastructure investment throughout the history of classical economics. Transportation infrastructure is believed to have a positive impact, promoting urbanization and expanding market access (Kim and Go 2017). A vast literature on transportation suggests new railway lines promote economic growth by reducing transaction costs. For example, investment in railroads in Portugal had a positive influence on output, employment, and private investments (Pereira and Andraz 2012). In India, railways reduced trade costs and price differences across regions, which in turn led to cross-regional markets and increased income levels (Donaldson 2018). In France and the UK, expanded railway systems promoted structural changes in agriculture (Schwartz 2010). Furthermore, it has been reported that construction and improvement of railways increased the volume of trade in the People's Republic of China (Xu 2016).

This chapter is a continuation of the recent work done by Yoshino and Abidhadjaev (2017). According to that research, new railway lines in southeastern Uzbekistan had a positive long-term effect on the gross domestic product (GDP) and agricultural output of regions located at the far ends of the system. In addition, this chapter investigates the comprehensive financial impact of new railway lines in southeastern Uzbekistan on enterprises and institutions. The impact is quantified by employing the difference-in-difference estimation technique independently for regions of provision (regional effect), for neighboring districts (spillover effect) and for regions located in the far ends (connectivity effect) of the current railway system in Uzbekistan (Figure 12.1). The discovery of positive influence on enterprises and institutions is important with regard to further infrastructure development in Uzbekistan, with its direct effect on the regions of intervention highlighting the ways of infrastructure financing. Understanding the impact of infrastructure funding can help policymakers to better allocate resources and come up with mechanisms of financing. In cases where the impact on the outcome variable turns out to be regionally positive, this might play as a rationale for implementing different financing tools such as tax increment financing.

DOI: 10.4324/9781003228790-15

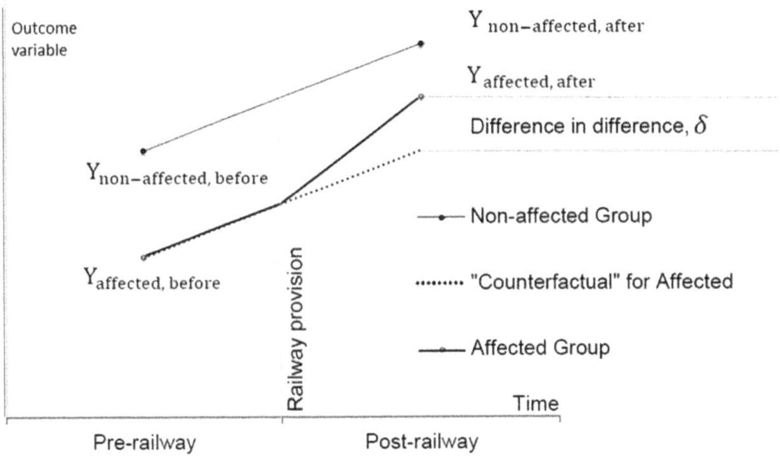

Figure 12.1 Graphical Representation of the DID Design.
Note: DID = difference-in-difference.
Source: Yoshino and Abidhadjaev (2017).

The rest of the chapter is organized as follows. In Section 12.2, we review the literature on the various effects of infrastructure development. Section 12.3 details the analytical methods, and Section 12.4 reviews the relevant data. Section 12.5 presents the results of the estimation. The description of the corresponding policy implications and the conclusion are given the Sections 12.6 and 12.7.

12.2 Literature Review

12.2.1 Notion of Infrastructure Capital and Performance of Enterprises

Infrastructure capital can be defined in many ways. In a narrow way, it consists of tangible capital stock such as highway, water and sewer lines, transportation facilities, and communication systems. A broader view additionally comprises investments in human capital and research and development. The literature emphasizes that well-developed infrastructure capital boosts the productive capacity of a nation through accelerated mobilization of resources and, at the same time, expanding those resources' productivity. In particular, transportation infrastructure can be involved in the production process in the form of "unpaid factors" that can reduce costs, allowing faster delivery of goods to the market, which in turn might also attract foreign investors (Pradhan and Bagchi 2013; Wheeler and Mody 1992). Transport infrastructure can also agglomerate external resources into the region. This is noticeable from the comparative economic superiority of coastal and riverbank areas throughout history. Transport infrastructure also impacts growth via aggregate demand. Typical cases include the increase in intermediate inputs needed for the construction.

With respect to the performance of enterprises, Hirschman (1958) claims that primary, secondary, and tertiary production activities cannot operate without infrastructure, which, in a broad sense, includes transportation, communication, power and water supply, etc. This is in line with the affirmation of Adenikinju (2005) that infrastructure development affects the performance of enterprises in terms of their output, profitability, and employment through the productivity channel. In addition, it has also been reported in Kessides (1993) that infrastructure increases the competitiveness of small and medium-sized enterprises (SMEs) through factors of production.

Barro (1990) incorporates the impact of policy variables such as infrastructure provision in the production function. Further, Kessides (1993) emphasizes that the contribution of infrastructure to economic growth occurs through supply and demand channels as a result of reduced production costs. Kessides (1993) also claims that proper infrastructure improves the quality of life through provision of transport, communication, health and other services. Consequently, the contribution of infrastructure to economic expansion takes place by means of private sector advancement. Transportation development makes it comfortable to bring modern technologies to enterprises and provide opportunities through economies of scale.

12.2.2 Methods for Analyzing

There are two systematic ways of investigating the linkage between infrastructure capital and economic growth: cost-benefit analysis, and macroeconomic modelling. The latter is subdivided into production function, cost/profit function, and causality (Vector autoregressions). Until the 1980s, infrastructure capital was not included in any economic growth models. Aschauer (1989) was among the first to incorporate infrastructure capital into the production function vis-à-vis economic growth in the US. Auschauer's findings set a baseline for further research in this area. Moreover, many other scholars came to the conclusion of positive return on infrastructure investment (Eisner 1991; Munnell 1992; Harmatuck 1996; Easterly and Rebelo 1994; Canning, Fay and Perotti 1994), while others questioned the robustness of these results (Hulten and Schwab 1991; Tatom 1993; Harmatuck 1996). Furthermore, Yoshino and Nakahigashi (2000) estimated the effect of infrastructure on productivity using data from Thailand and Japan and found it to be positive. From the perspective of enterprises, this implies that they can increase their output levels without making any changes to inputs, which is known as a direct effect. Further, firms can maximize their profits by altering the input structure, i.e., an indirect effect (Nakahigashi and Yoshino 2016). The systematic development of effective and efficient transportation policies depends on the comprehension of the interrelation between transport infrastructure and economic gains.

Table 12.1 Representation of the Simple Difference-in-Difference Estimator for the Periods 2005–2008 and 2009–2012

Regions	*Outcome variable (in billion sum)*	*Pre-intervention*	*Post-intervention*	*Difference*
Non-affected group	Profit/loss of enterprises and institutions	185	373	188
Affected group	Profit/loss of enterprises and institutions	175	496	321
Difference				133

Source: Authors.

Note
The affected group comprises of the Kashkadarya and Surkhandarya regions.

12.3 Methodology

Following the comprehensive methodology of Yoshino and Abidhajaev (2017), we employ a quasi-experimental design, i.e., the so-called difference-in-difference (DID) estimation. Typically, DID is used to estimate the impact of a specific treatment, like the introduction of a railway connection—in the case of Uzbekistan, the Toshguzar-Boysun-Kumkurgon line—by dividing the data into a control group and a treated group and comparing their changes in outcomes over time. Before analyzing the DID estimator, it is useful to look at the simple difference estimator, which is defined as the difference in average outcome in the affected group before after intervention, minus the difference in average outcome in the non-affected group before and after the intervention (Table 12.1).

The simple DID estimator shows an increase in the profits of enterprises and institutions for the regions where the new railway was introduced. This method allows capturing the time-invariant and region-specific effects. However, the problem is that other crucial factors defining the level of profit/loss of organizations might be missing, leading to over/under estimations. The list of other time-varying covariates might include the investment, terms of trade, labor force, etc. The incorporation of such covariates to our estimation framework allows us to fully define the notion of affected and non-affected groups:

Affected group, $F_{g=A}$

$$t = 0(\textit{before intervention}) : F_{A0} = a_{A0} + \gamma_{A0} + X_{A0}\beta' + \varepsilon_{A0} \tag{12.1}$$

$$t = 1(\textit{after intervention}) : F_{A1} = a_{A1} + \gamma_{A1} + X_{A1}\beta' + \varphi_{A1} + \delta + \varepsilon_{A1} \tag{12.2}$$

Non-affected group, $F_{g=N}$

$$t = 0(\textit{before intervention}) : F_{N0} = a_{N0} + \gamma_{N0} + X_{N0}\beta' + \varepsilon_{N0} \tag{12.3}$$

$$t = 1(\textit{after intervention}) : F_{N1} = a_{N1} + \gamma_{N1} + X_{N1}\beta' + \varphi_{A1} + \varepsilon_{A1} \tag{12.4}$$

These definitions facilitate the modelling of the outcome F_{it} for the panel data. The baseline regression specification is given in the Equation 12.5.

$$F_{it} = a_i + \varphi_t + X'_{it}\beta + \delta D_{gt} + \epsilon_{it} \tag{12.5}$$

Here, F_{it} is the financial performance of enterprises and institutions; X is a vector of time-varying covariates; D is the binary variable showing whether or not the observation is related to the affected group; i represents regions; g represents whether the group is affected=1, or non-affected=0; t represents treatment before ($t = 0$) and after ($t = 1$); a_i incorporates the constant term (a), which is assumed to be the same across groups (common trend assumption) and time-invariant unobserved region-specific effects (γ_i); φ_t is the year-specific effect and ϵ_{it} is the random, unobserved "error" term, which is assumed to be independently and identically distributed. The coefficient of interest– δ would be the DID estimate; in other words, the above-mentioned difference between observed "actual" outcome and "counter-factual" outcome.

12.3.1 Geographical Impact of the Railway Introduction

The extension of our analysis consists of questioning the impact of intervention based on cross-sectional and time series characteristics. In particular, the first stage includes the estimation of the geographical effects, including the regional, spillover, and connectivity effects. Regional effects are directly concerned with analyzing the impact of railway intervention in the location of intervention, mainly the Surkhandarya and Kashkadarya regions. Consequently, the spillover effects are related to the impact on neighboring regions. In this case, the affected group would be supplemented with the Bukhara and Samarkand regions. Finally, the examination of connectivity effects comprises the regions located at the end points (Samarkand, Surkhandarya, Tashkent region, Karakalpakstan) of the current internal railway system in Uzbekistan.

12.3.2 Timing of the Impact of Railway Introduction

We also check for the variations in outcome depending on the time basis. These include the anticipation effects, launch effects, and postponed effects of the intervention, which is further divided into short-, mid-, and long-term effects, with

2-, 3-, and 4-year spans, respectively. Specifically, the impact of the introduction of a railway is captured by the launch effect. Though the new railway line started operation in August 2007, the construction of two out of five main bridges was not finished until the end of 2008. Thus, the launch period was set to 2009. Considering these modifications, the regression specifications for the launch effect would be in the following forms:

$$F_{it} = a_i + \varphi_t + X_{it}'\beta + \delta_{\tau=0}\left(D_{gt\{2010:2009\}}\right) + \epsilon_{it}, \text{ short} - \text{term} \quad (12.6)$$

$$F_{it} = a_i + \varphi_t + X_{it}'\beta + \delta_{\tau=0}\left(D_{gt\{2011:2009\}}\right) + \epsilon_{it}, \text{ mid} - \text{term} \quad (12.7)$$

$$F_{it} = a_i + \varphi_t + X_{it}'\beta + \delta_{\tau=0}\left(D_{gt\{2012:2009\}}\right) + \epsilon_{it}, \text{ long} - \text{term} \quad (12.8)$$

In order to control for the positive shock of pre-launching the project, we refer to anticipation effects that incorporate one and two years in the regression framework. This is motivated by the existence of forward-looking agents who consider the future changes in making optimal decisions (Sargent 1987). The corresponding regression framework would be:

With one year of anticipation:

$$F_{it} = a_i + \varphi_t + X_{it}'\beta + \delta_{\tau=-1}\left(D_{gt\{2010:2008\}}\right) + \epsilon_{it}, \text{ short} - \text{term} \quad (12.9)$$

$$F_{it} = a_i + \varphi_t + X_{it}'\beta + \delta_{\tau=-1}\left(D_{gt\{2011:2008\}}\right) + \epsilon_{it}, \text{ mid} - \text{term} \quad (12.10)$$

$$F_{it} = a_i + \varphi_t + X_{it}'\beta + \delta_{\tau=-1}\left(D_{gt\{2012:2008\}}\right) + \epsilon_{it}, \text{ long} - \text{term} \quad (12.11)$$

With two years of anticipation:

$$F_{it} = a_i + \varphi_t + X_{it}'\beta + \delta_{\tau=-2}\left(D_{gt\{2010:2007\}}\right) + \epsilon_{it}, \text{ short} - \text{term} \quad (12.12)$$

$$F_{it} = a_i + \varphi_t + X_{it}'\beta + \delta_{\tau=-2}\left(D_{gt\{2011:2007\}}\right) + \epsilon_{it}, \text{mid} - \text{term} \quad (12.13)$$

$$F_{it} = a_i + \varphi_t + X_{it}'\beta + \delta_{\tau=-2}\left(D_{gt\{2012:2007\}}\right) + \epsilon_{it}, \text{ long} - \text{term} \quad (12.14)$$

In the end, there might be the possibility of postponed effects (one and two years) of an infrastructure provision, as it might take some time for some businesses and individuals to respond:

$$F_{it} = a_i + \varphi_t + X_{it}'\beta + \delta_{\tau=1}\left(D_{gt\{2012:2010\}}\right) + \epsilon_{it}, 1 \text{ year lag} \quad (12.15)$$

$$F_{it} = a_i + \varphi_t + X_{it}'\beta + \delta_{\tau=2}\left(D_{gt\{2012:2011\}}\right) + \epsilon_{it}, \text{ 2 year lag} \quad (12.16)$$

12.4 Data

The panel dataset used in our analysis is composed of yearly regional economic indicators starting from 2005 to 2012. The source of the data is the State Statistics Committee of the Republic of Uzbekistan (2014). The dependent variable, i.e., performance of enterprises and institutions, is proxied with the yearly financial results of activity in billions of sum. According to the official definition, the financial result is based on the accounting of all business operations. Moreover, it represents the amount of gross profit (loss) from the sale of products (services) and other income, reduced by the amount of expenses of the period (Statistics Committee of the Republic of Uzbekistan 2014).

The summary statistics for the variable of outcome are given in Table 12.2. The overall number of observations in the dataset is 112, the number of cross-sections is 14, and the repetitions per cross-section is eight. The panel dataset is strongly balanced. The mean and standard deviation for the full dataset, without considering the panel structure, are 286 and 562, respectively. The variation between cross-sections is higher (503) than within individual variations (280). The same tendency is observed in all other subgroups under consideration. The minimum value for outcome variable is -SUM57 billion and the corresponding maximum is SUM3.092 trillion. The group of explanatory variables includes total investment, external trade turnover, labor force and the number of small enterprises and microfirms for the respective regions (Statistics Committee of the Republic of Uzbekistan 2014). Summary statistics of the outcome variable for

Table 12.2 Summary Statistics for Outcome Variable—Financial Performance of Enterprises and Institutions (in billion sum)

Full data set	*Mean*	*Std. Dev.*	*Min.*	*Max.*	*Observations*
overall	286.8545	562.0853	-57.2	3,092.4	N=112
between		503.2296	12.725	1,908.5	n=14
within		280.4816	-1,058.746	1,470.754	T=8
Regional					
overall	335.1687	416.0853	18.8	1369	N=16
between		407.3907	47.1	623.2375	n=2
within		290.8799	-151.4687	1,080.931	T=8
Spillover					
overall	222.95	318.5191	-21.3	1369	N=32
between		271.3845	47.1	623.2375	n=4
within		210.7971	-263.6875	968.7125	T=8
Connectivity					
overall	165.6344	234.2716	13.9	920	N=32
between		228.0793	45.1625	507.55	n=4
within		120.8698	-175.4156	578.0844	T=8

Source: Authors.

Table 12.3 Summary Statistics of the Financial Results of Activity of Enterprises and Institutions

Affected group					
	Observ.	*Mean*	*Std. Dev.*	*Min.*	*Max.*
Before 2009	8	174.6	187.9024	18.8	507.4
After 2009 (included)	8	495.7375	526.0684	41.4	1,369
Non-affected group					
	Observ.	*Mean*	*Std. Dev.*	*Min.*	*Max.*
Before 2009	48	184.7104	326.9245	4.8	1,689
After 2009 (included)	48	372.8938	751.6732	-57.2	3,092.4

Source: Authors.

affected and non-affected groups before and after implementation of the project are provided in Table 12.3.

12.5 Results

To begin with, the estimation of four versions of the baseline specification model (Equation 12.1) is given in Table 12.4. Regression 1 includes only the total investment and volume of external trade turnover as explanatory variables and excludes time effects. In this particular case, the DID coefficient turns out to be significant at the level of 5% with coefficient around 199. The subsequent versions of regressions (2–4), follow the same positive tendency, with the DID coefficient of financial performance ranging from 252 to 319 on the same significance level. In particular, the inclusion of year-specific effects in regression 2 increases the DID coefficient, which might be explained by the overall business climate in the region or the changes in the legislation over the period.

We also observe a statistically significant DID coefficient for mid-term regional effects. As in the previous case, the estimation procedure comprises four regressions, and is formed by step-by-step inclusion of explanatory variables. In particular, the mid-term DID coefficient constitutes SUM245 billion when all regressors are included (Table 12.5). Moreover, the one-year postponed regional effect of infrastructure on financial performance of enterprises and institutions turns out to be significant and lies in the range from SUM356 billion to SUM491 billion for the corresponding four regression stages (Table 12.6).

Furthermore, Table 12.7 illustrates launch effects, anticipation effects and postponed effects for respective short, mid, and long terms, depending on the geographical location. We find statistically significant results for mid- and long-term launch effects for the newly introduced Kashkadarya and Surkhandarya railway systems. Turning to the anticipation effects, the long-term magnitude of

Table 12.4 Regional Financial Performance of Enterprises and Institutions and Railways Connection: Estimation Output for the Long-Term Regional Effects

Time period	*2005–2012 Regression 1*	*2005–2012 Regression 2*	*2005–2012 Regression 3*	*2005-2012 Regression 4*
State effects	Yes	Yes	Yes	Yes
Time effect	No	Yes	Yes	Yes
DID_regional	199.016	252.475	261.268	318.811
	(2.16)**	(2.63)**	(2.77)**	(3.53)**
Total investment	0.140	0.178	0.182	0.122
	(4.15)***	(4.50)**	(4.66)**	(3.04)**
External trade turnover	0.232	0.225	0.231	0.231
	(18.86)***	(17.50)**	(17.88)**	(18.93)**
Labor force			-0.093	-0.191
			(2.24)*	(4.05)**
№ of small enterprises and microfirms				0.008
				(3.74)**
Constant	-99.697	-78.462	12.805	-58.193
	(4.02)***	(2.89)**	(0.26)	(1.17)
R^2	0.90	0.90	0.91	0.92
N	112	112	112	112

Source: Authors.

Note
* p<0.1; ** p<0.05; *** p<0.01.

Table 12.5 Regional Financial Performance of Enterprises and Institutions and Railways Connection: Estimation Output for the Mid-Term Regional Effects

Time period	*2005–2012 Regression 1*	*2005–2012 Regression 2*	*2005–2012 Regression 3*	*2005–2012 Regression 4*
State effects	Yes	Yes	Yes	Yes
Time effect	No	Yes	Yes	Yes
did_regional	146.739	187.863	195.087	245.747
	(1.56)	(1.91)	(2.02)*	(2.64)**
Total Investment	0.127	0.155	0.157	0.105
	(3.75)***	(3.88)**	(4.99)**	(2.61)*
External trade turnover	0.240	0.235	0.242	0.242
	(19.09)***	(17.95)**	(18.22)**	(19.24)**
Labor force			-0.092	-0.185
			(2.12)*	(3.73)**
№ of small enterprises and microfirms				0.007
				(3.36)**
Constant	-92.766	-79.837	9.819	-48.141
	(3.81)***	(3.05)**	(0.20)	(0.96)
R^2	0.91	0.91	0.91	0.92
N	98	98	98	98

Source: Authors.

Note
* p<0.1; ** p<0.05; *** p<0.01.

Table 12.6 Regional Financial Performance of Enterprises and Institutions and Railways Connection: Estimation Output for the One-year Regional Postponed Effects

Time period	*2005–2012 Regression 1*	*2005–2012 Regression 2*	*2005–2012 Regression 3*	*2005–2012 Regression 4*
State effects	Yes	Yes	Yes	Yes
Time effect	No	Yes	Yes	Yes
did_regional	356.403	446.319	459.331	491.275
	(3.95)***	(4.81)**	(5.07)**	(5.68)**
Total Investment	0.132	0.185	0.188	0.164
	(4.14)***	(5.15)**	(5.36)**	(4.83)**
External trade turnover	0.236	0.225	0.232	0.229
	(20.03)***	(18.95)**	(19.49)**	(20.10)**
Labor force			-0.098	-0.168
			(2.54)*	(4.04)**
№ of small enterprises and microfirms				0.006
				(3.54)**
Constant	-98.075	-78.308	18.174	-21.429
	(4.16)***	(3.29)**	(0.41)	(0.49)
R^2	0.91	0.92	0.92	0.93
N	112	112	112	112

Source: Authors.

Note
* p<0.1; ** p<0.05; *** p<0.01.

DID stays positive at 10% significance level. Additionally, we observe statistically significant results for one-year and two-year postponed effects for the original location of intervention (Kashkadarya and Surkhandarya regions) and for spillover regions (Bukhara and Samarkand regions included).

The findings of this chapter indicate that the same intervention increases the financial performance of enterprises and institutions directly in the regions of intervention. On the other hand, previous ex-post analysis of the introduction of the Toshguzar-Boysun-Kumkurgon railway line in Uzbekistan reveals a positive long-term impact on regional GDP in the far ends of the railway system (connectivity effect) in Uzbekistan (Yoshino and Abidhadjaev 2017). Table 12.8 demonstrates the results of these findings: connectivity effects are around 2.8%, 2.5%, and 2% in the short-, mid-, and long-term periods, respectively. Besides, according to Yoshino and Abidhadjaev (2017), the hypothesis of spillover effects, which is also reported for different countries in other sources, such as Pereira and Andraz (2003) and Pereira and Roca-Sagales (2007), also holds in the case of Uzbekistan, with the long-term launch effect to be around 2.3%.

Interestingly, the results indicate that the introduction of a new railway system that connects Surkhandarya and Kashkadarya regions has a 2% regional GDP increase on average on the far end districts of Uzbekistan, mainly in Karakalpakstan, Tashkent, Surkhandarya, and Samarkand (mid-point), which is

Table 12.7 Difference-in-Difference Coefficients for all Cases

			Regional effect	*Spillover effect*	*Connectivity effect*
		D_i / D_t	D_g = *regional*	D_g = *spillover*	D_g = *connectivity*
Launch effects					
	Short-term	$D_{t=(2010:2009)}$	22.886	-101.619	-33.880
			(0.29)	(1.60)	(0.56)
	Mid-term	$D_{t=(2011:2009)}$	245.747	31.597	-29.421
			(2.64)**	(0.40)	(0.40)
	Long-term	$D_{t=(2012:2009)}$	318.811	81.156	-11.967
			(3.53)**	(1.03)	(0.16)
Anticipation effects					
1 year	Short-term	$D_{t=(2010:2008)}$	-29.616	-82.686	-3.214
			(0.40)	(1.42)	(0.06)
	Mid-term	$D_{t=(2011:2008)}$	137.818	-11.762	-6.277
			(1.44)	(0.15)	(0.08)
	Long-term	$D_{t=(2012:2008)}$	206.355	19.849	2.723
			(2.14)*	(0.25)	(0.04)
Postponed effects		$D_{t=(2012:2010)}$	491.275	156.736	5.601
			(5.68)***	(2.02)*	(0.07)
Anticipation effects					
2 years	Short-term	$D_{t=(2010:2007)}$	-33.313	-65.749	-33.678
			(0.42)	(1.08)	(0.56)
	Mid-term	$D_{t=(2011:2007)}$	95.749	-21.316	-35.996
			(0.91)	(0.25)	(0.44)
	Long-term	$D_{t=(2012:2007)}$	155.936	-0.905	-29.011
			(1.43)	(0.01)	(0.34)
Postponed effects		$D_{t=(2012:2011)}$	559.690	197.991	12.941
			(5.86)***	(2.32)*	(0.15)

Source: Authors.

consistent with other empirical studies on the positive role of distance for the use of rail as a transportation mode (Briffault et al. 2000; Jiang, Johnson, and Calzada 1999; Wang et al. 2013).

12.6 Policy Implications

The findings of this chapter highlight infrastructure, especially for the region where the intervention takes place. Since the main problem with infrastructure development is financing, this chapter questions whether the provision of capital and services should be financed centrally or locally. In many cases, the main beneficiary of such infrastructure refinements is the region where the construction takes place; since adequate resources or borrowing capacity are usually lacking in underdeveloped regions, ways and methods of attracting funds from other sources are needed.

Table 12.8 Difference-in-Difference Coefficients with the GDP Outcome Variable

			Regional effect	*Spillover effect*	*Connectivity effect*
		D_i / D_t	D_g = *regional*	D_g = *spillover*	D_g = *connectivity*
Launch effects					
	Short-term	$D_{t=(2010:2009)}$	0.70 (0.45)	1.33 (1.14)	2.83 (4.48)***
	Mid-term	$D_{t=(2011:2009)}$	0.36 (0.29)	1.27 (1.46)	2.5 (6.88)***
	Long-term	$D_{t=(2012:2009)}$	-0.42 (-0.29)	2.29 (2.94)**	2.06 (3.04)***
Anticipation effects					
1 year	Short-term	$D_{t=(2010:2008)}$	0.85 (1.75)	-0.18 (-0.20)	0.19 (0.33)
	Mid-term	$D_{t=(2011:2008)}$	0.64 (1.30)	-0.02 (-0.03)	0.31 (0.51)
	Long-term	$D_{t=(2012:2008)}$	-0.006 (-0.01)	0.50 (0.67)	0.07 (0.13)
Postponed effects		$D_{t=(2012:2010)}$	-1.49 (-0.72)	2.58 (2.03)*	1.76 (1.95)*
Anticipation effects					
2 years	Short-term	$D_{t=(2010:2007)}$	1.42 (0.78)	-1.32 (-0.92)	-1.54 (-1.66)
	Mid-term	$D_{t=(2011:2007)}$	0.84 (1.42)	0.13 (0.13)	0.32 (0.44)
	Long-term	$D_{t=(2012:2007)}$	0.10 (0.16)	0.87 (1.19)	0.11 (0.15)
Postponed effects		$D_{t=(2012:2011)}$	-1.71 (-1.35)	1.05 (1.44)	-0.14 (-0.20)

Source: Yoshino and Abidhadjaev (2017).

Note
GDP = gross domestic product.

There are many mechanisms for this, one being hometown investment trust funds, which attracts resources for local development (Yoshino and Taghizadeh 2014). Another process through which local financing occurs is Tax Incremental Financing (TIF), which is an economic tool for development purposes in a specific area using "incremental" local property tax revenues. Particularly for the sake of investment improvements in a specific district, the government could raise the funds by means of incremental increases in future property tax revenues of that region. Due to timing discrepancies of expenditure and collection of tax revenues, the regional tax authority usually borrows funds in the early stages of a project and then pays them off with the incremental tax revenues in the future. Theoretically, TIF can be described as a loop. In the initial stage, the incremental

Table 12.9 Pay-off Matrix: Simultaneous Effort

	Normal case	*Effort case*
Normal case	(50, r) Operating Investors entity	(50, ar) Operating Investors entity
Effort case	(100, r) Operating Investors entity	(100, ar) Operating Investors entity

Source: Nakahigash and Yoshino (2016).

revenues are used for the local infrastructure provision, which triggers the private investment, which in turn generates incremental revenues that would be used again for public expenditures (Briffault 2010). Besides, it is well documented that the returned additional tax revenues would increase the returns on infrastructure investments up to 16% in the case of Uzbekistan. Thus, Yoshino et al. (2017) emphasize the importance of injecting additional spillover tax revenues into infrastructure financing by illustrating the incentive mechanisms in the payoff framework. Table 12.9 shows how both infrastructure operating entities and investors increase their payoffs in the case of simultaneous maximum effort. Mainly, if the infrastructure investors improve the dividend system by injecting additional spillover tax revenues back to the operating entity, this would increase the income for both parties.

12.7 Conclusion

The main goal of this chapter was to investigate the impact of newly introduced Toshguzar-Boysun-Kumkurgon railway line on the financial performance of enterprises and institutions. The effect turned out to be positive for regions of origin, i.e., Surkhandarya and Kashkadarya. In particular, in the short term, there was, on average, a SUM246 billion increase in profits and a SUM319 billion increase over the long term compared with counterfactual scenarios. Moreover, the difference in financial performance for one-year, long-term anticipation effects of the original regions was SUM206 billion. Analysis also revealed differences for the regional and spillover postponed effects. In particular, for one-year regional and spillover postponed effects, the differences were SUM491 billion and SUM157 billion, respectively. The policy implication is that infrastructure development is important for the financial performance of enterprises and institutions. Therefore, it might be rational to employ TIF since the main beneficiary of the infrastructure is the region where it is introduced. The results follow the previous research on the impact of infrastructure development in Uzbekistan by Yoshino and Abidhadjaev (2017), where they find positive connectivity effects on regional GDPs.

References

Adenikinju, A.F. 2005. Analysis of the Cost of Infrastructure Failures in a Developing Economy: The Case of the Electricity Sector in Nigeria. AERC Research Paper 148. Nairobi: African Economic Research Consortium.

Aschauer, D.A. 1989. Is Public Expenditure Productive? *Journal of Monetary Economics* 23(2): 177–200.

Barro, R.J. 1990. Government Spending in a Simple Model of Endogenous Growth. *Journal of Political Economy* 98(5, Part 2), S103–S125.

Briffault, R. 2010. The Most Popular Tool: Tax Increment Financing and the Political Economy of Local Government. *University of Chicago Law Review* 77: 65.

Briffault, R. 2000. Localism and Regionalism. *Buffalo Law Review* 48: 1.

Canning, D., M. Fay, and R. Perotti. 1994. Infrastructure and Economic Growth. *International Differences in Growth Rates.* New York: MacMillan.

Donaldson, D. 2018. Railroads of the Raj: Estimating the Impact of Transportation Infrastructure. *American Economic Review* 108(4–5): 899–934.

Easterly, W., and S. Rebelo. 1994. Fiscal Policy and Economic Growth: An Empirical Investigation (No. 885). CEPR Discussion Papers.

Eisner, R. 1991. Infrastructure and Regional Economic Performance: Comment. *New England Economic Review*: 47–58.

Harmatuck, D.J. 1996. The Influence of Transportation Infrastructure on Economic Development. *Logistics and Transportation Review* 32(1): 63.

Hirschman, A. 1958. *Strategies of Economic Development.* New Haven: Yale University Press.

Hulten, C.R., and R.M. Schwab. 1991. Public Capital Formation and the Growth of Regional Manufacturing Industries. *National Tax Journal*, 121–134.

Jiang, F., P. Johnson, and C. Calzada. 1999. Freight Demand Characteristics and Mode Choice: An Analysis of the Results of Modeling with Disaggregate Revealed Preference Data. *Journal of Transportation and Statistics* 2.

Kessides, C. 1993. *The Contributions of Infrastructure to Economic Development: A Review of Experience and Policy Implications.* Washington, DC: The World Bank.

Kim, J., and S. Go. 2017. Impact of Railroads on Local Economies: Evidence from US History. *The Journal of Distribution Science* 15(4): 25–32.

Munnell, A.H. 1992. Policy Watch: Infrastructure Investment and Economic Growth. *Journal of Economic Perspectives* 6(4): 189–198.

Nakahigashi, M., and N. Yoshino. 2016. Changes in Economic Effect of Infrastructure and Financing Methods. *Public Policy Review* 12(1): 47–68.

Pereira, A.M., and J.M. Andraz. 2003. On the Impact of Public Investment on the Performance of US Industries. *Public Finance Review* 31(1): 66–90.

Pereira, A.M., and J.M. Andraz. 2012. On the Economic Effects of Investment in Railroad Infrastructures in Portugal. *Journal of Economic Development-Seoul* 37(2): 79.

Pereira, A.M., and O. Roca-Sagales. 2007. Public Infrastructure and Regional Asymmetries in Spain. *Revue d'Economie Regionale Urbaine* 3: 503–519.

Pradhan, R.P., and T.P. Bagchi. 2013. Effect of Transportation Infrastructure on Economic Growth in India: The VECM Approach. *Research in Transportation Economics* 38(1): 139–148.

Raghuram, G., and M.R. Babu. 1999. Alternate Means of Financing Railways. *Vikalpa* 24(1): 13–26.

Sargent, T.J. 1987. Rational Expectations. *The New Palgrave Dictionary of Economics* 4: 76–79.

Schwartz, R.M. 2010. Rail Transport, Agrarian Crisis, and the Restructuring of Agriculture: France and Great Britain Confront Globalization, 1860-1900. *Social Science History* 34(2): 229–255.

State Statistics Committee of the Republic of Uzbekistan. 2014. Yearly and Quarterly Reports on Growth Rates of Basic Macroeconomic Indicators of Uzbekistan.

Tatom, J.A. 1993. The Spurious Effect of Public Capital Formation on Private Sector Productivity. *Policy Studies Journal* 21(2): 391–396.

Wang, Y., C. Ding, C. Liu, and B. Xie. 2013. Intelligent and Integrated Sustainable Multimodal Transportation Systems. In *Procedia Social and Behavioral Sciences, Proceedings from the 13th COTA International Conference of Transportation Professionals (CICTP2013)* 96: 1239–1249.

Wheeler, D., and A. Mody. 1992. International Investment Location Decisions: The Case of US Firms. *Journal of International Economics* 33(1–2): 57–76.

Yoshino, N., and U. Abidhadjaev. 2017. An Impact Evaluation of Investment in Infrastructure: The Case of a Railway Connection in Uzbekistan. *Journal of Asian Economics* 49: 1–11.

Yoshino, N., and M. Nakahigashi. 2000. The Role of Infrastructure in Economic Development. Typescript Manuscript.

Yoshino, N., and F. Taghizadeh Hesary. 2014. Hometown Investment Trust Funds: An Analysis of Credit Risk. ADBI Working Paper series 505. Tokyo: ADBI.

Yoshino, N., U. Abidhadjaev, and M. Nakahigashi. 2018. Closing the Asia Infrastructure Gap. *Horizons: Journal of International Relations and Sustainable Development* 10: 62–75.

Yoshino, N., M. Nakahigashi, and V. Pontines. 2017. Attract Private Financing to Infrastructure Investment by Injecting Spillover Tax Revenues. *Nomura Journal of Asian Capital Market* 1(2): 4–9.

13 Government Initiatives to Unlock Private Participation in Infrastructure

Lessons from Indonesia's Public–Private Partnership in the Water Sector

Febrio Kacaribu, Yohanna M.L. Gultom, Nauli A. Desdiani, and Syahda Sabrina*

13.1 Introduction

Clean water is a major global issue, with around 47% of the world population, and 44% of the Asian population, not having access (UN Water Development Report 2018). With the inevitable population boom, Asia's demand for water will increase significantly. The United Nations Development Programme has estimated that at least one in four people will experience water scarcity in 2050. To meet the world commitment of achieving the Sustainable Development Goals (SDGs), which demand the widespread access to clean water, sanitation, and hygiene, the issue then is how to unlock investment in infrastructure in the face of unequal access to clean water.

The Asian Development Bank reported that developing Asia will need around $800 billion in infrastructure investment for water and sanitation over the next decade to maintain growth and eradicate poverty (Hasan, Yi, and Zhigang 2017). Unfortunately, public investment in water infrastructure has failed to keep pace with the demand for clean water during the past 50 years (Purbo et al. 2019; Winpenny and Camdessus 2003). The key issue, however, is often not the lack of public financing, but lack of political will, as water is rarely among the top priorities of governments (OECD 2009). Public authorities tend to focus on the other infrastructures, such as electricity and transportation, to push higher economic growth (OECD 2009). Meanwhile, the existing public provision of water is shadowed by inefficiency and poor performance due to low-level equilibrium, with governments tending to set a low price for a political reason, thus preventing the operators from financing business expansion.

In this context, private participation through public-private partnerships (PPPs) can help governments to not only overcome the financing shortfall, but also promote an efficient and sustainable clean water service. PPPs in water infrastructure development and investment have become more relevant as governments usually face challenges in providing infrastructure, including poor project selection,

DOI: 10.4324/9781003228790-16

poor infrastructure maintenance, inefficient pricing, the presence of state capture and corruption, poor institutional design, and inefficient renegotiation processes (Engel, Fischer, and Galetovic 2014).

However, the water sector is generally not competitive compared to other public infrastructure, making it more difficult to attract private participation, not only because the investments involve large sunk costs and large economies of scale that make full recovery of water tariffs difficult to attain, even in the long-term, but also because consumers are typically unwilling to pay at the cost recovery rates. Meanwhile, the fact that good water resources are not available equally has made the costs of producing clean water, and, consequently, the returns on investment, highly variable. As a result, it is even more difficult to attract private investment in the places where the returns are lower, notwithstanding the government's commitment to attaining SDGs of clean and accessible water for all.

Currently, over 110 nations have embraced PPPs as an acquirement technique for water and sanitation service provision (Purbo et al. 2019; Jensen 2017). Yet, in 2019, private participation in this sector is still low, at around 5% of total private investments (The World Bank PPI Database 2019). Studies over the determinants of PPPs show that institutions, governance, and political factors also play a crucial role in determining the level of private participation (Araya, Schwartz, and Andres 2013; Hammami, Ruhashyankiko, and Yehoue 2006; Moszoro et al. 2015). These studies demonstrate that the level of private participation in infrastructure development is associated with the level of freedom from corruption, the better rule of law, a better quality of regulations, and a lower number of court disputes. Thus, the institutional framework and the political economy underlying the water service provision are also keys to unlock private participation.

With this background, this study aims at answering the question of how to unlock private participation in clean water infrastructure, especially in the face of low return on investment, using the case of Indonesia's water sector PPP projects as an example. The Government of Indonesia (GoI) has attempted to promote private participation in water projects since 1995 by giving concessions to private firms for clean water supply in the Batam area. The contract was signed by GoI and a Singaporean company that has a high interest in providing water supply on the nearest of Indonesia's industrial areas to Singapore. The strong political will from both parties contributed to an efficient infrastructure development coming from more manageable structural risks, such as certainty and legal issues. Further, the strategic location has boosted the demand for clean water, and, thus, increased the tariff. The political will and high tariff have been the key success factors of the project.

The success story of Batam's clean water infrastructure motivated GoI to adopt PPPs in other regions. However, the second contract failed to execute because of the economic crisis and lack of a sufficient legal framework (Purbo et al. 2019). This failure discouraged the implementation of PPP schemes in water infrastructure, at least until 2015, when the government amended specific national regulation regarding PPPs under Presidential Decree No. 38. With this framework, infrastructure projects under the cooperation between the government and private entities are granted government support and/or guarantees to ensure the financial and economic viability of the investment.

In addition, the government allows regional-owned water supply company (Perusahaan Daerah Air Minum, PDAM) to directly contract with other private firms to provide clean water services. This scheme refers to standard Business-to-Business (B2B) partnership between a private entity and a government body or State-Owned Enterprise (SOE). Unlike the PPP contract, the B2B mechanism is omitted from the government support and/or guarantee. However, as of 2019, out of the 22 clean water supply system projects that were offered, only four water supply projects that have been successfully tendered and transacted, the rest of the projects were cancelled (Purbo et al. 2019).

It is then the interest of this study to extract lessons from the successful PPP water projects in Indonesia about how they address the financial, institutional, and regulatory challenges discussed above. This study will employ the World Bank database on Private Participation in Infrastructure (PPI) to conduct the quantitative analysis, while relying on in-depth interviews with government officials, as well as their private sector counterparts, to conduct the case study analysis. More specifically, this chapter will explore what can be learned from Indonesia for future projects in other emerging countries and further address possible improvements to current policies.

The rest of this chapter is structured as follows. Section 13.2 reviews water infrastructure investment in developing economies, especially developing Asia, with descriptive analysis of PPP projects investments and government initiatives. The results from quantitative analysis of how government support and/or guarantees might accelerate investments are detailed in Section 13.3. The lessons from Indonesia's water infrastructure development drawn through case studies from three water supply projects that have been successfully transacted, namely Umbulan Water Project in East Java Province, West Semarang Water Project in Semarang Province, and Bandar Lampung Water Project in Lampung Province, are presented in Section 13.4. Finally, some conclusions and policy recommendations are covered in Section 13.5.

13.2 Overview of Water Infrastructure Investment: Comparison Between Developing Asia and the Others

As water is a basic human need, the public sector in any given country has a tremendous interest in providing clean and accessible water. However, millions of people die each year from diseases associated with insufficient water supply, sanitation, and hygiene. Governments have barely kept pace with the rapid demand for clean water due to inefficiency and poor performance. In some countries, the low progress of conventional public service has led local investors to provide private water service. As indicated by Akhmouch and Kauffmann (2013), the global population served by private water infrastructure has developed consistently, from

5% of the total population in 1999 to somewhere in the range of 962 million people by the end of 2013. Finding the best value for money, as well as improving efficiency, is the main goal of developing economies in promoting private participation in water infrastructures (Petersen, et al. 2015).

Nevertheless, the private investment in the water sector, particularly in developing economies, is still subtle. According to the World Bank database on PPI of developing economies, only 1,045 PPPs for water and sewerage infrastructures were awarded since 1990, with the total global investment amounting to around $87 billion. The number is relatively small compared to other projects' investment, such as energy ($1 trillion), transportation ($656 billion), and information, communication, and technology (ICT; $115 billion). Figure 13.1 shows an increasing trend of private investment in overall infrastructures from 2004–2012. The improvement was mainly from the higher investment in energy and transportation infrastructures, with only a slight increase recorded in the water sector infrastructure. Further, PPI investment has doubled in 2019, increasing from $12 billion to around $52 billion during 1990–2019. Despite this striking growth, water PPI remains small compared to PPI in other sectors. In addition, since the 1990s, the number of cancelled or under distress projects has increased to 18% of total investment. This is the highest compared to the other sectors, showing a high risk of uncertainty in water infrastructure projects.

Of the several determinants of the private participation on each individual project, one of the main ones is investment return. High project return is always linked with a high private contribution. Unfortunately, clean water infrastructures are notorious for their low financial viability. Water projects are associated with

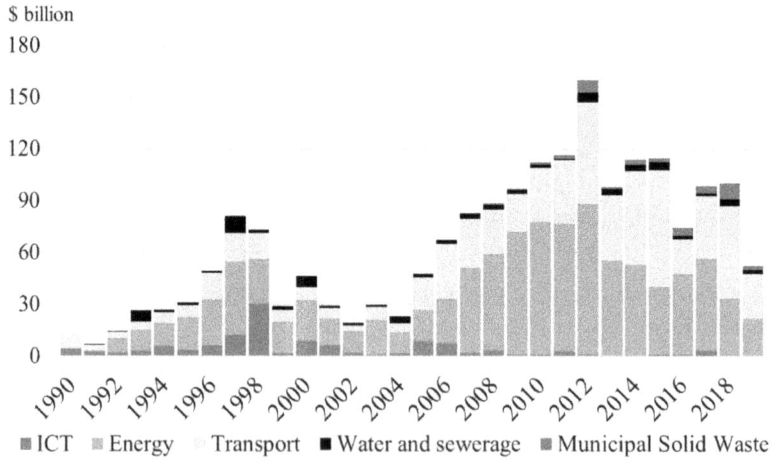

Figure 13.1 Private Investments in Developing Countries.

Note: ICT = information and communications technology.

Source: Authors' calculation based on World Bank Private Participation in Infrastructure (PPI) database (https://ppi.worldbank.org [accessed 27 February 2020]).

a high fixed cost, as well as a long-term initial investment due to their capital-intensive nature. They also involve long payback periods and low rates of return (Leigland and Shugart 2006).

The participation of the private sector is generally defined as involving some transfer of risk to the private partner. Allocating risk across partners is a key element of success in the co-operation between the public authorities and the private sector. To date, there is a wide range of risk-sharing arrangements available to policymakers, such as service contracts, management contracts, leasing contracts, Build-Operate-Transfer (BOT), joint ventures, as well as divestiture (OECD 2009). Moreover, the PPI database classified four main types of water infrastructure, i.e., brownfield projects, divestiture, greenfield projects, and management and lease contracts. Each of the arrangements is part of a range of risk, from a very limited transfer to the private sector, such as with the service contract, to the extreme case of complete divestiture where the assets are entirely transferred. Recently, the private sector has been more comfortable using the management and lease contracts or greenfield projects that provide lower risks and allow the public sector to retain more responsibilities. One of the backgrounds of this movement is the increasingly politicized debates and international arbitration in the water projects with the international private entities during the 1990s (Akhmouch and Kauffmann 2013). Figure 13.2 shows the trend of private water investments based on their type of arrangements or contracts. The proportion of greenfield as well as management and lease contracts are growing, while the brownfield and divestiture are declining.

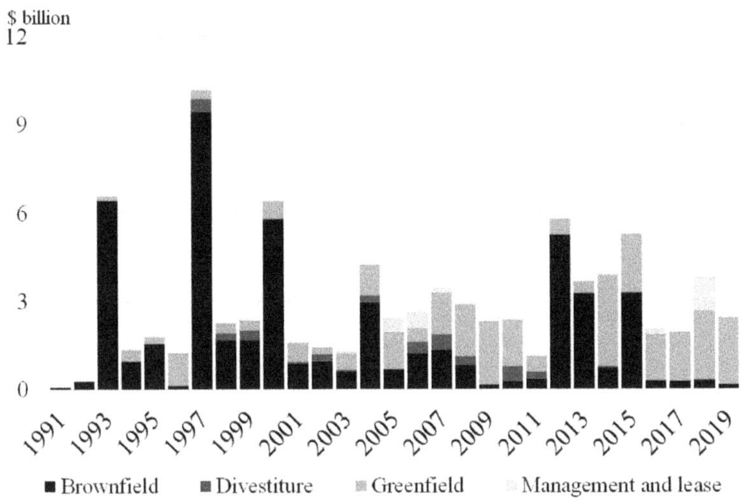

Figure 13.2 Private Water Investments in Developing Countries by Type of Private Participation.

Source: Authors' calculation based on World Bank Private Participation in Infrastructure (PPI) database (https://ppi.worldbank.org [accessed 27 February 2020]).

The various arrangements above stem from public authorities needing to be innovative in developing a set of agreements to provide a suitable allocation of risks to private investors. OECD (2009) has pointed out that low private appetite for water investment is often caused by poor understanding of the PPI opportunities and risks, as well as inadequate framework conditions from the government. The cooperation between the public and private sector is getting more complicated due to the commercial risk, contractual risk, foreign-exchange risk, sub-sovereign risk, arbitrary political interferences, and complex pricing policies with multiple objectives. The risks have retained investors' appetites for developing wider water services.

In the last 20 years, private sector involvement in water infrastructure has been challenged by the inherent complexities. The main challenges include high territorial and institutional fragmentation; inability of local stakeholders; weak legislative, regulatory, accountability, and transparency frameworks; as well as questionable allocation of resources; patchy financial management; weak accountability; unclear policy objectives, strategies and monitoring mechanisms; and an unpredictable investment climate (Akhmouch and Kauffmann 2013).

Based on the income groups, private water investment is higher in more developed economies, while the low-income countries experience extremely low private investment. Of the $87 billion investment in water during 1990–2019, $1 billion is contributed by the low-income group, $15 billion is provided by the lower-middle-income group, while the other $71 billion come from the upper-middle-income countries (Figure 13.3). Private participation in developing economies is mainly generated in upper-middle countries. This could be the result of a better investment climate and certainty in more developed economies. Araya, Schwartz, and Andres (2013) show that private participation, in terms of the

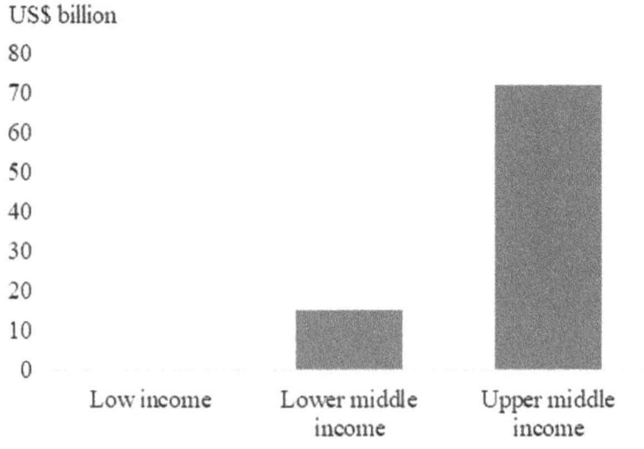

Figure 13.3 Private Water Investments in Developing Countries by Income Groups, 1990–2019.

Source: Authors' calculation based on World Bank Private Participation in Infrastructure database (https://ppi.worldbank.org [accessed 27 February 2020]).

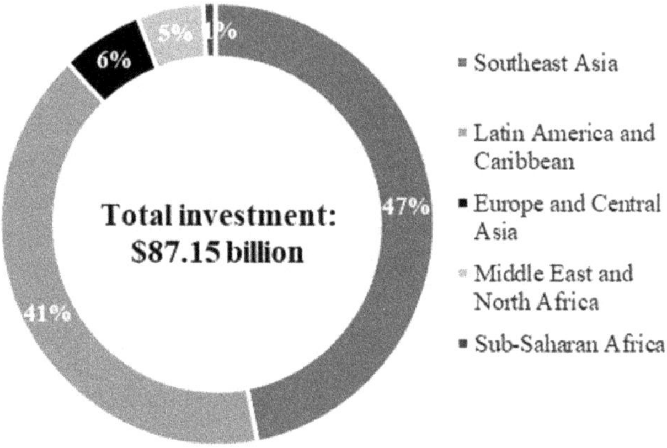

Figure 13.4 Private Water Investments in Developing Countries by Regions, 1990–2019. Source: Authors' calculation based on World Bank Private Participation in Infrastructure database (https://ppi.worldbank.org [accessed 27 February 2020]).

number of commitments, as well as the level of investment, is related to country risk. They find that a higher country risk index is associated with a lower private investment level, especially when the investment is related to assets that are difficult to secure. The country risks include several indicators, such as sound institutions framework, freedom from corruption, effective rule of law, and good governance. The level of corruption and the effectiveness of the rule of law in particular are also determinants affecting the level of PPI investment (Hammami, Ruhashyankiko, and Yehoue 2006).

Looking deeper, Figure 13.4 demonstrates that the proportion of water infrastructure investment in developing Asia is currently the highest (47%). It may be explained by the high demand for water in Asian countries, as their total population accounts for 71% of the global population. Countries within Asia use more than half of the world's water resources. With the projected positive economic growth in the region and the inevitable population boom, Asia's demand for water will continue to increase in the future.

Besides Asia (47%), the private water infrastructure is mostly found in Latin America and the Caribbean (41%) and Europe and Central Asia (6%), with sub-Saharan Africa the region with the lowest progress (1%). According to OECD, a wide range of contracts has been awarded in Africa; however, the types of contracts are dissimilar with the common private investment in developing Latin America and Asia. The concession contracts model has been widely used in Latin America and Asia, while only two concession contracts are found in Africa. The other types of contracts, such as BOT, shorter-term contracts, and lower-risk contracts (management or lease) are more common, reflecting the perception of high risk. This finding supports the earlier statement related to the country risks, as lower private investment in Africa is associated with the higher risks of the region.

To attract higher investment, the fair allocation of risk in a private-public model is demanded. Akhmouch and Kauffmann (2013) have summarized that good risk allocation is driven by an assessment of the party best able to manage it. It is traditionally agreed that the private sector is best suited to assume the commercial risk, while the public sector is better able to assume the legal, regulatory, and political risks. However, simply allocating risks is not enough to ensure that each of the parties will effectively bear their responsibilities. In this context, secure property rights and credible commitment become very relevant given the fact that a public-private agreement is usually related to a long-term contractual relationship. North (1990) has pointed out that the poorly defined and/or ineffective insurance of the property rights in developing economies has led to high transaction costs. Regarding managing the agreement between public authorities and private sector, the system of private participation requires a sound institutional framework that would secure the property rights, as well as facilitate the transaction and cooperation between parties during the contract. Such an institutional framework is also needed to avoid the higher transaction cost due to unreliable commitment (Williamson 1985).

A credible commitment is very relevant in the water sector due to the nature of its responsibilities that vary across tiers of public authorities, including local, national, and regional (Akhmouch and Kauffmann 2013). This has been exacerbated by some countries' heavy decentralization during the 1990s and 2000s. As a result, numerous multi-level stakeholders with different public policy and PPP motives may create difficulties for water sector governance (Purbo et al. 2019; Effah Ameyaw and Chan 2013; Wibowo 2015). This raises significant capability and consistency challenges across government levels in developing water infrastructure projects. If the institutions develop a mechanism that guarantees private property rights and strengthens credible commitments, the transaction costs will be low, thus enabling cooperation or transaction between parties in a long-term contractual relationship.

Nevertheless, even if the sound institutional framework is still inadequate, the relevant additional incentives and monitoring mechanisms are in place. Based on the PPI database, some projects are already provided with government support, both directly and indirectly. As shown in Figure 13.5 and Table 13.1, of the $668 million in government water infrastructure support during 1990–2019, $443 million has taken place in Latin America and the Caribbean; the other $205 million has occurred in Asia. High government support in Latin America stems from government guarantees to ensure creditworthiness since several banks do not consider water operator revenue as collateral for loans (OECD 2009).

Regarding developing Asia, only three countries—Indonesia ($122 mn), India ($78 mn), and the People's Republic of China ($5 mn)—implement government support. Indonesia is quite progressive on PPPs in the clean water sector compared to its peers in terms of the government support and facilities. High government support in Indonesia is associated with the government's desire to stimulate private investment amid the low financial viability of water infrastructure. Almost all water sector PPPs receive government support, either through

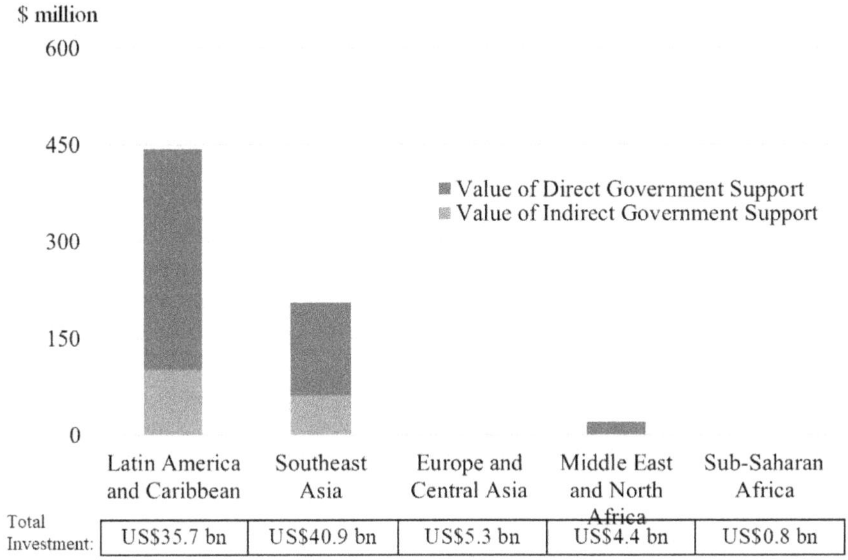

Figure 13.5 Government Support in Water Infrastructures of Developing Countries by Regions (1990–2019).

Source: Authors' calculation based on World Bank Private Participation in Infrastructure database (https://ppi.worldbank.org [accessed 27 February 2020]).

Table 13.1 Government Support in Water Infrastructures of Developing Asian Countries, 1990–2019

Country	*Total Investment ($ million)*	*Government Support ($ million)*
PRC	17,225	5
Malaysia	10,144	-
Philippines	8,816	-
Indonesia	1,729	122
India	1,258	78
Thailand	831	-
Viet Nam	560	-
Bangladesh	327	-
Papua New Guinea	71	-
Nepal	-	-

Source: Authors' calculation based on World Bank Private Participation in Infrastructure database (https://ppi.worldbank.org [accessed 27 February 2020]).

Note
PRC = People's Republic of China.

the Viability Gap Fund (VGF), the Project Development Facility (PDF), or both, in addition to government guarantees. To date, there are at least two PPP projects that have obtained VGF support in Indonesia. PDF serves as assistance to the Government Contracting Agency (GCA) to develop pre-feasibility studies and additional required documentation standards during the transaction-to-financial-close phase. To mitigate government-related financial risks, GoI provides guarantees to improve projects' bankability in the form of a credible feasibility study from PDF assisted by PT. Sarana Multi Infrastruktur (SMI) and assistance from the Indonesia Infrastructure Guarantee Fund (IIGF). Similarly, India's government also made several attempts to fill the wider gap between supply and demand for clean water. To increase the financial viability of the projects, the government provides the government assistance facility. More viable projects, thus, increase the returns on investment.

Nevertheless, the shift of public authorities toward applying government supports in developing Asia is mainly associated with political motives. Jensen (2017) records that, in several Asian countries' experiences with PPPs, politics plays an important role in switching between "supportive and critical" attitudes towards PPPs. High political will from Indonesia and India to boost the national infrastructure has led to strong government support. However, the impact of government on water infrastructure is still unclear, as the support pattern is relatively new. What is required is more comprehensive quantitative research and a case study analysis.

13.3 Quantitative Analysis of Government Initiatives on PPI

To evaluate whether government support affects PPI, this study used a regression analysis by employing the cross-section dataset from the World Bank. The dependent variable of interest is the level of PPI that captures the level of investment by a country in a specific period of time. However, the PPI database reports total project size in commitments that captures both public and private contributions. The natural logarithm value of PPI is used to meet the normality assumption of the error distribution. The main independent variable is government support, which is dummy of both direct and indirect. Direct government support is in the form of direct financial contribution, while indirect government supports are in the form of government guarantee and tax deduction. The other independent variable is Multilateral Lending Support (MLS), which is dummy of multilateral lending support. The control variables are economic conditions such as GDP, debt, and inflation in a country within a certain period in which the project is implemented.

The main finding in this section of the chapter is that government support matters to attract PPI in all sectors in infrastructure and specifically in water sector. The result from the basic model for all sectors (Model I) suggests that government support will increase PPI by 0.47% and this result is significant at 99% level of confidence. Likewise, the multilateral support will significantly increase private participation in infrastructure by 0.62% (see Table 13.2).

Table 13.2 Determinants of Private Participation in Infrastructure

PPI	*All Sectors*		*Water Sector*	
	I	*II*	*III*	*IV*
Government Support	0.4742***	0.0809***	0.6599***	0.3928***
Multilateral Support	0.6177***	0.5856***	0.3562***	0.6743***
GDP		0.0835***		0.2109***
Debt		0.2661***		0.5485***
Inflation		0.1807***		-0.0679***
Const.	3.9363***	1.3283***	2.3269***	-3.4938***
R-squared	0.0310	0.1116	0.0134	0.1066
N	8,851	8,833	1,150	1,150
F	171.5	354.8	8.45	79.6

Source: Authors' calculation.

Note
GDP = gross domestic product, PPI = Private Participation in Infrastructure.
Robust standard errors in parentheses.
*** p < 0,01, ** p < 0,05, * p < 0,1.

In the water sector, government support plays a bigger role in attracting PPI. The result suggests that the magnitude effect is greater compared to the effect of government initiatives in all sectors. The model for the water sector (Model III) and the model with control variables (Model IV) show that government support will significantly increase the level of PPI by 0.66% and 0.39%, respectively. The overall findings suggest that the government support—direct and indirect—has a stronger effect on the level of private participation in infrastructure provision.

13.4 Lessons Learned from Indonesia's Water Sector PPPs

The PPP concept in Indonesia is characterized by an individual private sector entity or more private parties consolidating into a consortium to finance and develop a project or asset required by the government on behalf of the public and to be paid overtime. The main regulation for PPPs in Indonesia is Presidential Decree No. 38 of 2015 regarding cooperation between the government and business entities in infrastructure provision. Under this regulation, PPPs broadly include partnerships between public agencies including the GoI, SOEs, private firms, or cooperatives.

Currently, the private sector can participate in water infrastructure development and investment in Indonesia through various PPP schemes and B2B schemes. PPP schemes, both solicited and unsolicited, may include projects with government support and/or guarantees (e.g., Umbulan clean water project) and projects without government support and/or guarantees. For the other scheme, the B2B scenario, the project partnership between a private entity and an SOE does not require any government support or guarantees due to its high return

(Ministry of Public Works and Housing Regulation No. 19 of 2016). As a consequence, under the B2B scheme, the parties involved must agree that the overall financing and all risks of the partnership are to be borne only by the parties involved in the collaboration.

The governance of water sector PPPs in Indonesia involves various stakeholders: regional governments as a contracting agency or GCA (mainly city or district or provincial government due to decentralization), regional legislators, PDAM, PDAB, and business entities. SOEs can also act as a GCA. Water supply services in Indonesia are served by PDAM or PDAB. In cases where PPP projects comprise more than one city or district, the governor will act as a GCA from the regional government and PDAB is the agency responsible for signing an agreement with the governor. Meanwhile, if the project belongs to a specific area or only one district, the mayor is responsible as a GCA for the development of the project and PDAM is the agency responsible for signing a contract agreement with the mayor. Last is the business entity which becomes the water infrastructure that is selected through a bidding process. A business entity could be a private corporation, a consortium, or a government enterprise, either state or regionally owned. This business entity constructs transmission pipelines or water treatment plant facilities. PPP arrangements are in the concession form, where the private agency will build and operate the infrastructure for some specific period of time, and after the concession period is over, they are obliged to transfer the facilities to the regional water supply company.

Investments in water sector projects in Indonesia are commonly based on the B2B scheme, considered to be the most favored option available since it offers a higher rate of return. Unlike PPPs, organizational structures in a B2B partnership involve only two parties: PDAM as the contracting agency and a private firm as the contractor. It is called B2B because the agreement is conducted between two business entities, where PDAM is considered a business entity that represents the government in this contract. The uncommon use of PPPs in Indonesia water infrastructure development at first is due to the inability of the private sector and governments to deal with several challenges such as institutional arrangements and water tariffs. Moreover, during the early decentralization era, no large-scale PPP projects were begun (Jensen 2017). Since 2015, after the implementation of a new regulation, PPPs began to reappear in the water sector and the trend has been rising along with the government shifting its main focus into infrastructure development by creating National Strategic Projects and Priority Projects. In an effort to meet the needs of high quality water resources and provide better services to the public, GoI initiated the Umbulan Drinking Water Supply System as a National Strategic Project, and a number of water infrastructures such as West Semarang Drinking Water Supply System and Bandar Lampung Drinking Water Supply System as Priority Projects.

In order to meet the high demand for clean water in Indonesia, reliance on government budgets alone is no longer possible, suggesting the need for private sectors or multilateral agencies to fill the funding gap. However, the relatively low Financial Internal Rate of Return (FIRR) water tariff, and the general public's low willingness to pay for water, discourages private entities to invest in the water sector. Hence, the government initiatives and incentives become essential.

From 2015 to 2019, along with the massive infrastructure development and investment, GoI has shown its strong commitment to initiate regulatory and policy reform to create a more conducive environment for private sector participation. To encourage private investors, GoI provides VGF and adds several tax incentives. A government guarantee is also available to mitigate risks that may come from the government, external factors such as demand and unforeseen circumstances, or the project itself during the construction and operation. IIGF becomes the SOE to provide guarantees for infrastructure development. Besides the government support, GoI also gives technical assistance in the form of PDF to help GCA during the preparation and implementation phase of the project through SMI and Danareksa as the responsible agencies. In order to accelerate the land acquisition process, GoI established an agency to support funding settle procurement issues. Compared with the other Asian countries (Table 13.3), Indonesia is above average in terms of government support and is the only country with an agency for financing land acquisition.

Table 13.3 Government Support in Five Asian Countries

Indicator	*Malaysia*	*Philippines*	*Viet Nam*	*PRC*	*Indonesia*
Government Support	• Facilitation Funds • Tax Incentives	• VGF • Direct Government Equity • Project Development and Monitoring Fund • PPP Strategic Support Fund	• VGF • PDF • Government Guarantee • Tax Incentives	• VGF • Land Acquisition Financing • Minimal Demand Guarantee • Tax Subsidies	• VGF • PDF • Land Acquisition Financing • Infrastructure Guarantee • Tax Incentives
Government Support in Land Acquisition	-	PPP Strategic Support Fund	-	Land Acquisition Financing (Not Obligated)	Land Acquisition Agency (LMAN) to funding for land acquisition and settle land procurement issues

Source: Authors' identification.

Note
PDF = Project Development Facility, PPP = Public-Private Partnership, PRC = People's Republic of China, VGF = Viability Gap Funding.

In this part, we examine how the institutional aspects, governance, and government support play a vital role to unlock private sector participation in water infrastructure. This study takes lessons learned from three successful water projects in Indonesia as case studies: Umbulan Drinking Water Supply System in East Java province, West Semarang Drinking Water Supply System in Central Java province, and Bandar Lampung Drinking Water Supply system in Lampung Province.

13.5 Umbulan Drinking Water Supply System

The provision of clean water to society is one of mandated responsibilities for a local government. Umbulan water supply is selected as the first water sector PPP project since it contains high quality water from Umbulan spring that could be best used for drinking water. Another interesting point is that the national government aims to alleviate poverty and inequality by expanding the service coverage of Umbulan water supply, which is located in East Java province, where only 75% of the population is served by a water supply system (Zen 2018). The need for additional secured supply of clean water, along with increasing numbers of potential new customers, incentivize implementing the project to affordably distribute clean water and improve sanitation.

The Umbulan project has a long development history. The initial idea started about 40 years ago, began in the 1980s, but ended in 1999. At that time three bidders were short-listed, but financial closures had never been successfully acquired. There was a lack of support to increase financial feasibility, especially without the supporting instrument and policy from the government. Learning from that experience, GoI now has prepared better support in terms of instruments, along with other facilities aiming to increase feasibility for the Umbulan water project. These government supports, however, can only be secured when they are implemented using PPP. Private sector involvement is expected to play an important role in providing technical know-how, innovation, and sustainable operations, as well as capital investment (APEC 2014). Final execution came when the Umbulan drinking water supply system was registered as National Strategic Project. The successful realization of the project was possible by the coordination and hard work of various parties from both the government and private sector. The project proposal was tendered in 2010, procured in 2015, and financially closed in December 2016. The construction was completed in early 2020 and operations have started.

Crossing five regencies in East Java province, lying from Pasuruan Regency to Pasuruan City, Sidoarjo Regency, Surabaya City, and finally ending in Gresik Regency, the Umbulan water supply project is expected to deliver about 4,000 liters per second of bulk water to serve 1.3 million people through the development of a 93 km transmission pipeline. It requires investments to around Rp2.05 trillion ($147 million) to build the system. However, the governor of East Java as the Government Contracting Agency, and PT. Meta Adhya Tirta Umbulan as the responsible private consortium are only able to finance 60% of the project. Given the social and economic impact of the project despite its low FIRR (around 12.09%), GoI decided to make this project as a PPP and take the necessary steps to make it financially feasible.

In this project, the Build-Operate-Transfer (BOT) scheme is chosen as the form of PPP partnership for a 25-year concession period. The private company is responsible for building, operating, and maintaining the required upstream infrastructures. The concessionaire then delivers bulk water to the East Java PDAB, where the water would then be distributed to five off-takers in five regional areas through a PDAM. Revenue streams for private companies come from PDAB bulk water payments, whereas PDABs basically receive payment from five PDAMs that collect water tariffs from the community through a user fees mechanism.

During its implementation, the project received government support in the form of partial funding such as VGF, which was valued at Rp818 billion from the Ministry of Finance. This support aims to ensure affordable tariffs for society. This incentive is available by request from the private consortium and acts as the only bidding parameter. Another fiscal tool from the Ministry of Finance is PDF, implemented by SMI, which assists the governor of East Java in preparing and executing the Umbulan project transaction. GoI also gives government guarantees through IIGF, with intention of mitigating any risks involved in a project development, particularly political and unforeseen risks.

The Ministry of Public Works and Housing has also provided support in the form of pipeline construction from the offtake point to the main distribution point; the construction of a treatment plant for water from Rejoso River with capacity of 300 liters per second; the provision of permits for installation of a pipeline along the toll road, among others, the Pasuruan-Gempol, Gempol-Pandaan, Surabaya-Gempol, Surabaya-Mojokerto and Surabaya-Gresik toll road segments; and reduced land lease fees on the toll roads. In realizing the projects, other supports such as land acquisition and environmental impact analyses are available from the provincial government of East Java to de-bottleneck the project. Without these government supports and facilities, the project was not feasible because the cost of production was higher than the tariff (see Table 13.4).

Table 13.4 Umbulan Water Tariff, With and Without VGF

PDAM/PDAB (water utilities)	*Without Viability Gap Fund (Rp/m3)*	*Tariff Affordability (Rp/m3)*	*With Viability Gap Fund (Rp/m3)*
Weighted average tariff	7,000	5,820	5,280
PDAM Pasuruan Municipality	3,850	3,000	2,510
PDAM Pasuruan District	4,600	3,300	2,820
PDAM Sidoarjo District	8,050	6,499	5,990
PDAM Surabaya Municipality	6,050	5,681	4,240
PDAM Gresik District	7,700	6,199	6,190
PDAB East Java Province	7,600	6,900	6,860

Source: Purbo et al. 2019, adapted from Government of East Java Province data, 2017.

Note

$1 = Rp14,000.

PDAM = regional water supply company, PDAB = provincial water supply company, VGF = Viability Gap Funding.

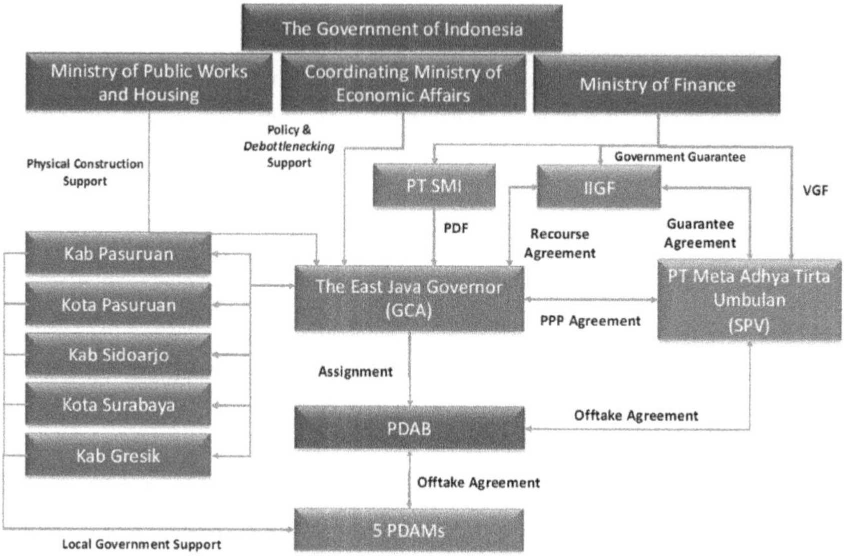

Figure 13.6 Umbulan Water Supply Project Structure.

Note: IIGF = Indonesia Infrastructure Guarantee Fund, PDAM = regional water supply company, PDAB = provincial water supply company, PDF = Project Development Facility, PT SMI = PT. Sarana Multi Infrastruktur.

Source: Adapted from PPP Book 2018, Ministry of Development Planning.

In addition to Umbulan's financial problems, there are other obstacles that hamper implementation. Since the Umbulan project is the first large PPP in the provincial level (consisting of five municipal areas), multiple layers of sub-national governments were also contributing to further delay implementation. Different mindset and knowledge capacity gaps among stakeholders require extra effort in managing the decision-making process. Multiple actors with different perceptions and objectives made the Umbulan project appear as a series of games played in different arenas (Klijn and Teisman 2003). The next obstacle comes from the lack of commitment from the GCA and its lack of understanding of PPPs. Another challenge was overlapping regulations when there is a dispute in the installation of a pipeline along the toll road.

As the first showcase PPP in the water sector, Umbulan project shows that political willingness together with the government initiatives and supports affect the success of a project. With strong support and synergy from various stakeholders, Umbulan water project has finally been realized in accordance with the prevailing laws and regulations (see Figure 13.6).

West Semarang Drinking Water Supply System

Our second case study, West Semarang drinking water supply system, became one of the pilot water sector PPP projects in Indonesia, with an availability payment scheme from the regional budget. This project is included as a priority project with a 25-year concession period and was built under the BOT PPP scheme for a two-year construction period. Located in Central Java Province, the West Semarang drinking water supply project will be the solution for the clean water shortage in Semarang, which is currently supplied by Kudus Regency, and as an effort to reduce land subsidence due to excessive groundwater usage. The project will use water from Jatibarang Dam, aimed at providing drinking water demand for around 60,000 families located in 31 villages in three sub-districts (West Semarang, Tugu, and Ngaliyan sub-district).

Given the project costs around Rp1.17 trillion ($34 million), the PDAM Tirta Moedal Semarang city acted as GCA in 2017, and invited the private sector to deliver the water services specifically to build raw water supply system, water treatment plant, and distribution network. After several rounds of bidding, PT. Aetra Air and PT. Medco gas consortium were declared as the winners. This decision was based on their offerings to not use the VGF support and instead rely on a 36% discount tariff on bulk water provision. FIRR for the project is relatively higher at 16% compared to Umbulan and Bandar Lampung water projects. Although in the end the government did not provide VGF support, the Ministry of Public Works and Housing provided support for the construction of the intake unit valued at Rp90 billion. The ministry also supported the construction of the main distribution network system worth Rp221 billion in order to increase the investment feasibility of the project. The construction is expected to be completed within two years (2019–2020), with the operation of West Semarang water supply expected to start in 2021.

West Semarang Drinking Water Supply System project was previously planned to use a PPP scheme in 2009, with technical assistance to develop a pre-feasibility study supported by the Japan International Cooperation Agency and financial assistance by Indonesia Infrastructure Finance. However, funding availability and land acquisition were sources of implementation delay. At that time, there was no private interest to build the infrastructure, as the offer from the B2B scheme often failed to guarantee a clear benefit due to uncertain tariff setting. In 2014, realizing the importance of the project, the government undertook several reforms to shift the financial source of this project to a PPP scheme. Eventually, the funding was decided to come from three different sources: state budgets, local government budgets, and private sector investment. However, even after the financial issues of this project were addressed, the land acquisition issue still remains complicated.

The success of the West Semarang water project is partly due to the independence of the local government to take greater responsibility and have the willingness to accelerate such a public service like clean water. The project also has clear stages and a relatively short construction period compared with other clean water projects such as Umbulan. Furthermore, minimum interference by local politicians, supported by the approval of the local government and parliament makes the PPP run smoothly. In realizing the project, the provincial government also helps to secure the land procurement process. Meanwhile, at the national level, GoI provides technical assistance through PDF for preparation and transaction advisory support. Government guarantees are also made available to both the central and local government, thus increasing the certainty of the private sector's participation (see Figure 13.7).

Bandar Lampung Drinking Water Supply

The rapid growth of Bandar Lampung city as the capital of Lampung province in Indonesia has implications on land use and population density. Notably, most of the households in the area use unsanitary groundwater to cover their daily needs.

Bandar Lampung Water Supply PPP Project was developed and listed as a priority project by GoI. The provision of the water supply system is implemented through a BOT-PPP scheme, enabling the private entities not only to build, finance, and operate the raw water and production unit, but also to have the rights to manage part of the distribution network. Assets that are built and managed by the business entity will be handed over to the PDAM in the end of concession period. The cooperation agreement was signed in February 2018 between PDAM Way Rilau Bandar Lampung as the GCA and PT. Adhya Tirta Lampung as the executing enterprise (consortium of PT. Bangun Cipta Sarana and PT. Bangun Cipta Kontraktor). The project costs around Rp1.1 trillion ($82.6 million) and has a 25-year concession period plus an additional two-year construction period. Since the project reached financial closure and started the construction phase in August 2018, it is expected to start operating by mid-2020.

Once completed, the Bandar Lampung water supply system will provide access to clean water to and improve the sanitation of about 60,000 households, with the capacity of the system rated around 750 liters per second. The service area will cover eight districts in Bandar Lampung namely Rajabasa, Labuan Ratu, Way Halim, Kedaton, Tanjung Senang, Sukarame, Sukabumi and Kedamaian. Raw water from the intake in Way Sekampung River will be pumped into the water treatment plant located in Rulung Helok village, approximately 500 m from the intake site. Further, raw water will be distributed throughout the transmission pipeline for approximately 21 km to the reservoir in Rajabasa district in Bandar Lampung as the offtake point from the project company to GCA. PDAM as GCA will purchase bulk water and distribute the water using a user fee mechanism.

Due to the relatively low financial feasibility of the project (showed by its 15.3% FIRR) and inadequate local government fiscal capacity, VGF is provided from the government at Rp259 billion or $18.78 million to improve the financial soundness and ensure the tariff remains affordable. In addition, the Bandar Lampung water supply project is also getting funding from the PDF of around $1.8 million by the Ministry of Finance through SMI to assist the transaction. Given the lack of technical knowledge about PPP in the local government, GoI

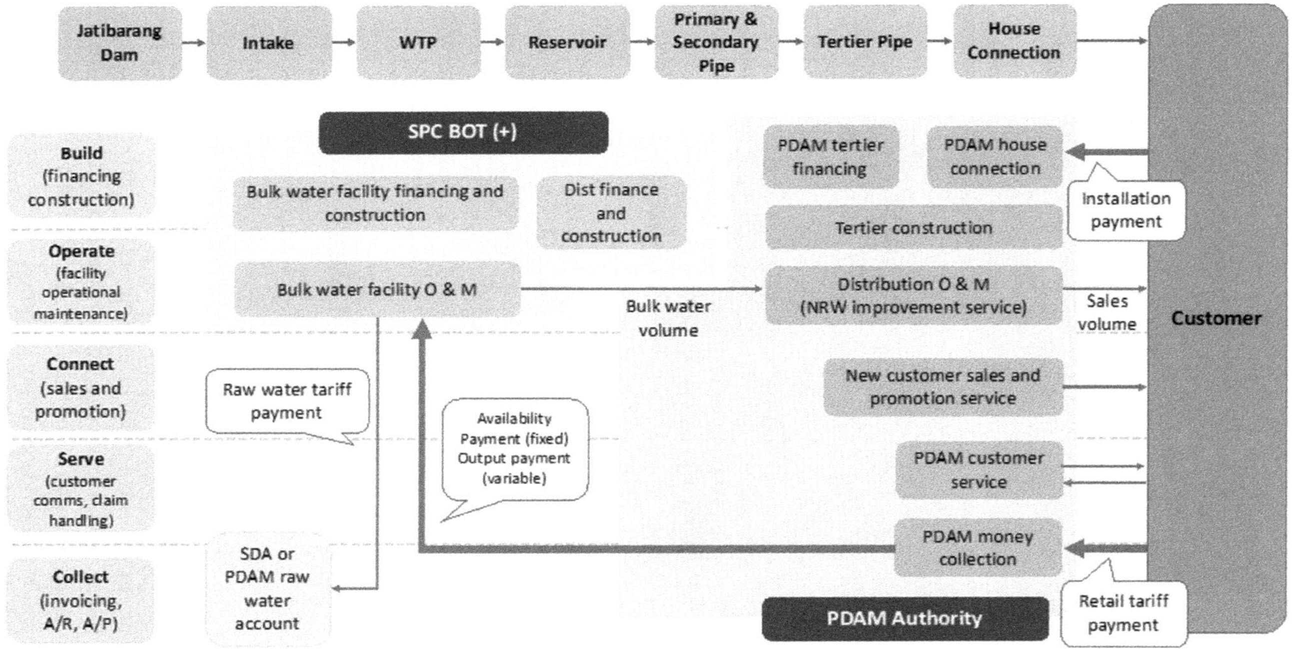

Figure 13.7 West Semarang Water Supply Project Structure.

Note: PDAM = regional water supply company, WTP = Water Treatment Plant, A/R = Account Receivable, A/P = Account Payable, SDA = Sumber Daya Air (Water Resources), O & M = Operation & Maintenance, SPC = Special Purpose Company, BOT = Build Operate Transfer, NRW = Non-Revenue Water.

Source: Adapted from PPP Book 2018, Ministry of Development Planning.

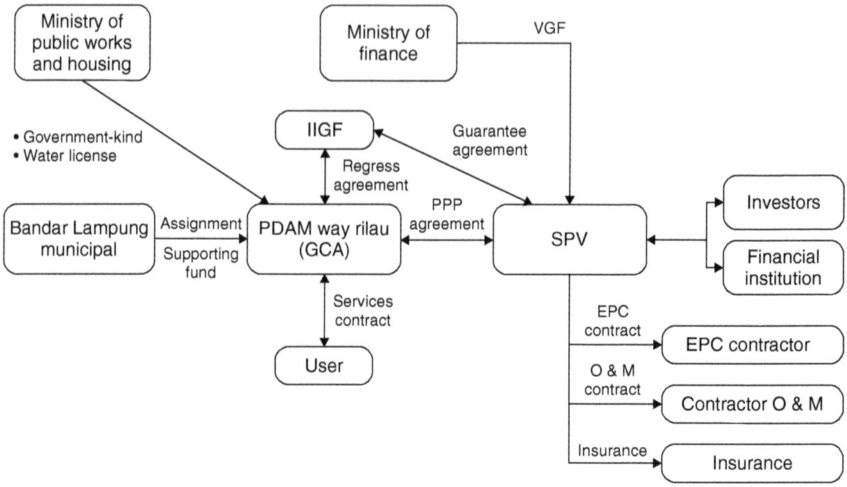

Figure 13.8 Bandar Lampung Water Supply Project Structure.

Note: IIGF = Indonesia Infrastructure Guarantee Fund, PDAM = regional water supply company, PPP = public-private partnership, VGF = Viability Gap Funding, GCA = Government Contracting Agency, SPV = Special Purpose Vehicle, EPC = Engineering, Procurement, and Construction, O & M = Operation & Maintenance.

Source: Adapted from PPP Book 2018, Ministry of Development Planning.

provides the capacity building and support for the PDAM and the local government to understand the technical and required contractual documents during the tender period and to facilitate the approval process of the project. To mitigate the project risks, a government guarantee is provided through IIGF, mainly to secure political risks including monthly payments from GCA and sudden termination (see Figure 13.8).

13.5 Conclusion and Policy Recommendations

The main policy implication of this study is that the institutional aspects, governance, and government support play a vital role in attracting PPI in clean water infrastructure projects. The government needs to address the issues by formulating the right instruments and setting up a workable arrangement in introducing these instruments to the market to unlock their potential. It is important to develop the right incentive system to involve all parties in a project from the start to the end. This study found several basic necessary conditions that must be fulfilled from public initiatives to unleash more PPI (see Figure 13.9).

First, multiple and multi-level actors are commonly involved in the adoption and implementation of PPPs in the water sector in Indonesia. This can create problems during the PPP adoption and implementation process, making it highly

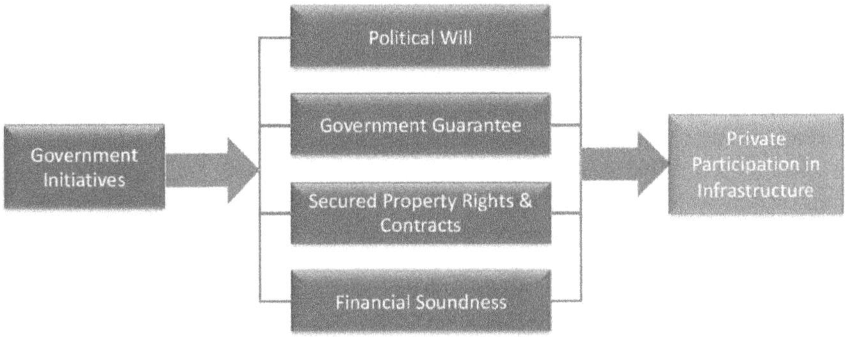

Figure 13.9 Basic Necessary Conditions to Unlock Private Participation in Infrastructure.
Source: Authors' identification.

important to manage interdependencies among these actors (Purbo 2019). Therefore, political will from the government matters to attract private participation in infrastructure.

Second, we found that land acquisition provided by the government is important to tackle property rights problems. Institutions, especially those that are ensuring private property rights, are necessary for the growing PPI. The government initiatives to solve property rights issues will result in significant decreases in transaction costs, which may further improve economic performance (North 1990). In Indonesia, over the last five years, the government has been undertaking reforms by establishing a land acquisition responsibility agency and revising regulations on the scope of land acquisition to solve any issues that might delay the project.

Third, a government guarantee should be provided to mitigate uncertainty problems and increase private investors' trust. Lastly, in order to increase financial soundness and projects' FIRR, government support in the form of a partial contribution in financing is necessary. In general, the water projects are economically viable but less financially feasible, hence the financial support from the government such as VGF becomes one of the breakthrough policies to accelerate the development of infrastructure.

Indonesia is relatively more progressive on PPPs in the clean water sector compared to its peers in the region in terms of government support and facilities. Driven by their high economic and social impacts, almost all of the PPPs in water supply projects receive government support, either through VGF or PDF or both, in addition to some government guarantee. VGF is the partial fiscal support, up to a maximum of 49% of the project costs from the government for projects with marginal feasibility to ensure tariffs remain affordable for users. Currently, there are two PPP projects that have obtained VGF support in Indonesia: Umbulan water supply system with VGF value of Rp818 billion and Bandar Lampung water supply system with VGF value of Rp259 billion. Another initiative, PDF, serves as assistance to GCAs to develop pre-feasibility studies and additional required documentation standards during the transaction phase to reach financial closure. To help mitigate the government-related financial risks, GoI also provides guarantee assistance to improve projects' bankability. Umbulan, West Semarang, and Bandar Lampung water supply system projects all received a credible feasibility study from PDF assisted by SMI and guarantee assistance provided by IIGF.

Note

* Corresponding author. E-mail address: febrio.nathan@ui.ac.id

References

Akhmouch, A. and C. Kauffmann. 2013. Private-Sector Participation in Water Service Provision: Revealing Governance Gaps. *Water International* 38(3): 340–352. doi: 10.1080/02508060.2013.793573

Araya, G., J. Schwartz, L. Andres. 2013. The Effects of Country Risk and Conflict on Infrastructure PPIs. *World Bank Policy Research Working Paper* No. 6569. Washington, DC: World Bank.

Asia-Pacific Economic Cooperation (APEC). 2014. Infrastructure Public-Private-Partnership, Case Studies of APEC Member Economies. An Outcome of the Asia-Pacific Economic Cooperation Finance Ministers' Meeting 2014. In *APEC Foreign Ministers' Meeting Secretariat*. Singapore: APEC.

Effah Ameyaw, E., and A.P.C. Chan. 2013. Identifying Public-Private Partnership (PPP) Risks in Managing Water Supply Projects in Ghana. *Journal of Facilities Management* 11(2): 152–182. doi: 10.1108/14725961311314651

Engel, E., R. Fischer and A. Galetovic. 2014. *The Economics of Public-Private Partnerships: A Basic Guide*. Cambridge: Cambridge University Press.

Hammami M., J.F. Ruhashyankiko, E.B. Yehoue. 2006. Determinants of Public Private Partnership in Infrastructure. IMF Working Paper WP/06/09. Washington, DC: International Monetary Fund.

Hasan, R., J. Yi, and L. Zhigang. 2017. Meeting Asia's Infrastructure Needs. Manila: Asian Development Bank. www.adb.org/sites/default/files/publication/227496/special-report-infrastructure.pdf (accessed 27 February 2020).

Jensen, O. 2017. Public-Private Partnerships for Water in Asia: A Review of Two Decades of Experience. *International Journal of Water Resources Development* 33(1): 4–30. doi: 10.1080/07900627.2015.1121136

Klijn, E.-H., and G.R. Teisman. 2003. Institutional and Strategic Barriers to Public-Private Partnership: An Analysis of Dutch Cases. *Public Money and Management* 23(3): 137–146. doi:10.1111/ 1467-9302.00361

Leigland, J., and C. Shugart. 2006. Is the Public Sector Comparator Right for Developing Countries? *Gridlines. Public Private Infrastructure Advisory Facility*. www.ppiaf.org/Gridlines/8africa.pdf (accessed 27 February 2020).

Marin, P. 2009. Public-Private Partnerships for Urban Water Utilities: A Review of Experiences in Developing Countries (English). *Trends and Policy Options*

8. Washington, DC: World Bank. http://documents.worldbank.org/curated/en/984921468182666780/Public-private-partnerships-for-urban-water-utilities-a-review-of-experiences-in-developing-countries (accessed 27 February 2020).

National Development Planning Agency, Indonesia (BAPPENAS). 2018. *PPP Book 2018.* Jakarta: Ministry of National Development Planning.

North, D.C. 1990. *Institutions, Institutional Change and Economic Performance.* Cambridge: Cambridge University Press.

Organisation for Economic Co-operation and Development (OECD). 2009. Private Sector Participation in Water Infrastructure: OECD Checklist for Public Action. *OECD Studies on Water.* www.oecd.org/env/resources/42350657.pdf (accessed 27 February 2020).

Purbo, R.K., C. Smith, and R.J. Bianchi. 2019. Lessons Learned from the Indonesian Public Private Partnerships Program in the Water Sector. *Bulletin of Indonesian Economic* Studies 55(2): 193–212. doi: 10.1080/00074918.2018.1550250

Wibowo, F.A. 2015. A Study on the Implementation of Public-Private Partnership (PPP) in the Socio-Economic, Political, Cultural and Islamic Context of Indonesia. Durham University. http://etheses.dur.ac.uk/11347/ (accessed 28 February 2020).

Winpenny, J., and M. Camdessus. 2003. Financing Water for All: Report of the World Panel on Financing Water Infrastructure. Washington, DC: World Bank. www.worldwatercouncil.org/fileadmin/wwc/Library/Publications_and_reports/CamdessusSummary.pdf (accessed 27 February 2020).

Zen, F. 2018. Public-Private Partnership Development in Southeast Asia. ADB Economics Working Paper Series, No. 553. Manila: Asian Development Bank http://dx.doi.org/10.22617/WPS189496-2.

14 Land Pooling

A Public–Private Partnership Model for Sustainable Infrastructure Investment in Delhi

Gaurav Verma

14.1 Background

Infrastructure plays a vital role in economic development of a city or state or nationwide. It promotes economic development and enhances welfare of the society. In the past decade, Asian countries have built more infrastructure than any other developing regions. Nevertheless, there are major differences in the quantity and quality of infrastructure in developing Asia, both across economies and compared to other developed regions. Central or state budgets are an obvious source of investment in infrastructure, which includes not only national and state governments, but also public sector companies. How much investment is needed in Asia or can one quantify investments in infrastructure?

Viable options are federal budget records, national accounts with an adequate breakdown of gross fixed capital formation (GFCF) data, and international databases of private sector infrastructure expenditures. Developing Asia will need $26 trillion investment from 2016 to 2030, or $1.7 trillion per year, if the region is to maintain its growth momentum, eradicate poverty, and respond to climate change (climate-adjusted estimate) (ADB, 2017). Without climate change mitigation and adaptation costs, $22.6 trillion will be needed, or $1.5 trillion per year (baseline estimate) (ADB, 2017). The $1.7 trillion annual estimate is more than double the $750 billion Asian Development Bank (ADB) estimated in 2009 (ADB, 2017).

The analysis from Figure 14.1 covers the transport, power, telecommunications, and water supply and sanitation. The report describes how much the region will need to invest in infrastructure to continue its economic growth momentum, eradicate poverty, and respond to climate change. It examines how much countries have been investing in infrastructure, using data from a variety of sources—including government budget data, components of gross fixed capital formation, and information on private sector investment. It concludes with a discussion of the financial and institutional challenges the region must overcome to meet future infrastructure needs.

If we consider climate adjusted estimated of infrastructure investments and gaps for 2016–2020 from Figure 14.2, India would require $261 billion, making

DOI: 10.4324/9781003228790-17

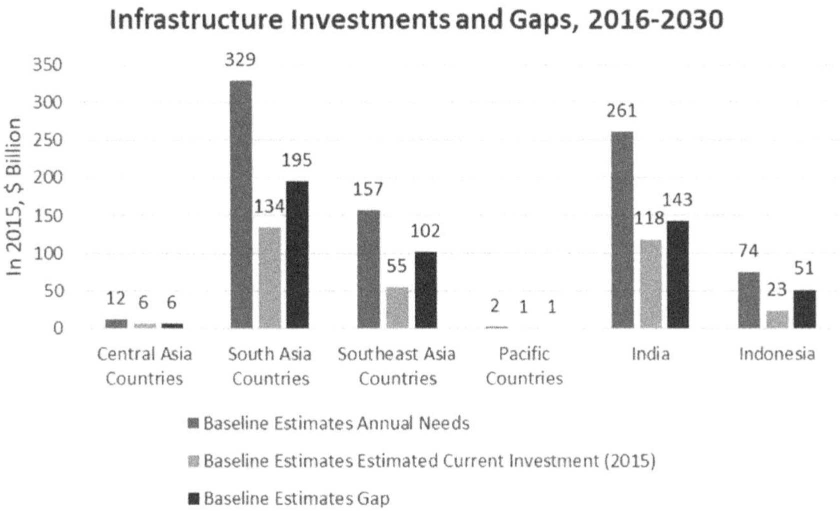

Figure 14.1 Baseline Estimate of Infrastructure Investments and Gaps, 2016–2030.
Source: ADB Data Library.

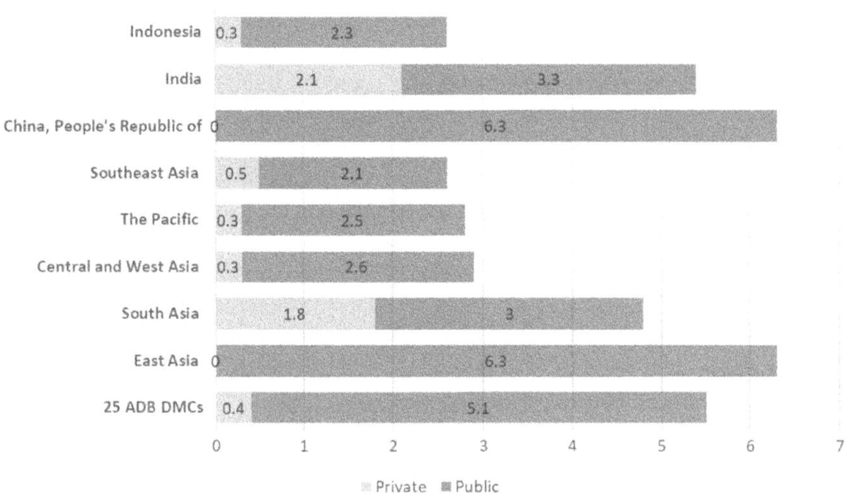

Figure 14.2 Climate-Adjusted Estimate of Infrastructure Investments and Gaps, 2016–2030.
Source: ADB Data Library.

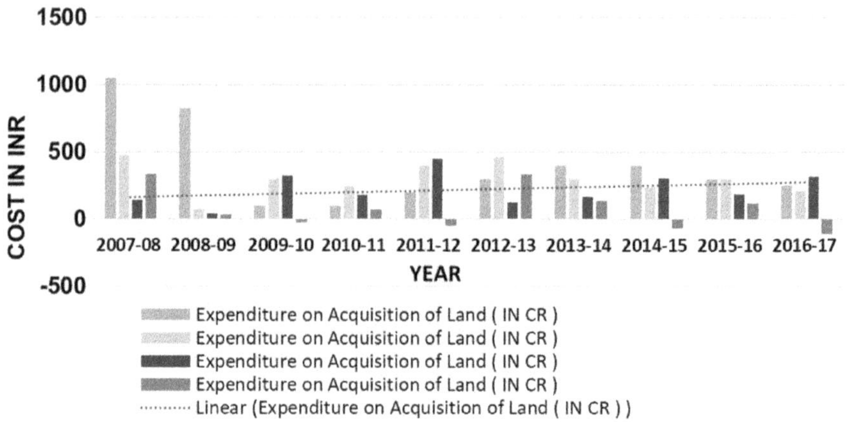

Figure 14.3 Public and Private Infrastructure Investments in Asia, 2010–2014 (% of GDP).
Note: ADB = Asian Development Bank, DMC = developing member country.
Source: ADB Data Library, https://data.adb.org/dataset/infrastructure-needs-asia-and-pacific (accessed 27 June 2021).

it fall short by $143. Analysing Figure 14.3 shows over 90% of the region's overall infrastructure investment is still primarily done by the public sector. This constitutes 5.1% of gross domestic product (GDP) annually, which is far above the 0.4% of GDP coming from the private sector.

From Table 14.1, it can be deduced that there are huge infrastructure investment needs in Asia and the Pacific. In many regions of Asia and the Pacific, these infrastructure needs are very high compared with tax revenues. Based on the above estimations in the baseline, it is clear that Asia and the Pacific as a whole needs 26.3% of the total tax revenue for infrastructure investment. Fully 49.1% of the infrastructure projects are financed by tax revenues in South Asia. In this situation, private sector investment is the key to the sustainable development in infrastructure.

Land acquisition is one of the main obstacles for infrastructure development in many Asian countries such as Bangladesh, India, Indonesia, and Thailand, which delays the completion of projects and lowers the rate of return of private investment. By contrast, if we take the example of Japan, land trust has been extensively used in the field of commercial building and apartment buildings. Like, for a project of high-speed railway linking Narita Airport with the center of Tokyo city, which got delayed due to the opposition of a few landowners who did not want to sell their land, results in construction of the high-speed rail project was hindered. Borrowing the concept of land trust and sustainable infrastructure, this chapter will discuss the potential framework for land pooling in Delhi, using a framework that unlocked private investments in sustainable infrastructure in Delhi.

Table 14.1 Estimated Infrastructure Investment Needs by Region, 2016–2030 ($ billion in 2015 prices)

Region/Sub-region	*Projected Annual GDP Growth*	*2030 Projected GDP per Capita (2015 $)*	*Baseline Estimates*				*Climate-adjusted Estimates*		
			Investment Needs	*Annual Average*	*Investment needs as % of GDP*	*IG/TAX (% of 2015)*	*Investment Needs*	*Annual Average*	*Investment needs as % of GDP*
Central Asia	3.1	6,202	492	33	6.8	29.6	565	38	7.8
East Asia	5.1	18,602	13,781	919	4.5	21.4	16,062	1,071	5.2
South Asia	6.5	3,446	5,477	365	7.6	49.1	6,343	423	8.8
Southeast Asia	5.1	7,040	2,759	184	5.0	36.4	3,147	210	5.7
Pacific	3.1	2,889	42	2.8	8.2	30.9	46	3.1	9.1
Asia and the Pacific	5.3	9,277	22,551	1,503	5.1	26.3	26,166	1,744	5.9

Source: ADB- Meeting Asia's investment needs.

14.2 Introduction

Land is the most basic asset for revenue generation by development authorities and urban local bodies (ULBs). Intervention in infrastructure appreciates the adjoining property value in and around the area. A city can capture rising land values by owning land or taxing it. In many developing cities, the government does not own much land and large-scale acquisition is a political impossibility (Paul Collier, July 2018). ULBs can utilize the value addition by providing infrastructure, and in turn, can capture its value partly or wholly. Property development at the station nodes and development of air space are some ways to capture land value to finance transit-supportive infrastructure.

In 2013, India's Ministry of Urban Development carried out a study on land-based fiscal tools and practices for generating additional financial resources for ULBs. To meet the Rs 3,250,000 (INR) annual urban infrastructure investment under the smart city mission was keenly felt by the ministry. Thus, the Ministry prepared a "value capture policy framework" in 2017. Simultaneously, the Metro Rail Policy 2017 requested the state government to adopt this policy to fund the infrastructure projects (MoHUA- Ministry of Housing and Urban Affairs, Government of India, 2017). The fundamental concept underlying land value capture is that owners legally generate value. Thus, if there is an increase in the valuation of immovable assets due to investment in infrastructure investment by the government, the government has the right to catch this increase in value.

At present, while private developers are interested in making use of the benefits of land value increment, ULBs are yet to capture this rise in land value (Abhishek Das 2016). Gujarat is seen to be extremely proactive to provide urban, land services and trunk infrastructure. It exhibits a successful model of land pooling mechanism for a self-sustaining financial tool for the provision of infrastructure. Since its inception in AUDA (Ahmedabad Urban Development Authority) Development Plan 2021, under the Gujarat Town Planning and Urban Development Act (GTPUDA), land pooling is gaining wider acceptance as a tool to improve the existing peri-urban areas of Gujarat and Maharashtra. After the division of Andhra Pradesh into the states Telangana and Andhra Pradesh, the state has opted for land pooling over land acquisition for its new capital Amravati. Also, with MoHUA's recent initiative for expanding this tool in Delhi, it has received nationwide recognition.

Since British rule, Delhi has had a long history of land acquisition with the objective of building infrastructure to transfer the army to different parts of the country. With an intention to extend, control, and further consolidate its rule throughout the country, the government acquired land belonging to rural landowners. Ownership and control of the infrastructure built after land acquisition remained completely with the government for utilization in public purpose.

After independence, the government acquired land from farmers for developing housing colonies, and industries. Even in the recent decades, large-scale land acquisition has been made for companies proposing to use it for a public purpose. In the name of development projects, large chunks of land belonging to farmers have been acquired by the government at throwaway prices. Changing of land use regulations results in land being handed over to private builders for construction of residential and commercial complexes, industries, etc. Even if landowners/farmers are paid by the government, they do not receive any monetary gain, as the money they receive is either lost or expended unwisely restricting it to landless/unemployed people. Moreover, there are many more obstacles in this land acquisition act by which many projects have been undergone delay in the past decades as they are not compensating individuals enough or are making acquisition mandatory.

On 7 September 2018, the Delhi Development Authority (DDA) approved the long-awaited Delhi Land Pooling (DLP) policy; the policy has received approval from the housing ministry. The new system will replace the existing policy of government land acquisition, which became increasingly unpopular because the high compensation payouts were uncompetitive (DDA, DELHI LPP, 2016). Land pooling has a strong potential for unlocking the private investments for infrastructure in land pooling zones of Delhi.

In land pooling, land monetization could be a significant tool to capture value. The revenue generated in rural areas is so low that they are unable to fund the infrastructure projects. The collection of these levies results in loss of revenue. Because of this, the levies, which are capable of financing up to 90% of infrastructure projects are left with only 5%–6% in practice. Robust, development-based value capture strategies need to be formulated as a self-financing/sustainable model for developing infrastructure that can overcome these pitfalls.

14.3 Concept Study

14.3.1 Overview of Financing Alternatives for Urban Development in The Region

There is a need to understand the value capture strategies for exploring the development-based value capture (DBVC) as a self-financing model for developing sustainable infrastructure in transit-oriented development (TOD) areas in land-pooling zones for Delhi. To capture value, there is a need to first create value. As ULBs need funds for development, they depend upon state and central grants to a significant extent. The development in the TOD zones requires infrastructure; land acquisition is required, which of course adds additional cost to it. There is a need to liberate the burden of land acquisition cost. Land pooling could be a better alternative because it is not only cheaper but also generates higher revenue as compared to land acquisition. A generous amount of capital is required to develop infrastructure and amenities around the TOD zones and thus prompts the need to calculate the expenditure cost for sites. To cover the cost of expenditure and generate revenues, value capture tools must be worked out extensively for developing sustainable infrastructure investments in Delhi's Land Pooling zones. Although Delhi has numerous value capture tools based on taxes and fee charges yet none of them contributed in the development of the TOD.

In Indian cities, infrastructure investments and development are carried out by different hierarchies like the central government, state governments, and private agencies. Sometimes for large projects, such as metro rails, special bodies are created. These bodies do not have the power to impose a tax on land, and often do not coordinate with ULBs. This raises the question of possible solutions to make ULBs capable of generating sustainable revenues to improve or promote sustainable infrastructure development in areas of Delhi. It is in light of the current predicament situation solution that land pooling has emerged as a viable and popular alternative to direct land acquisition in India. Land pooling could be the best DBVC tool for the state to allow this mechanism to be implemented. Land monetization would be the purest form for unlocking the private investment for sustainable infrastructure in TOD zones in land pooling zones of Delhi.

The selling of property would generate some income, and compensation comes from homeowners now opening up land that has risen in value after growth. It also makes it possible to rebuild irregularly formed and small parcels of land as more suitable plots for development. Land pooling is not new in India, having been used in Gujarat under the mechanism of Town Planning schemes (TPS), where the area of single TPS would range from 100 to 1,200 ha and cover around 1,000 to 2,000 individual land parcels. It has allowed Ahmedabad to both build a 76 km ring road and to amass the land needed for developing the Dholera special investment region.

This chapter will conclude that land monetization would be the purest form of value capture for unlocking the private investment for sustainable infrastructure in land pooling zones of Delhi around the TOD influence areas. The next section will provide an understanding of DBVC for Delhi. Also, assessing the need for an alternative to the current land development approach in Delhi which identifies appropriate DBVC tools for sustainable infrastructure development in TOD areas of Delhi's Land Pooling zones.

14.3.2 Assessment Framework

The assessment of the research framework focuses on formulating a sustainable model for developing infrastructure around TOD zones in Delhi's land pooling zones under PPP. It articulates the contexts through which DBVC mechanism can contribute to developing infrastructure around TOD zones and complementary land use of the surroundings. Identifying a model that allows the authorities and local bodies to capture value from the increase in land and property prices by the provision of infrastructure in and around the TOD zones. The research synthesizes transit's impact on property values, financial instruments, and supportive legislation related to land value capture.

The methodology follows an understanding of the need for DBVC strategies for Delhi, with the need for an alternative to the current land development approach. Also, it focuses on land pooling as a value capture tool to finance sustainable infrastructure investments for Delhi. With the concluding new framework of simplified Development Based Value Captured Strategies and recommendations for sustainable development investments in land pooling zones of Delhi. The expected policy implications make land pooling an emerged way as a PPP model to finance and develop sustainable infrastructure in TOD influence areas/zones of Delhi.

14.4 Identification and Designing of Instruments—Assimilation of Analysis

14.4.1 Assessing the Need for an Alternative to the Current Land Development Approach in Delhi

The need for an alternative to current land development (land acquisition to land pooling) in Delhi is acute, with a population projection of 37.2 million by 2030 as per a 2018 UN Department of Economics and Urban Affairs report (Affairs, 2018). From 1961–1981, the total proposed acquired land in Delhi was 27,487 ha, out of which only 15,540 ha were actually acquired. During 1982–1992, 6,763 ha of land were acquired, and from 1992–2000 another 2,744 ha were acquired. The pace of acquisition was far short of the requirement. The annual acquisition during 1981–2001 was 475 ha as compared to the planned requirement, which is 1,200 ha. Land acquired during 2002–2011 was even less than what it was during 1981–2001. The resulting need to acquire more land for the projected population and expanding the urban limits naturally concerns higher budget allocations.

Reviewing the Ministry of Housing and Urban Affairs' audit during the years 2005–2010 reveals that there were abnormal variations (up to 70% in respect to acquisition of land and up to 49% in case of development of land), which indicates the budget provisions were not realistic. The variations were higher than the permissible limits of 10% during 2006–2007, 2007–2008, and 2008–2009 in cases of land acquisition and all five years in cases of development. The DDA clarified that the budget is requisitioned based on the land acquired in the previous year and the amount of compensation paid.

Table 14.2 and Figure 14.4 show details from the Ministry of Urban Development regarding funds allocated for acquisition and development of land during the last 10 years.

This whole unspent amount under the budget allocation is due to landowners being reluctant to sell off their lands because of conflict of interests. Thus, for such development projects, the consent of landowners is skipped and the intention of acquiring the land is not disclosed or defined. Previously, "public purpose" was not defined but after the LARR Act, 2013 Right to Fair Compensation and Transparency in Land Acquisition, Rehabilitation and Resettlement Act, the government can take land only for national security, natural calamities or any other emergency with parliament's approval.

Though the rate of compensation was as per the market rate was not defined, it ended up being much less (after the reformation of 1894 Land Acquisition Act, the rate of compensation has been fixed for rural areas at four times the rate

Table 14.2 Expenditure on Acquisition of Land (Amount in CR-INR)

Financial Year	*Budget Estimate*	*Revised Budget Estimate*	*Actual Expenditure*	*Unspent amount*
2007–08	1,050.0	475.0	141.29	333.71
2008–09	825.0	75.0	40.41	35.41
2009–10	100.0	300.0	324.10	-24.10
2010–11	100.0	246.0	175.75	70.25
2011–12	200.0	400.0	447.71	-47.71
2012–13	300.0	459.0	124.75	334.25
2013–14	400.0	297.0	163.50	133.50
2014–15	400.0	234.30	300.57	-66.27
2015–16	300.0	300.0	182.73	117.27
2016–17	250.0	210.0	317.34	-107.34

Source: Ministry of Urban Development, and Ministry of Housing and Urban Affairs.

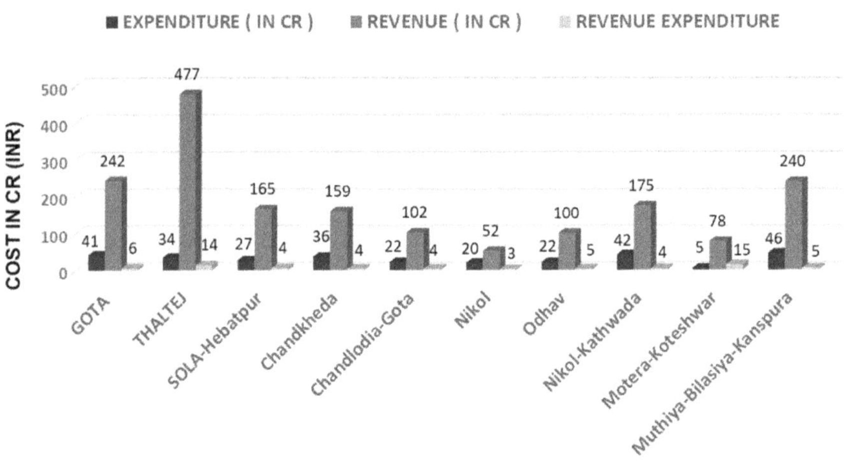

Figure 14.4 Expenditure on Acquisition of Land in India.
Source: Author.

of market value whereas for urban land it is twice the market rate). The acquisition of agricultural land needs serious attention, since there will be a shortage of agricultural land for cultivation if not checked upon seriously, thus food security becomes a major concern. Therefore, the agricultural land which needs to be acquired should not exceed 2% of the sown area in a district and the total acquisition in the state should not exceed 5% of the sown area in the state and no irrigated multi-crop land should be acquired.

Another major issue with high compensation is that there is no government procurement for rehabilitation and resettlement. The compensation on the acquisition of agricultural and non-agricultural land cannot be the same, unlike the present scenario. The compensation on acquisition of agriculture land is determined on the basis of yielding capacity of land and, in the case of non-agriculture land, it is determined on the basis of the market value of the land. With all of above, the government has not even stopped but also imposed income tax on enhanced compensation for the compulsory acquisition of the agricultural land, which is even worse for the land-owners.

In addition to the acquisition of land, the expenditure of Rs. 84.98 CR was incurred for the construction of just 100-meter road and the lackadaisical approach of DDA resulted in Rs. 8.86 CR as damage charges from landowners; Rs. 25.69 CR was incurred on account of excess payment of compensation to the landowners.

14.4.2 Land Pooling as a Cheaper Alternative

As per Table 14.3, the expenditure for developing raw infrastructure in the town planning schemes of Ahmedabad usually lies between Rs.1,000–1,200 per sq.

Table 14.3 Cost of Work of TPS of Prahaladnagar, Ahmedabad Gujarat, India

DRAFT TOW PLANNING SCHEME NO 23-26 TPS PRAHALADNAGAR	
ABSTRACT OF ESTIMATE FOR COST OF WORKS	
SUBMITTED UNDER SECTION 48(1) OF THE G.T.P AND UD ACT-1916	
TPS AREA- 162 HA	
Name Of Work	*TOTAL COST IN CR (INR–RS.)*
Construction of bituminous road including excavating, carting, filling, watering, hammering, soiling, metalling, carpentering and prime coat, tack coat, etc., complete including footpath, central verge and tree plantation	36
Providing electricity street light with underground wiring, painting, cow lamp fitting, etc., completely provided at every 30 m. distance	12
Providing and laying of appropriate size drainage line including treatment plant etc.	40.5
Providing and laying of appropriate size water pipeline including tube well, sump well, pump room with pump in connection to adjoining schemes, etc.	21
Green Development	18.8
Storm Water	25
Administrative Overheads	8
Grand Total	**161.3**
Say	**Rs. 1025/ Sq. m.**

TPS = Town Planning Schemes.

Source: Ahmedabad Municipal Corporation (AMC).

Table 14.4 Revenue Generation of TPS Prahaladnagar, Ahmedabad, Gujarat

Revenue Category	*INR RS (IN CR)*
Sale of commercial purpose @60,000 sq_m plot @rate 1,25,000 INR Rs per so.rn	750.0
Sale of residential purpose @50,000 sq_rri plot @rate 95,000 INR Rs per sq.m	475.0
Sale of neighborhood purpose @8,000 sq.m plot @rate 75,000 INR Rs per sq.m	60.0
Betterment charges @203 INR Rs per sq.m of reconstitute i.e. @67.6% at 10,95,120 INR Rs per sq.m	21.9
Collection by the AUDA	1306.9

TPS = Town Planning Schemes.

Source: Ahmedabad Municipal Corporation (AMC).

m. Taking the example of TPS of Prahalad Nagar, Ahmedabad, Gujarat, the whole development of TPS has been done within INR 161 CR investment for 162 ha of land. Nearly Rs.1,000 per sq. m. was devoted to the construction of bituminous roads, street lighting, drainage lines, water pipelines, and garden development, including maintenance and administrative overheads. Land was assembled through voluntary pooling by its owners, which could be consolidated, thereby permitting the local agency to develop infrastructure according to a layout plan. This would not be possible if land acquisition was occurring, which may result in a contradictory situation for landowners. Thus, land pooling is not only a cheaper alternative, but also revenue generation is quite high, as shown in Table 14.4.

Analyzing the different TPS in Ahmedabad, the revenue generation here is remarkable as compared to the cost of expenditure in making TPS. Revenue collection from the sale of land, which means land monetization, is the highest rate, whereas the betterment levy is also an additional tool for collecting revenue, as shown in Figures 14.5 and 14.6.

14.4.3 Land Trust and Spillover Effect

With the amendment of land pooling, land trusts would enhance the development of the region. Land trusts are a contractual vehicle for transferring the title of a property to an appointed trustee. The original property owner does not lose their claim of ownership, but the trustee becomes the titleholder for legal purposes. In theory, the landowners can keep the land, but lease it to the infrastructure company for the development against the selling price. A trust bank is the intermediary between landowners and infrastructure companies that monitors whether the land is properly used and pays rent to landowners based on project revenues. The total cost of infrastructure investment will become the land rent cost, replacing the land purchase cost, the construction cost, as well as the

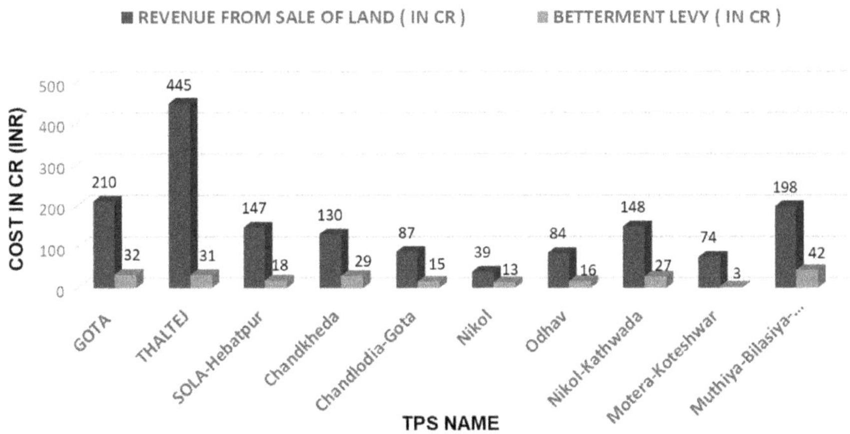

Figure 14.5 Expenditure versus Revenue Generated in Ahmedabad TPS—Prahaladnagar. Source: Ahmedabad Municipal Corporation (AMC).

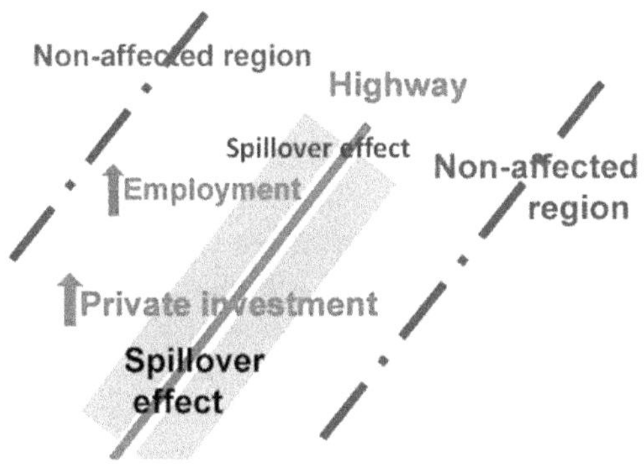

Figure 14.6 Revenue Collection in TPS—Prahaladnagar, Ahmedabad, Gujarat. Source: Ahmedabad Municipal Corporation (AMC).

operation and maintenance costs under this scheme. The benefit of infrastructure investment is not only of user charges but also the spillover tax revenues created by infrastructure investment.

With the development caused by spillover effects, new businesses will come into the region and create new employment, new restaurants open, and the services sector can be developed. This regional development will increase tax revenues along the infrastructure projects. Infrastructure development has both direct and indirect impacts. An increase in road capacity due to the development of transport infrastructure may constitute a direct impact, while indirect impacts are the short- and long-term effects, such as the improvement of capital inputs

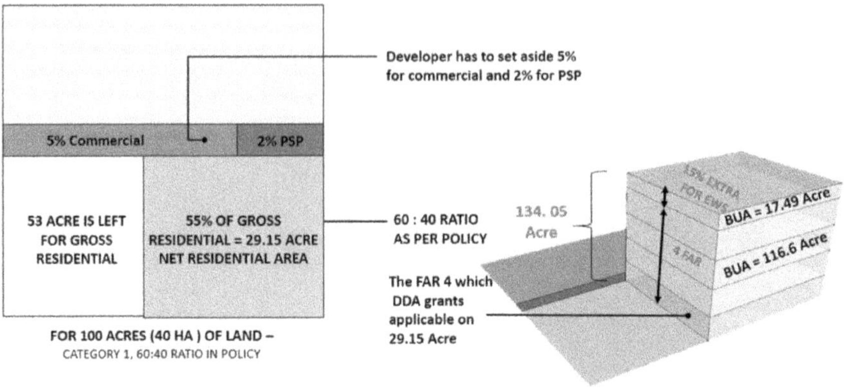

Figure 14.7 The Spillover Effects of Infrastructure Investments.
Source: Naoyuki Yoshino and ADBI.

and employment from regional economic activities, which usually take time. The indirect impact is assumed to be the spillover effect.

For example: The orange line in the middle of Figure 14.7 shows transport infrastructure development, for example, a highway or high-speed rail. The yellow regions along this infrastructure development line represent the area into which new businesses opportunities will come, employment will be created, and small and medium-sized enterprises will be established. The spillover effect around the region by the infrastructure investment will increase the local tax revenues compared with the non-affected regions outside of the blue dotted line. Successful examples include the highway project in Manila City and the high-speed rail project in the Kyushu region. It is usually seen that tax revenues increased along transport infrastructure projects. This increment of tax revenue is the spill-over tax revenue.

14.5 Empirical Analysis

14.5.1 Comparative Analysis of Delhi Land Pooling Policy with Different States

A comparative analysis has been done with different states having a land pooling policy, Development Control Regulations (DCR's), finance, revenue for deeper analysis and conclusions. Three cities have been selected for analyzing the policy along with Delhi: the first is Magarpatta, Pune, which is India's first example of land pooling done by a private individual; the second is Ahmedabad, where land pooling is done by authorities and the municipal corporation; and the third is Amravati, which is being built from scratch (Table 14.5).

Table 14.5 Comparative Analysis of Delhi Land Pooling Policy

CRITICAL ANALYSIS OF LAND POOLING POLICY WITH DIFFERENT CITIES/STATE OF INDIA				
PARAMETERS	*PUNE—MAGARPATTA*	*GUJARAT*	*ANDHRA PRADESH-AMRAVATI*	*DELHI*
GENERAL				
LEGAL BACKUP	Developed under MTDCCL, 1993	Developed under GTPUDA, 1976	Developed under APCRDA ACT, 2014 (Under section 43 subsection- 4)	Developed Under MPD 2021, supported by DDA act 1957
SECTION / ACT	Special township notification,2006 under Maharashtra Regional and Town Planning act, 1972	Chapter 5 under section 40	CRDA ACT	Chapter 19- MPD 2021
AREA	430 Acre	It extends to the whole of the state of Gujarat	38,581 Acre	6 land pooling zones of Delhi
OWNER'S INVOLVED	123 Farmer's family (800 individual)	Vary to different-different TP schemes	24 village farmers	Land parcels of any size brought under pooling provided they fall in land pooling area
REHABILITATION	Every native peasant got a parcel of land for house or flat within the Magarpatta City SEZ based on their land and every native peasant got a parcel of land for a house or flat within the Magarpatta City SEZ based on their land.	Within the close vicinity of original plot (minimum displacement) and with at least minimum previous benefits	Plots within the same village with a maximum displacement of 5km	Within the close vicinity of original plot (minimum displacement) and with at least minimum previous benefits

(*continued*)

Table 14.5 Cont.

CRITICAL ANALYSIS OF LAND POOLING POLICY WITH DIFFERENT CITIES/STATE OF INDIA				
PARAMETERS	*PUNE—MAGARPATTA*	*GUJARAT*	*ANDHRA PRADESH-AMRAVATI*	*DELHI*
ELIGIBILITY	Landowners of Magar area	Greenfield site under public domain with scope/ propose a development project	No eligibility criteria on plot size but all 24 villages near Krishna riverbank are included	Landowner having land 2–20 ha and 20 ha above in Delhi land pooling zones, 70% contiguous pooled land, Min 30m wide road on one side expect forest land, unauthorized colonies, Lal Dora villages, heritage, and natural features
DEVELOPED BY	Developed by MTDCCL	Government Body	Government Body	Developer entity
LAND POLICY MODEL	Co-operative movement	Public Participation model	People Public Partnership	Joint Development model
PROJECT SCHEME	Township project	Neighborhood planning scheme	City development scheme	Zonal development scheme
MINIMUM AREA	Land pooled for 162 HA	100 HA	---	2 ha
MAXIMUM AREA	---	100 HA ABOVE	38,581 Acre	20 ha above
LAND DISTRIBUTION UNDER PUBLIC DOMAIN	---	Roads-15%, Parks and open spaces- 5%, Social infrastructure-5%, sale of residential and commercial- 15% (it may be altered to the nature of development)	Roads and utility services-30%, Parks and open spaces- 10%, EWS- 5%, social amenities—5%	Roads-12%, Recreational—16%, PSP- 10%

LAND DISTRIBUTION UNDER PRIVATE DOMAIN	---	---	---	Gross Residential- 53%, Commercial- 4%
DEDUCTION POLICY	---	40:60 ratio (commonly- but may vary to the site) where 60% is retained by an appropriate authority and 40% by landowners but the ratio cannot be reduced by min 30:70 and maximum by 50:50	50: 50 ratio	40: 60 ratio
COMPENSATION	Company stockholder	Shared amenities, Better transportation connectivity, Infrastructure development, Increased land, and property value	Residential and commercial plots, Annuity, Training and employment and debt waiver of 1.5 lakh to farmers one time	Shared amenities, Better transportation connectivity, Infrastructure development, Increased land, and property value and TDR
SUPPORTING AGENCIES	Pune Municipal Corporation	Gujarat town planning and valuation department	Singapore government-appointed Surbana International consultants	NIUA
BENEFICIARY	Farmers (FDI—Farmers Direct Investment)	State government, Authority, ULB's and Landowner	Farmers (FDI—Farmers Direct Investment) and APCRDA	Centre and State government, Authority, ULB's and Landowner

(*continued*)

Table 14.5 Cont.

CRITICAL ANALYSIS OF LAND POOLING POLICY WITH DIFFERENT CITIES/STATE OF INDIA				
PARAMETERS	*PUNE—MAGARPATTA*	*GUJARAT*	*ANDHRA PRADESH-AMRAVATI*	*DELHI*
ADDITIONAL BENEFITS	Authorized Registration, Employment, Annuity, Entrepreneur, SEZ	---	Free higher education, Singapore trip, Pension, Free health camps	Tradable FAR—is allowed and can be transferred to another DE in the same planning zone having a licence of a project more than 20 Ha
OWNERSHIP AFTER FP	7/12 registration, part of the land remains with farmers, including companies stock	2 or more original plots which are owned by several persons or owned by persons jointly be held in ownership in common as a final plot	Ownership of residential and commercial	7/12 registration, part of the land remains with original landowners
TRANSFER OF LAND RIGHTS / SHARES	Allowed within native peasants	Possible	---	Not possible
RESERVATION OF LAND	---	Up to 10%	---	---
CHANGE OF LAND USE	---	Land allotted for the purposes referred shall not be changed by variation of schemes for the purposes other than a public purpose	No under section 99 CRDA ACT	Not possible
AMALGAMATION	---	---	Joint/ Individual allotment plot size	Amalgamation and subdivision of plots shall be allowed as per norms of a master plan

DEVELOPMENT CONTROL NORMS				
SCHEME PREPARATION BY	Developer Entity	Appropriate Authority (In case of Ahmedabad- AMC &AUDA)	APCRDA	DDA
GREEN BUILDING REGULATIONS	---	---	---	10% Energy consumption by solar fittings and green building norms
DELINEATION	---	Based on roads, No. of land parcels, and development zone	Based on the urban population	Based on sector
DENSITY	---	---	---	800-1000 persons/ hectare
EWS HOUSEHOLD SIZE	---	As per DP	---	32–40 sq. Meter
GROUND COVERAGE	---	---	---	40%
FAR	As per DP	As per DP	As per DP	FAR 400 for group housing and additional 15% EWS in that, Commercial, Industrial and PSP- as per MPD 2021
FINANCE				
FINANCE BY	HDFC LOAN	Appropriate Authority (Grants, loans, impact fees, and state government)	APCRDA	Appropriate Authority (Grants, loans, impact fees, and central government)
EXPENDITURE	By MTDCCL	The net cost of scheme borne by the appropriate authority	The net cost of scheme borne by the appropriate authority	The net cost of scheme borne by the appropriate authority

(*continued*)

Table 14.5 Cont.

CRITICAL ANALYSIS OF LAND POOLING POLICY WITH DIFFERENT CITIES/STATE OF INDIA				
PARAMETERS	*PUNE—MAGARPATTA*	*GUJARAT*	*ANDHRA PRADESH-AMRAVATI*	*DELHI*
MARGIN	---	20% of the amount of cost of the infrastructure provided in the adjacent area of the scheme	20% of the amount of cost of the infrastructure provided in the adjacent area of the scheme	---
REVENUE				
MONETIZATION OF LAND	Sale and auction of land (30% cost of construction get by the cost of the land)	Sale and auction of land	Sale and auction of land	Not mentioned in the policy
DEVELOPMENT CHARGES	Paid by MTDCCL (No discloser of rates)	Paid by individual landowner @ Rs50,000 / hectare for land and Rs 15/ sq. Meter for building	Rs 3,38,825/- and city level impact fee Rs 6,12,490/-	Paid by DE (No discloser of rates)
BETTERMENT CHARGES	Paid by MTDCCL (No discloser of rates)	Paid by the individual landowner (No discloser of rates)	---	---

STAMP DUTY	---	---	---	yes
RESULT SUCCESS	Win-win-situation	Win-win-situation	Win-win-situation—85% rate	Win-No-win-situation as DE is not getting any beneficial profit
INSPIRATION	Inspired many other projects in Pune like Nanded city SEZ, Videocon SEZ	Foundation of land pooling which Inspires many other states like Madhya Pradesh, Delhi, Andhra Pradesh, and Maharashtra	Amravati is one of the largest greenfield ventures in India	---

Source: Author.

14.6 Conclusion

Delhi's land pooling policy lacks the potential to create long-term wealth for its landholders, whereas Magarpatta creates long-term wealth for both peasants and landholders. In Delhi, entrepreneurial or investment opportunities to turn into an entrepreneur or shareholders or the possibility of a permanent job in the company somehow were lost in the policy, unlike Magarpatta. The lack of flexibility of plot sizes and of house sizes has proved unattractive to landowners, which is not the case with the Amravati model. In Amravati, farmers hold equal partnership rights with the state/city government, whereas, in Delhi's policy, the capital expenditure will be raised by external development charges (EDCs). It was found through field interviews that there was unwillingness to pay taxes as EDCs were extremely high. Therefore, land pooling in Delhi is a win-no-win situation, as developers are not getting any profit out of the policy.

14.6.1 Empirical Findings - Delhi Land Pooling Policy Challenges

Failure of land pooling of Delhi will undermine other master plans similar to MPD 2021. This makes it imperative to secure sufficient land for providing housing and infrastructure to the forecasted population of Delhi. Higher land and property prices will eventually spur out-migration to satellite cities like Noida, Gurugram, Faridabad, Meerut, and Ghaziabad. The major challenges to land pooling are:

- Statutory Law
- Spotted development—lead by the developers
- On-the-ground reality of Floor Area Ratio—what the policy says
- Unwilling to pay EDC—by landowners

14.6.1.1 Statutory Law

The policies produced by the Government as well as other planning-related documents and reports become statutory law when written by a legislative body. It's a law that a government deliberately creates through elected legislators in a formal legislative process. It's up to the judiciary to interpret and enforce statutory law, but the judiciary can't create it. Delhi's land pooling policy is not a statutory law set down by a body of the legislature, but rather is part of Delhi's 2021 master plan that might get modified or deleted in the future. Policy needs to have a legal backing for the implementation. States like Gujarat have a separate land pooling legal origin, i.e., GTPUDA Act, 1976 section 65, which makes it statutory and provides validity for the scheme. Further, Andhra Pradesh has the APCRDA Act, 2014 section 52, Rajasthan has its land pooling scheme act, 2016, and the Punjab has its town planning and urban development Act, 1995. Delhi also has a DDA Act, 1957, which gives the legal authority of DDA to formulate planning policies, despite there being no legal statutory legal backup as other cities have. It is imperative to designate the Delhi land pooling policy in DDA Act, 1957 as land acquisition.

14.6.1.2 Spotted Development

In Delhi's land pooling policy, the phasing in of land-pooled areas was not mentioned, thus it does not attract many developers. A developer might be more interested in a sector that has high potential or has a major earning scope like around the metro stations, leading to spotted development. To combat this, Gujarat and Amravati are phasing in development, keeping in mind the market growth patterns.

14.6.1.3 On-the-Ground Reality of Floor Area Ratio

According to DDA, developers get a Floor Area Ratio (FAR) incentive of four in zones demarcated for land pooling but in reality, they only achieve 1 to 1.3 FAR. While fixing FAR for the land pooling policy, DDA made it attractive for the builders by including community and commercial facilities in the area they would be developing and selling.

> If in DDA's scheme, community and commercial facilities are part of F.A.R (saleable built-up area), then developers will assume that they will be able to utilize more F.A.R than what will actually be available for them if the Apartment Ownership Act is factored in. There is a need for clarification on this subject from DDA to all stakeholders that the developers can't sell community and commercial facilities. The only saleable built-up area is the apartment in the group housing project.
>
> (Source: http://delhi-masterplan.com)

> Citing the scarcity of water, the Delhi Development Authority (DDA) has proposed to reduce the Floor Area Ratio (F.A.R) for residential areas from 400 — as approved in 2013 — to 200 in its land-pooling policy that has been hanging fire for five years.
>
> (Source:http://delhi-masterplan.com)

This decline of FAR will create a negative impact on the model as it defeats the whole purpose of the land pooling, which is to create housing for all and better infrastructure for the forecast population of Delhi. The reduction in FAR makes the houses more expensive; this diminishes the profit margins of developers, forcing them to raise the cost of unit prices, and undermining the affordability factor.

In addition to the FAR strictures, the waste of land in the current land pooling policy is quite high. Figure 14.8 shows how a developer can only build 36.15 out of 60 acres (60%); analysis of the overall use of the land reveals 48.15/ 100 acres, only 48%. Other cities' land deduction policies are around 60%–70%.

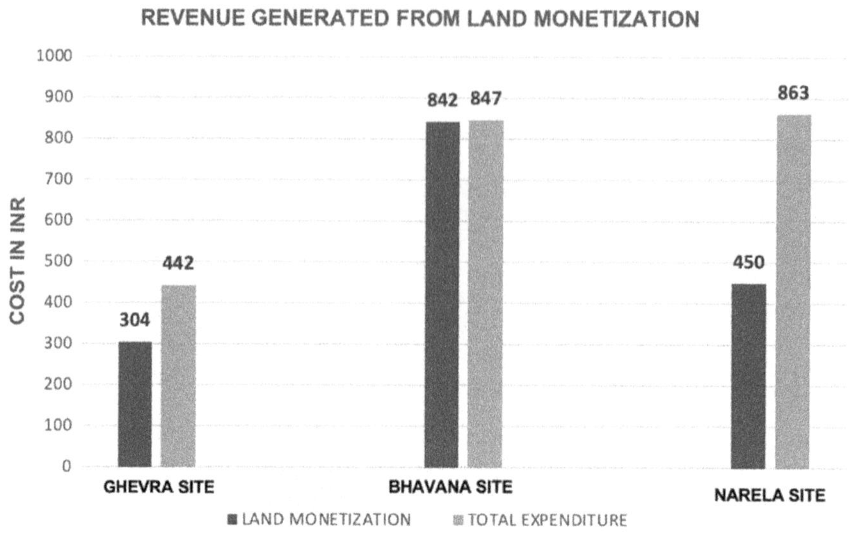

Figure 14.8 On-ground FAR Calculation of Delhi Land Pooling Policy.
Note: FAR = floor area ratio.
Source: DDA & Author.

14.6.2 Unwilling Payment of External Development Charges

As per DDA, EDCs will support the cost of infrastructure in Delhi land-pooling zones as per land rates in different zonal areas. Rates have been worked out after factoring in the cost of acquisition, holding, and EDCs for the non-saleable portion. Both EDC and Internal Development Charges (IDC) are statutory charges, which are levied by the respective state governments; that can differ from state to state. The charges are also variant depending on the location (zone) and type of the land-use within the city. For example: in Gurugram, Haryana, under the residential category, the IDCs are different for hyper-potential zones (Rs. 500 per sq. m), high-potential zones (Rs. 350 per sq. m), medium-potential zones (Rs. 250 per sq. m) and low-potential zones (Rs. 70 per sq. m). Under the commercial category, IDC rates range from Rs. 1,000 per sq. m. for hyper-potential zones and Rs. 190 per sq. m. for low-potential zones.

As per the Delhi land pooling policy, the expenses of the capital investment will be raised from the EDCs levied on landowners and consortiums. In an earlier draft of the policy, DDA had earmarked a charge of Rs 2 crore to be paid by land owners for every acre of pooled. This amount was later scrapped as the policy was revised in 2018. As per the revised policy, EDCs are to be calculated on the basis of "actual cost of providing city-level infrastructure" for the pooled land.

The costs of EDC per acre are hidden and Delhi's are quite high. As per the field interviews, the land holders are not willing to pay the EDCs as there is no declaration of them in land pooling policy and they do not get any attractive benefits like other states' policies. So, the challenge for DDA will be to incur/ tackle the cost of expenditure if the imposed taxes on landowners are not being paid.

14.6.3 Existing Value Capture Tools in Delhi

Currently, Delhi has numerous tax and non-tax-based value capture tools which are collected neither by the Municipality nor by DDA. DMRC is also expanding its efforts in capturing the land value by property development. Delhi has mainly focused on tax-based value capture tools, which are quite reliable. The value captured by non-taxed-based tools is less compared to tax-based tools. ULBs are dependent upon taxed-based value capture like property tax which is highest among all. About 60%–70% of revenue is being collected by property tax only in tax-based tools, whereas DDA relies on fee-based value capture, which only occurs once. Despite having numerous land value capture tools, none go for the developing infrastructure. Therefore, a new institutional framework is necessary for selected value capture tools of development in the TOD context.

14.6.4 Appropriate Land Value Capture Tools for Delhi

Table 14.6 identifies the numerous tools that currently exist in Delhi, are efficient and have the highest potential to work in the TOD context in Delhi land pooling zones. Based on market and statistical analysis, the following tools are appropriate:

1. DEVELOPMENT BASED VALUE CAPTURE TOOLS
   a) Sale of Land
   b) Land lease agreement
   c) Land Readjustment
   d) Air rights sale / TDR

   These tools are the most effective forms of capturing land value, i.e., Land monetization.
2. TAX-BASED LAND VALUE CAPTURE TOOLS
   a) Land value tax
   b) Vacant land tax
   c) Property tax
3. FEE-BASED LAND VALUE CAPTURE TOOLS
   a) Impact / Development fees (IDC's)
   b) Betterment charges
   c) External Development Charges (EDCs)

Table 14.6 Existing Value Capture Tools in Delhi

TOOLS	*LEGISLATION*	*LVC IN THEORY*	*LVC IN PRACTICE*	*BASE*	*RATE*	*FREQUENCY*	*COLLECTED BY*	*CAN WORK (YES/NO)*
TAX-BASED VALUE CAPTURE TOOLS								
Property Tax / Land Value Tax	Wealth Tax act, 1957	YES	YES	Area Based	7% Residential, 20% Commercial,10% Industrial	Yearly	Municipality	YES
Vacant Land Tax	Wealth Tax act,1957	YES	YES	Area Based	Included in Property Tax	Yearly	Municipality	YES
Tax-Increment Financing	Delhi Township Board	YES	NO	Area Based	-	Recurring for area based	-	NO
NON-TAX / FEE-BASED VALUE CAPTURE TOOLS								
Stamp Duty Fees	Registration Act,1908	YES	YES	Area Based	6%—Men, 4%- Women	when there is a transaction of property	Authority	Yes
Development / Impact fees	DDA ACT,1957	YES	YES	Area / Project Based	Sewer and water = RS100 square meter	One-time charge	Authority	Yes
Change of Land-use	No law	NO	YES	Area / Project Based	Residential = 14,000–24,777; Commercial and Industrial = 1.5 Times of Residential	One-time charge	Authority	Yes (working but very less)
Lease of Land And Development	Property Act,1882	YES	YES	Area / Project Based	As per market rate	One time charge	Authority	Yes
Property Transaction Fees	Registration Act,1908	No	YES	Area Based	6%—Men, 4%- Women	when there is a transaction of property	Authority	Yes (working but very less)

Sale of Naming Rights To Stations	DMRC ACT	No	Yes	Area Based	10 X Fixed annual license fees	For a period of 10 Year	DMRC	Yes
External Development Charges	**No law**	No	Yes	Area / Project Based	**As per Hectare or Acre**	One time charge	Authority	Yes
Land Pooling	MPD 2021	YES	YES	Area / Project Based	As per EDC charges	One time charge	Authority	Yes (working but very less)
Air Rights / F.A.R	No law	YES	YES	Area Based	As per category	One time charge	Authority	Yes
Fee for regularizing unauthorized development	DDA Act 1957, Section 57	No	YES	Area Based	As per category	One time charge	Authority	Yes (working but very less)
Betterment Charges	DDA ACT,1957	YES	YES	Area Based	RS 150/ SQ.MTR.	One time charge	Authority	Yes (working but very less)

Source: Author.

The above tools have been identified based on statistics efficiency, amount of revenue collected, popularity or people's willingness to pay the levy and the extent the levy is being charged for collecting the revenue.

14.7 Conclusion and Policy Recommendations - Establishing Land Value Capture Potential for Financing a Project

14.7.1 Implementing Urban Projects Through Land Value Capture

The recommendations are derived from the selected sites of Delhi land pooling zones. The illustrations on the site represent analysis of the cost required to develop the TOD influence area of 500 m. The cost of developing the whole sector is compared with the cost of developing a TOD influence zone. Applying land-based value capture tools on the sites gives a perception of the reliability of these tools. Three sites have been selected in land pooling zones based on three criteria: first, it should fall under Delhi land pooling zones; second, there should be a greenfield site; and third, there should be an existing or proposed metro station in the land pooling zones. The sites are:

1. Ghevera Metro Station—Existing (Zone- L)
2. Bawana Metro Station—Proposed (Zone- N)
3. Narela Metro Station—proposed (Zone- P1)

14.8 SITE 1—GHEVRA METRO STATION (ZONE—L)

The Ghevra site has an existing character of unplanned industrial area around sector 1 and 2 have noxious industries which fall under Nazafgarh zone, Mundaka ward; having circle rate under category H. The cost of expenditure of sector 1 has been analyzed for a total area of 440 ha with a vacant area of 228 ha, which is compared with the cost incurred for developing sample area of 50.3 ha around the 500-meter TOD influence zone.

Table 14.7 suggests that the capital expenditure for developing sector 2 near Ghevra site is approximately 1,188 CR (INR). It includes road construction, street lighting, water supply network, sewerage, storm water network, recreational development, and maintenance costs. Calculating the capital expenditure for developing a sample area of 50.3 ha would be around 442 CR considering the percentage of roads (25%) and recreational (16%). As analyzing the percentage of roads nearby developing the areas is not the same as the percentage of land pooling policy, one cannot apply for sample area as it may or may not have an equal percentage of roads and recreational spaces in the considered sector. So, 37.2% would be the total cost for developing the TOD area on a sample area of the cost of the sector 2.

Table 14.8 suggests the appropriate LVC tools on sample site at sector 2 have been illustrated to capture land value, keeping the potential of workability according to the past trends. Since each tool cannot be applied on the same

Table 14.7 Capital Expenditure for Sector 2 (Ghevra site)

	Const. of Roads	*Street Lighting*	*Sewerage Network*	*Storm water*	*Water Supply*	*Recreational*	*Cost of Publication*	*Manpower Cost*
RATE (INR)	50,000/Sq.m.	70,000	2,601/ Rmt	10.9 CR/Km	2,516/ Rmt	1,1604/ Sq.m.	10 LAKHS	1 CR
AREA (HA)	27.36	27.36	27.36	27.36	27.36	36.48	27.36	27.36
COST (INR)	227 CR	12 CR	11 CR	497 CR	11 CR	426 CR	10 LAKHS	1 CR
CAPITAL EXPENDITURE FOR AREA 228 HA- 1,188 CR (ROADS- 12%, RECREATIONAL-16%)								
CAPITAL EXPENDITURE FOR SAMPLE AREA 50.3 HA- 442 CR (ROADS- 25 %, RECREATIONAL-16%)								
37.2% of the total cost for developing TOD area on a sample area of the cost of sector area								

Source: Author.

Note: The total cost is the multiplication of quantity with respect to its unit and rate in addition to 20% cost of infrastructure of adjoining schemes, 10% escalation rate for 3 years and 7% miscellaneous cost.

Table 14.8 Value Capture from Selected LVC Tools (Ghevra site)

REVENUE FROM LVC TOOLS								
	Development Based Tools		*Tax Based Tools*			*Fee Based Tools*		
	Land For Sale	*Air Rights*	*Land Value Tax*	*Land Vacant Tax*	*Property Tax*	*Impact Fees*	*Betterment Charges*	*EDC*
REVENUE (INR)	280.75 CR	23.65 CR	38.02 CR	42.25 LAKHS	2.86 CR	84.33 LAKHS	15.55 CR	67.29 CR
68.8% REVENUE FORM DEVELOPMENT BASED TOOLS								

Source: Author.

plot, the total value capture done by all three categories, i.e., development-based tools, taxed based tools and fee-based tools, cannot be compared with the capital expenditure analyzed for sample area of 50.3 ha. If we adopt the purest form, development-based tools would be most appropriate because taxed and fee-based tools are not reliable for capturing the value of any land or developed sector. 68.8% is the total value captured if considering only development-based tools, which is quite sufficient revenue for development infrastructure in an area by the ULBs.

14.9 SITE 2—BAWANA METRO STATION (ZONE—N)

The Bawana site has an existing character of planned industrial area around sector 17. It has noxious industries which fall under Narela zone, Bawana ward, having a circle rate falling under category G. The cost of expenditure of sector 17 has been analyzed having a total area of 193 ha in which the total vacant area is 188 ha. It is being compared with the cost incurred for developing sample area of 79.2 ha around the 500-meter TOD influence zone.

Table 14.9 suggests that the capital expenditure for developing sector 17 near Bhavana site is approximately 978 CR (INR). It includes road construction, street lighting, water supply network, sewerage, storm water network, recreational development, and maintenance costs. Calculating the capital expenditure for developing a sample area of 72.9 ha would be around 847 CR considering the percentage of roads (35%) and recreational (16%). As analyzing the percentage of roads nearby developing the areas is not the same as the percentage of land pooling policy, one cannot apply for sample area as it may or may not have an equal percentage of roads and recreational spaces in the considered sector. So, 86.5% would be the total cost for developing the TOD area on a sample area of the cost of the sector 17.

Table 14.10 suggests the appropriate LVC tools on sample site at sector 17 have been illustrated to capture land value, keeping the potential of workability according to the past trends. Since each tool cannot be applied on the same plot, the total value capture done by all three categories, i.e., development based tools, taxed based tools and fee-based tools, cannot be compared with the capital expenditure analyzed for sample area of 72.9 ha. If we adopt the purest form, development-based tools would be most appropriate because taxed and fee-based tools are not reliable for capturing the value of any land or developed sector. At least 99.4% is the total value captured if considering only development-based tools, which is quite sufficient revenue for development infrastructure in an area by the ULBs.

14.10 SITE 3—NARELA METRO STATION (ZONE—P-1)

The Narela site has an existing rural fabric, having agricultural land around the proposed metro station, which falls under Narela zone, Alipur ward. Its circle rate falls under category H. The sample site has been analyzed as having total area

Table 14.9 Capital Expenditure for Sector 17 (Bhavana site)

	Const. of Roads	*Street Lighting*	*Sewerage Network*	*Storm water*	*Water Supply*	*Recreational*	*Cost of Publication*	*Manpower Cost*
RATE (INR)	50,000/Sq.m.	70,000	2,601/ Rmt	10.9 CR/Km	2,516/ Rmt	1,1604/ Sq.m.	10 LAKHS	1 CR
AREA (ha)	22.56	22.56	22.56	22.56	22.56	30.08	22.56	22.56
COST (INR)	187 CR	10 CR	09 CR	408 CR	09 CR	351 CR	10 LAKHS	1 CR
CAPITAL EXPENDITURE FOR AREA 188 ha- 978 CR (ROADS- 12%, RECREATIONAL-16%)								
CAPITAL EXPENDITURE FOR SAMPLE AREA 72.9 ha- 847 CR (ROADS- 35 %, RECREATIONAL-16%)								
86.5% of the total cost for developing TOD area on a sample area of the cost of sector area								

Source: Author.

Note: The total cost is the multiplication of quantity with respect to its unit and rate in addition to 20% cost of infrastructure of adjoining schemes, 10% escalation rate for 3 years and 7% miscellaneous cost.

Table 14.10 Value Capture from Selected LVC tools (Bhavana site)

REVENUE FROM LVC TOOLS								
	Development Based Tools		*Tax Based Tools*			*Fee Based Tools*		
	Land For Sale	*Air Rights*	*Land Value Tax*	*Land Vacant Tax*	*Property Tax*	*Impact Fees*	*Betterment Charges*	*EDC*
REVENUE (INR)	808.31 CR	34.29 CR	109 CR	109 CR	8.31 CR	1.22 CR	22.55 CR	99.29 CR
99.4 % REVENUE FORM DEVELOPMENT BASED TOOLS								

Source: Author.

of 74.3 ha. The site cannot be compared with the cost incurred for developing sector area around the 500-meter TOD influence zone as the sector plan for Narela zone is still in draft phase and has not been published officially.

Table 14.11 suggests that the capital expenditure for developing a sample area of 74.3 ha would be around 863 CR considering the percentage of roads (30%) and recreational (16%). As analyzing the percentage of roads nearby developing the areas is not the same as the percentage of land pooling policy, one cannot apply for sample area as it may or may not have an equal percentage of roads and recreational spaces in the considered sector. At least 86.5% would be the total cost for developing the TOD area on a sample area of the cost of the area.

Table 14.12 suggests the appropriate LVC tools on sample site at Alipur ward have been illustrated to capture land value, keeping the potential of workability according to the past trends. Since each tool cannot be applied on the same plot, the total value capture done by all three categories, i.e., development based tools, taxed based tools and fee-based tools, cannot be compared with the capital expenditure analyzed for sample area of 74.3 ha. If we adopt the purest form, development-based tools would be most appropriate because taxed and fee-based tools are not reliable for capturing the value of any land or developed sector. At least 52.1% is the total value captured if considering only development-based tools, which is quite sufficient revenue for development infrastructure in an area by the ULBs.

14.10.1 Conclusion

The above section presents a researched-based scenario for the implementation of urban projects through LVC for both public and private sectors. The sampled sites in section 14.6 show that the revenue generation from value capture tools are economically, financially, and institutionally sustainable. The above section is also intended to generate discussion amongst key stakeholders and serves as a basis for research and experimentation for unlocking the private investments in sustainable infrastructure in Asia. Since the chapter limited its scope of work to some of the indicators of economic and institutional framework, certain obsolete types of infrastructure may occur due to innovative technologies and business models. New sources of private investments would increase the legal and regulatory challenges faced by government agencies looking to increase investments in sustainable infrastructure.

More private sector involvement may enhance performance and increase efficiency of infrastructure services in addition to reducing the fiscal burden of public budgets. It is evident from the past that governments will not be able to meet projected demand for investment in a sustainable way. Increasing access to long-term capital at adequate rates to support sustainable investments will require enhanced participation from the private sector. This establishes the distinction between standard and sustainable infrastructure.

Table 14.11 Capital Expenditure for Sample Site (Narela site)

	Const. of Roads	*Street Lighting*	*Sewerage Network*	*Storm water*	*Water Supply*	*Recreational*	*Cost of Publication*	*Manpower Cost*
RATE (INR)	50,000/Sq.m.	70,000	2,601/ Rmt	10.9 CR/Km	2,516/ R mt	1,1604/ Sq.m.	10 LAKHS	1 CR
AREA (ha)	26.01	26.01	26.01	26.01	26.01	11.89	26.01	26.01
COST (INR)	216 CR	12.13 CR	11.24 CR	472 CR	10.87 CR	138 CR	10 LAKHS	1 CR
CAPITAL EXPENDITURE FOR AREA- SECTOR PLAN IS NOT PUBLISHED								
CAPITAL EXPENDITURE FOR SAMPLE AREA 74.3 ha- 863 CR (ROADS- 30 %, RECREATIONAL-16%)								
86.5% of the total cost for developing TOD area on a sample area of the cost of area								

Source: Author.

Note: The total cost is the multiplication of quantity with respect to its unit and rate in addition to 20% cost of infrastructure of adjoining schemes, 10% escalation rate for 3 years and 7% miscellaneous cost.

Table 14.12 Value Capture from Selected LVC Tools (Narela site)

REVENUE FROM LVC TOOLS								
	Development Based Tools		*Tax Based Tools*			*Fee Based Tools*		
	Land For Sale	*Air Rights*	*Land Value Tax*	*Land Vacant Tax*	*Property Tax*	*Impact Fees*	*Betterment Charges*	*EDC*
REVENUE (INR)	415.12 CR	34.89 CR	1019 CR	1.23 CR	4.23 CR	1.24 CR	22.94 CR	99.27 CR
52.1 % REVENUE FORM DEVELOPMENT BASED TOOLS								

Source: Author.

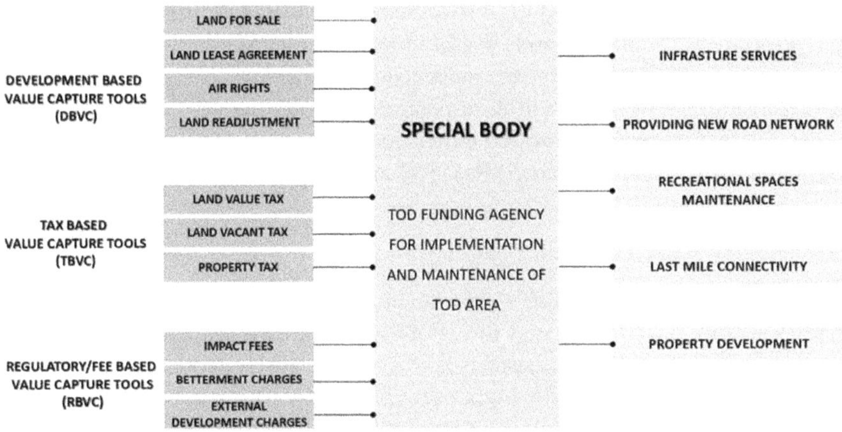

Figure 14.9 Revenue Generation from Land Monetization (Ghevra, Bhavana, and Narela). Source: Author.

14.10.2 Recommendations and Policy Implications

(i) APPROPRIATE DBVC TOOLS FOR DEVELOPMENT IN TOD AREAS OF DELHI'S LAND POOLING ZONES

Development-Based Land Value Capture Tools

The sale of land, land lease agreements, and land readjustment are the purest development-based land value capture tools. In other words, land monetization is the purest form for value capture in the TOD context.

Figure 14.9 analyzes all three selected sites with their value capture being generated by only land monetization; if we take an average of all three sites, 74.3% of the revenue is being generated by land monetization only. Therefore, it is appropriate to say that land monetization is the purest form of doing land value capture in the TOD context in Delhi land pooling zones.

14.10.2.1 Tax-Based Land Value Capture Tools

Property taxes, land vacant taxes, and land value taxes are the most significant tax-based land value capture tools. Land vacancy taxes should be segregated from property taxes as land vacant tax is not compulsory to pay it if there is no construction on a land parcel (as per Delhi property tax). Thus, there should be a segregation of both the taxes so that it can contribute in addition to value capture as vacancy tax is creating a negative impact in the development of an area. Taking an example in Bihar, where vacant land in urban parts of the state would now come under the aegis of the state, lands located in municipal areas on the main principal road, main road and local roads would be Rs5, Rs4 and Rs3 per square feet respectively. Similarly, lands available in Nagar Parishad areas and located either on the main principal road, main road and local roads would be charged Rs4, Rs3, and Rs2 per square foot, respectively. In a similar way lands available in Nagar Panchayat areas and located either on the main principal road, main road and local roads would be charged Rs3, Rs2 and Rs1 per square foot respectively.

14.10.2.2 Fee-Based Land Value Capture Tools

Sale of impact/development fees, betterment charges, and external development charges are the purest fee-based forms of capturing land value. Seeing the past trend in Delhi, the fee or tax-based is not as reliable as the people are not willing to pay any taxes because of the higher fee charged by Municipal Corporation or by the authority. So, there is a need to minimize the fee if we need to capture the land value as minimizing the fee-based levy people might be willing to pay a levy which is imposed on them. Hence, there is a need for analyzing how much EDC a person gives and how much a betterment charge a person should give as per the range of TOD influence area.

In the current scenario, the betterment levy is executed as same for different F.A.R. at different radius but on practical implementation, it cannot be the same. For example, the betterment levy imposed on commercial or residential land use around the 100 meters of influence zone of TOD area cannot be same as the around the 800 meters as the distance varies the land value also varies so, there cannot be the same levy for the same radius (Table 14.13). There should a FAR range that decides the percentage of levy imposed on particular land use based on the distance of land from the metro station.

1. **NEW ADMINISTRATIVE FRAMEWORK**—Simplified and direct Institutional framework (who collects and division of LVC tools must be subdivided)

   Figure 14.10 shows the new administrative framework to capture value from different land-based value capture tools is of no use unless it is transferred or imposed for development in the TOD context. It can only be

Table 14.13 Distribution of Betterment Levy Based on Floor Area Ratio

Band	*Range of far*	*Betterment Levy*
1	5–4	50%
2	4–3	40%
3	3–2	35%
4	2–1	25%

Source: Author.

Figure 14.10 New Administrative Framework for TOD areas in Delhi.
Source: Author.

workable if there is a simplified institutional framework that directly collects some amount to capture value. It can be mandated by various revenue-collecting agencies so that the amount can be used in the development of TOD influence zones.

2. **STATUTORY LAW**—Delhi Land Pooling policy should be included in the DDA Act, 1957 to be legally backup as Land Acquisition Act, 1984.
3. **PHASING**—Phasing should be mandated and given by DDA to developers to avoid the spotted development in land pooling zones of Delhi.
4. **DECLARATION OF EDC CHARGES OR REVENUE SOURCES IN POLICY**—There should be a declaration of fees or charges for each tool where revenue is being generated.
5. **INCREASE THE F.A.R IN DELHI LAND POOLING POLICY**– Capacity building of agencies like Delhi Jal Board and other agencies for improving infrastructure and making viable for developers as well.
6. **DEVELOPMENT-BASED VALUE CAPTURE TOOLS**—The purest form to capture DBVC is by land monetization with property development, land trust and sale of air rights.

References

ADB. 2017. *Meeting Asia's Infrastructure Needs*. www.adb.org/publications/asia-infrastructure-needs (accessed 27 June 2021).

Authority, D.D.A. 2007. Master Plan for, *2021*, 1–306.

Bank, W. 2015. Urban land Management and Tenure, *5*(7), 143–152.

Centre for Policy Research. 2015. The Intersection of Governments in Delhi, (April), 1–3. http://cprindia.org/sites/default/files/policy-briefs/The-Intersection-of-Governments-in-Delhi.pdf (accessed 27 June 2021).

Collier, P. 2018. *Land and Property Taxes for Municipal Finance*. IGC.

Economic Survey of Delhi, D., Delhi, N., Corporation, M., Delhi, S., Corporation, M., Delhi, E., … Council, M. 2017. *Economic Survey of Delhi*.

Gupta, S. 2018. All You Need To Know About DDA Land Pooling Policy. www.proptiger.com/guide/post/all-you-need-to-know-about-dda-land-pooling-policy

Law, F. (n.d.). How the Government Takes Property. Retrieved from https://realestate.findlaw.com/land-use-laws/how-the-government-takes-property.html

NIUA. 2016. Value Capture From Infrastructure Investments for Smart Cities.

Olajide, O. 2015. Transit Value Capture Finance: A Global Review towards Measuring Monetary Efficiency.

Smolka, M.O. and D. Amborski. 2000. Value Capture for Urban Development: An Inter-American Comparison. www.lincolninst.edu/sites/default/files/pubfiles/1279_Smolka Final.pdf (accessed 27 June 2021).

Town and Country Planning Organisation. 2007. Model Guidelines for Town and Country Planning Organisation. July 40.

UN General Assembly. 2015. Addis Ababa Action Agenda of the Third International Conference on Financing for Development. Addis Ababa Action Agenda, Resolution A/RES/69/313, undocs.org/A/RES/69/313 (accessed 2 June 2016).

APPENDIX: DEFINITIONS

1. **Property Tax:** "Property tax is the annual amount paid by a land owner to the local government or the municipal corporation of his area. The property includes all tangible real estate property: house, office building and the property he has rented to others. In India, the Municipal Corporation of a particular area assesses and imposes the property tax annually or semi-annually. The tax amount is based on the area, construction, property size, building, etc. The collected amount is mainly used for public services like repairing roads, construction schools, buildings, sanitation. Central government properties and vacant properties are generally exempt." The formula for property tax is **Property tax or House Tax = Annual value * Rate of tax.**

   Annual Value = Unit area value per sq. mtr * unit area of property * age factor * use factor * structure factor * occupancy factor

2. **Vacant Land Tax:** This is also a variant of property tax, which charges owners who have not carried out development on their land. This tool particularly gains importance given to the fact that land is scarce and must be monetized to reap benefits. For example, the Greater Hyderabad Municipal Corporation charges 0.5% of the registration value of the land if the land is not utilized for agriculture or is left un-built. The Tamil Nadu State of India has the legal backing for levying the vacant land as with the Land Ceiling Act of 1976. Vacant land is levied under the Gujarat Provisional Municipal Corporation Act 1949 section 455. It is levied on non-agriculture plots which have infrastructure facilities but no buildings.
3. **Tax-Increment Financing:** "Tax Increment Financing or TIF is one of the most popular value capture tools in many developed countries, especially the United States. In TIF, the incremental revenues from future increases in property tax or a surcharge on the existing property tax rate are ring-fenced for a defined period of time to finance some new investment in the area." TIF makes use of a predicted future increase in tax revenue in order to finance improvements that will, in turn, reap the predicted benefits.
4. **Stamp Duty Fees:** Stamp duty is a tax imposed on the sale of property/property ownership by the state government. It is payable under Section 3 of the Indian Stamp Act, 1899. The duration of the stamp duty at the time of registration shall be based on the value of the house/property. It also varies

based on the state or area where the property is located, and whether it is a new or old house. Stamp duty is an additional cost incurred when purchasing immovable property.

5. **Development/ Impact Fees: Impact** fees are charges that are imposed upon new development as a state of development approval to pay for a proportionate share of the cost in the city's infrastructure wherever it is necessary for new growth and development. Impact fees are one-time payments used to construct system improvements. Impact fees are collected to provide public services to a new development, fund capital improvements required to serve the growth, and benefit new development by maintaining current levels of service. This is a widely used land-based value capture tool that is used in Indian States like Andhra Pradesh, Gujarat, Maharashtra, and Tamil Nadu and they been collecting it upfront while granting development permission. Impact fees are widely used in the United States to fund infrastructure.
6. **Change of land use:** Land use change is a process which transforms the natural landscape by direct human-induced land use such as settlements, commercial and economic uses and forestry activities.
7. **Lease of land and development:** A land lease, also called a ground lease, is a lease agreement that permits the tenant to use a piece of land owned by the landlord in exchange for rent. Land leases work very similarly to the way traditional property leases operate, and tenants can enter into both residential and commercial agreements. Most land leases are vacant, allowing the tenant to construct a temporary—or in some arrangements, permanent—structure at his own cost. However, some land leases do already have structures, partial structures, or other objects on them for the tenant's use.
8. **Property transaction fees:** Property transaction fees is the total transaction costs that includes the costs of buying a property plus the costs of selling of a property or land.
9. **Sale of naming rights:** Naming rights are a financial transaction and form of advertising whereby a corporation or other entity purchases the right to name a facility or event, typically for a defined period of time. The distinctive characteristic for naming rights is that the buyer gets a marketing property to promote products and services, promote customer retention and/or increase market share.
10. **External Development Charges (EDC)**: The EDC is the fee that builders have to pay to the civic authority for development of basic facilities in and around housing projects. These include supply of water, electricity, sewerage system, waste management system, landscaping, roads, etc.
11. **Land pooling:** This concept originated in Germany with a supporting legal structure was enacted in 1902. Since it has been used extensively across East Asia, land pooling was adopted in Japan, the People's Republic of China, and Taipei,China. Land pooling is a form of land procurement where all the land parcels in an area are pooled for the infrastructure development and share land in proportion to original ownership returned as reconstituted parcels. In India, states such as Gujarat and Haryana are using land assembly

mechanism where the owner agrees to exchange their land for infrastructure development. Gujarat is using this tool for the development of infrastructure in Ahmedabad and recently, Andhra Pradesh has also used LPS to get land for its new Capital Amravati.

12. **Air rights:** Rights to the airspace above a building or lot, regarded as the real property of the one who owns the building or lot.
13. **Fee for regularizing unauthorized development:** The charges incurred from an unauthorized colony or development comprising of a contiguous area, where no permission has been obtained for approval of layout plan or building plans and has been identified for regularization of such colony in pursuance to the notification number S.O. 683(E) dated the 24th March, 2008 and includes colonies as identified by the Delhi Development Authority under these regulations as specified in Annexure II (1797 colonies).
14. **Betterment charges:** A betterment levy is a onetime upfront charge on the land value gain caused by public infrastructure investment. And is considered equitable as the payer is charged for the benefits received. The levy can be charged as revenue for improvement schemes or as project-based tax. In Hong Kong, China, the betterment taxes are based on market value whereas in Mumbai the MMRDA collects it on a project basis. Another form of being through it is town planning schemes. Under this, the Development Authority is empowered to collect betterment charges at the time of building permit for laying trunk water lines, development of major roads, etc. but sometimes, they do not have the estimates of investment. Thus, they collected charges after the development of infrastructure as it gives total expenditure amount. Great Britain has imposed a betterment levy equal to 40% of the land value gain attribute to public investment.

15 Tax Incentives to Attract Private Investment in Infrastructure

The Indonesian Perspective

Wawan Juswanto and Yanuar Falak Abiyunus

15.1 Introduction

In half a century, Asia's population more than doubled from 1.8 billion in 1966 to 4 billion in 2015. The rapid growth of the population urged the need for infrastructure to support the basic needs of living, such as water treatment, energy, education, and healthcare. Sufficient road infrastructure is also needed to support the mobility of goods and services, which is essential to maintain growth.

In terms of economic performance, developing Asia[1] has shown stable and robust economic growth, especially for its developing countries. As shown in Figure 15.1, developing Asia is expected to grow by 5.5% in 2020, far beyond emerging markets (4.1%) and the world average (2.5%). Infrastructure development is essential to support economic performance by reducing factors that may negatively impact the economy, such as inequality and poverty.

To meet infrastructure needs, developing Asia will need to invest $1.7 trillion each year from 2016 to 2030 (ADB 2017), which is generally grouped into energy, transportation, telecommunications, water, and sanitation. The estimated amount was rising rapidly, reaching more than double the 2009 estimate of $750 billion per year (ADB and ADBI 2009). Currently, the region annually invests an estimated $881 billion in infrastructure. However, the current level of investment is not sufficient, with a financing gap equal to 2.4% of gross domestic product (GDP) from 2016 to 2020. Unfortunately, the gap is wider for low to lower-middle-income economies, which can be around 5.6% of projected GDP (ADB 2017).

The role of the public sector in infrastructure funding is still prominent compared to private sector contributions. Around 90% of infrastructure funding in developing Asia is sourced from the public sector (ADB 2017). However, limited fiscal capacity generates considerable challenges if the governments are relying heavily on the public sector for infrastructure investment. To fund the rising spending for infrastructure, governments should classify the budget among high-priority programs. If the government wants to allocate more infrastructure spending without sacrificing other spending items, it needs to raise its revenue. Although governments can raise their debt level, they need to keep it reasonable to make the budget sustainable.

DOI: 10.4324/9781003228790-18

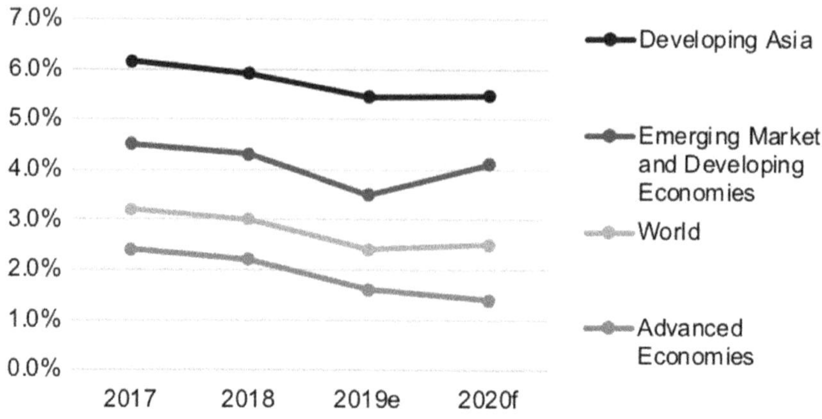

Figure 15.1 Economic Growth(%).
Source: ADB (2019) and World Bank (2020).

Similar to the above situation, Indonesia is facing challenges to improve its infrastructure development despite its economic potential. Currently, Indonesia is the largest country in Southeast Asia, with a GDP of more than $1 trillion. Amid global uncertainty, the economic growth of Indonesia remained above 5% in recent years. Furthermore, Indonesia is projected to be one of the developed countries with a GDP of $7.3 trillion in 2045. However, economic development is still unequally spread across the country. The development in Indonesia is still heavily concentrated in Java, with more than 55% of GDP concentrated in it. Data from the Central Bureau of Statistics show that, in 2018, Jakarta has the most significant regional GDP of Rp2.6 trillion ($1.765 billion). Meanwhile, the regional GDP of the least-developed region in Indonesia (North Maluku) only amounted to 1.4% of it (See ANNEX A). Inequal development across Indonesia can also be seen from its electricity distribution. On average, as much as 98.3% of households in Indonesia had electricity in 2018. Among 34 provinces in Indonesia, Bali is the only one with all households having access to electricity. West Nusa Tenggara, with the lowest electricity ratio, is far behind, with only 62.7% of households having access to electricity (Ministry of ESDM 2019).

In terms of infrastructure quality, Indonesia is still trailing its neighboring countries. According to the Global Competitiveness Report 2019 (Schwab 2019), Indonesia ranked 72 out of 141 countries in overall infrastructure quality, behind Thailand (71), Malaysia (35), Brunei Darussalam (58), and Singapore (1). Although Indonesia scored a positive result in airport connectivity (5th position), several aspects need to be improved, especially road connectivity (109th position), exposure to unsafe drinking water (98th position), electricity access (95th position), and railroad density (85th position).

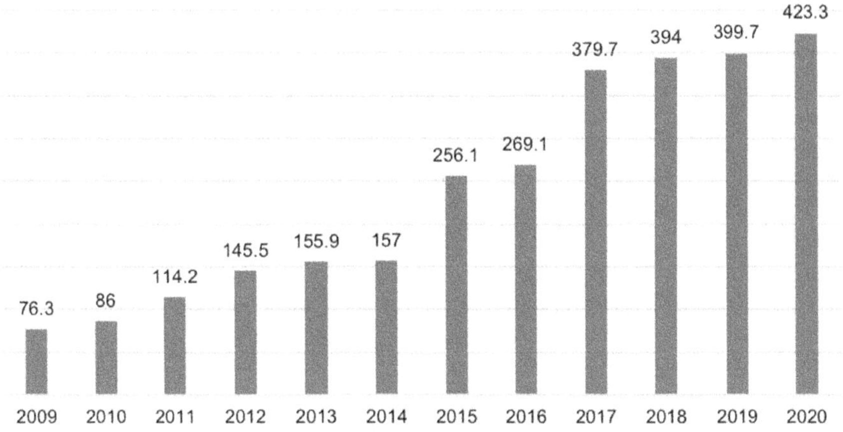

Figure 15.2 Infrastructure Spending (Rp trillion).
Source: Ministry of Finance. The figure for 2019 is an estimation. The figure for 2020 is the budgeted amount.

In the mid-term development plan, the lack of infrastructure development is mentioned as one of the main challenges of economic development. Therefore, the government put infrastructure as one of the general policies of national development for equitable economic growth (Bappenas 2015). Since 2015, the government has increased the budget allocation for infrastructure spending budget significantly. From 2014 to 2020, infrastructure spending increased by almost triple from Rp157 trillion ($10.7 billion) to Rp423.3 trillion ($28.7 billion), with average annual growth of 11.8%. See Figure 15.2.

Indonesia continued to emphasize infrastructure as one of the strategic options in order to accelerate the growth and equity of the economy. In its mid-term development plan of 2020–2024, Indonesia focused on three infrastructure frameworks:

1. Basic service infrastructure, which is prioritized to ensure equitable development in all regions of Indonesia, including adequate housing supported by water supply and sanitation systems, improvement of on-grid and off-grid network services for electricity access, provision of telecommunications and internet services for public facilities, development of past safety systems transportation, pioneer transportation services, as well as the construction of multi-purpose and irrigation reservoirs.
2. Economic infrastructure, which will focus on the development of transportation, electricity and energy, and information technology with a large enough capacity and high enough speed to exploit Big Data, the Internet of Things, and artificial intelligence.

3. Urban infrastructure, which includes improvement of facilities and infrastructure that will support the convenience of living in cities such as the construction of mass public transportation, construction of city gas pipelines, drinking water and sanitation pipes, and waste management.

However, although the budget for infrastructure has risen significantly it only constitutes a small portion of the financing needs. In the following five-year period (2020–2024), Indonesia needs around $433.6 billion (6.08% of GDP) to finance its infrastructure. However, the government is only expected to contribute 37% of that amount (Bappenas 2020). Another estimation by ADB (2017) shows that Indonesia will need an annual investment of $70 billion in infrastructure for the next five years. However, the current level of investment can only provide $23 billion, or about 32% of the total financing needs, creating a gap equivalent to 4.7% of GDP. If the estimate includes climate factors, the gap may be increased to 5.1% of GDP.

In utilizing the budget as infrastructure financing, Indonesia should consider its limited fiscal space. The government should consider other necessary expenditures, especially for mandated ones such as education and health. By law, the central government and local government must allocate 20% of its budget for education purposes and 5% of the budget for health purposes. Meanwhile, on the revenue side, tax performance still cannot support the need for spending. In 2017, the tax-to-GDP ratio of Indonesia was only 11.5%, far below the Organisation for Economic Co-operation and Development (OECD) average (34.2%), as well as the Latin America and Caribbean average (22.8%) and the African average (18.2%) (OECD, 2019).

Therefore, the government must increase the role of the private sector in infrastructure development. One of the policies taken by Indonesia is providing tax incentives to attract direct investment in certain sectors, including infrastructure. The government also provides value added tax (VAT) exemption for certain residence types to provide decent housing that is affordable for low-income households. This paper will describe tax incentives related to the infrastructure sector and evaluate its utilization by covering the policy perspective as well as its administrative matters.

15.2 The Role of Tax Incentives

Tax incentives are widely used to attract private investment in various sectors. Tax incentives reduce the cost of investment, thereby increasing the profit of investors. In the Asia and the Pacific region, incentives can reduce the effective tax rate by 8.6 percentage points (Nicolay and Wiedemann 2016). With reduced investment costs, incentives are expected to attract investment, especially direct investment. Furthermore, direct investment, not limited to infrastructure sectors, can affect the availability of infrastructure, as found by Wang (2019) in ASEAN countries.

From the direct tax perspective, tax incentives are provided by reducing the corporate income tax. The most popular types of income tax incentives are the tax holiday and investment allowance. Tax holidays exempt the taxpayers from income tax liability within a specified period. Taxpayers wishing to enjoy tax holidays are required to meet certain eligibility criteria. In most cases, tax holidays are granted to newly established enterprises or target specific sectors or activities (Muyaa 2018).

The government can reduce income tax based on a certain amount of investment, including (i) deducting a certain amount of investment to the tax liability (investment tax credit), (ii) deducting a certain amount of investment to the taxable profit (investment allowance), or (iii) allowing a faster schedule of depreciation for certain assets (accelerated depreciation) (James 2013). These kinds of tax incentives determine the benefit granted to taxpayers based on the amount of investment, as opposed to a tax holiday that completely exempts the eligible taxpayers from income tax liability.

Tax incentives can also be given in the form of value added tax/general sales tax (VAT/GST). In contrast to direct tax incentives, which impact a company's profits, VAT/GST incentives affect the prices of goods or services. The exemption eases the burden on consumers by giving exemptions of VAT/GST for specific goods and services related to the investment in selected sectors.

Although the tax is not considered as the main determinant of investment location, it is still becoming one of the considerations (Baggerman-Noudari and Offermanns 2016). Klemm and Parys (2009) found that tax incentives have a positive impact on attracting FDI in developing countries. Furthermore, tax incentives are needed in competing for FDI with other countries that also provide them (OECD 2008).

Tax incentives are favorable because their costs (in the form of foregone revenue) will occur only when the investment generates profit (Easson 2001). In contrast, other kinds of incentives, such as financing incentives, will burden the budget from the beginning of its utilization. While developed countries tend to offer financial incentives such as grants, subsidized loans, or loan guarantees, developing countries usually do not have the same possibilities to provide capital upfront (Muyaa 2018). James (2013) and Juárez and Manrique (2018) found that tax incentives are more prevalent in Asia, Africa, and Latin America than in OECD countries. Tax incentives have also become an essential part of policies in the Middle East and North African countries in attracting investment (OECD 2008).

The tax holiday is the most used tax incentive in the world, followed by reduced tax rates and investment allowance and tax credits. Each of those incentives is implemented by more than 50% of countries around the world. In Latin America and the Caribbean, Asia and the Pacific, and Africa, around 60% of the countries are using those incentives. Otherwise, only a limited number of OECD countries (8%) are utilizing a tax holiday. Deduction of research and development is the most common incentive used in OECD countries. See Figure 15.3.

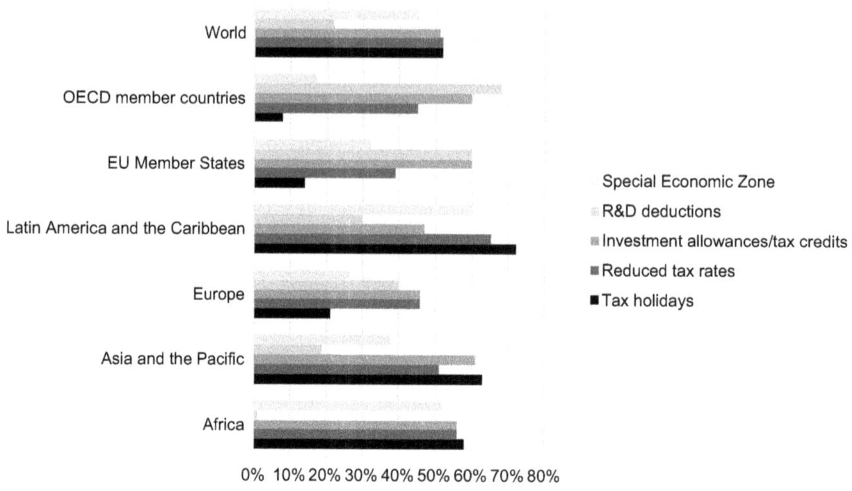

Figure 15.3 Prevalence of Selected Tax Incentives.

Note: EU = European Union, OECD = Organisation for Economic Co-operation and Development, R&D = research and development.

Source: Juárez and Manrique (2018).

Indonesia is one of the countries that offer fiscal incentives to attract direct investments, including in infrastructure sectors. From the direct tax perspective, Indonesia offers tax holidays for pioneer industries and tax allowance for investment in certain sectors or certain locations. Indonesia also offers VAT exemptions for certain goods and services. However, the amount of tax foregone as an impact of implementing tax incentives only resulted in Rp221.1 trillion (1.5% of GDP) of revenue foregone, relatively low compared to other developing countries (see Figure 15.4). Furthermore, tax incentives to attract investment only comprise 12.3% of the tax foregone. Although the government has generously offered tax incentives, its utilization is still relatively low.

15.3 Tax Holiday

The tax holiday was first introduced in Indonesia in 1967 with Law number 1 of 1967. The introduction of the tax holiday was intended to attract foreign investors after the government had prohibited foreign investment in the first half of 1960. At the time, the tax holiday was considered necessary due to the high rate of corporate income tax (Wells et al. 2001). In the later amendment, domestic investors were also eligible to obtain tax holiday. During its 15 years of implementation, 473 projects from foreign direct investment utilized tax holiday, with 75% of them realized (Makmun 2010). The tax holiday was abolished by the implementation of Income Tax Law number 7 of 1983.

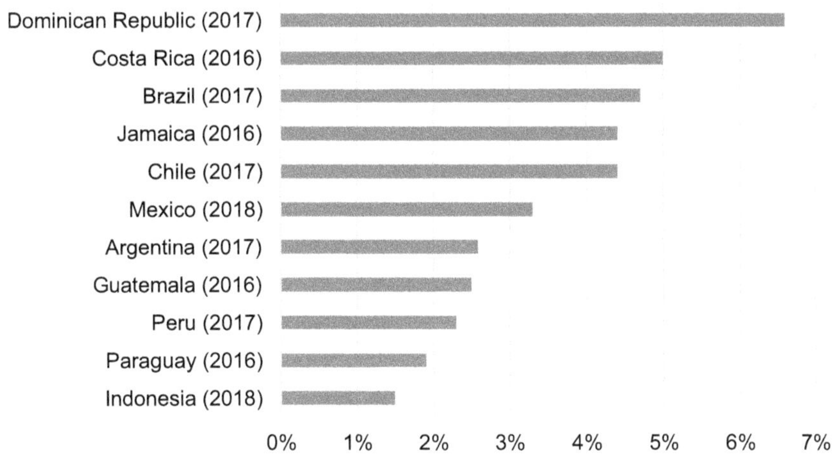

Figure 15.4 Tax Expenditure (% of GDP).
Note: GDP = gross domestic product.
Source: Longinotti (2018) and BKF (2019), processed by authors.

More than two decades later, the government reintroduced the tax holiday through Investment Law number 25 of 2007. Article 18 of the Law stated that the government might grant pioneer industries a total exemption or a certain amount of reduction of corporate income tax for a particular period. A pioneer industry is one that has broad connection and linkage, generates added value and high externalities, introduces new technology, and provides strategic value for the national economy.

The implementing regulation for tax holiday (MoF Regulation 130/2011) was enacted in 2011, which was later amended once in 2015 and twice in 2018. In general, the amendments modified the scope of eligible sectors, the investment threshold, the benefit, and the administration procedures. Economic infrastructure has been listed as one of the pioneer industries since the 2015 amendment. The main features of the tax holiday in Indonesia are described in Table 15.1. Furthermore, the sectors covered by tax holiday are described in ANNEX B.

15.3.1 The 2011 Tax Holiday

The 2011 tax holiday was regulated under Ministry of Finance (MoF) Regulation 130/2011 and was effective from 15 August 2011. At the time, tax holiday was only granted for new investments with a minimum amount of Rp1 trillion ($67.9 million). For eligible taxpayers, the concession period is between five fiscal years up to 10 fiscal years. After the concession period ends, the taxpayer would be granted 50% of corporate income tax reduction for two more fiscal years. The Minister of Finance has the authority to expand the concession period to be more

Table 15.1 Main Features of Tax Holiday in Indonesia

Year	*2011*	*2015*	*2018*	
Ministry of Finance Regulation	130/2011	159/2015	35/2018	150/2018
Eligible Sectors	5	9	17	18
Income Tax Reduction	100%	10%–100%	100%	50%–100%
Concession Period	5–10 years	5–15 years	5–20 years	5–20 years
Investment Threshold	Rp1 trillion ($67.9 million)	Rp500 billion ($33.95 million)	Multiple thresholds, from Rp500 billion to Rp30 trillion ($33.95 million–$2.03 billion)	Multiple thresholds, from Rp100 billion to Rp30 trillion ($6.79 million–$2.03 billion)
Determinant	Based on analysis	Based on analysis	Based on Investment value	Based on Investment value

Source: Ministry of Finance Regulation 130/2011, 159/2015, 35/2018, and 150/2018. Processed by authors.

than 10 fiscal years, with consideration of strategic value and national competitiveness of the investment.

In the 2011 regime, the application process of the tax holiday was relatively complicated. To submit a tax holiday application, the investor must have completed the investment approval process and registered as a taxpayer in Indonesia. Investment approval documents and taxpayer identification number are part of the required documents for tax holiday submission. Besides, the investor must deposit 10% of their investment plan in an Indonesian bank, which cannot be withdrawn until the investment has been realized.

The taxpayer must submit a request for tax holiday and the required documents to the Minister of Industry or Chairman of the Investment Coordinating Board (BKPM). The Ministry of Industry or the BKPM chairman reviews the application and coordinates with other relevant ministries to decide whether the taxpayer is eligible to obtain a tax holiday.

If the taxpayer is eligible, the Ministry of Industry or the BKPM chairman will submit a recommendation letter to the Minister of Finance. The recommendation letter must include related information, including infrastructure conditions at the investment location, potential absorption of the domestic workforce, a review result of the fulfillment of the criteria for a pioneer industry, a clear and concrete plan for the transfer of technology, and information whether the home country of the investor would acknowledge a tax reduction that is given in Indonesia in the calculation (tax sparring).

The Minister of Finance forms a verification committee to analyze and verify the application based on the recommendation letter. The analysis determines whether the investment has a strategic impact on the national economy. In conducting the analysis, the committee consults with the Coordinating Minister of Economy. Based on the analysis, the committee proposes its recommendation to the Minister of Finance. The recommendation includes how long the concession period should be given to the taxpayer (between 5 to 10 fiscal years). Based on the recommendation, the Minister of Finance will consult the president in the decision-making process. Finally, the Minister of Finance issues a decree to grant or revoke the tax holiday application. Unfortunately, in the 2011 tax holiday regime, the government did not regulate a specific period from submission until the decree of tax holiday was issued.

Taxpayers who have obtained a tax holiday must submit periodic reports to the Department of General Taxation (DGT) and the verification committee. The report must mention the use of funds deposited in an Indonesian bank. The taxpayer must also report the realization of audited investments. The DGT may revoke the tax holiday if they identify that the realization of investment is not in line with the requirements, or if the taxpayer does not report accordingly.

15.3.2 The 2015 Tax Holiday

The government amended the 2011 tax holiday by issuing MoF regulation 159/2015, which was effective from 16 August 2015. In this regime, the government offered more flexibility and relaxation than the previous regulation by giving an income tax exemption that ranged from 10% to 100%. The government also extended the concession period to a maximum of 15 years. The Minister of Finance was able to extend the period to 20 years by considering the strategic value and national competitiveness of the taxpayer. The government also expanded the scope of pioneer industries to nine sectors. Furthermore, the investment threshold for the information and communication sector was lowered to Rp500 billion ($33.95 million).

The government also offered more relaxation by relieving the deposit requirement in an Indonesian bank (previously, the investor must deposit 10% of its investment value). The investor was only required to submit a letter of commitment, which stated that the investor can deposit 10% of the investment value. Furthermore, the government also simplified the process of granting tax holiday. The Minister of Finance could issue a tax holiday decree without consultation with the president.

On the other side, the government added more requirements for the taxpayer. In order to apply the tax holiday, the investor must fulfill a debt-to-equity ratio, which is regulated in MoF Regulation 169/2015. According to the rule, a corporate taxpayer should have a maximum debt-to-equity ratio of 4:1. However, the requirement is not applied to (i) taxpayers in banking, financing, insurance, and oil and gas sectors with a contract that has debt-to-equity ratio provisions, (ii) taxpayers that are subject to final income tax, and (iii) taxpayers from infrastructure sectors. Another added requirement was a tax clearance certificate from the DGT for the taxpayer that is owned directly by other domestic taxpayers or permanent establishments.

In the 2015 regime, the economic infrastructure was first listed as one of the pioneer sectors. However, only the projects that were not under a public-private partnership (PPP) scheme can apply for the tax holiday.

15.3.3 The 2018 Tax Holiday

The government amended the tax holiday regulation twice in 2018. The first amendment was done through MoF regulation 35/2018, which was effective from 4 April 2018. The last amendment was done through MoF Regulation 150/2018, which was effective from 27 November 2018.

15.3.3.1 MoF Regulation 35/2018

The notable changes in this regime were the certainty and simplicity of the procedure. The Minister of Finance no longer decides the amount of income tax exemption and the concession period. Rather, the government provided a clear list of exemption rates and the period of concession based on the investment amount (see Table 15.2). Through MoF Regulation 35/2018, the government reintroduced a "single rate" of 100% reduction of corporate income tax, rather than the ranged rate as offered in MoF Regulation 159/2015. The government also reduced the general threshold from Rp1 trillion ($67.9 million) to Rp500 billion ($33.95 million). The concession period was also extended to a maximum of 20 years. After the concession period is exceeded, there is an additional reduction of 50% of the income tax for two fiscal years.

The list of pioneer industries was extended significantly to 17 sectors. The exclusion of investment under the PPP scheme for economic infrastructure sectors was removed. Detailed regulation of business activities and production types of each sector is under BKPM Regulation. For the economic infrastructure sector, covered production types are renewable energy power plants, highway construction, port construction, and investment activities and operation of an oil

Table 15.2 Concession Period Under MoF Regulation 35/2018

Concession Period	*Investment Threshold*
5 years	Rp500 billion ($33.95 million)
7 years	Rp1 trillion ($67.9 million)
10 years	Rp5 trillion ($339.5 million)
15 years	Rp15trillion ($1.02 billion)
Up to 20 years	Rp30 trillion ($2.03 billion)

Source: Ministry of Finance Regulation 35/2018.

tank. For highway and port construction, eligible projects are those with a low internal rate of return.

In Mof Regulation 35/2018, a taxpayer that is not covered in the list of pioneer industries is able to apply for the tax holiday, if the taxpayer fulfills the other requirements. For this application, the decision of whether the taxpayer can be classified as pioneer industries is subject to inter-ministries meeting. The meeting is coordinated by BKPM and, at minimum, involves the Ministry of Finance and another related ministry. If the taxpayer can be specified as a pioneer industry, BKPM submits the recommendation to the Minister of Finance.

The government also substantially simplified the application process by implementing a "trust and verify" paradigm. Through MoF Regulation 35/2018, the government shifted the verification process from the verification committee to field audit, which is performed by the DGT tax auditors (the Ministry of Finance was no longer required to form a verification committee to review the recommendation from BKPM). The audit, which is conducted when the taxpayer starts its commercial production, will determine the starting point of the commercial production, the investment realization, and the suitability between realization and the plan. From the administration perspective, the taxpayer is no longer required to submit a commitment letter of bank deposit. Furthermore, the government offered more certainty by limiting the processing time to five working days (since the receipt of the BKPM recommendation until the issuance of tax holiday decree).

15.3.3.2 MoF Regulation 150/2018

In this amendment, the government introduced a "mini tax holiday" for an investment of more than Rp100 billion ($6.79 million) but not exceeding Rp500 billion ($33.95 million). However, for investors in this category, the government only offers a 50% reduction of corporate income tax for five fiscal years and a 25% reduction of corporate income tax for the next two fiscal years. The government offered relaxation in terms of the scope of sectors. The government extended the list of pioneer industries to 18 sectors.

A taxpayer appointed by the government under the national strategic project can apply to obtain tax holiday. The appointment must be based on a ministerial level decree. Currently, the national strategic projects are regulated by Presidential Regulation 56/2018, which generally covers large-scale infrastructure programs, including toll road projects, national roadway projects, railway projects, airport projects, ports, housing, water treatment, air transportation, and other sectors.

The taxpayer can submit their tax holiday application through the Online Single Submission (OSS) system. The OSS will notify whether the investor meets the criteria of tax incentives since registering their investment. Once the taxpayer meets the criteria, they must submit digitalized documents to obtain tax holiday, including detailed fixed assets in the capital investment plan, the amount of debt and equity as the basis of debt-to-equity ratio calculation, and fiscal statement letters before the Commercial Production. The DGT will issue the decision to grant the tax holiday to the company for and on behalf of the MoF within five business days after it receives the complete proposal.

15.4 Evaluation of Tax Holiday

During its initial periods, tax holiday had a limited ability to attract direct investment in Indonesia. There were only five taxpayers utilizing the 2011 tax holiday with a total investment plan of Rp39.4 trillion ($2.8 billion) that affected 4,855 workforces.

In the 2015 tax holiday, the government's effort to attract more investors by expanding the list of pioneer industries (including the infrastructure sector) and simplifying the application process gave unexpected results. None of the companies received tax holidays based on MoF Regulation159/2015. The ranged rate of corporate income tax reduction (10%–100%), rather than a single rate 100% reduction, raised uncertainty for the investors.

The government successfully acquired a significant result in the implementation of the 2018 tax holiday, with the improvement of certainty and simplicity as the most critical factors. In this regime, the time needed to process the tax holiday application was greatly reduced to only five days. The government also improved certainty by providing the duration of the concession period based on the investment amount. By implementing the "trust and verify" paradigm, the long and uncertain process of analysis was revoked, and the verification process was shifted to the audit process when the investment is realized. Moreover, in the last amendments (MoF Regulation 135/2018) the taxpayer can submit the tax holiday application online through the OSS system.

Although the "economic infrastructure" has been listed as one of the pioneer industries since the 2015 regime, the tax holiday recipients from the infrastructure sector were only recognized following the implementation of the 2018 tax holiday. In addition to the complicated and uncertain process, the government only allowed investors from economic infrastructure sectors that were not in the PPP scheme to apply for the tax holiday.

As of February 2020, the 2018 tax holiday has been granted to 67 taxpayers with a total investment of Rp1,102 trillion ($78 billion) and opened up 54,086 employments. From the economic infrastructure sector, 23 taxpayers have utilized tax holiday covering Rp247 trillion ($16.7 billion) of investment and 6,641 workforces. The tax holiday has a positive impact on the distribution of infrastructure development, as the investments in the economic infrastructure sectors utilizing tax holidays are distributed evenly throughout Indonesia. See Table 15.3.

Although the tax holiday has attracted significant direct investments to Indonesia, its impact on state revenue was relatively small. From 2011 until 2017, there was no revenue foregone as the impact of tax holiday implementation. The government recorded the first tax foregone from tax holiday implementation in 2018, with Rp1.1 trillion ($74.5 million) (BKF 2019).

Table 15.3 Tax Holiday Recipients from the Economic Infrastructure Sector

No	*Province*	*Number of Taxpayer*	*Investment Amount (Rp trillion)*	*Workforce*
1	Aceh	2	9.6	965
2	Banten	2	57.2	376
3	Bengkulu	2	6.0	87
4	Central Java	1	55.7	30
5	Central Sulawesi	1	9.8	2,250
6	East Kalimantan	1	5.4	200
7	East Nusa Tenggara	2	2.1	70
8	Jambi	1	12.5	500
9	North Sumatera	3	33.1	981
10	Papua	1	0.1	98
11	South Sulawesi	2	7.2	250
12	South Sumatera	3	41.3	505
13	West Java	1	2.0	19
14	West Kalimantan	1	4.5	310
	Grand Total	**23**	**246.6**	**6,641**

Source: Ministry of Finance.

15.5 Tax Allowance

Tax allowance in Indonesia is offered to investors in certain sectors and certain regions. The benefits of tax allowance are stipulated in Article 31A of the Income Tax Law. The implementing regulation of tax allowance is Government Regulation, MoF Regulation, BKPM Regulation, and related ministries' regulation. There are four benefits provided by the incentive:

1. Reduction of net taxable income by 30% of the total investment of tangible fixed assets (including land). The reduction is distributed in 6 fiscal years equally (5% per year). Investment as a calculation base only covers the amount used for main business activity, which is defined as a production type declared when the taxpayer applies for a tax allowance. The main business activity is also stated in principle license, investment license, and capital investment registration issued by BKPM.

   Calculation example: If PT. X has an investment value of Rp500 billion in the form of land, building, and machinery, the reduction of net taxable income is 30% * Rp500 billion = Rp150 billion. That amount will be distributed equally in 6 fiscal years, with an annual reduction of Rp150 billion / 6 = Rp25 billion.
2. Accelerated depreciation for tangible fixed assets and amortization for non-tangible fixed assets, as described in Table 15.4.
3. A reduced withholding tax rate of 10% for dividend payment to non-residents. If the tax treaty provides a lower rate, the tax treaty rate is applied.

Table 15.4 Accelerated Depreciation Table for Tax Allowance Purposes

Asset Category	*Useful Life (without incentives)*	*Useful Life (with incentives)*	*Straight-line depreciation*	*Declining balance depreciation*
Category 1	4 years	2 years	50%	100%
Category 2	8 years	4 years	25%	50%
Category 3	16 years	8 years	12.5%	25%
Category 4	20 years	10 years	10%	20%
Permanent Building	20 years	10 years	10%	
Non-Permanent Building	10 years	5 years	20%	

Source: Government Regulation 78/2019.

Under the Income Tax Law, the withholding tax rate for dividend payments to a non-resident is 20%. If the payment is made to a resident of the tax treaty partner, the applicable rate will be the one stated in the treaty. However, if the tax treaty rate is higher than 10%, the applicable rate under tax allowance will be 10%.

Currently, Indonesia has 70 effective tax treaties. As many as 46 of them has a tax rate above 10% for dividend with substantial ownership and 18 have a tax rate above 10% for dividend with non-substantial holding. The substantial holding threshold varies across treaty partners. Most of them are 25% of ownership.

4. An extended period to the carrying forward of tax losses, beyond the standard five years but not exceeding 10 years with certain guidelines; see Table 15.5.

Eligible sectors for tax allowance are divided into two categories. The first is "certain business sectors," as described in Annex I of the government regulation related to tax allowance. Taxpayers in business sectors, as listed in Annex I, only need to fulfill the criteria of business classification and scope of products. Meanwhile, Annex II listed "certain business sectors and a certain region." Taxpayers within the business sectors in Annex II must fulfill business classifications, the scope of products, and particular region (province). Annex II is in line with the purpose of tax allowance, i.e., equitable development across regions in Indonesia.

15.5.1 Development of Tax Allowance

Since 2007, there has been no difference in benefits provided on tax allowance incentives, provided that the benefits were regulated in Income Tax Law Article. If the government needs to change the benefits under tax allowance, they must seek permission from the parliament and amend the tax law. Eligible sectors had been increasing from 72 (GR 1/2007) to 183 (GR 78/2019). Eligible sectors under Annex I (dark gray in Figure 15.5) are higher under GR 1/2007 and GR 62/2008. However, eligible sectors under Annex II (light gray in Figure 15.5)

Table 15.5 Guide for Extended Loss Carry Forward

1-Year Addition	*2-Year Addition*
1 Capital Investment; 2 Capital Investment that is conducted in an industrial estate or bonded zone; 3 Capital investment on the new and renewable energy business sectors; 4 Disbursed at least Rp10 billion ($677,000) for economic or social infrastructure in the business location. Social infrastructure is non-commercial facilities for the public interest; 5 Utilized at least 70% of local material or components no later than the second fiscal year; or 6 Recruited at least 300 local employees and maintains that number for 4 consecutive years.	1 Recruited at least 600 local employees and maintains that amount for 4 consecutive years; 2 Disbursed research and development expenses in Indonesia for at least 5% of the capital investment amount within 5 years, for product development or production efficiency; or 3 If a business outside the bonded zone exports at least 30% of its total sales value within a fiscal year.

Source: Government Regulation 78/2019.

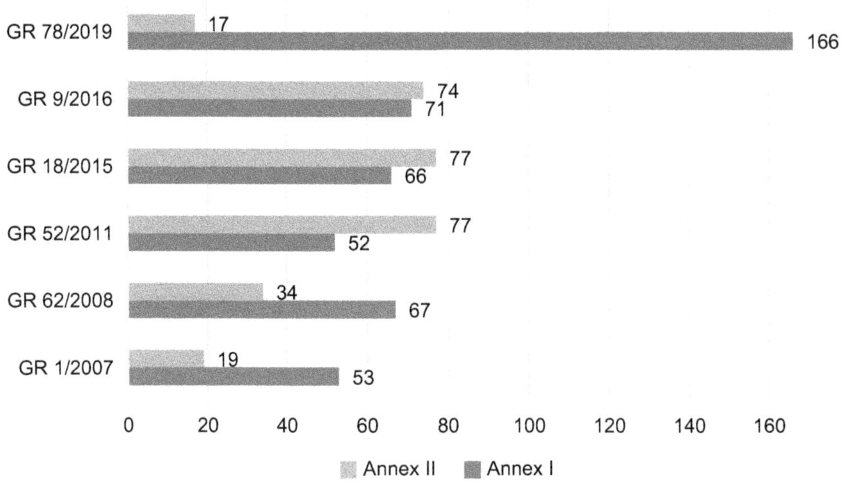

Figure 15.5 Number of Eligible Sectors for Tax Allowance.

Notes: GR = government regulation.

Annex I refers to certain sectors; Annex II refers to certain sectors and certain locations.

Source: Government Regulation 1/2007, 62/2008, 52/2011, 18/2015, 9/2016, 78/2019. Processed by authors.

rise significantly in the period of GR 52 of 2011 until GR 9 of 2016. In GR 78 of 2019, there are 166 business sectors in Annex I and 17 business sectors in Annex II. Initially, tax allowance was only given to *Perseroan Terbatas* (Limited Corporation) taxpayers. In the 2011 tax allowance, the scope was expanded to cover cooperation. Since the 2015 tax allowance, all corporate taxpayers are eligible to apply, regardless of its legal form.

The changes were made regarding the administration process. In the 2011 tax allowance, the taxpayer must submit their application to BKPM. If the taxpayer meets the criteria, the Chairman of BKPM sends the recommendation to the Minister of Finance. The Director-General of Taxes will issue tax allowance approval in 10 days after the recommendation from BKPM is received by the Minister of Finance. However, the government did not specified how long the processing time will occur in BKPM until they submit the recommendation to the Ministry of Finance.

In GR 18/2015 and its implementing rules, the government set more specific procedures for the overall tax allowance submission process. To decide whether an application meets the specified criteria, BKPM might held trilateral meetings with the Ministry of Finance and related Ministry. The overall process also specified to 28 days, including 15 days of processing in BKPM, 3 days of trilateral meetings, and 10 days of processing in the Ministry of Finance. The period was later shortened to 25 working days through the implementation of Economic Policy Package II (Bappenas, 2015). After completing the process, the taxpayers should apply to commercial production to the DGT to determine investment realization and how much investment is counted. See Figure 15.6.

In the 2015 tax allowance, the change was also made in terms of its utilization. Under GR 52/2011, eligible taxpayers can utilize tax allowance only when they have realized 80% of their investment commitment. The requirements have

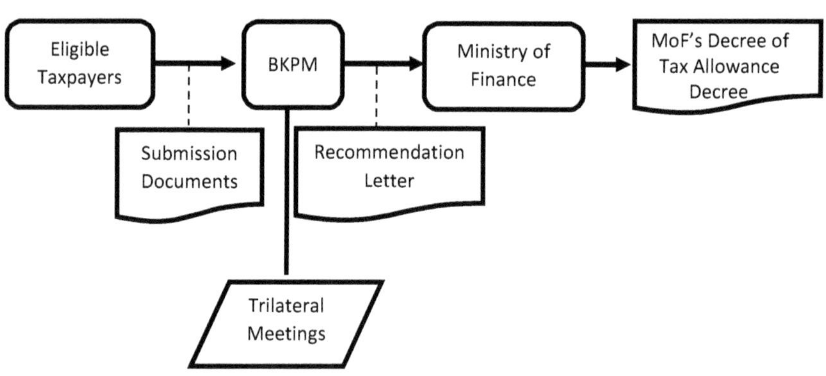

Figure 15.6 Tax Allowance Application Process.

Notes: BKPM= *Badan Koordinasi Penanaman Modal* (Investment Coordinating Board), MoF=Minister of Finance.

Source: Ministry of Finance Regulation 89/2015. Processed by authors.

Table 15.6 Utilization Time for Benefit under Tax Allowance

No.	*Benefit*	*Utilization Time*
1.	Investment allowance	When the taxpayer starts the commercial production
2.	Accelerated depreciation and amortization	Date of asset acquisition
3.	Reduced rate of dividend	Forever
4.	Extended period of loss carry-forward	Subject to requirements

Source: Ministry of Finance Regulation 89/2015.

the potential for complexity and uncertainty since the calculations are subject to disputes between taxpayers and tax auditors. The time of utilization, according to the GR 18/2015 regime, is described in Table 15.6.

In the current tax allowance regime (GR 78/2019), the application of tax allowance is utilizing the OSS system. Through the OSS system, taxpayers can find out whether they are eligible for tax incentives when they are applying for an investment permit. Furthermore, the process can be completed online, without the need to submit physical documents. After OSS clarifies the eligibility, taxpayers must submit a fiscal clearance letter of stockholders and list of fixed assets included in the investment plan through the system. Tax allowance decrees will be issued in only five working days after the required documents are submitted to BKPM through the OSS system.

DGT will conduct the field audit after the first year of commercial production is ended. The audit will determine when the commercial production is commencing, the investment amount as the basis of tax allowance calculation, and whether the taxpayer has fulfilled the criteria. However, the impact of the application of OSS in a tax allowance request cannot yet be seen clearly as the implementation rules (MoF Regulation 11/2020) took effect in February 2020.

The number of infrastructure-related sectors changed in every amendment of the tax allowance regulation. The infrastructure sector was included for tax allowance since 2008 (Geothermal Powerplant). In GR 52/2011, geothermal powerplants were no longer listed as an eligible sector included. Instead, the government mentioned five infrastructure-related sectors, which are (i) power plants, (ii) collection, purification and distribution of freshwater, (iii) building construction of processing, distribution, and collection of drinking water, wastewater, and drainage, (iv) highway construction, and (v) tourism areas. However, construction sectors are no longer included in later regulations (highway construction and processing, distribution, and collection of drinking water, wastewater, and drainage). See Table 15.7.

15.5.2 Evaluation of Tax Allowance

Although the government provides tax allowance for a wide range of business sectors, its use was limited. From 2007 to February 2020, tax allowance was

Table 15.7 Infrastructure Sectors in Tax Allowance

	Business Sectors	*Scope of Products*	*Regulation*
1	Geothermal Powerplant (11102)	Exploration, drilling, and processing of geothermal energy into electricity	GR 62/2008
2	Power Plant (35101)	Conversion of new energy and renewable energy into electricity	GR 52/2011 GR 18/2015 GR 9/2016
		Micro and mini-power plant	GR 78/2019
3	Collection, purification, and distribution of freshwater (36001)	Taking drinking water directly from springs and groundwater, purifying surface water from water sources, and channeling water directly through piping networks and from water terminals, tank trucks for sale to consumers.	GR 52/2011 GR 18/2015 GR 9/2016 GR 78/2019
4	Management and Disposal of Hazardous Wastewater (37022)	All related products	GR 78/2019
5	Building construction of processing, distribution, and collection of drinking water, wastewater, and drainage (42212)	Construction, maintenance, and repair of sewerage structures in municipalities and wastewater treatment buildings, residential drainage networks, retention basins, pumping buildings, and construction of similar buildings	GR 52/2011
6	Highway Construction (42111)	Construction, enhancement, maintenance, and improvement of toll road outside Java Island	GR 52/2011
7	Tourism Area (68120)	Excluding those in Special Economic Zone	GR 52/2011 GR 18/2015 GR 9/2016 GR 78/2019

Source: Government Regulation 1/2007, 62/2008, 52/2011, 18/2015, 9/2016, 78/2019. Processed by authors.

Note
GR = government regulation.

utilized by 167 taxpayers with a total investment of Rp957 trillion and $112 billion. The amount of foregone tax revenue related to the use of tax allowance decreased from Rp1.06 trillion in 2016 to Rp791 billion in 2018 (BKF 2019).

In the tax allowance regime before GR 18 of 2015, the average number of utilizing taxpayers was only five per year. A significant increase occurred after 2015. Between 2015–2019, the number of taxpayers utilizing tax allowance reached 15 per year. See Figure 15.7.

The utilization of taxpayers in the infrastructure sector was started in 2016. To date, there are a total of 11 taxpayers in the infrastructure sector, with a

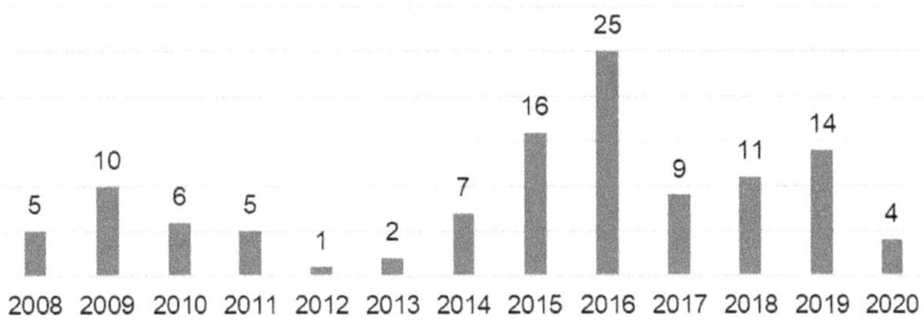

Figure 15.7 Number of Tax Allowance Recipients.
Source: Ministry of Finance.

Table 15.8 Tax Allowance Recipient from Infrastructure Sectors

	Year	*Sector*	*Location*	*Investment (Rp billion)*
1	2016	Power Plant	North Sumatera	497
2	2016	Power Plant	South Sumatera	2,469
3	2016	Power Plant	West Java	150
4	2017	Power Plant	Bengkulu	200
5	2017	Power Plant	West Java	302
6	2018	Power Plant	West Sumatera	141
7	2019	Power Plant	West Sumatera	258
8	2019	Power Plant	North Sumatera	452
9	2020	Power Plant	Gorontalo	225
10	2020	Power Plant	West Nusa Tenggara	142
11	2019	Collection, purification, and distribution of freshwater	West Nusa Tenggara	330
	TOTAL			5,167

Source: Ministry of Finance.

total investment of Rp5.2 trillion ($349.8 million). Those taxpayers are spread in Sumatra, Java, Sulawesi, and West Nusa Tenggara. See Table 15.8.

15.6 Vat Exemption for Residential Buildings

Indonesia has VAT for any consumption of taxable goods. The rate for VAT is 10%. However, to support national development, the government provides VAT exemption for certain types of residences. VAT exemption was given through Presidential decree number 18/1986, as last amended by GR 38/ 2003.

For a simple house, the criteria are as follows:

a. The building area is not exceeding 36 square meters.
b. The land area is not exceeding 60 square meters.

c. The selling price is not exceeding the following threshold:
d. For the owner, the unit the first-owned residence.
e. The owner is categorized as low-income.
f. The unit is used as a place of residence.
g. The unit is not transferrable in four years.

For residential buildings, VAT exemption applies for simple buildings that are built and financed by individuals or labor cooperatives or employee cooperatives, intended to be built for permanent workers or low-income informal sector workers with agreed rental fees. The unit is not transferable within four years since it was obtained.

For student dormitories, VAT exemption is given for simple buildings that are built and funded by universities or schools, individuals, or local governments, which are specifically designated for student accommodation, and not transferable within four years.

For other residential houses, VAT exemption is given to the worker's house, which is built and funded by a company for its employees and is not commercial. The building is not transferable within four years from the acquisition. The government also gives exemption for building construction that is designated for victims of natural disasters.

In Indonesia's mid-term national development plan 2004–2009, simple apartment programs were expected to provide low-income housing at affordable prices. To support the supply of simple apartments, the government provides VAT exemption by the listed simple apartment as one of the strategic goods, according to GR 31/2007 (as last amended by GR 81/2015).

Simple apartments covered by the incentive are in high-rise buildings and that are equipped with a bathroom and kitchen with the following criteria:

a. The sale price is not exceeding Rp250 million ($16,925).
b. The unit area is more than 21 square meters but not exceeding 36 square meters.
c. The Individual bought the apartment has a monthly income of a maximum of Rp7 million ($474).
d. The unit is first-owned residence.
e. The unit is used as a place of residence (the unit cannot be rented).
f. The unit is not transferrable.

From 2016 to 2018, VAT exemption for housing resulted in Rp985 billion ($66.7 million) of tax foregone, or Rp9.85 trillion ($667 million) in turnover volume. See Figure 15.8.

15.7 Conclusion and Policy Recommendations

Increasing private sector involvement in infrastructure development is an urgent matter. One way the government encourages private sector involvement is by

Table 15.9 Price Threshold for VAT Exemption of Simple House

No.	*Zone*	*2019*	*2020*
1.	Java and Sumatera	Rp140 million ($9,478)	Rp150.5 million ($10,188)
2.	Kalimantan	Rp153 million ($10,358)	Rp164.5 million ($11,136)
3.	Sulawesi, Bangka Belitung, Mentawai Islands, and Riau Islands	Rp146 million ($9,884)	Rp156.5 million ($10,595)
4.	Maluku, North Maluku, Bali and Nusa Tenggara, Jakarta, Bogor, Depok, Tangerang, Bekasi, and Anambas Islands, Murung Raya Regency, Mahakam Ulu Regency	Rp147 million ($9,951)	Rp168 million ($11,373)
5.	Papua and West Papua	Rp212 million ($14,352)	Rp219 million ($14,826)

Source: Ministry of Finance Regulation 81/2019.

Note
VAT = value added tax.

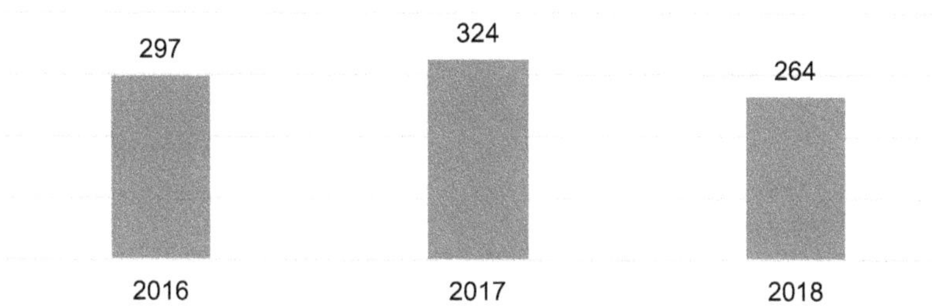

Figure 15.8 Revenue Foregone from VAT Exemption of Housing (Rp trillion).
Note: VAT = value added tax.
Source: BKF (2019).

providing tax incentives. Income tax incentives (tax holiday and tax allowance) are given to attract direct investment, including from infrastructure sectors. The government also provides VAT exemptions to ensure the availability of decent housing for low-income households.

The development of tax holiday and tax allowance in Indonesia shows that the simplicity of procedures and certainty play an essential role in attracting investment. Regarding tax holiday, this can be seen from its soaring use in 2018, when the government simplified procedures to only five days with a certainty of the concession period based on investment value. On the other hand, tax allowance users have also increased since 2015, when the government set the time limit of the tax allowance application process. The OSS system complements administrative simplification efforts that have been made by the government in providing incentives. These results are in line with the principles of good tax policy, as stated by Association of International Certified Professional Accountants (AICPA 2017), which includes certainty, simplicity, and transparency. Those factors are essential in implementing policies and administration. Investors often consider more important things than incentives (OECD 2008).

In terms of the scope, the government has included infrastructure sectors as tax holiday and tax allowance recipients. Infrastructure sectors included as pioneer industries are renewable energy power plants, highway construction, port construction, and investment activities and operation of an oil tank. Infrastructure projects outside the above-mentioned sectors can still apply for tax holidays if other requirements, other than listed as pioneer industries, are fulfilled. Based on GR 78/2019, infrastructure sectors that are eligible for tax allowance are micro and mini-power plants, collection, purification, and distribution of freshwater, management and disposal of hazardous wastewater, and tourism areas.

The government should consider adding more infrastructure sectors as eligible for tax holiday and tax allowance by referring to the mid-term development plan of 2020–2024. The government should pay more attention to basic service infrastructure, economic infrastructure, and urban infrastructure. Furthermore, the government should consider designating more infrastructure sectors for tax allowance, even if they have already been listed as tax holiday recipients, to accommodate taxpayers with smaller-scale investments.

Note

1 Developing Asia refers to 45 developing ADB members: Afghanistan; Armenia; Azerbaijan; Bangladesh; Bhutan; Brunei Darussalam; Cambodia; Cook Islands; Federated States of Micronesia; Georgia; India; Indonesia; Fiji; Hong Kong, China; Kazakhstan; Kiribati; Kyrgyz Republic; Lao People's Democratic Republic; Malaysia; Maldives; Marshall Islands; Mongolia; Myanmar; Nauru; Nepal; Pakistan; Palau; Papua New Guinea; People's Republic of China; Philippines; Republic of Korea; Samoa; Singapore; Solomon Islands; Sri Lanka; Taipei,China; Tajikistan; Thailand; Timor-Leste; Tonga; Turkmenistan; Tuvalu; Uzbekistan; Vanuatu; Viet Nam.

References

ADB. 2017. *Meeting Asia's Infrastructure Needs.* www.adb.org/sites/default/files/publication/227496/special-report-infrastructure.pdf (accessed 1 July 2020).

ADB. 2019. *GDP Growth in Asia and the Pacific, Asian Development Outlook ADO.* https://data.adb.org/dataset/gdp-growth-asia-and-pacific-asian-development-outlook (accessed 3 November 2020).

ADB and ADBI. 2009. *Infrastructure for a Seamless Asia: A Joint Study of the Asian Development Bank and the Asian Development Bank Institute.* www.adb.org/sites/default/files/publication/159348/adbi-infrastructure-seamless-asia.pdf (accessed 1 August 2020).

AICPA. 2017. *Guiding Principles of Good Tax Policy: A Framework for Evaluating Tax Proposals.* www.aicpa.org/advocacy/tax/downloadabledocuments/tax-policy-concept-statement-no-1-global.pdf (accessed 13 December 2020).

Baggerman-Noudari, K., and R. Offermanns. 2016. International – Foreign Direct Investment in Developing Countries: Some Tax Considerations and Other Related Legal Matters. *Bulletin for International Taxation* 70(6): 310–26.

Bappenas. 2015. *National Mid-Term Development Plan 2015-2019.* www.bappenas.go.id/files/rpjmn/RPJMN%202015-2019.zip (accessed 7 September 2020).

Bappenas. 2020. *National Middle Term Development Plan 2020-2024.* www.bappenas.go.id/files/rpjmn/Narasi%20Rancangan%20RPJMN%202020-2024.pdf (accessed 11 March 2020).

BKF. 2019. *Tax Expenditure Report 2018.* https://fiskal.kemenkeu.go.id/dw-taxexpenditure.asp (accessed 6 March 2020).

BPS. 2020. *[Seri 2010] Produk Domestik Regional Bruto Milyar Rupiah, 2017-2019.* www.bps.go.id/indicator/52/286/1/-seri-2010-produk-domestik-regional-bruto-.html (accessed 7 September 2020).

Easson, A. 2001. Tax Incentives for Foreign Direct Investment Part II: Design Considerations. *Bulletin for International Taxation* 55(8): 365–375.

James, S. 2013. Effectiveness of Tax and Non-Tax Incentives and Investments: Evidence and Policy Implications. http://dx.doi.org/10.2139/ssrn.2401905 (accessed 10 March 2020).

Juárez, L.G.O., and D.C. Manrique. 2018. Chapter 1: Introduction to Tax Incentives in the BEPS Era. In *Tax Incentives in the BEPS Era* edited by M. Cotrut, K. Munyandi, W. Choi, V. A. Ferreira, and J. Rienstra. https://research.ibfd.org/#/doc?url=/document/tib_p01_c01 (accessed 4 September 2020).

Klemm, A., and S. Van Parys. 2009. *Empirical Evidence on the Effects of Tax Incentives* WP/09/136; IMF Working Paper.

Longinotti, F.P. 2018. *Overview of Tax Expenditures in Latin America: Main Statistics of the CIAT Database.* www.ciat.org/Biblioteca/DocumentosdeTrabajo/2018/WP_05_2018_pelaez.pdf (accessed 11 March 2020).

Makmun. 2010. *Menimbang Tax Holiday.* Kajian Fiskal. https://fiskal.kemenkeu.go.id/dw-konten-view.asp?id=20100326083732000953792 (accessed 5 March 2020).

Ministry of ESDM. 2019. *Electricity Statistics 2018* 32nd ed. Secretariate General of Electricity. http://alpha.djk.esdm.go.id/index.php/statistik-ketenagalistrikan (accessed 9 March 2020).

Muyaa, E. 2018. Chapter 2: Tax Holidays. In *Tax Incentives in the BEPS Era,* edited by M. Cotrut, K. Munyandi, W. Choi, V. A. Ferreira, and J. Rienstra. https://research.ibfd.org/#/doc?url=/document/tib_p02_c02 (accessed 4 September 2020).

Nicolay, K., and V. Wiedemann. 2016. Asia-Pacific/International – Taxing Investments in the Asia-Pacific Region: The Importance of Cross-Border Taxation and Fiscal Incentives. *World Tax Journal* 8(2). https://research.ibfd.org/#/doc?url=/document/wtj_2016_02_int_2 (accessed 5 March 2020).

OECD. 2008. Tax Incentives for Investment: A Global Perspective Experiences in MENA and Non-MENA Countries. In *Making Reforms Succeed: Moving Forward with the MENA Investment Policy Agenda* pp. 225–261. OECD Publishing. https://doi.org/10.1787/9789264052826-11-en (accessed 11 March 2020).

Schwab, K. 2019. *The Global Competitiveness Report 2019.* www.weforum.org/reports/global-competitiveness-report-2019 (accessed 23 January 2020).

Wang, X. 2019. FDI and Infrastructure Improvement in ASEAN. *International Journal of Economics and Finance* 11(10). https://doi.org/10.5539/ijef.v11n10p140.

Wells, L.T.J., N.J. Allen, J. Morisset, and N. Pirnia. 2001. Using Tax Incentives to Compete for Foreign Investment – Are They Worth the Costs? In *Foreign Investment Advisory*

Service occasional paper FIAS 15. http://documents.worldbank.org/curated/en/164401468770722428/Using-tax-incentives-to-compete-for-foreign-investment-Are-they-worth-the-costs (accessed 5 March 2020).

World Bank. 2020. GLOBAL ECONOMIC PROSPECTS: In *Global Economic Prospects Slow Growth, Policy Challenges.* https://doi.org/10.1596/ 978-1-4648-1468-6

APPENDIX

Table 15A.1 Eligible Sectors for Tax Holiday in Indonesia

MoF Regulation 130/2011	*MoF Regulation 159/2015*	*MoF Regulation 35/2018*	*MoF Regulation 150/2018*
1. Basic metals 2. Oil refinery or basic organic chemicals derived from oil and gas 3. Machinery 4. Renewable energy 5. Communications equipment.	1. Upstream metal *previously basic metals* 2. Oil refinery 3. Basic organic chemicals derived from oil and gas 4. Machinery 5. Telecommunications and information 6. Sea transportation—added 7. Processing industries for agriculture, forestry, and fishery products—added 8. processing industries which represent a primary industry in an SEZ—added; 9. economic infrastructure other than those under a PPP—added Removed: Renewable Energy	1. Integrated upstream basic metal; 2. Integrated oil and gas refinery; 3. Integrated petrochemicals from oil, gas, or coal; 4. Integrated inorganic basic chemicals; 5. Integrated organic basic chemicals from agriculture, plantation, or forestry products; 6. Integrated pharmaceutical raw materials; 7. Semi-conductor and other main components of computers such as semiconductor wafer, backlight for liquid crystal display, electrical driver, or liquid crystal display, which are integrated with computers manufacturing; 8. Main components of communication equipment such as semiconductor wafer, backlight for liquid crystal display, electrical driver, or liquid crystal display, which are integrated with smartphones manufacturing	1. Integrated upstream basic metal; 2. Integrated oil and gas refinery; 3. Integrated petrochemicals from oil, gas, or coal; 4. Integrated inorganic basic chemicals; 5. Integrated organic basic chemicals from agriculture, plantation, or forestry products; 6. Integrated pharmaceutical raw materials; 7. Irradiation, electromedical, or electrotherapy equipment—change 8. Main components of electronics or telematics equipment such as semiconductor wafer, backlight for liquid crystal display, electrical driver, or liquid crystal display—change 9. Machinery and main components of machinery—change 10. Robotics components that support the creation of manufacturing machinery—change

(continued)

Table 15A.1 Cont.

MoF Regulation 130/2011	*MoF Regulation 159/2015*	*MoF Regulation 35/2018*	*MoF Regulation 150/2018*
		9. Main components of health equipment, which are integrated with irradiation, electromedical or electrotherapy manufacturing	11. Main components of power plant machinery—change 12. Motor vehicles and main components of motor vehicles—change 13. Main components of vessels—change 14. Main components of trains—change 15. Main components of aircraft and activities supporting the aerospace industry; change
		10. Main components of industrial machinery, which are integrated with machinery manufacturing 11. Main components of machinery such as piston, cylinder head, or cylinder block, which are integrated with motor vehicles manufacturing 12. Robotics components, which are integrated with the manufacturing industry 13. Main components of vessels, which are integrated with vessel manufacturing	16. Agricultural, plantation, or forestry-based processing that produce pulp; added 17. Economic infrastructure; 18. The digital economy, which includes data processing, hosting, and related activities—added Note: Certain taxpayers who are assigned for the National Strategic Projects can apply for the tax holiday.

14. Main components of aircraft such as the engine, propeller, rotor, or structure components, which are integrated with aircraft manufacturing
15. Main components of trains such as engine or transmission, which are integrated with train manufacturing
16. Power plant machinery
17. Economic infrastructure.

Note:

a. The economic infrastructure sectors under PPP are no longer excluded.
b. The government is also open to input on pioneer industries that have not been listed should the applicant fulfill the remaining requirements.

Source: Ministry of Finance Regulation 130/2011, 159/2015, 35/2018, and 150/2018. Processed by authors.

Note

MoF = Ministry of Finance, PPP = Public-Private Partnership, SEZ = Special Economic Zone.

Index

Note: Page numbers in *italic* and **bold** indicate figures and tables, respectively. Page numbers followed by 'n' indicate a note.

Milton Keynes UK
Ingram Content Group UK Ltd.
UKHW022136070524
442378UK00003B/89

9 781032 133454